Spooky Archaeology

SPOOKY ARCHAEOLOGY

Myth and the Science of the Past

JEB J. CARD

University of New Mexico Press • Albuquerque

First paperback edition, 2019
Paperback ISBN: 978-0-8263-5914-8

Library of Congress Cataloging-in-Publication Data
Names: Card, Jeb J., author.
Title: Spooky archaeology: myth and the science of the past / Jeb J. Card.
Description: Albuquerque: University of New Mexico Press, 2018. | Includes
bibliographical references and index. |
Identifiers: LCCN 2017053368 (print) | LCCN 2018021191 (e-book) |
ISBN 9780826359667 (e-book) | ISBN 9780826359650 (printed case: alk. paper)
Subjects: LCSH: Parapsychology and archaeology. | Archaeology and history. |
Mysticism.
Classification: LCC BF1045.A74 (e-book) | LCC BF1045.A74 C37 2018 (print) |
DDC 930.1—dc23
LC record available at https://lccn.loc.gov/2017053368

Cover photograph: *Tomb*, by Keith Yahl, licensed under CC by 2.0
Designed by Felicia Cedillos
Composed in Minion Pro 10.25/14

CONTENTS

ILLUSTRATIONS

ACKNOWLEDGMENTS

The following institutions provided access to sites, artifacts, images, documents, and other valuable resources that made this volume possible: Miami University; the Middle American Research Institute (MARI) at Tulane University; the Glenn G. Bartle Library and Special Collections at Binghamton University; the Broome County Public Library; the British Library; Glastonbury Abbey; the Museo Nacional de Antropología Dr. David J. Guzmán, Secretaría de Cultura de la Presidencia, San Salvador, El Salvador; the British Museum; the National Trust of the United Kingdom; the National Archives of the United Kingdom.

A number of individuals provided intellectual, emotional, and other support for *Spooky Archaeology*. The Invisible College of Mystery Investigators includes Ken Feder, Serra Zander, Jason Colavito, Sharon Hill, and Blake Smith. Each of these intrepid investigators helped in the discovery or contextualization of some clues in this volume. Chris Begley has done much of the pioneering work on the historical and social context of Ciudad Blanca, and his help has been invaluable. April Beisaw and Gabe Moshenska both led the way in exploring why haunted archaeology is important. Fellow Tulane graduates David Anderson and Stacy Dunn have followed their own paths into the history and weirdness of archaeology in ways that have stimulated the ideas in this volume. In addition to helping with the Niven correspondence at MARI, Marcello Canuto and Marc Zender provided valuable feedback and help with various aspects of this project. Donovan Loucks not only provided the Lovecraft texts underlying chapter 10, but also showed me the Providence haunts of HPL.

My colleagues at Miami University suffered through my bizarre flights of absurdity, and also provided solid assistance, suggestions, and support as I finished this volume: James Bielo, Cameron Hay-Rollins, Linda Marchant, Leighton Peterson, Mark Peterson, and Homayun Sidky. My entire squad of students, as well as numerous other students in classes, provided helpful feedback and insights. I'd like to particularly thank Emily Ratvasky for her wonderful illustrations in chapter 10. Brandi McConahay road-tested *Spooky Archaeology* for a live studio audience.

Outside of the classroom, I would like to thank readers Nicole Thesz, Heidi Schran, Brandon Ney, and Bodhi Ney. Joseph and Sandy Card provided feedback on *Spooky Archaeology* as well as welcome support and encouragement throughout the project. And I would like to thank John Byram at the University of New Mexico Press for seeing the value in this project from its origins in a blog post and conference paper through to the book you now hold.

1

Time, Memory, and Myth

The Foundations of Spooky Archaeology

ARCHAEOLOGY AS A field of science and scholarship, amateur or professional, is based on the principle that we can recognize and understand the material remnants of past human activities. A stone spear point can be analyzed to understand who made it, where they obtained the raw stone, when they made it, what it was used for, and the outlines of the larger society in which all of this occurred. A ceramic vessel might tell us what it contained, how it was transported around the world, or what the images painted on its sides might reflect about the identity of the person who used it and how they saw the world. Stone wall foundations tell us where people once lived, how they organized their community, and perhaps what happened that made them leave. The promise of archaeology as a science is that through these insights, we may better understand what it is to be human and learn from past human decisions about how we might engage with ecological, economic, and social challenges in the future.

This is not how most people have approached the archaeological record. The objects of this record are seen as the magical technology of fairies, jinn, *aluxob'*, and extraterrestrials. Abandoned buildings are thought to be home to ghosts, mythic ancestors, and lost races. Remnants of the past provide luck, curses, and magical powers. Ancient writing can control the universe, reveal the secrets of creation, and define who we are. To access all of these things, people have called on spirits, unlocked mystical earth energies, and undertaken secret missions.

An archaeologist might scoff at the description I just provided of our shared professional field, relegating it to pulp fiction, old legends, and pseudoscience. Another archaeologist, however, might admit that spooky archaeology is unavoidable in pop culture. Our most famous fictional counterparts in movies, television shows, books, games, and other media seek mystical artifacts, fight strange cults and secret societies, and navigate earthly and unearthly dangers. These characters deposit their treasures in haunted museums whose specters transcend death. In nonfiction, archaeologists have a long and complicated history of contributing to and inspiring such ideas in news, books, and documentaries. Increasingly, we find representations of the past filled with conspiracies and curses, with aliens instead of ancestors. A professional archaeologist might blame "Hollywood" or people's inherent love of mystery and sensationalism. They might tell an audience that real archaeology isn't like that, that it is deliberate and considered, maybe even boring (please, don't do this), that it isn't like the movies.

That archaeologist is right: our scientific, scholarly, academic, and professional lives are typically not like the movies. But they are wrong in thinking that there is no connection between those practices and the spooky popular image of our field. Nor is that image limited to fiction and mass media. Almost half of Americans believe that ancient advanced civilizations like Atlantis existed, and another third are undecided, making it one of the more popular beliefs dubbed paranormal by mainstream scholars.[1] This book excavates archaeology, digging into past practices and practitioners that have been quietly occulted and into the inherently spooky nature of the material past.

About This Book

The core argument of this book is that inherent and historical characteristics of the archaeological record (material remains from the past, including artifacts, monuments, buildings, and archaeological sites) and of the practice of archaeology (the study of the material remnants of the past and related forms of investigation) continue to give archaeology a mysterious and supernatural profile. Some of the history of archaeological practice reflects a larger social history. In these pages, I examine psychic mediums and spies who blended spiritualism and espionage with their archaeology. These individuals were not the only people in their society or social class to

undertake these unusual behaviors, though I argue that aspects of archaeology made these more common and less surprising than if those people
had been, say, lawyers or medical doctors or chemists. I also examine the
impact of modernity, colonialism, and nationalism on archaeological theory and museum practice. Most important, I examine the inherent qualities of material remnants of the past and the study of those remnants that
create mysterious, supernatural, mystical, or spooky results. I discuss two
of these concepts—collapsed protohistory and extrahumans—at some
length here since they will reappear throughout the volume.

Extrahumans are the subject of chapter 2, "Supernatural Relics." Around
the world, artifacts, monuments, and archaeological sites are commonly
interpreted not as the material culture created and used by past people just
like those living today, but instead as the material evidence of past or present extrahumans. Well into the modern era Europeans attributed stone
tools and monuments to fairies and elves, and the mythology of these entities persists today. In the Middle East potent and dangerous jinn haunt
abandoned places. The jinn are believed to have built many of the great
monuments of the past from the pyramids of Egypt to the Temple of
Solomon. Angels and demons in the Abrahamic faiths may have derived
from archaeological relics, and they were able to possess such objects. In
Mesoamerica, the aluxob' and the *itzaj* were and to a lesser extent still are
believed to be supernatural entities that built and live in ancient Mayan
cities. Even before the Spaniards arrived, the Aztecs understood the material remains of the past as supernaturally charged, as remnants of a world
of jade and fertility. Despite or perhaps because of archaeology, many people now view ancient artifacts and cities as evidence of extraterrestrial visitors. Not only are these kinds of entities—more than people but less than
gods—commonly associated with the archaeological, but it is possible that
the archaeological has played a significant role in the development of this
extrahuman lore.

With the past given a mystical bent and archaeology's development
during the emergence of modern science, it is no surprise that some archaeologists have blended the mystical and occult with their work. In chapter 3,
"Occulted Archaeologists," and elsewhere throughout this volume, I examine several examples who have been purposely forgotten or who have had
their supernatural activities minimized.

In the three middle chapters of this book, I argue that archaeology transgresses social and mythic time and cannot be easily separated from mythic narratives that resonate with meaning. In chapter 4, "Hieroglyphs, Magic, and Mummies," I discuss the power that is granted to writing, especially ancient writing. The notion of writing, and by implication named history, is critical for concepts of historical place and identity. Europe in particular came to venerate Egyptian hieroglyphs, or divine signs, long before they could be read, as being innately closer to creation and containing metaphysical wisdom and powers. This idea sits at the base of a main strand of Western occultism: Hermetic magic, the notion that ancient hidden wisdom derives from Egypt. Beginning with the classical Greeks, Hermeticism has shaped many conceptions of archaeology and the past, including the creation of the mummy's curse in real life and in cinema. Less well known is the rooting of the mummy's curse in real events and people in ancient Egypt. Beyond Egypt, the very existence of an untranslated ancient writing system has provided tremendous interpretive potency to those who claim to be best at not being able to read that writing. Such alleged experts will often resist subsequent efforts of decipherment. Finally, we can see the exotic power of hieroglyphic writing in the new blank space on the map, the stars, in the form of extraterrestrial writing found in Martian meteorites and crashed UFOs.

Chapter 5 is "Myth and Protohistory." The power of writing and history creates a social time of people in contrast with ahistorical mythic time, which is larger than people. The extrahumans of chapter 2 act like people (because they were actually human) but are temporally located in mythic time. The boundary of these two temporal domains, protohistory, has had a dramatic methodological and theoretical impact on how and why archaeology is undertaken. Because of the critical importance of the edge of history in creating identity, the resulting distortion of the archaeological record has been used to create national and ideological identities of all sorts. Some of the most horrific abuses involving archaeology resulted from protohistoric nation making. Atlantis, a staple of alternative archaeology, is the ultimate form of collapsed protohistory, providing a lost island in which modernity and its uncomfortable truths do not exist.

I unexpectedly discovered physical evidence of another mythic place, the lost continent of Mu, while preparing this book. That story is told in chapter 6,

"The Creation of a Lost Continent." The mythology of Mu began in early Maya archaeology and passed through the professionalization of the field into alternative mythmaking and hoaxing. The Mu stones detailed in this volume were part of a massive collection once thought to be almost entirely lost. Finding several of them has uncovered some, but not all, of their secrets.

The last half of this book deals in mystery. In chapter 7, "Relic Hunters and Haunted Museums," I examine the common perception of museums as haunted by spirits and by cursed objects. Early museum practices, especially the wholesale collection of looted artifacts from colonized lands, turned museums from promoters of rationality into the heart of the Western occult underground. The erasure of an object's history leaves a mental vacuum that is filled with mystery and the history of those who acquired the object. Some museum agents were of dubious backgrounds and were valued for their ability to obtain rare antiquities in difficult places. These liminal individuals often embroidered their personae with mystery, intrigue, and occultism.

Shady characters continue in chapter 8, "Time Detectives and International Intrigue." Archaeology is commonly assessed, and promoted, as being similar to whodunit and forensic crime stories due to the collision of careful science, clever sleuthing, and mystery. For this and other reasons, quite a few archaeologists have been intelligence agents and spies. In chapter 9, "Digging Up Witches and Murder," I find that this image of intrigue lends itself to supernatural and occult connotations. The chapter concludes with the story of an archaeologist turned undercover detective and conspiracy theorist on the hunt for a timeless, murdering witch cult. She didn't find her ancient witches, but in the process she helped create a modern religion and a new mythology.

The last two chapters explore the impact of that mythology and the related concepts spread throughout this book. In chapter 10, "Cthulhu and Cosmic Mythology," I analyze the archaeological science fiction of H. P. Lovecraft. Lovecraft's pulp fiction created a new mythology that has been called the "Cthulhu mythos," tales of hidden ancient sciences and eons-old extraterrestrial civilizations lurking in archaeological sites and secret societies. I provide a new analysis of that mythos and its origins, finding evidence that archaeology was the primary inspiration for this new mythology, which reflected the state of archaeology at the time.

In creating this fictional mythology, Lovecraft gave a material boost to older occult ideas once found within the archaeological community but increasingly driven out by newly minted professionals. This process culminated in the middle of the twentieth century, producing the academic and professional archaeological fields we know today. However, these occulted ideas did not vanish into the ether. They returned as alternative archaeology or, as its critics call it, pseudoarchaeology, the "living incarnation of the skeletons in [our] historical closet."[2] In this form, it has successfully competed for control of the symbols of archaeology, of the past, and of the charter myths that archaeologists once presented to the public. In chapter 11, "The Revenge of Alternative Archaeology," I conclude the book with a brief examination of the nature of alternative archaeology, and I pose questions about what this development means for the archaeological community and what steps may be taken in the future.

Time and Myth

Humans engage with the past differently depending on whether it persists as words or objects. Written or recorded documents can contain tremendous amounts of information, but as objects they should be mistaken neither for truth nor memory.[3] Even for events happening in our lifetime, documents present massive challenges. Documents always lack information relevant to historical understanding, and they often contain errors. Documents are created for specific reasons in specific times and contexts and may make little sense to later interpreters. An unimportant document can become invested with great meaning simply by surviving for centuries. Oral histories have all the same issues of context but are not literally anchored inside physical objects, making them even more susceptible to change. Archaeologists have fluctuated back and forth on the usefulness of oral traditions for reconstructing the past.[4] Yet as we shall see, documents and texts have informed and empowered many misconceptions about archaeological sites, objects, and traditions.

In discussing the nature of ancient construction of the past, Gosden and Lock refer to both oral and textual sources as history.[5] They emphasize the importance of human agency, anchored to named individuals, Herodotus's "time of men," as the defining principle of historical time.[6] This is the period of chronological time, of cause and effect. Objects of chronological time fill national museums of art while archaeological materials, especially of colonized peoples, are displayed in natural history museums.[7] By contrast, myth describes a time very different from now, a time outside of history, reaching back to before we can trace the present to the past names of people and their objects. This is a time of actors larger than the everyday, larger than normal humans. Myth explains how things originated and why things are the way they are.[8] Chronological time focuses on past events, though the events may be chosen to satisfy present desires. Mythic time somewhat paradoxically focuses on the present by enveloping it in a more profound past.

The dichotomy between chronological and mythic time appears in a number of cultural contexts.[9] Eviatar Zerubavel examined national memory via the national calendars of 191 countries, cataloging what their holidays commemorated and when these events occurred. A striking bimodal pattern emerges. National memory celebrates early mythic events tied to a nation's origins or to early religious figures, on the one hand, and nationalist and other events of the previous 200 years, on the other. The span of 200 years coincides nicely with Eliade's discussion of the loss of historicity to mythic time in popular memory.[10] With one exception, everything in Zerubavel's survey between these landmarks is almost entirely forgotten. The one exception is the European colonization of the Americas after Columbus. Even this exception mirrors mythic time in commemorating the declaration of a "new world." In absolute terms, this means that throughout the world most national calendars ignore the period from about 680 CE to 1776 CE, other than the momentous expansion of the global map after Columbus. It is also notable that most of the early dates are religious in nature, while the later ones commemorate national histories.[11] This is mythic time versus the time of people, which is variously called chronological, social, or historic time.

The boundary between these two temporal realms has a particular power over the material objects of archaeology and notions of antiquity. Archaeologists use the term "protohistory" to refer to contexts that can be understood at least in part through historical documents but are not directly part of a literate society.[12] For example, indigenous people in eastern North America in the sixteenth and seventeenth centuries, who may have been in contact with Europeans and who were probably living in ways somewhat related to those described in European documents, have been considered protohistoric. Likewise, much knowledge of the "Celtic" world comes from the accounts of invaders like Julius Caesar. The relationship between writing and states inevitably grounds protohistory in colonialism and informs both the myth of the vanishing native and criticisms of the idea of prehistory.

Dependency on history inherently projects recent colonialism into the past, explaining the present. It also encourages narrative. Historical records can reveal complex and chaotic events, but a successful historical tradition that influences how people understand the past is not going to be formless and random. Gaps are filled with intelligible narratives and impersonal entities, such as "peoples," "nations," and "religions." These entities receive personal characteristics that turn a mass of facts into a morality tale. As gaps grow with temporal distance, narrative or legend becomes more important.

Dependency on textual or oral historical traditions tends to collapse time, to place most or all of human agency within the time of names.[13] The time before words, "prehistory," collapses into a somewhat flat palimpsest of protohistory and antiquity. Names, labels, and descriptions from the beginning of history are projected deeper into unspoken time. Adrienne Mayor argues that a similar phenomenon drove the classical Mediterranean world's understanding of fossils.[14] Without a concept of deep time and biological change, fossils were seen as the bones of relatively recent or existing creatures or of mythic individuals from earlier and more heroic times.

Concepts and identities from the beginning of history become primordial, unchanging, and often mystical.[15] Ancient objects become associated with the most prominent early labels known to a region's historical tradition, attributed to the first people with names known to outsiders. Celts, Germans, Inkas, and Aztecs come to mind, but there are many more. Since this almost always occurs in a colonial context, the effect is profound and can be extremely damaging. The colonized people become symbols of the unchanging primitive past, and if they deviate from this unchanging past, they may be condemned as inauthentic.[16] The common placement of the material culture of colonized peoples in natural history museums alongside dinosaurs, dodos, and diamonds underlines their less than historical, not entirely human status.

The Extrahuman Past

This knowing relegation of real people and their relics to an unchanging past is not inherent to the human experience and is an anomaly of colonialism. The archaeological record from before history is typically treated in one of two ways. The first is this collapsed protohistory, in which material remnants of the past are condensed into the primordial beginning of history, the time before written or oral accounts of the relatively recent past.

Alternatively, archaeological objects not assigned to historical figures take on the characteristics of myth from before history. Gabriel Moshenska suggests that this recognition is key to the uncanny nature of the archaeological.[17] Moshenska cites Freud's notion of the *unheimlich* or uncanny, suggesting that the presence of recognizable elements of human life in the realm of the dead—the excavated pit in the earth or the sterile stage of the museum exhibit—produces the uncanny effect of the archaeological. I would argue that this effect is primarily strong among relatively recent remains and artifacts. Moshenska notes that the antiquarian and master ghost story author M. R. James largely limited the supernatural traps sprung by his archaeological protagonists to recent contexts, typically the medieval period at the earliest and more often the early modern era.[18] These are within historical time and produce the effect of the misplacement of the living among the dead. It is notable that when the early Maya archaeologist Thomas Gann felt a pang of regret at having disturbed Maya human remains, he compared them with the sixteenth-century *Relación de las Cosas de Yucatán* of Archbishop Diego de Landa and its description of everyday Mayas comparable to those of today. Gann showed no such consideration for the bones of ancient Maya priests and rulers that he also excavated, noting "it would never do for an archaeologist to become a sentimentalist, for the two are incompatible."[19] It is no coincidence that real world ghost stories also limit themselves to the relatively recent past. Ghost stories typically reach back at most a few hundred years. The trope of native burial grounds, examined later in this volume, is the alleged exception that proves this rule.

Mythic time is before human society, and its end can set the stage for human time, such as the end of Ra in Egyptian myth or the triumph of the Hero Twins in the K'iche' Mayan Popol Vuh. Myth is the time of natural and supernatural forces and is divorced from human agency and historical time.[20] An Australian park demonstrates this difference. For the indigenous Waanyi, a World Heritage property is a place of "personal histories, individual and collective memories, kinship relations and cultural knowledge" in which a human past with extinct animals becomes part of the Dreamtime. Non-indigenous Australians speak of this same place, known for its Oligo-Miocene fossils, in spiritual and mythic terms as being greater than humans even though this space has been inhabited by people for tens of thousands of years.[21] The first perspective shades into the legendary or even mythic, but the latter explicitly ties a prehuman existence to the spiritual. These attitudes contrast strongly with the ideals and motivations considered "historical." Archaeological practices have played a role in enforcing this dichotomy, such as by emphasizing indigenous people's interactions with the environment as the major goal of research in pre-European California, but emphasizing in the historical archaeology of the state how indigenous people coped with European-driven changes.[22]

This division is also found within archaeology in the distinction between "social time" and "science time," a division between a human-focused social reality tied to everyday life and a less-human (though not necessarily less-than-human) time of deeper explanatory significance. The traditional model of anthropological archaeology leans toward science time, the universal comparative study of the creation of humanity often using "prehistoric" non-Westerners and their ancestors as the conceptual construction material for illustrating cultural evolution and the rise of Western civilization. Much of the theoretical development of archaeology since the mid-twentieth century has been an attempt to emphasize social time, to analyze past humans' social life.[23]

One of my arguments in this volume is that science time holds a powerful mythic resonance for Western societies. It is a truism that the oldest example of something is overly emphasized in the popular consumption of archaeology.[24] Origins are a charter. The mythic past explains.[25] To know the origins of warfare, sexism, religion, or consciousness gives one power to explain the importance and nature of these things. The abandonment by professional archaeologists of that mythic ground does not mean that Western archaeology consumers followed professional archaeology into a paradigm of social time. Instead, the legacy of archaeology and its association with mythic science time has been co-opted. Anyone willing to wear the old symbols of preprofessional archaeology can claim the archaeological legacy and its mythic social currency even if their ideas or methods have no significant tie to actual archaeological practices past or present.

Archaeology since the end of the nineteenth century is the anomaly in placing real humans before names, in a prehistory of archaeological cultures constructed out of material objects. The very notion of prehistory is inherently part of modernity.[26] Within archaeology, the utility and accuracy of such constructions is questioned. Outside of archaeology, these units have become literal peoples or nations, and as we see in chapter 5, have been transformed into the tools or weapons of nationalists.

The more common approach to the time before names is to understand it as the time of nonhumans. The origins of this time are often attributed to powerful supernatural entities and forces glossed as "gods." The naming of mythic time, and the retrieval of material objects from that time, has powered the popularity of archaeology. As the most human-focused of the material sciences studying the past (versus geology, paleontology, and evolutionary biology), archaeology directly handles the stuff of sacredness. Archaeology's intellectual dominion over the biblical and then evolutionary origins of humanity and civilization has made it powerful and transgressive.[27] This dangerous or transgressive supernatural aspect of archaeology is the most persistent and popular representation of the profession in fiction. The most successful big-budget film treatments of archaeology, those that connect best with audiences, feature supernatural or paranormal forces playing a significant role in the human past. The supernatural past empowers archaeology in these films with the ability to trigger or prevent modern catastrophe through mystical relics and knowledge.[28]

The goods of the gods (the Holy Grail, the Ark of the Covenant, Pandora's box) are popular in fictional accounts of archaeology. Some real-world artifacts are assigned to the gods, such as the fourteenth-century idea that Arretine ware or other classical pottery was too fine in manufacture to have been made by humans.[29] But the archaeological record is generally not assigned to such entities. Adrienne Mayor argues that even in myth, Greek observers recognized the principles of biology in fossils.[30] Instead, ancient objects are generally attributed to neither gods nor mortals but to extrahuman beings or "nonpeople," who may still exist today. Nonpeople may have magical powers, may be partially nonmaterial, and may not always cohere to the principles of biology. Cultural insiders or outsiders might call them "spirits." Other times, they are considered to be something closer to people, but they are not "us." These entities often live in societies and have personal desires and needs but not necessarily specific personal names, simply being anonymous members of a community or realm, not unlike the members of a neighboring tribe.

Remnants of the living in the realm of the dead within historical time can produce a morbid uncanny.[31] By contrast, the recognition of something human-like in mythological time produces extrahumans. The artifacts of nonpeople are similar enough to known human material culture to be recognizable, yet they are foreign to any known people. The presence of constructed things on a human scale within mythological time produces a profound mystery. Similarity to the natural world makes supernatural entities more successful in terms of cultural transmission. Modern fantasy and science fiction are populated by human-like aliens and magical societies created in the image of past human cultures. The creation of such supernaturals may be part of a cognitive module of folk biology.[32] Mayor documents the embodiment of mythic heroes and creatures in nonhuman fossils.[33] The interpretation of ancient tools and constructions as extrahuman extends this impulse to folk archaeology.

This equation carries over to the exoticization and atemporal nature of colonized people. If the colonized people on the edges of history are made primordial and unchanging—and therefore not part of the present modern world—then the relics of their ancestors from before protohistory can become transformed into the haunts of spirits, goblins, and, in the twentieth century, aliens. This is the same phenomenon that populates the imagined spaces of the lost worlds of South America, Congo, or Indonesia with dinosaurs and other prehistoric survivals.[34] Archaeological writings are not immune to this exotic collapsing of time, such as Thomas Gann's suggestion that a saurian survival might not be out of place, which he made during the exploration of a Belizean cave filled with the shadows of spirits and grotesque monsters.[35]

Reincarnating Sacred Origins

Theosophy is a key concept to understanding the history of archaeology, though the specific word is no longer in common use. Many of the ideas and practices once associated with theosophy are today labeled "New Age." Theosophical concepts underpin large swaths of popular fantasy tales as well as alternative archaeologies. The theosophical movement had superficially similar goals to early anthropology: to recover a universal human religion out of the study of religions around the world. It also desired to work in an evolutionary framework, though theosophy was more concerned with spiritual than physical evolution and believed in cyclical races rather than lineal evolution. The word "theosophy" first appeared in the sixteenth century, and the first theosophical society was founded in London in 1783, influenced by Emanuel Swedenborg. Theosophists critiqued imperialism and celebrated the cultures and beliefs of colonized peoples, at least as they interpreted and constructed such beliefs. More than a few anthropologists were among the intellectuals who found one of the several strands of nineteenth-century theosophy appealing.[36]

Ultimately, the most influential form of the movement was led by Helena Petrovna Blavatsky, a Ukranian émigré who founded the Theosophical Society in the 1870s. Her theosophy included anthropologists, but its larger impact was on the occult fringes of the intellectual world, including archaeology. It was a romantic countercultural movement reacting against Christian authorities, on the one hand, and scientific authorities, on the other, to recover a shared origin of all religions.[37] The occult and esoteric philosophy of theosophy rejected mainstream research, including archaeology, into non-Western cultures as only understanding superficial forms of Eastern philosophies and not their true internal or hidden meanings. Theosophy incorporated spiritualism, the contemporary beliefs and practices associated with contacting the spirits of the dead. Much of theosophical interest derives from older occult concepts, including kabala, alchemy, and especially the Hermetic Greek appropriation of Egyptian religion. Theosophy also incorporated the scientific racism pioneered by anthropologists in the late Victorian period, creating a series of semiphysical and physical races sharing ancient wisdom in places like Atlantis and other planets and passing it down to the

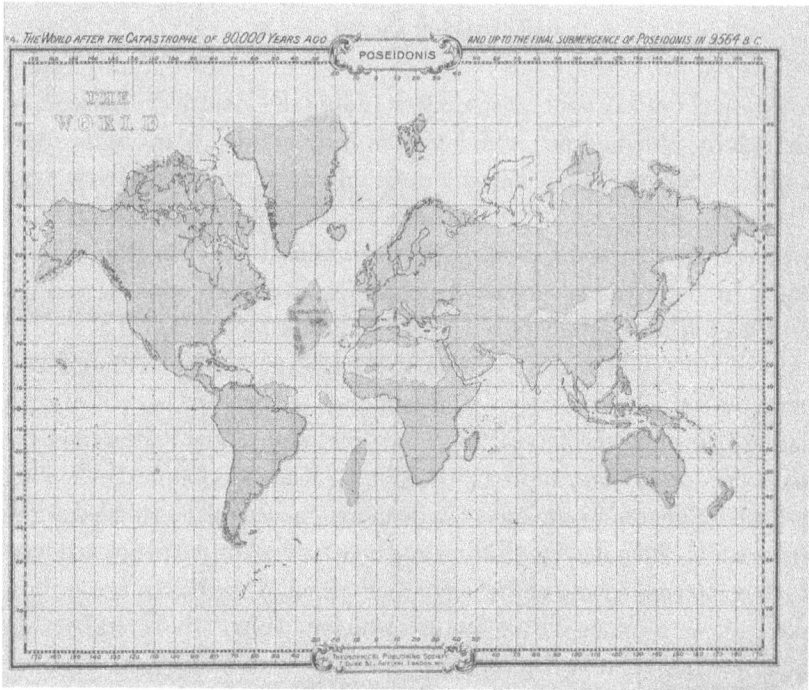

FIGURE 1.1. Map showing the continent of Poseidonis, home of Atlantis.
From W. S. Elliot, *The Story of Atlantis: A Geographical, Historical, and Ethnological Sketch* (N.p.: Theosophical Publishing Society, 1896), 91.

present. However, while anthropology came to critique and reject racism, the racial themes found in theosophy continued to inform later paranormal and alternative archaeological descendants of the movement. The movement also preserved pre-continental drift geology, building its mythic histories out of sunken continents (figure 1.1).[38]

Blavatsky's first book, *Isis Unveiled*, is informed by the Hermetic idea going back to the Greeks that Egypt was the heart of wisdom, and an early name for the movement was the Brotherhood of Luxor. Blavatsky increasingly focused on Asian religions and philosophies, especially after she traveled to India in search of secret masters from whom she learned the contents of her second book, *The Secret Doctrine*. First Egypt and then Tibet acted as mental playgrounds for intellectually conservative elements of European society, utopian fantasies into which they could retreat from the onrush of Darwinism, industrialization, and modernity.[39]

Blavatsky's writings were inspired in part by fiction author Sir Edward Bulwer-Lytton.[40] Bulwer-Lytton's 1871 novel, *The Coming Race*, set the model for the "lost world" adventure fiction that came to dominate the popular imagination of anthropology, archaeology, colonialism, and the past. *The Coming Race* tells of a lost race of underground dwellers who can accomplish superhuman feats through control over the mystical force of Vril. The book's imitators profoundly affected the superhero and space opera genres.[41] It and the theosophy it helped inspire have also been major influences on paranormal and conspiracy culture, especially the emergence of the UFO myth in the 1940s. Almost every element of modern alternative archaeology can be found in Blavatsky's *Isis Unveiled* and especially *The Secret Doctrine*: giants; ancient space travelers; magic as occult science and wisdom; druids; megaliths; poor "sounds alike, is alike" linguistics; secret texts in unknown languages; a particular interest in the Aryan race; lost continents; "looks alike, is alike" comparisons between places like Egypt, the Maya homeland, Peru, and Easter Island; myth as history; and a high-handed disdain for foolish, materialist scientists and benighted religious leaders. It may be worth noting that Bulwer-Lytton is famous for coining the phrase "It was a dark and stormy night." A prize for bad writing is awarded annually in his honor.

What This Book Is Not

The subject of this book is broad: the roots of the mythic and supernatural in archaeological practice, and the impact of the mythic and supernatural on archaeology. But this book is not all-encompassing. A number of case studies are presented as evidence in these pages, but most of them have been covered in more detail by other researchers and authors. Numerous studies, some quite rigorous, others sensational, have examined the nationalist abuses of archaeology. Entire libraries could be filled with the arguments over archaeological looting and the ethics of museums. The more information that has been published about any given case has typically resulted in less detail here: please read those articles and books. I fully expect that I have missed evidence in one mystery or another. This is all right: archaeology is about new discoveries of old things.

This book is not a collection of scary things from the past. It is not a parade of human sacrifice, or pagan statues, or creepy dolls. Many such finds are simply normal things out of cultural context. A "demonic" image may be someone else's sacred focus. A creepy old doll was beloved by a child when it was shiny and new and was probably given to them by someone dear. Reveling in the strangeness of the old is no different from the Romantics who commissioned their servants to build already ruined follies in order to experience the uncanny and mystical right in the comfort of their own home. Frankly, it cheapens the prospect.

Last, this both is and is not a debunking book. I am good friends and colleagues with archaeologists and others who expend tremendous and often insightful effort in solving ancient and modern mysteries. Those who wish to profit in some fashion from mysteries, be it for money or ego, often call this "debunking." I call it investigating, and I respect the real investigators. I take part in such efforts. Yet that is not the primary mission of this book. Yes, I examine the material aspects of some of these mysteries. Crystal skulls are only about a century old. Glastonbury monks almost certainly did not dig up King Arthur. The inscriptions from the lost continent of Mu are likely fakes from the 1920s. But saying so is not the point of this book. Instead, I aim to debunk some of the conventional wisdom about archaeology, including the following:

- Archaeology has nothing to do with the mystical. There is a clear history that it does.
- Archaeologists study just the old trash of people like us. That has come to be true, but that's not why people started doing archaeology and that's not why people care about archaeology.
- The fantasies that swirl around archaeology are the fault of crazy people, or Hollywood, or crazy Hollywood people. They aren't; we inspired them. Mass media are the primary mechanism of the education the public receives about archaeology,[42] but as much of this book shows, mass media take notes from us, not the other way around.

The most important error about spooky archaeology is that it will go away if we ignore it. These ideas have been with archaeologists since before the word "archaeology" existed, and if we ignore that, we will likely be ignored ourselves. To look under the rocks, to examine the evidence, and to investigate the myths are what archaeologists do. For the rest of this volume, I'm going to do a little archaeology of the weird past and the mythic future of archaeology itself.

STONEHENGE FROM THE NORTH.

FIGURE 2.1. Stonehenge as depicted in *Our Own Country: Descriptive, Historical, Pictoral* (London: Cassell, 1885), 29.

2

Supernatural Relics

European Fairy Traditions and Archaeology

In 2011 the *Belfast Telegraph* asked if the bankruptcy and ruin of Ireland's richest man, Sean Quinn, was caused by the disturbance of a Neolithic megalithic monument. In 1992 Quinn's cement company had relocated the Aughrim wedge tomb as part of a quarry expansion and rebuilt it on the grounds of Quinn's hotel on the other side of the village of Ballyconnell. Quinn later lost the quarry, the hotel, other businesses, and his fortune. The *Belfast Telegraph* reported that some locals blamed the fairies, a manifestation of commonly held Irish beliefs according to University of Ulster folklorist Seamus MacFlionn.[1] A similar legend has arisen to explain the failure of John DeLorean, his car company, and his Belfast factory.[2]

Eighty-two years earlier, a young occultist, Marie Emily "Netta" Fornario, was found dead on a fairy mound on the island of Iona, Scotland. Fornario was naked except for a robe and silver jewelry; there was a knife nearby. Despite some scratch marks on her toes, she appeared to have died of exposure in the cold November Scottish sea air. The spot where Fornario was found was the Sithean Mor, or Great Fairy Hill, which until probably the nineteenth century had boasted a megalithic ring of stones.[3] Her role as a healer in the British occult community, some of whom I discuss below in their intersections with archaeology, led to mythmaking of astral journeys and psychic attacks.[4]

Over millennia and well into the modern era, European megalithic sites have been modified physically and spiritually into liminal places connected to the otherworld and the sites of fairy sightings. New cultural and religious paradigms renamed or even literally reinscribed carved texts onto megalithic sites, relabeling the ancient places in a new supernatural narrative. The more visually spectacular the site, the more likely it has attracted a rich body of folklore (figure 2.1).[5]

One important name in Irish Gaelic for the fairies is *sidhe* (*sith* in Scottish Gaelic), which refers to mounds. Archaeological sites like Newgrange in Ireland, and particularly those associated with wells or forest groves, are traditionally regarded as sacred spots or houses of the divine Aes Side, the people of the *sid* or *si*, the "mounds" or "seat."[6] Many of these traditional ideas became part of the Celtic Revival by intellectuals like the Irish poet W. B. Yeats, contemporary with the growth of antiquarianism. Romantic mythmaking was common in the nineteenth century with ghost and fairy stories made up or modified to fit spectacular archaeological discoveries.[7] Nonetheless, early Anglo-Saxon shrines may have been constructed on ancient barrow mound sites in attempts to gain information from the supernatural entities that dwelt within the mounds.[8]

The association of fairies and ancient sites reflects one folkloric explanation for the nature of European fairies, elves, and related entities: they are the souls of the dead, especially those of the pre-Christian dead unable to enter heaven or those not claimed by the church.[9] In the Icelandic *Bard's Saga*, probably recorded in the late medieval period, tomb robbers are unable to open a king's tomb because their excavations refill each night. The robbers eventually enter this unhallowed ground after a priest employs holy water and a crucifix, and they find the king's body moving and speaking with the spirits, trolls, and dwarves that live in the tomb.[10]

Archaeological investigation reveals how the meaning of Neolithic and Bronze Age mounds have changed through time. Megalithic chambers in northeastern Germany continued as burial sites into the Bronze Age and for secondary burials around the main burials into the Slavic era, while similar practices occurred in England into the Anglo-Saxon period. After Christianity arrived in Germany and Britain, megalithic sites were associated with giants, demons, and the devil. Scottish *howe* chamber tombs were not only reused in the early Iron Age, but new structures were built at the entrances to ancient tombs, possibly to control access.[11]

As also occurred in Latin America, Christian authorities fostered a

FIGURE 2.2. The tomb of Maeshowe was looted by "Norse crusaders," as they called themselves in runic inscriptions left behind. The image of an animal scratched into the wall cannot be fully interpreted, but the scales suggest it might be a dragon. Tomb interior illustration by Captain W. St. G. Burke. From *Proceedings of the Royal Society of Antiquaries of Ireland* (Dublin: Royal Society of Antiquaries of Ireland, 1899), 343; animal effigy on 284.

break with the historical knowledge and religious practices of pagan Europe, branding ancient burial mounds as the homes of elves, demons, and dragons. The modern image of a dragon sprawled atop a golden treasure secreted in a subterranean lair derives in large part from the story of *Beowulf,* in which a dragon lives in a barrow surrounded by an old king's burial treasure. The treasure in *Beowulf* is described in detail and resembles the artifacts found in tombs, and Beowulf meets his doom as the supernatural punishment for just such a looting. Later Norse plunderers of the Maeshowe chambered cairn in Scotland left behind runic inscriptions recording the treasures within the chamber as well as a zoomorphic image interpreted as either a lion or, due to apparent scales on its back, a dragon. The site was believed into the nineteenth century to be home to a goblin (figure 2.2).[12]

The folklore of treasure guarded by spirits, fairies, or dragons was broadly associated with archaeological ruins from all eras in Britain and Scandinavia whereas Roman ruins in southern Europe were associated with treasure and demons.[13] Medieval laws about treasure ownership lie at the foundation of treasure trove laws, which preceded archaeological preservation laws. Treasures left unclaimed due to death or other calamity would likely attract fairies and elves. The looting of prehistoric tombs for magical objects became so commonplace in Europe that spells for obtaining treasure troves can be found in grimoires such as the seventeenth-century *Janua Magica Reserata* (Keys to the Gateway of Magic).[14] These spells call up, control, and exorcise dark spirits in order to obtain treasures made in the past by humans and hidden in secret places under the earth. The lord admiral of the British fleet used spirits and fairies to search for legendary jewels described in the Bible.[15] Holy benedictions and prayers cleansed antique objects and "vessels found in heathen barrows and in other somewhat unorthodox ways" of pagan association, and one officially authorized barrow excavation began by finding the site with a crystal ball, under the administration of parish priests.[16]

Anglo-Saxons called British Neolithic sites names like "elf barrow" or "goblin hill." These were the most haunted and demonic places in the Anglo-Saxon landscape, and condemned criminals (possibly executed on the sites of barrow mounds) were buried in intrusive graves to suffer torment from the demonic inhabitants. Only thieves and outcasts would dare enter an ancient tomb, and in later centuries a barrow might be destroyed if it was feared to be a haunt of criminals. Barrow diggers could suffer from curses, but this did not stop clergy from building on or near barrow mounds so that they could exorcise demons from the ancient tombs.[17] Research by antiquarian Augustus Jessopp into haunted or demonic treasures from the earth inspired the artifact- and ruin-oriented ghost stories of M. R. James.[18]

Megalithic sites, such as the Callanish Standing Stones of the Western Isles of Scotland, are said in folklore to be people or giants turned to stone, and Stonehenge may have once been known as the Giant's Dance, but by the twelfth century Geoffrey of Monmouth recorded its magical construction by the wizard Merlin.[19] In medieval Denmark, giants built the megalithic sites, and fairies subsequently lived in the ruins.[20] Even sea creatures, such as mermaids, could be associated with terrestrial archaeological sites. In one legend, after a woman is abducted by the Finfolk, her vengeful husband finds their vanishing island home by performing a ritual at the Odin Stone at Stenness in the Orkneys of Scotland.[21] The Odin Stone continued to be associated with traditions of love and was used to join couples without

FIGURE 2.3. Elf shot mounted in a silver charm and worn by a Scottish woman in the nineteenth century. Illustration by F. C. Lukas. From John Evans, *The Ancient Stone Implements, Weapons, and Ornaments of Great Britain* (New York: Appleton, 1872), 325.

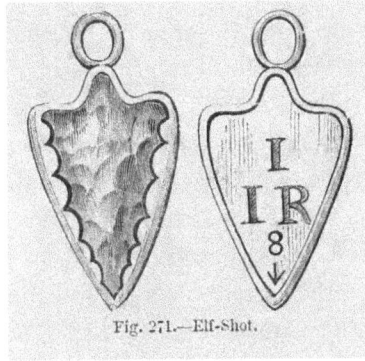

Fig. 271.—Elf-Shot.

a formal marriage until it was removed on Christmas Day 1814, angering local residents to the point of violence. The removed Odin Stone survived in storage for more than a century before being destroyed by a young man unaware of the stone's history.[22]

Enchanted Artifacts in Europe

Europeans also viewed portable artifacts as potentially supernatural. Roman era coins, potsherds, keys, and other objects, along with crystals and fossils, were deposited in Anglo-Saxon burials in Britain as what appear to be apotropaic (protecting from magic) charms worn in particular by women and children.[23] Mesolithic and Neolithic chipped-stone projectile points became magically poisonous fairy or elf missiles, shot by malign elves to cause illness (figure 2.3). Healers removed the poison from victims in the form of hair, rags, or bits of bone or crockery, similar to the modern practices referred to as "psychic surgery."[24] By the end of the seventeenth century, contact with stone-tool-making societies, such as indigenous North Americans, turned "elf arrows" back into stone tools made by ancient humans.[25]

Elf shot appears in witch trial testimony as both a gift from the devil and fairies and an aid in healing. In Scotland, Katherene Ross was accused in 1590 of going to the hills to get "elf-arrow-heidis," while in 1628 accused witch Stein Maltman described a healing cure, intended for an "elf-shot" woman, which contained an elf arrowhead. Fairy arrows had to be carefully handled because they lost their efficacy if they touched the ground or were struck by sunlight.[26] The notion of elf shot is echoed in modern fiction by the magically poisonous, evil Morgul blade, whose cut is only curable by elves, of Tolkien's *The Fellowship of the Ring*.[27] The first weapons used by the hobbits in *The Lord of the Rings* are barrow blades taken from the tomb of a wight buried in the Barrow-downs marked by megalithic standing stones, and one of these weapons injures the witch-king of Angmar because of its ancient magic.[28]

The narrative of a man stealing a fairy cup is common in England and other Danish-influenced areas of Europe and is reminiscent of the theft of the dragon's cup in *Beowulf*. Stories about the theft of fairy cups go back at least as far as the twelfth century when William of Newburgh recorded the legend of a man who raided the barrow of Willy Howe in East Riding, Yorkshire, for a fairy cup that ended up in the hands of Henry I and other kings.[29] The Oldenburg Horn, on display at Rosenborg Castle in Copenhagen, is linked to a story recorded in the nineteenth century by the Grimm brothers of a medieval count who stole the horn from a fairy woman. The cup was acquired by the king of Denmark in 1689. In one version of the tale, damage to the tip of the horn could not be repaired because the fairy metal was unknown to human smiths.[30] This detail is reminiscent of the modern legends of indestructible alien metals recovered from the Roswell UFO crash and hoarded by the American government, several versions of which involve archaeologists.[31]

The most famous of the fairy cups was old, foreign, and exotic. Stories about the Luck of Edenhall appeared as early as 1600. The Musgrave family kept the ornate glass goblet and protective case at their family seat of Edenhall in Cumberland. Either a Musgrave or a family servant had stolen the cup from fairies drinking at St. Cuthbert's well (figure 2.4). In one version, the cup was stolen for use in curing the lady of Edenhall, which is reminiscent of contemporary "elf arrow" cures. The fairies cursed the family that "if this cup should break or fall, farewell the luck of Edenhall."[32] The story become popular after it was recorded in 1721, and the cup outlived the estate, which was demolished in 1934 due to financial troubles. The Luck is today described by the Victoria and Albert Museum as the most famous glass in the world. Examination of the Luck has revealed that it was made by Syrian craftspeople of the thirteenth century and was probably a souvenir of the Crusades.[33]

THE LUCK OF EDEN-HALL.

ɴ Eden's wild romantic bowers,
    The summer moonbeams sweetly fall,
And tint with yellow light the towers —
    The stately towers of Eden-Hall.

FIGURE 2.4. A noble Musgrave ancestor steals the fairy cup that came to be
called the Luck of Edenhall. The cup was in reality a medieval glass goblet made in
Syria. From *The Book of British Ballads*, edited by Samuel Carter Hall
(London: Henry G. Bohn, 1853), 401.

Fairies, Evolution, and Archaeology

As early as the seventeenth century fairies were becoming a symbol of a simpler premodern time. Yet as part of the modern struggle between rational inquiry and traditional belief, antiquarianism and archaeology did not initially extinguish the fairies but adapted them.[34] Influential antiquarian John Aubrey recorded in *Natural History of Wiltshire* in the latter half of the seventeenth century a fairy assault account from a firsthand experiencer.[35] Sir Walter Scott's 1830 volume, *Letters on Demonology and Witchcraft*, is an early major publication suggesting that fairies were euhemeristic memories of earlier people in European lands, such as Lapps, though a form of this idea dates at least as far back as 1803. Euhemerism, the notion derived from the fourth-century BCE Greek philosopher Euhemerus that ancient gods were misremembered mortals, is at the core of many ideas about myths and legends of the past.[36]

Sir Walter Scott and his fellows created a fairy scholarship that in many ways resembles today's ancient extraterrestrial and UFO research, including the painful tension between the Enlightenment and a desire for the enchanted and sacred. The key difference is that fairies were studied by respected scholars rather than by outsiders bent on devaluing academia. These scholars began with the notion that perhaps the druids or the Celts defeated by the Romans were inspiration for fairies. Like the witch cult (see chapter 9), the fairies became survivals of ancient primordial religions and cultures that had to be documented before science and industrialization swept them away.[37]

Darwin's revolution made the idea of a biologically distinct fairy race popular among Victorian and Edwardian antiquarians and intellectuals. The already existing idea that the Lapps of Arctic Europe may have inspired some dwarf and fairy legends was transformed into a cross-continent pre-Indo-European or, more commonly, pre-Aryan race. The recognition of an Indo-European language family cast the non-Indo-European Lapps and the Basques of Spain as remnants of a non-Aryan Mongoloid/Turanian pygmy race who had been replaced by taller, metal-using colonists. The Stone–Bronze–Iron scheme of European prehistory lent itself to the fairy lore of iron vulnerability, though folklorist Sabine Baring-Gould suggested that the pygmies were metalworkers, skills they taught to the Norse who remembered them as magical smiths. The smaller indigenous inhabitants were driven to hide in caves, mounds, and other wild haunts of the fairies, their fires providing the source of fairy lights. These ideas spurred the interpretation of some archaeological remains as pygmies and the theory that modern Central African pygmies are a survival of this Turanian primeval race.[38] One antiquarian even suggested that relic Neanderthals hid in Ireland.[39] The Victorian colonial, racial, and evolutionary cast of all of these ideas (vanishing natives, technologically superior colonists, domestication of the wild, hidden pagan survivals, evolution of religion from savagery) is unmistakable.

The most developed version of this idea was folklorist David MacRitchie's "realist" perspective in *The Testimony of Tradition* and *Fians, Fairies, and Picts*. MacRitchie laboriously trawled through etymology and folklore to find proofs of his claims, such as the notion that the sealskins of shape-changing selkies were the skin-boat kayaks or currachs of Lapps and other Northern Europeans. Rather than burial places, barrow mounds and chambered cairns were Pict and fairy houses. There may be formal and metaphorical similarities between megalithic structures and houses, but MacRitchie suggested that these were primarily houses into historic times. His lost pygmy race hid in these chambers into early modern times, developing low-light vision that made it difficult to tolerate sunlight.[40] The folklore of supernaturally built cathedrals was evidence of the immense strength of the conquered Pictish dwarfs. Stories of castles haunted by brownies and banshees were memories of the colonial subjugation of this pygmy race, who became servants and wives to the iron users.[41] This methodology is akin to the cherry-picking of pseudoscientific endeavors like cryptozoology. Would-be monster hunters uncritically appropriate convenient parts of legends of water or forest spirits to create flesh-and-blood creatures like Bigfoot and the Loch Ness monster, ignoring supernatural or contradictory elements of these legends. Searching for the primordial at the edge of the modern world, MacRitchie mostly used accounts from rustic or "primitive" people (his descriptions are less kind, invoking illiteracy, stupidity, and drunkenness).[42]

The pygmy fairy race hypothesis went unresolved after formal debate by the Folklore Society in 1891 and did not long survive the professionalization of British archaeology. MacRitchie's second piece on the topic, *Fians,*

Fairies and Picts, was read to the Folk-Lore Society in 1892 and was published as a pamphlet the following year after the society rejected it as an article.[43] But the notion survived in fiction. The influential fantasy and horror author Arthur Machen wrote several stories about a hidden survival of the subterranean Mongoloid/Turanian Little People, who still abduct and abuse surface-dwellers and who are responsible for witchcraft lore. All of MacRitchie's lost race can be found in Machen's fiction stories and in his beliefs about prehistory, including the notion of Lapp sealskin boats as selkie skins.

Machen featured archaeology in many of his stories. He was born in Caerleon-on-Usk in Wales, also known as Isca Silurum, one of the most important Roman archaeological sites in Britain. Machen's haunted rural landscape mirrored his antipathy toward industrial society, secularism, and the disenchantment caused by science. Machen explicitly condemned the banishment of the supernatural from science and believed that hypnotism and other quasi-psychic experiences were the basis of magic, though he mocked spiritualists as ineffective and domesticated. Machen sought out the esoteric, was a lifelong friend of occultist Arthur Edward Waite, and was a member of the Order of the Golden Dawn alongside the influential fantasy author Algernon Blackwood and fellow Celtic fairy-lore author Yeats.[44]

Machen's 1895 "The Shining Pyramid" is an archaeological horror tale, beginning with the title. Two investigators in the mold of Holmes and Watson investigate a strange series of designs composed of chipped flint tools at a rural estate. Decipherment leads them to a hollow in which the pygmies ravage a woman who had gone missing, before sacrificing her on a shining pyramid of flame. The fairies are only quasi human and, per MacRitchie, have eyes adapted for darkness.[45] The survival of the Little People and their modern stone tools also feature in the detective story "The Red Hand," originally published in *The Three Impostors*.[46]

The theme is treated more thoroughly in "The Novel of the Black Seal," also in *The Three Impostors*. Ethnology professor Gregg brings his family to Caenlaen, a thinly veiled version of Machen's own Caerleon-on-Usk. Gregg has studied scattered pieces of information, including the disappearances of young women and strange hints from archaeological reports and antiquarian meetings, hoping to discover a new world, like Columbus discovering the Americas or the hypothetical discovery of Atlantis.[47] The key to the mystery is the Black Seal, an inscribed black stone described in Roman records and found near Babylon. Baffled for years, Gregg is able to crack the code after he encounters a Rosetta Stone-like key in an English museum, inscribed with both cuneiform and a corrupted form of cuneiform found on the Black Seal and written in ocher at the spot where a man was murdered with an unusual prehistoric-style ax. Gregg discovers that the writing on the seal is the key to an ancient science/magic of degeneration, embodying the colonial obsession with devolution.[48] The language of the stone, as spoken by a local fairy-human hybrid boy, is like that of "a tongue dead since untold ages, and buried deep beneath Nilotic mud, or in the inmost recesses of the Mexican forest."[49] As discussed in chapter 4, Egyptian and Mayan hieroglyphs were believed for centuries to have a kinship with the earliest writing and, in the case of Egyptian, to preserve symbols with magical powers.

It is difficult to ignore a remodeling of the British past as a reflection of more recent encounters between indigenous people and technology-wielding colonizers. That fairy reports surged in the sixteenth and seventeenth centuries, at the very time that the world was expanding and becoming more wondrously strange because of these encounters, may not be a coincidence. Likewise, the idea of the fairy race driven underground or to another realm bears more than a passing resemblance to the "vanishing native" of such importance to colonial myth and popular culture. The remaining house fairies and brownies that MacRitchie reconstructs as more domesticated are tricky but ultimately servile, a disturbing reflection of colonial house servant stereotypes.

As archaeology rejected the fairy race theory, more exotic natures emerged in the context of psychical research. The codiscoverer of natural selection, Alfred Russel Wallace, was one of many who suggested there may be "discarnate" beings that psychically evolved alongside humans, a concept that dominated much of theosophical thought.[50] The Oxford-trained anthropologist W. Y. Evans-Wentz collected a tremendous amount of folkloric and ethnographic data on fairy beliefs in his 1911 tome, *The Fairy-Faith in Celtic Countries*, data that he ultimately concluded were evidence of a nonhuman fairy reality. Evans-Wentz practiced a form of fairyosophy, blending Celtic and non-Celtic materials (usually from Asia since Evans-Wentz was a pioneer in spreading Buddhism in the West) and arguing that if these beliefs could be so easily meshed together, they must describe a common external reality.[51] Evans-Wentz collected testimony that the fairies were extraterrestrial in origin, mirroring the idea that fairies and other similar beings were a separate creation cast to earth when they were neutral in Satan's war in heaven. The separately created fairies merged with the elemental spirits of Western occultism and alchemy. These in turn blended with the theosophical astral beings and thought forms of the Victorians that became the occupants of UFOs in the twentieth century.[52]

Mesoamerican Ruins and Supernaturals

Pre-Columbian Mesoamericans had a deep historical tradition. Preclassic (1200 BCE–300 CE) Olmec artifacts, especially those made of jade, were kept as heirlooms and modified with later writing or sculpture and were depicted in Classic (300–1000 CE) and Postclassic (1000–1550 CE) artwork. Mexica (also known as Aztec, a later term for the Triple Alliance that dominated Mexico in the sixteenth century) scholars equated jade with greenery and herbs, and they searched for jade antiquities in places with such greenery. The parallel with the modern stereotype of the lost city blanketed by jungle growth is striking. Ancient jades and other antiquities were reused in the Postclassic to celebrate the nobles and kings who derived their right to power from Toltec descent. The term "Toltec" has been specifically applied to the 800–1200 CE site of Tula in the Mexican state of Hidalgo, and sculpture and objects from this site were recovered by later Mexica diggers. The word and concept "Toltec" had the broader meaning of the "people of Tollan," the Place of Reeds, a term used to refer to Teotihuacan, Cholula, and other ancient sites of urban civilization. Artwork in the Mexica language of Nahuatl was *toltecayotl* ("the Toltec thing"), and an artist was a *toltecatl* ("a Tollan person").[53]

The Place of Reeds refers to a deep Mesoamerican belief in an origin site, a sacred mountain in a marshy land of sustenance and fertility. This place was replicated in many Mesoamerican artificial mountains, or pyramids, including the Templo Mayor of the Aztec Empire in what is now Mexico City. However, the Classic Mayas referred in written records to anyone associated with contemporary Teotihuacan as *aj puj*, "he of the reeds."[54]

Postclassic Aztec kings and priests visited Teotihuacan as a shrine on a regular basis, removed Teotihuacan masks and sculptures, and left new sculptures at the base of the Pyramid of the Sun. Entire buildings were uncovered to copy ancient artworks and to remove monumental art and human remains, and Teotihuacan artwork was deposited in Aztec temple offerings.[55]

Ancient heirlooms and archaism in Mesoamerican artwork were ties to a sophisticated past comparable to the European notion of the "classical age."[56] Jade, as a substance innately associated with the ancient past, recalls the classical connotations of marble. The classical association with marble began in the Middle Ages with a fixation on the large, strong, squared, and polished nature of classical marble construction, equating it with ancient authority and the exotic and foreign.[57] A related analogue may be the association in the archaeological era of gold with ancient idols or buried treasure from faraway places. The antiquities cached in the Mexica Templo Mayor temporally range from Middle Preclassic Olmec jades to Early Postclassic Toltec ceramics. Most came from conquered tributary provinces rather than the Mexica heartland.[58] The analogy between this collection buried in the Mexica symbolic mountain of creation in the heart of the empire, and the museums erected in the imperial capitals of Europe and America in the nineteenth and twentieth centuries, is obvious.

Despite this sophistication, there was a broader Mesoamerican notion that the present had vanquished an immoral or uncivilized past, with heirloom objects depicted in association with defeated captives. Teotihuacan means "the city of the gods" in Nahuatl. Aztec chronicles describe it as the place where the gods began the current age by sacrificing themselves in an immense fire to ignite the sun.[59] Archaeologically, Teotihuacan's governmental and religious heart was destroyed by several days of organized burning and iconoclasm in the seventh century CE. The traditional Mesoamerican sign of a city's defeat was firing its temple, but the Teotihuacan burning also resonates with the later origin myth. Postclassic Mixtec books from Oaxaca depict the "stone men" of an earlier era being defeated in war, a mythic narrative that has been interpreted as referring to the defeat of the Classic order. In the Mixtec books, these stone men share a number of traits with a more supernatural original people, the *xolotl* or "earth men." Mixtec people today still remember the stone men as the beginning of history, who were followed by the pre-Columbian "ancient dead" and finally by the more recent ancestors since the arrival of Christianity.[60]

Important places of the previous age were still supernaturally powerful. Classic Maya reuse of older sites, such as the Late Preclassic San Bartolo, reflects a persisting understanding of ancient places and the sacred geography of shrines and burials.[61] The Preclassic and Classic period Oaxacan capital of Monte Albán may be the inspiration for the defeated stone men of the Mixtec books, but it continued to be a sacred pilgrimage and burial site up to the Spanish conquest. Around 1500 CE flooding and drought compounded problems with the Chapultepec aqueduct, which provided water to the Mexica imperial capital of Tenochtitlan. A carving was made at this time at Tula, the Toltec city associated with Quetzalcoatl, depicting the Mexica emperor Ahuitzotl asking the goddess Chalchihuitlicue to help with these problems. Chalchihuitlicue, "She of the Jade Skirt," is the goddess of the waters and consort to the rain/storm god Tlaloc, and she ruled the previous era, which was destroyed in a flood.[62] Her importance in antiquity, her jade symbolism, and her watery significance all make sense of the ritual return to a former Tollan, a place of older civilization.

Classic Maya texts and later accounts describe how spirits could inhabit ancient and sacred objects. The Aztec Empire kept god images captured from its enemies in a "prison temple" or *coateocalli*.[63] In at least some cases, ancient ruins were considered the work of giants. Sixteenth-century Spanish chronicles of Nahua culture also attribute the first age and the great pyramids of Teotihuacan to giants.[64]

Post-Columbian Mesoamerican Prehistory

Mesoamerican knowledge was doubly threatening to the Spanish colonial regime. Historical pride could bolster indigenous resistance and was considered inseparable from pagan religion. Christian kingdoms had expelled the last Muslim ruler from Granada the same year that Columbus landed in the Caribbean, and the Spanish Inquisition was dedicated to rooting out secret Jewish or Muslim practices hidden under allegedly insincere conversion to Christianity. Missionaries in Mesoamerica burned books, destroyed "idols," and wrote manuals for identifying hidden Mesoamerican cultural practices that were similar to the 1487 *Malleus Maleficarum* guidebook to the practices of supposed witches. The mass baptisms of thousands of Mesoamericans at a time and a severe shortage of trained and dutiful Christian teachers did little to quash millennia-old worldviews and religious practices, which survived underground by blending Mesoamerican deities and rituals with Christian saints.[65]

Indigenous cultures have continued to be targeted, especially during the revolutions and civil wars of the twentieth century but also in less violent manners, such as the persistent myth in El Salvador of the disappearance of the Nahua Pipil, a phenomenon similar to the vanishing-native ideology of North America.[66] Political disenfranchisement was behind the propagation in the colonial era of the "bearded white god" myth that equated the legendary god/historical figure Quetzalcoatl with Europeans such as Cortés. This idea has continued to be prominent in alternative archaeology circles. Mayas' cultural activism in the context of violence and warfare in the 1980s led to legal protection for indigenous religion, though it is caught up in a complicated struggle between Maya identity, Catholic reform, and evangelical Protestants who view indigenous religious specialists as witches.[67] In Colombia centuries of promoting the equivalence between indigenous religion and the demonic has created the "cacique disease," a fear that the remains of ancestors can cause physical sickness. Indigenous archaeology has recently begun to renew some connections between natives' needs in the present and the material past.[68]

The net result has been the erasure of the Mesoamerican historical tradition, although colonial Spaniards recorded some of the late history of Mexico and the "Aztecs." Like the folklore recorded in the European countryside by educated elites, this material was suitable for creating a Mexican national identity.[69] As in Europe, the collapsed protohistory phenomenon compressed the archaeological imagination into the Aztecs and Toltecs of the region around Mexico City and its educated historians. European folklore of magic and treasure lights at archaeological sites replaced Mesoamerican notions of ancient green places of jade, water, and fertility. Early Mesoamerican archaeologists recorded tales of cocks that crow at midnight to mark Christian golden treasure in pre-Hispanic mounds.[70] I have heard almost identical stories from contemporary archaeologists who work in Peru and Honduras. Other modern examples align midnight lights over archaeological sites with UFOs, ancestors, sky people, and indirect riches through archaeological tourism.[71]

The colonial impact on historical tradition was profound even in the colonially peripheral Maya region. Early anthropological work among the Yukatek Mayas grew around the archaeological projects at Chichén Itzá in the twentieth century, documenting ideas about the ruins of Yucatán before the "ancient Mayas" became a globally famous historical construct and a renewed identity among the Mayas themselves.[72] Chichén Itzá was primarily built and occupied in the Late to Terminal Classic (600–1000 CE) but was a site of pilgrimage into the sixteenth century.

Yukatek villagers of the twentieth century believed that the monumental structures were built by the *chak winikob'* (the "red people"), who were at times associated with the Itzá ethnic group and at other times with the American archaeologists themselves. More recent discussions of ancestors describe the Spaniards.[73] The Itzás were a historically documented political and ethnic group (Chichén Itzá means "The Mouth of the Well of the Itzás") in the pre-Columbian and early colonial eras. They moved south and dominated northern Guatemala until 1697, 176 years after the Aztec Empire surrendered to Cortés.[74] In Yucatán the reconstruction of the memory of Yukatek and Itzá nobility has sufficient symbolic power to have played a role in recent political struggles.[75]

However, the early twentieth-century Mayas of the village of Chan Kom (near Chichén Itzá) saw the Itzás as something else. They were a race of men who had lived in the "Good Times," distinct from modern Yukatekos. They had mysterious wisdom and supernatural powers and could command stones to build monumental structures and roads on their own, firewood to deliver itself, and corn to cook itself. Similar magical beings allegedly built pre-Hispanic structures in the Mexican state of Oaxaca.[76] The Yukatekos of Chan Kom said these wise men were destroyed or punished as the current "Bad Times" began, and their secret knowledge was lost. These Itzás continue to exist under the floors of archaeological ruins and are destined to return, reflecting the long Mayan tradition of burying the dead under structures.[77] According to men in Chan Kom, the ancient Itzás sacrificed people for Xkukican, also known as Kukulkan, the feathered serpent of Mesoamerica prominently displayed in the monuments of Chichén Itzá.

Some indigenous villagers of Yucatán believe that the ruins were built by giants or the dwarves called *ppuzob'*, who turned to stone when the sun rose or who were swept away by the biblical flood. Archaeologists have found the stone boats of the ppuzob', though they interpret the stones as metates, corn-grinding stones, worn into a canoe shape through use. The excavation of the remains of a young person likewise can spark talk that the ancient people of the peninsula were small.[78] The pattern of interpreting ancient statuary or bones as petrified during the rise of the first sun of the current era is widespread throughout postconquest Mesoamerica.[79]

Aluxes, Ghosts, and Aliens of the Mayas

In the Yukatekan stories, the ancient Itzás burned incense in front of clay images to make spirits come to life. These are the aluxob' (singular, alux), who reside in clay figurines and incense burners. Even the discovery of potsherds, associated with the little clay people, could be dangerous and should be avoided. Some equate the aluxob' (*aluxes* in Spanish) with the magic-wielding dwarves who built large stone buildings like the Pyramid of the Dwarf, or Magician, at Uxmal. Others suggest that they are two distinct classes of entities, both potentially harmful to archaeological sites if not propitiated.[80] Rituals to propitiate them also were required to heal certain illnesses.[81] In 1992 a government-sponsored ritual petitioned the aluxob' of the Sacred Cenote at Chichén Itzá in advance of ceremonies marking Columbus Day and the quincentennial of the end of the pre-Columbian era.[82]

Early twentieth-century Yukatek Mayas, at the time when archaeology was first becoming established in Yucatán, believed in the supernatural nature of stone tools in a manner virtually identical to "elf shot" in Europe. Spirits of the land (some from farm fields, some from villages, some from beehives) known as balams (meaning "jaguars" or "stars," a prestigious pre-Columbian word) or *nucuch winikob'* ("great men"), protected humans from evil spirit winds and animals. In the dark, these little men would flick a magic stone blade at the evil spirits, a practice called *piliz dzonkab'*. Ancient chipped stone tool fragments were believed to be the result of piliz dzonkab' and could be placed in ritual deposits by healers in village protective ceremonies or placed above the door of a new house. The same spirits could also punish humans who did not offer them a tribute of corn, or those who trespassed or stole from another family's field. These spirits also replaced children with changelings.[83] The possibility of syncretism or the adoption of European fairy beliefs seems strong, but the balams are integrated with a number of traditional Mesoamerican practices involving directionality and color. In other ethnographic work, the aluxob' are the ones who steal children, but rather than replacing them with changelings, they teach the children positive healing techniques.[84]

Many twenty-first-century Mayas associate the aluxob' or similar spirits and creatures, as well as serpents and mysterious music, with archaeological ruins.[85] Nonetheless there is some notion that the aluxob' and other invisible entities are diminishing in number due to neglect.[86] The aluxob' are still spoken of around Xunantunich in western Belize but in a manner similar to *duendes*, the European Spanish elves or fairies, and more broadly associated with the forest than with archaeological sites. One archaeologist has suggested to me that once archaeological sites are cleared and reconstructed for tourism, they seem to lose their grassroots supernatural value.[87] This mirrors the Weberian "thinning" of magic and fairy folk from the world, a common trope in folklore and fiction.[88] Some stories of aluxob' compare them with UFO aliens.[89]

One early source for these stories was Thomas Gann, the chief medical officer for British Honduras in the early twentieth century, an early archaeologist, and an intelligence agent for the British and the Americans. His less-than-careful archaeology and dubious associates gave him a clouded reputation in life, and his sensational writing style suggests caution regarding his observations, especially on the supernatural. Some of his tales do echo other descriptions of Mayan folk beliefs. He was told that disturbing ancient ruins in the Yucatán peninsula might anger the souls of the dead buried there. Maya men refused to enter a cave with Gann since they believed it to be the burial place of ancient Maya nobility, whose souls still enacted rites and rituals and who would curse interlopers to become lost forever in the labyrinthine passages.[90] Gann had the temerity to call the Mayas "degenerate" for being a "ghost-haunted, spirit-obsessed people, living more in the past than in the present, concerned more with the spirits of the dead than with the living."[91] Not only was Gann obsessed with the past as an archaeologist, but he masqueraded as the devil and terrified

Maya villagers in order to "test" local folklore.[92] Gann wrote with an air of haunted mystery and dread about purchasing masks and regalia from a K'ekchi' Maya "Devil Dance."[93] His accusations that others were ghost-obsessed or superstitious were the height of hypocrisy.

In Belize (then British Honduras) Gann described a group of K'ekchi' Maya workers as being afraid of a limestone mask discovered immediately before an earthquake, while others blamed an epidemic on the opening of the tombs at Lubaantun.[94] Gann's digging partner F. A. Mitchell-Hedges, who as we shall see had a far worse reputation, also described curses, vengeful ancestors, and evil spirits killing K'ekchi' Maya laborers and literally shoving Mitchell-Hedges over the edge of a pyramid at Lubaantun.[95] The ruins of Xunantunich, Belize, were particularly haunted, and the site is named after a spectral "stone maiden" reported to appear at the mouth of a tunnel in the main pyramid at the site. Mitchell-Hedges described the stone maiden in ways reminiscent of La Llorona or the Mayan Ixtabai, a wandering temptress of the forest that is feared in Belize even today.[96] Tour guides still tell this story to my students who visit the site. When I stayed with the archaeological project at Xunantunich in the 1990s, no one mentioned the maiden, though I did not know about the story and so did not ask. At the large archaeological parks, scientific narratives fill the guidebooks, signs, and approved materials used by licensed tour guides, but in my experience any visitor will also hear informal narratives (including by tour guides) of evangelical Christian perspectives, extraterrestrials, power vortices, and local legends. Gann described other spirits at Xunantunich, including shape changers and a little old man with a gray beard, who drove the first settlers of the modern community to move their town away from the ruins.[97] Though Gann did not record a name for this little man, he sounds like the dwarves reported elsewhere in Mesoamerica.

Lost Secrets of the Middle East

Akkadian and Babylonian mythology and monumental art may have inspired some images and stories of angels in Aramaic and biblical records. Hellenistic observers in the third century BCE interpreted monumental Bronze Age inscriptions in Lebanon as records of the Watchers, the mysterious sons of God who mated with the daughters of man in the book of

Genesis. In some traditions it is the Watchers and their gifts of knowledge that constitute the sin and corruption of humanity wiped away by the deluge. These extrahuman figures in the noncanonical book of Enoch resemble the earlier sages of Babylonian lore, the Akkadian *apkallu*. These earlier entities were depicted wearing bird wings or, amusingly to modern viewers, fish on their heads to mark their origin in the sky or emerging from the Apsû sweet water abyss to give the gifts of civilization to humanity. Their images magically protected Assyrian households. Like the later depictions of Olmec jades or even our own persistent depiction of supernatural entities as wearing the garb of past centuries, figurines of the sages resembled older sculptural styles, reinforcing the primeval, supernatural nature of the sages.[98]

In later biblical traditions the cannibalistic offspring of the Watchers and human women, the giants, became demons after the death of their physical forms and are comparable to the Mesopotamian demons the *utukku-s*. Early Christians used the myth of the Watchers to demonize pagan teachings, casting non-Christian entities as fallen angels purveying forbidden knowledge. The Watchers were bound away and the deluge destroyed most of their offspring, but their knowledge of civilization was transmitted on inscribed stones buried or left in high places. Noah's son Ham, the progenitor of the people of Egypt and Asia, supposedly left magical secrets on these inscribed stones or plates.[99] The book of Jubilees speaks of ancient forbidden Watcher stones of astrology using the sun and moon, possibly matching the common use of a tripartite icon of the sun, a crescent moon, and a star on neo-Babylonian monuments. Babylonian monuments from Brisa in Lebanon may in particular have inspired the "dream" stories of the Qumran texts, the book of Giants, and Daniel 4, stories about the destruction of a cedar forest, about an inscribed stone, and about Watchers fighting animals.[100] The Watchers later provided a model for ancient extraterrestrials authors, and in the early twenty-first century there was a resurgence of interest in the Watchers or Nephilim in Christian and paranormal communities.[101]

The Great Sphinx of Giza has been excavated repeatedly since the time of the Egyptian pharaohs, only to be reburied by the desert winds. Egyptians and Nubians into the early first millennium CE continued to remember, honor, and play creatively with monuments, imagery, and concepts from earlier millennia.[102] However, as in Europe and Mesoamerica, the disruption of historical continuity in the Middle East and North Africa transformed archaeological sites into places of supernatural mystery and danger. In Arabic the Sphinx and other ancient monuments, such as the massive statue of Ramesses II at Memphis or the statues at the entrance to Luxor, are known as Abū 'l-Hawl or the "Father of Terror," potentially due to a linguistic confusion with the Egyptian Per-Hol, the "Place of Horus."[103] There is little difference between the panic of an Egyptian archaeological worker who "found himself in the presence of two heads of living human beings whose eyes stared back at him" when he was excavating painted sculptures in the Fourth Dynasty mastaba of Rahotep and Nofret,[104] and the fear of fairies living in Scottish howes or the clay aluxob' in Yukatekan ruins.

In classical times the Sphinx was thought to be a god, constructed before the pyramids, an idea that still dominates alternative ideas about Egypt.[105] As with the Christian demonization of monuments in Europe, the cultural colonization of Egypt by the Greeks, the Romans, Christians, and Muslims produced a stratigraphy of ruptures in meaning. After the arrival of Christianity, the pyramids became tombs for biblical figures or granaries built by the biblical Joseph. Egyptian Coptic Christian monks described hieroglyphic texts as magical and demonic, written in blood and consisting of dangerous nonsense, though more recently Coptic scholars have embraced continuities from pharaonic Egypt.[106] Christianity elsewhere treated classical monuments and other images as dangerous magical talismans and potential physical vessels for demons, and they were liable to be destroyed.[107]

The Sphinx could ward off evil spirits or provide riches in medieval Egypt, and the nearby pyramids likewise became associated with treasures guarded by spirits. Some medieval Arab scholars examined the monuments for their construction techniques, but most interpretations were more divine or magical since Egypt was seen as a place particularly full of divine wonders. One suggestion credited the pyramids to the tribe of 'Ād, which also allegedly built the mythic lost Arabian city Irem of the Pillars discussed in the Qur'an. A more persistent notion is the Hermetic idea that the pyramids preserved antediluvian knowledge and were built either by Hermes or King Surid, who may be a form of Hermes.[108]

Secret knowledge hidden in the pyramids is one of the key tropes of alternative archaeology. The American "sleeping prophet" and faith healer Edgar Cayce declared that a Hall of Records rests under the Giza plateau. Efforts to find this chamber have dogged mainstream archaeological activity at Giza for decades due to official tolerance of theosophically minded expeditions alongside more mainstream foreign scientists.[109] The journalist and alternative archaeology author Graham Hancock expanded this idea, claiming that monuments around the world were memories of a precatastrophe global civilization. Amazingly, his techniques of dating monuments according to alleged alignments with past locations of constellations in the sky are virtually identical to those of medieval Arab scholars. In the twelfth century Abū 'Mushrif 'Alawi al-Ḥafāfī interpreted the Egyptian winged sun-disc as the zodiacal Cancer and the Eagle as symbolized by the star Altair. By calculating the last time Altair had entered the zodiac sign of Cancer, he determined that the Egyptian ruins were built 20,000 years ago.[110]

The Abandoned Landscape of the Jinn

The Sphinx is not the only supernatural terror to be feared at Giza. Jinn and *ghuls* are also afield in the Old Kingdom necropolis on the edge of Cairo.[111] Jinn derive from pre-Islamic Arab traditions but spread globally through the Qur'an, Islamic beliefs, and the Western appropriation and construction of the "genie" from *The Arabian Nights*. They are a separate race that originated before humans who are able to perceive and act upon the unseen world of God and other unearthly beings, but they are materially of the earthly realm. They inhabit other realms, particularly under the earth, but also live alongside humans. Composed of scorching wind or smokeless fire, jinn have supernatural powers and can become invisible, shapeshift, move at high speed, walk through walls, and live for a long time.[112]

Like other extrahumans, such as fairies, aliens, and aluxob', jinn have the ability to magically build ancient monuments. Before Islam, jinn had been worshipped for their access to knowledge overheard from heaven as well as knowledge of crafts, such as superior medicine and metallurgy. Corrupted jinn who escaped angelic justice allegedly built several monuments and giant constructions.[113] The classical Egyptian magical protector/

god Bes is reflected in modern stories of dancing afreets (a type of jinn) at Karnak.[114] The construction of ancient monuments, divine magical knowledge of civilization, corruption, and subsequent purging by angels also mark the Judeo-Christian Watchers and Nephilim and their modern descendants the giants and ancient extraterrestrials of alternative archaeology and conspiracy theory. Theosophy author H. P. Blavatsky incorporated the legend of Ishmonia, the Petrified City, in her 1877 landmark occult work, *Isis Unveiled*. Her source only mentioned a ruined city of petrified people, but Blavatsky expanded this into a library of antediluvian knowledge and magic where afreets and jinn study ancient scrolls. Ishmonia is the Egyptian site of Ashmunein, located near Tuna el-Gebel and later called Hermopolis due to it being a late cult center of Thoth/Hermes. It is marked by catacombs filled with mummified ibis and baboons.[115]

The jinn and their abilities could be controlled through a mix of knowledge and sacred artifacts. The belief that archaeological ruins are the product of jinn was recorded in tenth-century Yemen. According to the historian al-Hasan al-Hamdani, one jinn made an inventory of all the structures the jinn had built in the region and the methods they employed. King Solomon possessed a ring with which he commanded jinn to build his temple and possibly a number of castles. He also commanded these spirits either to build the city of Palmyra (in some traditions, the resting place of the queen of Sheba) or to rebuild it from the ruins of an older city on the spot. The association of jinn with artifacts such as rings has entered into the Western imagination through *The Arabian Nights* and the story of Aladdin's lamp, but jinn were also part of the negotiation over the sale of artifacts to Western travelers in the nineteenth century.[116]

The link between jinn and magical treasure extends to lost cities, such as the City of Brass and its jinn-filled bottles recounted in *The Arabian Nights*; archaeological ruins; other abandoned buildings; and the desolate wastes of the desert. The first Saudi Arabian World Heritage designation was granted in 2008 to Al-Hijr, "The Stony Place," a stone-cut Nabataean site similar to the more famous Petra in Jordan. Al-Hijr is believed to have been destroyed for rejecting God and has long been considered an extremely dangerous place haunted by jinn and ghuls. Seeking treasure there can be fatal, and some Saudis still avoid the site.[117]

Modern Egyptians may be cautious around or even avoid archaeological sites because ancient monuments are believed to be the products of jinn and those who controlled them, an extension of modern practices of appealing to jinn for supernatural assistance.[118] The magical reputation of ancient Egyptian sites helped protect many of them from being plundered. Many modern Egyptians echo the medieval view that the pharaoh and other ancient Egyptians were masters of diabolism and witchcraft who bound jinn to protect their tombs and build monuments.[119] Information about treasure sites, and how to defeat the magic protecting them, is contained in the medieval *Book of Buried Pearls and Precious Mysteries: On the Indications of Cachettes, Finds, and Treasures*, a volume that continued to be used into the twentieth century.[120]

In order to dig in such places, a sheik with special knowledge in excavation must be employed (for 5–20 percent of the profit from a given excavation) to placate the jinn, who otherwise might drive intruders mad. These men not only have specialized knowledge, they are also in league with jinn. Such transgressions in black magic are sufficiently unclean that the better and more experienced (or less cautious) excavation sheiks are believed to be foreigners. In Egypt, the best sheiks to control jinn come from Morocco. This is comparable to the stereotype of the supernatural gypsy or the continental vampire expert Abraham Van Helsing in *Dracula*. In the wake of the 2011 Egyptian Revolution, archaeological looting has dramatically increased due to political instability, a lack of governmental oversight, and declining foreign tourist spending. Men who once sold souvenirs are hired by organized looting gangs to dig into ancient ruins. A sheik guides the excavations by "sensing" the objects and converses with jinn to stop them from harming the looters, though many continue to die in unsafe digging operations.[121]

Haunted Burial Grounds

The trope of the native burial ground is deeply embedded in colonialism and is part of the larger myth of the vanishing native and the extinction of indigenous people. Later colonial writings, of unknown authenticity, describe how in the first year the Puritans colonized Plymouth, the sachem (leader) of Passonagessit protested against English grave robbing for pottery and other goods by invoking his mother's ghost, who appeared to him in a dream. The sachem's speech became a persistent motif in colonial and early republic American literature, setting a standard for describing indigenous Americans as spirits, demons, and ghosts. However, hauntings may be more broadly associated with British colonialism globally, and the phenomenon of haunting is intimately tied to the transformations of landscapes in Europe.[122]

The sympathetic nature of the haunted native burial ground—that such places victimize white intruders—becomes both a form of appropriation of indigenous identity and oppression and a convenient way of mythologizing the landscape. The appropriation aspect echoes a long history of spiritualists' reliance on ethereal "Indian guides" as well as genuine activism for indigenous rights during the nineteenth century.[123] More concrete appropriation includes the transformation of indigenous sites into cemeteries. The European settlers of Middletown, Connecticut, explicitly placed their cemetery on "Indian Hill" after indigenous burials were removed and the area's former people were reduced to the status of a legend who had gone extinct. Monuments like these provide a charter myth involving fictive ancestors and the ownership of land.[124]

Mound Cemetery in Marietta, Ohio, contains not only a very large number of graves of Revolutionary War officers but a large indigenous monumental site that was possibly still being modified at the time of European contact. As the burying ground for the first permanent American settlement in the Northwest Territory, this appropriation had symbolic value in creating a new American identity. The British policy to prohibit settler encroachment into the territories of indigenous allies past the Appalachian Mountains had been a major impetus for the Revolutionary War, making Marietta a powerful symbol of victorious defiance. The Ohio Company of Associates preserved the monuments found there, but described them as heathen temples, possibly associated with Mexico and likely used for human sacrifices.[125] Early in the American imagination, North America was seen as the origin for Central American civilization, often ultimately derived from Aryan Eurasia.[126] To further emphasize their exotic antiquity, the Marietta mounds were given classical Latin names.[127]

Doubtful or blatantly invented Native American legends are a staple of North American paranormal tales with otherwise clear European roots, such as classically inspired sea serpents.[128] The Mothman legend, a fixture of paranormal, UFO, and conspiracy subculture, is entangled with the dubious "curse" of Chief Cornstalk, an actual person killed in what would become Point Pleasant, West Virginia.[129] The Amityville haunting hoax included dubious claims that the house was built on the demon-haunted place reserved for mentally ill members of the Shinnecock community, echoing the belief among ghost hunters that mental hospitals or asylums are particularly haunted places.[130] The success of *The Amityville Horror* in book and film versions spawned other successful fictional stories that invoked cursed indigenous burial grounds, such as Stephen King's *Pet Sematary*, or the power of indigenous spirituality (the second *Poltergeist* film features a Native American shaman fighting the evil spirit of a dooms-day Christian preacher). The revival of the cursed native burial ground occurred within the larger Satanic panic of the 1980s and 1990s, part of an American Christian movement of spiritual warfare. Native American sites, objects, and spirituality have been targeted by these spiritual warriors as demon-infested.[131]

The reassertion of indigenous agency inverts the haunted status of indigenous places. The "discovery" of indigenous remains can be a reemergence, a form of ancestral spiritual resistance to colonialism. One approach to a postcolonial archaeology is to engage with the spiritual experiences and perspectives of indigenous communities.[132] An archaeological survey in the traditional Hopi landscape conceptualized ruined structures, stone tools, and petroglyphs as metaphorical footprints left as sacred messages to the future by the Hopis as they left the place of emergence. These are important places of memory, sites of clan pilgrimage to remember and honor a migratory history. This kind of work explicitly acknowledges scientific chronological information as well as subjective intuition or phenomenological practice, and elides the boundary between the metaphorical and literal. In this living tradition, ancient pottery may be ground up for reuse in modern potting, and turquoise or stone tools may be incorporated into new objects rather than showing them off on the walls of museums or galleries, while the removal of artifacts can lead to curse-like illnesses and death. Rock paintings serve as reminders of mythic time when the Holy People walked among the Navajos and as possible evidence of strategic symbolic art made during a time of change and ethnogenesis.[133]

Colleen Boyd describes unease and hauntings during the excavation of human remains at Tse-whit-zen in Washington state. Some indigenous participants and archaeologists countered the impact of these revealed ancestors through the protective measures of smudging and using corpse berries associated with the dead. Personal experiences with the entity categorized in the twentieth century as Sasquatch occurred during the excavation, sparking a community debate over whether it was a guardian or a dangerous being.[134] Perhaps because Westerners have reimagined Sasquatch as a physical being, it has become a particular nexus between the material and the spiritual, a teaching moment for both evolutionary anthropology and collaborative archaeology.[135] However, others in and around anthropology have gone beyond using Sasquatch as a pedagogical tool and have argued for the physical reality of ancient hominids, such as *Paranthropus*, Neanderthals, or *Gigantopithecus*. The debate raged in the 1970s in the pages of *Current Anthropology*.[136]

The fossil hominin Bigfoot, created out of a blend of indigenous traditions and European wildman tales, resembles other supernatural folk archaeologies I have described in this chapter. Bigfoot and related humanoid cryptids act like people but aren't quite people, are reminiscent of tales of ancestors and the dead but are something distinct, and are a reimagining of ancient materiality (fossils, petroglyphs, sculptures) and folklore as entities with spirit-like capabilities. The popular conception of Bigfoot is of a mystery primate or apeman, but within the "Footer" community esoteric beliefs about the entity are much more common, such as its ability to cloak and become invisible, to stun prey or hunters with an electromagnetic force, or to walk between parallel planes of reality. Archaeologist Kathy Strain researches "hairy man" pictographs in relation to Bigfoot and participates in Bigfoot-focused expeditions outside of her work with the US Forest Service as a Forest Heritage Resource and Tribal Relations program manager. Strain does not claim physical evidence of a Bigfoot entity, but emphasizes its role in disparate indigenous narratives of various beings potentially related to the Western idea of Bigfoot.[137]

One nonparanormal and explicitly multivocal investigation blending indigenous beliefs and archaeological practices suggests that some extremely remote archaeological sites in the territory of the Squamish Nation of the Pacific Northwest may be tied to the "wild people" or Smaylilh. Reimer/Yumks explicitly rejects a giant primate explanation for the Smaylilh as pseudoscientific, instead researching potential hermit sites of unkempt human shamans-in-training learning to spiritually engage with the nonhuman world. Yet this shaman hypothesis was included in a History channel documentary promising to provide "definitive evidence" regarding Bigfoot and emphasizing an apelike reconstruction by anthropologists and biologists. Cryptozoology enthusiasts did not accept the indigenous engagement approach and bitterly complained about "hyper-empirical claptrap from the mainstream," preferring talk of conspiracies or citing pro-hominid Bigfoot anthropologist Jeffrey Meldrum.[138]

This mismatch mirrors a debate among those engaged in collaborative archaeology with indigenous communities. On the one hand, hauntings and similar phenomena can be seen to challenge Western approaches to science and to dislodge an academic authority rooted in colonialism.[139] On the other hand, some prefer a secular indigenous approach to antiquity, concerned that just as the mystical Celt stereotype is inherently colonial, a focus on the supernatural may stain indigenous political power as "spectral" and reinforce Euro-American stereotypes of the mystical native.[140]

3

Occulted Archaeologists

IN JUNE 2015, I accompanied a tour group to Stonehenge, Avebury, and other tourist sites in the Wiltshire area of England. Both the prerecorded narration and the tour guide significantly featured paranormal elements alongside archaeological information. Paranormal topics were not an advertised aspect of the tour but were not questioned by the guests. Prior to arriving at Stonehenge, we were treated to ghostly tales as well as discussion of the surrounding Salisbury Plain as "Britain's Area 51." The reference to the secretive US military base in Nevada is apt in two respects. Both rural areas are home to significant military exercises and installations, and both are connected with UFOs and associated phenomena.[1] Crop circles were born as a cultural phenomenon in this part of England, perhaps inspired by the circular henge sites and other mysterious archaeological monuments sprouting from the fields. By 1980, when crop circles began appearing in earnest, the UFO subculture was familiar with the notion that fairy accounts had strong similarities to modern UFO reports and alien abductions. Many cereologists have suggested parallels between accounts of fairies and other spirits dancing in the fields, "saucer nests" found near UFO sightings in the 1960s, the more intricate crop circles of the 1980s, and pictogram designs emerging around 1990.[2] The latter designs—circles and swirls of energy connected by lines—could easily be taken as gigantic representations of the core concepts of ley lines.

Why is Wiltshire home to crop circles? Why is Stonehenge associated with UFOs and the paranormal? To answer these questions, I had to go to the heart of the New Age, to the nearby town of Glastonbury. I had to excavate the hidden history of psychic archaeology.

Frederick Bligh Bond and Glastonbury

If archaeological remains commonly gain supernatural and spiritual qualities, we should not be surprised that archaeologists would participate in occult practices and have occult beliefs. Frederick Bligh Bond was an early spirit-talking archaeologist and arguably the originator of psychic archaeology. Bond was an architect with medieval antiquarian experience and a background steeped in Freemasonry, theosophy, psychical research, and esotericism, such as numerology and sacred geometry.[3] At the age of forty-four, Bond was hired to restore the Abbey of St. Mary at Glastonbury.

Archaeological evidence of Paleolithic and Neolithic settlement occurs broadly in the Glastonbury area. Twenty-first-century research calls into question claims of a possible Roman occupation on the site of the abbey, but there was likely a modest Roman settlement in the surrounding environs. The earliest structure at the actual abbey is post-Roman, possibly fifth or sixth century CE, with the early church probably dating to Anglo-Saxon times.[4] A Christian shrine was established on the imposing hill known as Glastonbury Tor by at least Anglo-Saxon times if not earlier (figure 3.1). Like many prominent archaeological sites and natural features in Europe, the tor was associated with fairies and was considered the entrance to the fairy underworld guarded by King Gwyn ap Nudd. It was also the legendary stronghold of Melwas, who had kidnapped Queen Guinevere for ransom.[5] The kidnapping of wives to the underground or undersea homes of the fairies or selkies is a common folklore motif. The tor would have risen above marshlands in earlier centuries, a quality that may have made it sacred in both pre-Christian and Anglo-Saxon times. This semipermanent island has become widely associated with the Isle of Avalon, where the wounded King Arthur rested until he returned to aid Britain.[6]

It wasn't on the tor but in the abbey that in 1191 Glastonbury's monks allegedly discovered Arthur's and Guinevere's remains. A lead cross, made in an anachronistic tenth- or eleventh-century style, marked the burial of Arthur's gigantic bones (figure 3.2). The search for Britain's mythic defender may have been spurred by the need for pilgrimage revenues after a devastating fire leveled most of the abbey in 1184. The monarchy supported and may have inspired the find. Edward I built a monument to Arthur at the abbey (figure 3.3), perhaps to undercut prophecies that Arthur would return

FIGURE 3.1. The remaining tower of an Anglo-Saxon church dedicated to St. Michael on Glastonbury Tor has become an icon of the English countryside and the New Age. The tor has become the focus of fairy, Arthurian, and Christian folklore. Image by author.

FIGURE 3.2. Drawings and descriptions are all that survive of a lead cross allegedly excavated by the Glastonbury monks, which supposedly marked the burial of King Arthur. Analysis of the writing has suggested an anachronistic style too late for Arthur but appearing old at the time of the discovery or, more likely, creation of the cross in 1191. From *Brock's Avalonian Guide: A History and Description of the Town and Abbey of Glastonbury* (Glastonbury: J. Brock, 1881), 17.

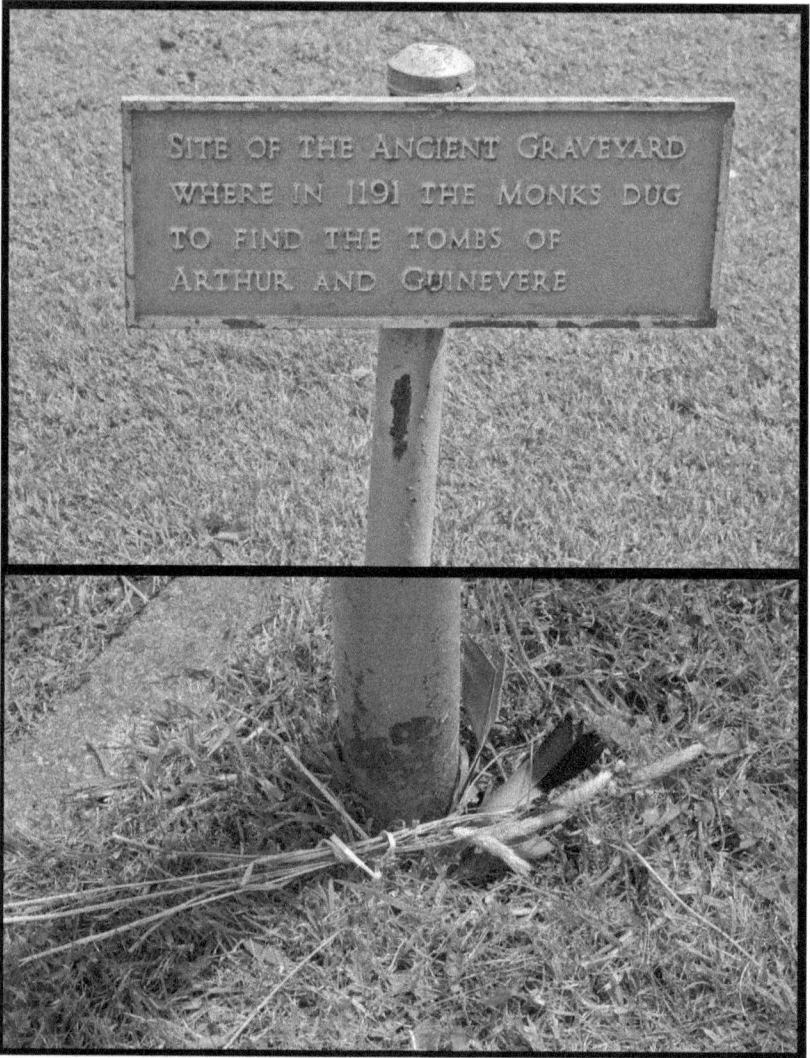

FIGURE 3.3. The sign in the upper photo marks where Ralegh Radford's excavations determined that the Glastonbury monks had dug in 1191 for Arthur's and Guinevere's graves. Analysis has suggested that this feature is not related to the digging. The lower photo is of an offering left on the day I visited the subsequent reburial tomb of Arthur, which was commissioned by Edward I. Images by author, used with permission of Glastonbury Abbey.

to defend the conquered Welsh.[7] Arthur was not alone in being fortuitously discovered. In 1164, the Three Magi were "discovered" outside of Milan and then taken to Cologne for Frederick I.[8]

Glastonbury already had a constructed legendary past as an extremely old Christian place possibly dating to the apostles, but after the excavation Arthurian and Holy Grail themes rose in prominence. The abbey eventually claimed the remains of more than 300 saints, and by the fourteenth century the full myth of Joseph of Arimathea bringing the Holy Grail to Glastonbury manifested. One legend associated with Joseph, that his staff miraculously blossomed into a perennial thorn tree, may be reflected in the fragments of a gilt rod found at the abbey, though the thorn legend may postdate the destruction of the abbey.[9] These legends were part of a larger mythology of an English church that had always been separate from Rome. A purposefully retrospective approach to ecclesiastical architecture was common at this time in this part of England, but Glastonbury Abbey exaggerated this tendency.[10] The massive Roman Catholic abbey, the second richest in England, was dissolved by Henry VIII in 1539, and its last abbot was drawn and quartered on the tor before his head was impaled on a spike above the abbey gate.[11]

The myth of a separate English church grew in strength after the Reformation and later joined with Victorians' interest in Arthur, the medieval, and folklore to increase antiquarian and esoteric attention in Glastonbury.[12] In 1907 the Church of England acquired the abbey and charged Bond with restoring the ruins and writing a guidebook (figure 3.4). Unbeknown to his employers, Bond took the opportunity to test automatism (automatic writing). The erudite Bond conceived of his activities as more than invoking spirits. He and his sensitive friend John Allen Bartlett (also known as John Alleyne) were accessing the Great Memoria, a timeless cosmic memory or consciousness. Bond believed that automatism blended rationalism, the "stifling incubus" of the West, with imagination and the important spiritual insights that could be made by trained minds of the East.[13]

Bond's automatism encapsulated the simultaneous European internal struggle with modernity and the colonial confrontation with global cultural diversity. This tension has driven much of the Western occult tradition from its roots in Hermetic magic, a legacy of the Greek reconceptualization of Egyptian wisdom and knowledge after Alexander's conquest of Egypt. The

FIGURE 3.4. Glastonbury Abbey reconstruction by Frederick Bligh Bond. From his *The Gate of Remembrance*, 4th ed. (New York: Dutton, 1921), plate III.

upheaval of industrialization and the foundational surprises of geology, evolution, and prehistoric archaeology shocked the European imagination, just as Europeans recoiled from the culture shock of colonial interaction with Africa, the Americas, and the East. European intellectuals and occultists reacted by appropriating new scientific findings and exotic cultural elements as independent proof of myths of psychic survival after death, an ancient golden age, and the limitless potential of the human consciousness to exceed its earthly bounds. An important classical Greek scholar of the first half of the twentieth century, Gilbert Murray, was considered telepathic and conducted psychical research experiments that were cited for decades as the best evidence of extrasensory perception, though even Murray wasn't sure if his abilities were due simply to his extraordinary hearing.[14] It is all but impossible to find a form of alternative or spooky archaeology that does not trace back to this crisis in modern and especially Victorian thought.

Bond was steeped in occult practices and theosophical appreciation for the mystical East, but he also emphasized Christianity, citing the presence of glossolalia (speaking in tongues) and prophecy in the New Testament.[15] Bond was not alone in mixing spiritualism, archaeology, and Christianity. At the same time that Bond was accessing the Great Memoria to reconstruct England's greatest Christian shrine, the British aristocrat Montague Brownlow Parker was following spirit guides to find the Ark of the Covenant and other treasures in Jerusalem. The Finnish medium Valter H. Juvelius provided spirit clues and alleged codes in the book of Ezekiel. Parker organized lavish and controversial excavations into the Temple Mount based on these clues, paying bribes to access the Dome of the Rock until local residents discovered his excavations. Rumors flew that he had found the holiest treasures in the Abrahamic faiths, such as the Ark of the Covenant and the regalia of King Solomon, including the ring with which Solomon controlled jinn. Days of rioting ensued in Jerusalem, and the incident further strained relations between Britain and the Ottoman Empire in the run-up to the First World War. Parker and his expedition escaped to their boat through trickery and with little to show in the way of treasure or profit.[16]

Back in Glastonbury, Bond was tapping into the Great Memoria with automatic writing akin to Ouija board conjurings. A few weeks after the death of John Bartlett's father, Bond discovered that Bartlett had the apparent ability to receive automatic writing from the spirit world.[17] Bartlett would hold a pencil over a piece of paper, and Bond would gently touch or hold Bartlett's hand and conduct a conversation with Bartlett about unrelated topics so as to not influence the information being received from a mélange of historical minds. The first message from beyond time was "All knowledge is eternal and available to mental sympathy."[18] In addition to accessing the mental impressions of various monks and other people of historical Glastonbury, Bartlett also contacted the Watchers, a group of ancient intelligences, which prompted Bond's most profound philosophical work. Bond even felt compelled to bring his revelations to the attention of a man he thought had discovered similar principles, Albert Einstein.[19] The exact identity of these Watchers is uncertain, but they seem cut from the same cloth as the ascended masters of theosophy rather than the biblical entities. Bond was familiar with theosophy, the spirit contacts claimed by Aleister Crowley, and the Enochian experiments of John Dee.[20]

Bond expected errors and ignored many of the sessions with Bartlett because they provided impossible architectural data that could not fit the abbey. It was not until the thirty-second reading that automatic writing from the original architect of the Edgar Chapel began to provide useful information (figure 3.5).[21] A skeptical observer would note that Bond was an expert on medieval religious architecture, that there are only so many ways to plan a church, and that sections of Glastonbury were still visible on the surface.[22] One might also note that the language of the ancients fluctuated among more modern English, an old-fashioned dialect, and shaky Latin.[23] These and other historical problems did not concern Bond, who was more interested in learning from mystically melding imagination and deduction. If fiction resulted, so be it.[24] When one of these sessions told Bond that some bones he had excavated belonged to the executed last abbot of the monastery, he hid the bones and removed their discovery from his report.[25]

Bond shared his psychic archaeology with Everard Feilding, the secretary of the Society for Psychical Research, who urged him to publish despite recognizing the potential bias of Bond's authoritative knowledge of church architecture. With the increased popularity of spiritualism in the wake of World War I, Bond published his experiment as *The Gate of Remembrance*. Already engaged with the world of psychical research, spiritualism, and theosophy, Bond became a psychical celebrity. He was inducted into the exclusive Ghost Club, founded in the nineteenth century as a private club for British elites to gather and tell ghost stories, where he presented his belief that automatic messages led Lord Carnarvon to discover Tutankhamun's tomb.[26] Bond may have been the inspiration for a "quaint little man from the Psychical Research Society" in the mystery novel *Strong Poison* (1930) by Dorothy L. Sayers. Bond had met Sayers in 1917 and told her stories of investigating haunted houses and exposing mediums.[27]

Spirit archaeology went over poorly with the trustees of the abbey, and the project was halted. After the publication of news stories about Bond's interest in dowsing, the abbey trustees disowned him completely in 1924.[28] Bond believed that the Catholic Church was plotting to deny Glastonbury

FIGURE 3.5. The drawing of Glastonbury Abbey that Bond and Bartlett obtained through automatic writing. From Bond, *The Gate of Remembrance*, 4th ed. (New York: Dutton, 1921), 34.

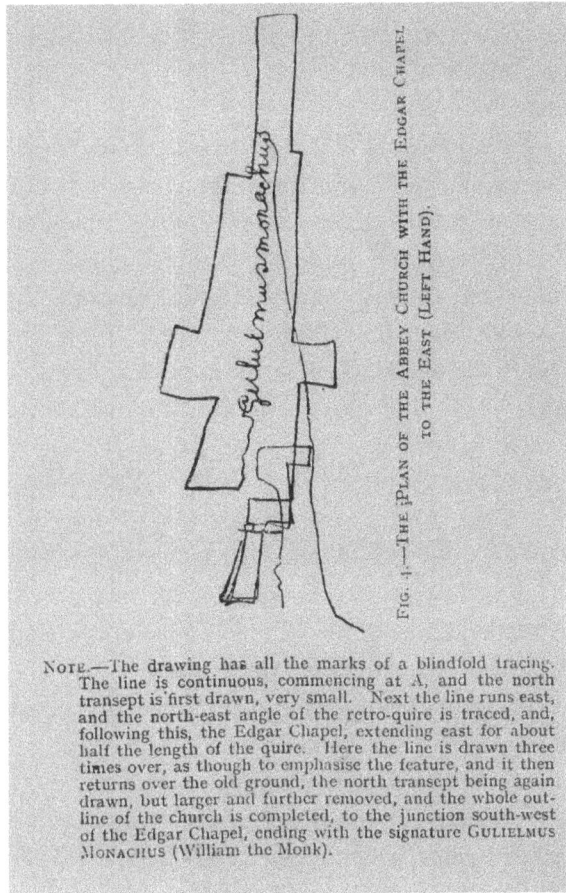

NOTE.—The drawing has all the marks of a blindfold tracing. The line is continuous, commencing at A, and the north transept is first drawn, very small. Next the line runs east, and the north-east angle of the retro-quire is traced, and, following this, the Edgar Chapel, extending east for about half the length of the quire. Here the line is drawn three times over, as though to emphasise the feature, and it then returns over the old ground, the north transept being again drawn, but larger and further removed, and the whole outline of the church is completed, to the junction south-west of the Edgar Chapel, ending with the signature GULIELMUS MONACHUS (William the Monk).

as the original home of Christendom and the Holy Grail, a potential global shrine where racial and religious differences could be reconciled.[29] Despite being forced to buy a ticket to visit his own reconstructions, Bond was able to raise funds from esoteric enthusiasts to return to Glastonbury and dig where dowsing had indicated the presence of gold. The Second World War prevented Bond's project, but the same donors sponsored very similar excavations by Ralegh Radford in the 1950s and 1960s.[30] These digs explicitly sought the excavation pit over the grave of King Arthur, and Radford believed he found it in 1962. His evidence was the presence of chips of Doulting stone in the pit, a construction material believed at the time not to predate 1191 but now known from the Anglo-Saxon constructions on-site. There is no reason to link these excavations to the 1191 Arthur hoax.[31]

The trustees of the abbey minimized Bond's psychical findings and dismantled his reconstruction of the apse of the Edgar Chapel.[32] Subsequent excavation determined that the "chapel" foundations were a post-abbey drainage system.[33] Today, Bond's work is quietly noted in the abbey's visitor center, but a label in smaller type describes his "increasingly unscientific" research. The Edgar Chapel is visible in some of the reconstruction maps and in the model found in the abbey's visitor center, but the site itself is unmarked. The other major automatic-writing discovery, the Loretto Chapel, is labeled, unlike other parts of the abbey, as "probable," though twenty-first-century analysis suggests this is also unlikely.[34]

Magical Glastonbury and Ley Lines

After Bond, Glastonbury became a major center of New Age, neo-pagan, and magical practices and communities. Since at least the nineteenth century pilgrims have gone to take the healing waters of the Chalice Well at the foot of the tor. Bond designed the wellhead for the Chalice Well, two interlocking circles that have come to symbolize the two traditions of Christian antiquarianism and esoteric questing found in Bond's work and in Glastonbury today. A pocket guide to the ley lines and earth energies of Glastonbury features Bond's psychical research and an image of the wellhead.[35] In June 2015 I wanted to try the waters myself, but the well spout was too busy with pilgrims for me to wait if I wanted to catch my bus. I was headed back to Bath, another ancient community with healing waters and extensive if questionable archaeological reconstruction. The centerpiece of the Roman baths exhibit there includes idealized Victorian sculptures of Roman emperors and an anthropomorphized Britain. These imperial and stuffy Roman sculptures fit the Enlightenment era Georgian atmosphere of Bath but lack the medieval Romantic basis for myth and magic found in Glastonbury.

Arthurian antiquarianism led to the "discovery" by theosophist Katharine Maltwood that Glastonbury was at the center of a "zodiac" of landforms. This notion is part of a larger construction of ley lines that dominates much of alternative archaeology in the United Kingdom. In 1921 Alfred Watkins, an archaeological editor and a former president of the Woolhope Naturalists Field Club in Herefordshire, began drawing lines between antiquarian points of interest. Watkins suggested that these alignments were the surviving traces, in an increasingly industrialized landscape, of ancient trackways. Later ley line enthusiasts suggested that John Dee, the infamous court astrologer to Elizabeth I, seeker of the philosophers' stone, and archetypal wizard, knew of the phenomenon.[36] More solidly, others had noticed some of Watkins's alignments perhaps as early as the late eighteenth century.[37]

The increasingly professional archaeological community resisted ley lines. *Antiquity*'s editor, O. G. S. Crawford, refused to accept a paid advertisement for the bible of the ley hunters, *The Old Straight Track*.[38] Crawford is best known as a pioneer of aerial archaeology and helped create the very ordinance survey maps that Watkins and his followers used to trace leys. Crawford's own schoolboy interest in archaeology grew from his fascination with the Neolithic monuments of Avebury and Stonehenge in the English landscape.[39]

Tom Williamson and Liz Bellamy provide a thorough examination of ley lines as a social phenomenon and archaeological possibility (which they ultimately discredit), and they note the importance of amateurs' access to archaeology through outdoor hobbyist activities. Many aspects of ley hunting are reminiscent of the social and intellectual elements of ghost hunting. Watkins's contemporary Donald Maxwell featured ley lines in a series of antiquarian rambles by "topographic detectives" in the English countryside. Maxwell humorously suggested that as a form of bureaucratic occultism, the official experts of the ordinance survey purposely removed philological details from maps in order to hide Roman roads. Maxwell's volumes were framed as detective work and explicitly critiqued expert archaeologists for too much hubris and for projecting certainty onto antiquarian "clues."[40] Maxwell accused archaeologists of a skeptical antagonism toward new discoveries, a common theme in the pseudoarchaeology discussed in chapter 11. However, he also foreshadowed some modern concerns of public archaeology, desiring cooperation between amateurs and professionals in gathering archaeological data.[41]

Watkins may have conceived of his ley lines as simple trackways, but the first amateur ley hunters prior to the Second World War appreciated diffusionist and Atlantean theorizing.[42] Ley lines became an energy grid by the 1930s and were revived in the 1960s in association with Aimé Michel's notion that UFOs follow straight magnetic lines of force.[43] It is fitting that after Frederick Bligh Bond and his mystical geometry and math, Glastonbury became a center of ley line practice and belief. Ley hunters combine the abbey with St. Michael's Tower on the tor as one end of a 300-mile-long "dragon path" ley line also known as St. Michael's Line.[44] There is little surprise that the tor, once believed to be the entrance to the fairy underworld, would become the focus for LSD-fueled UFO seekers.[45]

It is worth noting that both Bond's Glastonbury and Watkins's ley lines began in a theosophically flavored Christianity before being associated with neo-paganism and paranormal beliefs, such as fairy paths. Watkins cited the Bible as the most important evidence in *The Old Straight Track*, but he later professed psychic ability and a potential psychic tie to ley lines.[46] A countercultural turn to deeper pagan roots was inevitable. In his antiquarian rambles Maxwell excitedly proclaimed the modern relevance of ley lines as the ancient pre-Christian British foundations of modern English geography and daily life, including the rail lines.[47] Paul Devereux has spent decades investigating ley and other folkloric lines around the world for "archaeoacoustic" capabilities that at times approach the paranormal. His research, most famously the Dragon Project, has generally been accepted in paranormal circles as a more sophisticated form of psychic or UFO lines, though Devereux has moved away from more paranormal explanations, suggesting that dowsing for ley lines is both bad ley line work and bad dowsing. Yet he writes of encounters with indescribable anthropomorphic figures and floating balls of light.[48]

Occult Tourism at Glastonbury

The growth of the hippie, Avalonian, and "Glastafarian" populations of Glastonbury in the 1970s brought substantial interest in global, alternative, and newly minted spiritualities.[49] On the main thoroughfares, Buddhist- and Hindu-inspired meditative spaces rub shoulders with angelic kabalistic treatment centers and aura-reading photography studios. Free newsletters and pamphlets in the town hall advertise upcoming pagan and

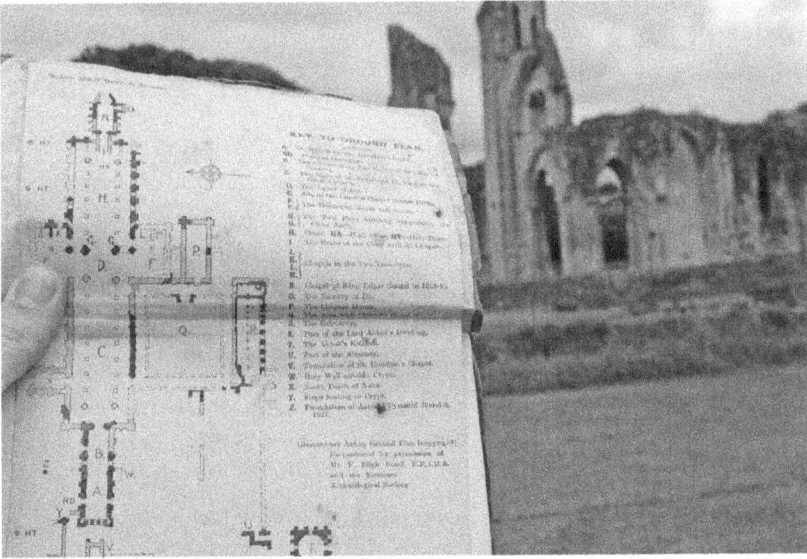

FIGURE 3.6. Searching Glastonbury Abbey for Bond's hidden archaeological features using a 1921 guidebook. My thumb is resting over the Loretto Chapel. Bond's psychically guided excavations led him to declare the chapel a reality, but subsequent analysis of the archaeology has suggested otherwise. Image by author, used with permission of Glastonbury Abbey.

artistic spiritual events. The streets around the entrance to the abbey are full of stores selling books on the paranormal and alternative medicine alongside physical materials for witchcraft rituals, incense, and dreamcatchers, ostensibly from indigenous North America.

I found my key for exploring Glastonbury Abbey in one of these occult bookshops, a guidebook to the ruins based largely on Bond's work and written shortly after the controversy erupted.[50] My treasure map allowed me to pace out the locations of the suppressed Loretto and Edgar Chapels (figure 3.6). I am not alone in following in Bond's footsteps. The parapsychologist Hans Holzer organized a psychic archaeological investigation of Glastonbury with the renowned psychic/witch Sybil Leek. Holzer claimed that he introduced psychometry to archaeology in 1967 and that the technique became a "legitimate adjunct of archaeology." The notion of psychometry, the ability to gain information psychically from objects, emerged with spiritualism in the mid-nineteenth century and became a staple of theosophy. Holzer described using the technique with various psychics to solve crimes, investigate haunted houses, and "read" archaeological sites like "America's Stonehenge" (a disputed site in New Hampshire discussed in the final chapter of this book) or Viking landfalls in the United States.[51]

A significant part of Holzer's biography is that he studied archaeology, making discoveries in both classical archaeology and numismatics (the study of coins) before moving into parapsychology.[52] Holzer did not like the strictures of archaeology, specifically that the field would not embrace a much deeper chronology for "civilization." Later in this book, I return to the desire to create a deep global past out of historical myth rather than the science of material remains.

Was Glastonbury's medieval legacy of Arthur and the Holy Grail the key foundation for the blossoming New Age in the late twentieth century? Glastonbury had a substantial impact on archaeologists like Frederick Bligh Bond, Ralegh Radford, and Margaret Murray who, after taking ill following a stint as a nurse during the First World War, visited Glastonbury, contemporary with Bond's work. Murray's creation of the witch cult owed inspiration to perceived similarities between Glastonbury's Holy Grail lore and her Egyptological study.

To heal in Glastonbury is to travel to the Chalice Well and drink its bloodred, iron-rich waters. The experience of engaging with the physical adds a powerful component to the ritual and pilgrimage activities. I believe that the materiality of Glastonbury and its archaeology was key to its becoming the heart of the New Age. Arthur's links to Glastonbury transcend legend. Arthur archaeologically manifested here, complete with sarcophagus, bones, and mysterious inscribed cross. The tor is a natural hill, but the sole surviving tower of St. Michael acts as the stark beacon welcoming pilgrims to Glastonbury. A locally published guidebook to the "grail quest" at Glastonbury recognizes this, simultaneously using the physical and historical landscape to lead metaphysical pilgrims while decrying that applying the material, explicitly the archaeologist's trowel, cheapens transcendent myth.[53] Bond's fusing of the physical, the archaeological, the psychic, and the esoteric must be considered a key prelude to the paranormal Glastonbury of today.

Stonehenge and Psychic Archaeology

In private tours' narrative and official site information, including an audio file in the guided tour presented by English Heritage at Stonehenge in 2015, the "druid connection" to Stonehenge was repeatedly dismissed to the point of protesting perhaps a bit too much.[54] In the seventeenth and eighteenth centuries, antiquarians John Aubrey and William Stukeley (who took on the character of an archdruid in the Society of Roman Knights) promoted the notion that the druids built Stonehenge. Prior to the archaeological invention of the concept of prehistory, Caesar's druids were logical antiquarian representatives for early Britons though many other alleged builders of Stonehenge were plucked from textual history.[55] The association with "named" or "protohistoric" peoples has persisted to the present, hence the "no druids" declarations made to visitors both in signage and on tours at Stonehenge.

Stukeley and his friend Sir Isaac Newton both suspected that the ancient builders of Stonehenge had special sacred wisdom about the nature of the universe and represented divine knowledge with their circular temple. Stonehenge as a literally magical place built by mystical druids became the primary understanding of the site until academic archaeology emerged, and that is probably the most popular understanding of the site to the present. The druid controversy re-erupted in the flesh in the early twentieth century as neo-druids openly challenged archaeological authority over the interpretation of and access to the monument.[56]

Outside English Heritage's tightly controlled Stonehenge site, the association of folklore, the New Age, the paranormal, and archaeological ruins becomes even stronger. The most common refrain I have heard from current and former visitors to the Salisbury Plain is that Stonehenge is sterile, roped off, and ruined by the presence of a nearby highway. I personally found the highway a minimal distraction, but then I am used to digging alongside roads, train tracks, occupied homes, active farm fields, and even an abandoned mini-golf course on the edge of an amusement park. The palpable sense of control and exclusion at Stonehenge can be traced to the growth of a countercultural festival at the site from 1974 until it was banned in 1984, culminating in the confrontation with police that came to be known as the Battle of the Beanfield.[57] Touching the stones may not have parapsychological importance, but I agree that the inability to physically engage with Stonehenge negatively changes the experience. The inability of visitors to touch mummies in museums also creates doubts about their authenticity.[58]

Almost to a soul, those who complained to me about Stonehenge enthusiastically suggested that one should instead visit Avebury. Lacking the impressive trilithon lintels balanced atop other megaliths, Avebury encloses a larger henge (circular monument) than Stonehenge and is the largest standing megalithic circle in Europe.[59] Antiquarian William Stukeley tried to promote a sacred Avebury, but the site did not gain the name recognition of Stonehenge.[60] Outside of the glare focused on Stonehenge, visitors to Avebury can walk among the stones. They can touch the stones. Never mind that the stones had to be heavily reconstructed due to past destruction by residents;[61] the open and tactile experience of Avebury provides a visceral authenticity.

Like the materiality of a pilgrimage to Glastonbury, physical access to the stones of Avebury has buried the site in ley lines, geomantic energies, and other mystical concepts. An early guidebook disdainfully described the henge as a protective circle to trap spirits.[62] The narrative presented to my tour group featured the magical folklore of naked rituals to make the devil appear in the Devil's Chair, and of former visitors who had successfully applied the henge's fertility powers to conceive a child. I should not have been surprised when our guide produced a set of copper dowsing rods and, after a brief demonstration of their alleged potential to interact with geomagnetic or ley line energies, encouraged others to give it a try (figure 3.7). Lest you think I lucked upon a particularly esoteric tour guide or am mischaracterizing the site, the major store catering to Avebury visitors primarily sells esoteric books, magical working materials, and other New Age or paranormal objects and information like that on offer in Glastonbury. Grimoires, crystal skulls, ley line pamphlets, journals about UFOs, and other materials were the takeaways du jour at Avebury. I purchased my own set of dowsing rods—a steal at six pounds!

I am not the first archaeologist to hold divining rods. My set now rests with other souvenirs, but serious scholars have championed water witching as an archaeological technique. Archaeology professor Byron Cummings supervised the use of dowsing in the discovery of mammoth remains in

FIGURE 3.7. The author dowsing at Avebury. Courtesy of author.

Arizona in 1926.[63] One in eight archaeology instructors in the 1980s were favorable to dowsing, and ethnographic work in the 1990s found widespread sympathy for dowsing among English and Dutch archaeologists.[64] These professionals may not have supported dowsing methods, but they recognized that other archaeologists do. Some suspected that perhaps there was something to it due to magnetic effects rather than to paranormal forces. Historical archaeology pioneer Ivor Noël Hume discussed the technique in his book *Historical Archaeology* a few years before John Coles praised dowsing in his manual of British archaeology.[65] Noël Hume portrayed dowsing as a time-tested and cost-effective form of magnetometry found "in every Williamsburg archaeologist's box of tricks" and used by American soldiers to find tunnels in Vietnam.[66] In 1990 a group of amateur archaeologists used dowsing to find an unusual Triple Goddess sculpture in an Anglo-Saxon monastery on the Isle of Sheppey, Kent. Rather than suffering a curse, archaeologist Ian White and his wife were blessed with two daughters despite difficulties conceiving, sparking local belief in the site as a fertility talisman.[67] Dowsing for treasure goes back centuries. In 1634 the king's clockmaster, David Ramsay, led a party of treasure hunters, including a dowser, at Westminster Abbey. Plagued by demons, the hunters found no treasure.[68]

Some parapsychologists believe that psychometric information comes from spirit informants, while others believe the "stone tape" notion that physical objects acquire a psychic or electromagnetic residue. The phrase derives from the 1972 television film *The Stone Tape*, which features archaeological imagery and is likely based on the writings of T. C. Lethbridge. Geologist William Denton tested his wife with material from Pompeii in an early attempt to employ psychometry.[69] Another psychic archaeologist, who quickly embraced the realm of Atlantis, the lost continent of Lemuria/Mu, the timeless Akashic records, and distinctive racial origins for indigenous Americans, declared Bond to be the father of psychic archaeology.[70]

Double-blind tests of psychic archaeology produced similar results to those of other "remote viewing" or psychic programs, such as the Central Intelligence Agency's Project Star Gate. Some results were striking in interpretation but were not consistent or clear enough to be useful, an attitude that persisted among archaeologists.[71] Even alleged successes have raised eyebrows, such as the psychometric reading of South African and Indonesian artifacts by the Dutch psychic Gerard Croiset working with the philologist Marius Valkhoff. Croiset produced sensational imagery of savage human sacrificial rituals in 1953, pleasing Valkhoff enough to continue the experiments in 1957. Treasure divers Mel Fisher and Bob Holloway experimented with psychic Olof Jonsson with allegedly positive results during the dive on the rich *Atocha* Spanish galleon wreck. Jonsson had previously conducted an ESP experiment with *Apollo* astronaut and New Age and UFO enthusiast Edgar Mitchell.[72] Careful testing regimens have often robbed dowsing and other psychic methods of any efficacy.[73]

T. C. Lethbridge and Gogmagog

One of the more contentious cases of an archaeologist experimenting with dowsing also involved many of the larger issues of this volume. Thomas C. Lethbridge and the Gogmagog affair mark a division between archaeology's antiquarian roots in landscape and folklore, and scientifically oriented professionals. Lethbridge participated in the birth of an independent, alternative archaeology with a disdain for academia and bureaucracy, a "scientification" of the supernatural into the paranormal, and an emphasis on physicality and personal adventure and experience over contextual research. This new style successfully appropriated the symbols of archaeology and in many ways overshadowed professional archaeology.

After indifferent study at Trinity College, a stint of Arctic fieldwork sold Tom Lethbridge on archaeology. Lethbridge referred to his Arctic adventure as real investigation in contrast with professional bureaucratic science.[74] However when the British Admiralty tasked him with searching for German naval activity near Iceland, Lethbridge performed poorly and preferred to amuse himself with antiquarianism.[75]

From start to finish Lethbridge characterized the Gogmagog affair as being in defiance of academic and scientific archaeology. Lethbridge was a volunteer keeper of Anglo-Saxon antiquities at Cambridge's Museum of Archaeology and Ethnology (now the Museum of Archaeology and Anthropology). The highly skilled but nonacademic, "gnome-like" museum restorer Sammy Cowles first told Lethbridge of the medieval legend of a ghostly knight who appears in the anthropomorphic earthworks at Wandlebury.[76] Lethbridge surveyed and excavated in 1954, discovering highly symbolic earthworks, a female counterpart to the male geoglyphs nearby. Lethbridge considered the site to be a premedieval folkloric survival in the manner of James George Frazer's *The Golden Bough* (1890) and the pagan Old Religion, which I revisit in chapter 9. Lethbridge cited Flinders Petrie as "one of the great men of the last generation." Petrie had connected geoglyphs in England with Hindu theology to reconstruct a Eurasian myth of a heroic figure slaying a "Dark Force," a morality ritual Lethbridge tied to Guy Fawkes Day.[77] Lethbridge's site derives its name from the medieval legend of Gogmagog, a blended version of the biblical Gog and Magog that acts as a condensed British version of the Watchers and giants of Genesis and the subsequent destruction of the Canaanites, a myth that became integral to the ritual celebration of London.[78]

Druids, human sacrifice, and witches inevitably entered the mix. In 1936 Lethbridge suggested in a letter to the *Times* that Elizabethan era secret rites near Wandlebury were a pagan survival. Lethbridge also hid with a small party of antiquarians near the giant geoglyph at Cerne during the May Eve night (Beltane) to spy on any surviving pagan rituals. They were disappointed.[79] Witch cult authority Margaret Murray had known

Lethbridge from her time at Cambridge and supported him with letters to the *Times* and site visits during the controversy. Lethbridge later wrote a volume on the witch cult largely in the Murrayite vein but with more emphasis on comparative evidence from Asia.[80] Sir Mortimer Wheeler, Britain's most media-popular archaeologist of the mid-twentieth century, reported on his own Cerne pagans stakeout to the Cambridge Antiquarian Society in 1931.[81]

Nocturnal encounters with secretive sects did not end with Lethbridge and Wheeler. In the 1980s, Glynis Reeve headed an excavation on Mouselow Hill in the Peak District of northwestern England. The site had long been associated with curious carved stones and other legends, and things escalated when Reeve began working. Public confrontations and threatening phone calls led Reeve and others to believe they had disrupted the ritual site of a hidden pagan survival cult. Accidents among workers on the project led to concern over ethereal persecution. The harassment ended after Reeve ventured up to Mouselow Hill on May Eve/Beltane and declared to the night sky, "You have nothing to fear from us." Subsequent press and television investigations appear to have driven the practitioners of the old ways underground.[82]

What set Lethbridge apart from other archaeologists with an interest in survivals was not so much his ideas, which he derived from Petrie, Murray, and Frazer, among others, but his disdain for the practices of scientific archaeology and modern anthropology.[83] Lethbridge's icon Sir Flinders Petrie had begun his archaeological career in Egypt in 1880 by searching in the pyramids of Giza for the "pyramid inch." This mystical notion suggested that the dimensions of the pyramids concealed ancient and even prophetic knowledge. Like many forms of pseudoarchaeology, the idea of a mathematically perfect pyramid rested heavily on scriptural literalism and resistance to scientific materialism. Twenty-first-century research has found the Great Pyramid at Giza to be slightly lopsided.[84]

The idea that there is lost knowledge of the supernatural past encoded in Egyptian monuments dates back in Europe to the Greeks, subsequent Hermetic lore, medieval Muslim explorations, and later occultism.[85] Contemporary with Petrie's search for the pyramid inch was the notion that the ratios and measurements of the Cerne Abbas giant encoded Roman surveying data.[86] Versions of a mathematically perfect Great Pyramid still prosper in pseudoarchaeology, with construction guidance alternatively offered by fallen angel Nephilim, Atlanteans, extraterrestrials, and interdimensional visitors.

Petrie was inspired by the Scottish royal astronomer Charles Piazzi Smyth, a family friend who believed that the pyramid inch was so close in size to the British inch that it was proof of British Israelism, the notion that the British were the true Lost Tribes of Israel. British Israelism has obvious themes of nationalism blended with race, and some related theologies can be openly anti-Semitic. Flinders Petrie did not share these sentiments, and after careful measurements he found no pyramid inch or other hidden messages. The British Israelites suggested that accuracy was overrated.[87]

Petrie perhaps became most famous for his scientific ceramic chronology of prehistoric Egypt. Lethbridge, however, derisively contrasted his own research into ancient mythology and folklore with the search for potsherds by archaeologists obsessed with digging in square holes. He railed against the "fussy little" men who stopped local archaeological societies from investigating because they might harm a national antiquity.[88] One of the first lessons in any archaeology class is that excavation is destructive. Evidence removed from its context cannot be put back, and information will be lost. This reality informs the sometimes-restrictive guardianship of archaeological sites.

Lethbridge championed traditional and, importantly, textual antiquarian sources of evidence, such as maps, place names, and church graffiti. For Lethbridge, it was the volunteers like the Cambridge Antiquarian Society and not the professionals in the Department of Archaeology who made the important discoveries.[89] Physically and morally weak academic archaeologists were too high-minded to conduct backbreaking work and too interested in studying inferior "primitive" people outside of Europe.[90] During his Gogmagog survey, Lethbridge got into altercations with a team of archaeologists working at the Wandlebury site.[91]

Above all, Lethbridge condemned archaeologists for not using "the bar," an auger thrust into the ground to detect softer or harder deposits. The bar thus becomes a rite of passage of rural masculine robustness.[92] Lethbridge reconstructed the Gogmagog site by driving the bar into the earth in thousands of spots to detect depressions, which he then excavated. A Freudian read of Lethbridge's behavior in the Gogmagog affair seems unavoidable.

He painted the entire event as a battle between the conservative scholars with more interest in European antiquities and the weak "fussy little" men from cities, academic departments, and bureaucracies who would rather study African anthropology. Lethbridge praised the old scholars like Petrie and as a volunteer undertook the Gogmagog work at the age of fifty-three whereas the committee of academic archaeologists that passed judgment on Lethbridge's findings averaged forty-seven years old. Lethbridge had his "great adventure" (his words) through manly, virile backbreaking work: repeatedly thrusting a rod into a chthonic female fertility figure. A cigar may be a cigar, but the Cerne giant almost certainly has a phallus.

Lethbridge's long-running disdain for the academy had led him to promote Gogmagog in the national press. In response, the Council for British Archaeology assembled a committee on the matter, finding that the "geoglyphs" were natural glacial phenomena, a conclusion supported by subsequent research. One notable dissenter was committee member Christopher Hawkes, who found neither the natural explanation nor Lethbridge's geoglyphs to be proven. At that time Hawkes was sympathetic to an Old Religion scheme for prehistory, researching a great goddess as a major aspect of Neolithic European culture before patriarchal Indo-Europeans invaded and destroyed old Europe. Gogmagog had turned into a symbolic fight for a science-based prehistory.[93]

Lethbridge resigned his post at the museum in 1957 feeling he had no place in an archaeology of "trade unionism" that had thrown away chances at "great adventure" and "thrilling discoveries" because they would not discard carefully laid plans when presented with "clues."[94] The pro-folklore, anti-academic nature of Lethbridge's career, especially after Gogmagog, was inherently antiquarian. His archaeology became almost entirely consumed with interpretation through historical accounts of myth and legend.[95] His disdain for professional science and his elevation of earlier traditional historical evidence for the past strongly resembled what was becoming typical pseudoarchaeological rhetoric and practices. Many of Lethbridge's contemporaries, early neo-pagan enthusiasts, were intelligent but not highly educated and also rejected mainstream academia. Colin Wilson, a fellow paranormal outsider from intellectual elite society, championed Lethbridge.[96]

After the success of Erich von Däniken's *Chariots of the Gods?* (1968),

Lethbridge jumped on the ancient extraterrestrials bandwagon. He suggested an ancient atomic war fought by Martian and lunar humans, and subsequent hybridization explained the biological inferiority of the "aborigines of New Guinea."[97] Lethbridge was instrumental in bringing the Westford Knight, a pecked stone carving in Massachusetts likely created in the nineteenth century, along with a complex mythology of Templars and other European settlers in New England, into the realm of alternative archaeology. On other occasions Lethbridge debunked alternative claims. For example, he recognized that the "sacrificial altar" at Pattee's Caves, New Hampshire (discussed later in this volume), was really a cider press like those of the English West Country, and he acknowledged that a real Atlantis would have left evidence.[98]

Psychic matters and ghostly encounters interested Lethbridge for much of his life, and he experimented with occult research after retiring to a house he believed to be haunted. Lethbridge was an influential proponent of the stone-tape theory that materials such as rock could store and replay energy or "hauntings" for those with psychic sensitivity. He suggested that megalithic circles stored bioenergy from frenetic dances by witches, who could raise storms in defense of Britain.[99] Margaret Murray suggested a version of this idea in her autobiography, speculating that ghosts are particularly prevalent in humid regions of the world (the US South, the British Isles) due to increased conductivity in the atmosphere.[100]

Lethbridge's ideas and interests show striking similarities to those of Frederick Bligh Bond, including belief in a timeless, universal shared consciousness, which Lethbridge claimed he could analyze with a pendulum. Dowsing with a pendulum for psychometric purposes became a major focus of Lethbridge's post-Gogmagog writing, and he was filmed dowsing in his garden for a 1964 BBC segment entitled "Ghost Hunting with T. C. Lethbridge." He claimed that the pendulum could determine if a stone had been manipulated by a man or a woman. Parapsychological beliefs about poltergeists informed much of this worldview, and Lethbridge came to believe that critics of the paranormal were physically incapable of interacting with dowsing or ghosts and were driven by anger at not being "completely human."[101]

Hieroglyphs, Magic, and Mummies

"¿Puede usted leer glifos Mayas?"

By January 2014 I had conducted archaeological research on and off for more than fifteen years in El Salvador. Six months earlier I had been granted permission for a temporary, nondestructive loan from the National Museum of Anthropology of eighty-four ceramic sherds I had previously studied as part of my dissertation research on the earliest Spanish colonial settlement in the country. Miami University's Department of Anthropology had purchased a three-dimensional scanner that could not leave our archaeology laboratory, and I wanted to expand my analysis of the transformation of Nahua Pipil pottery manufacture and use in the sixteenth century. This work had refined the archaeological chronology of the early colonial period in the Americas and helped us understand the transformation of society and identity in the wake of the Spanish invasion of Mesoamerica, a topic that could provide historical background to the present political and ethnic issues in Latin America. My short visit in early 2014 was to return the sherds and, once that was done, to provide any help I could with the museum's creation of a ceramic comparative reference collection (a *ceramoteca*). These were all activities and projects worthy of present-day archaeology, engaged with international scholarship and having relevance to modern social issues.

On the penultimate day of my visit, I was treated to lunch at a sushi restaurant by some of the staff of the Registration Department, and we got to talking about my earlier work in archaeology. When I mentioned I had dabbled in Mayan epigraphy, the study of hieroglyphics, the flow of the conversation changed. Unbeknown to me, this had been a point of recent interest due to some community education projects. Hieroglyphs are one of the key icons of Mayan civilization, and as I told my hosts, they were what had drawn me into a career studying the past of Central America.

Hieroglyphs had not been terribly vital to my work in El Salvador. Archaeologists are notorious for drawing distinctions between archaeological "cultures," which may or may not correlate with any differences actual people might recognize. Does a stone tool type or a ceramic motif define someone's identity or dictate what language they speak? As I write this on a rainy night in Ohio, I notice that my boots were made in Vietnam and my jacket was made in Cambodia. This speaks to my participation in an unequal global economy in which it makes profitable sense to produce and ship goods halfway around the world for lower labor costs. But my possession of these products doesn't make me Southeast Asian. These kinds of global economic issues were the heart of my colonial work.

The word "Maya" would not have been recognized by the vast majority of people in the Yucatán peninsula and surrounding region at the time of the Spanish invasion, and perhaps by none a thousand years earlier. It has become a powerful symbol since a handful of explorers began writing, drawing, and photographing their evocative experiences with "lost" cities in the forests of Mexico, Guatemala, Belize, Honduras, and El Salvador in the eighteenth century. Mexican national identity has focused on the Aztecs, the political hegemon of Mexico immediately prior to Cortés, one of many examples of protohistoric archaeology providing raw material for the creation of national symbols. The "Mayan" region that became so beloved and studied by outsiders was in a state of turmoil as the first European and North American archaeological explorers accompanied a wave of US influence and intervention that would define the phrase "banana republic." The Federal Republic of Central America was disintegrating, and Yucatán's indigenous people erupted into open revolt against the rest of Mexico. Rather than becoming a major part of national identity for Mexico or the other countries of northern Central America, pre-Hispanic Mayan imagery was largely defined by American and European scholars, who transformed the Classic Mayas, with their glyphs and text-rich remains, into the "Greeks" of the New World.

The word "Maya" has since become valuable. It can elevate an academic profile, draw tourists, or support bizarre notions about the past and the universe. El Salvador was on the edge of the Mayan world, a region with a complicated history of everyday artifacts, linguistic heritage, architecture, and other evidence that sometimes "looked Maya," sometimes "looked Nahua," and sometimes "looked Central American." One inscribed Early Classic Maya jade celt (a form of polished stone ax) had been retrieved from Lake Guija on El Salvador's border with Guatemala; its original provenance was presumed to be the Mayan heartland to the north. An earlier inscribed monument from western El Salvador is in a still poorly understood script with ties to Maya and other languages. The vast majority of the other glyphic artifacts in El Salvador are typically a phenomenon called "pseudo-glyphs," glyph-like imagery that visually references the elite inscriptions but is not legible.

Pseudoglyph-decorated ceramic vessels were what I expected when my friends from the National Museum in El Salvador asked me to look at the inscribed objects in the collection. And that was largely what I encountered (figure 4.1). Largely. One vessel, however, smaller and more delicate than the others, stood out. That small gray bottle covered in carvings dominated my interest that afternoon and in the coming months (figure 4.2). It does have Mayan glyphs, some of which I could read. On my first pass most of the text was opaque, but I could recognize one section, the name of a holy king, the *k'ul ajaw* of the great Mayan city of Copán to the north in Honduras. My rusty Mayan epigraphic skills didn't serve me perfectly, and I reached out for help from epigrapher Marc Zender from Tulane University. He corrected my reading from the fourteenth king of the city, K'ahk' Joplaj Chan K'awiil, to the powerful twelfth king, K'ahk' Uti' Witz' K'awiil. This vessel, recovered sixty years earlier from the biggest pyramid in El Salvador but never analyzed or published, had been made specifically for a great Mayan king.

I had chanced onto a significant find, one that extended Mayan history and political influence south into El Salvador. My mission of working on important everyday fragments of the colonial transformation of Central America was largely forgotten. All of the things that had enticed me, that had dedicated me to understanding the ancient Mayas, were in my hands: a king's personal object, an ancient tomb, a massive pyramid, hieroglyphs. I felt like an *archaeologist*.

FIGURE 4.1. Collection of ceramics in the National Museum of Anthropology of El Salvador. The inscribed bottle is peeking out from the back (see fig. 4.2). Image by author, used with permission of the Museo Nacional de Antropología Dr. David J. Guzman, Secretaría de Cultura de la Presidencia, San Salvador.

What had created this feeling? My intellectual life for the previous decade had been tooled for understanding the colonialist underpinnings of the modern world and the subversive aspects of hybridity and colonial critique. And yet in a heartbeat a king's tobacco flask had pulled me back to the search for the mysteries of, as I call my introductory course on world archaeology, Lost Cities and Ancient Civilizations. Perhaps I would (or should) have felt guiltier about this impulse, but it is so foundational in archaeology's history and public representation.

How does a civilization become lost? The word "lost" is shorthand for "lost from history." Two topics dominated early archaeological exploration of the past. With the discovery and acceptance of deep time and then evolution, the origin of humanity was hotly investigated and debated. The other topic was the origin of "civilization," which meant literate and urban societies like those inventing archaeology during the period of high imperialism.

FIGURE 4.2. Two views of the Tazumal hieroglyphic bottle found in a tomb in Chalch-uapa, El Salvador, but dedicated to K'ahk' Uti' Witz' K'awiil, the twelfth dynastic ruler of the city of Copán. Image by author, used with permission of the Museo Nacional de Antropología Dr. David J. Guzman, Secretaría de Cultura de la Presidencia, San Salvador.

These archaeologists focused on early centralized, class-based state societies. The regalia from early public ritual demonstrations of elites' affiliation with supernatural forces became the treasures of archaeological museums.

Investigating these early states or "civilizations" placed archaeology at the boundary of historical and mythic time, an inherently spooky place. That boundary, between history and the newly invented prehistory, a term first used in 1851,[1] was demarcated by writing, a feature that emerged in the earliest centralized state societies in North Africa, South and East Asia, and Central America. In focusing on early writing and the border of history and prehistory, Western archaeologists were reentering a deep tradition of European engagement with the mythic past and the veneration of the secrets of ancient writing.

Power of Secret Writing

The origin of writing was an obsession of those seeking to understand the past long before formal archaeology existed, and it continued to haunt the profession. The presence of text is the key here, not the contents of those texts. The simple existence of undeciphered texts at Indus sites is enough to differentiate these sites as protohistoric rather than prehistoric.[2] Moreover, ancient writing has its greatest symbolic power when it is undeciphered. To decipher a writing system opens it to all. The test of a decipherment is whether others can apply it to new texts in the same system and get intelligible results. A researcher who claims to understand an undeciphered system better than anyone else is laying claim to a tremendous amount of power. They are simultaneously deploying the symbol of the written word, with thousands of years of cultural value,[3] and claiming a nearly mystical insight into a mystery with esoteric overtones. From such a position, one can project hopes and fears onto the tabula (almost) rasa of an inscribed object, giving it the symbolic power of scripture.

Sir Arthur Evans carved the Minoan culture of ancient Crete out of his excavations at Bronze Age Knossos after he bought it from Turkish authorities in 1899. He was driven by mysterious masons' marks, seal stones, and an apparently indigenous European writing system owing nothing to alphabets from the East. The creation of the Minoans as separate from the Greeks was in no small part due to Evans's suggestions about the nature of the unreadable Linear B documents found in the palace. He compounded this situation by guarding most of the tablets he discovered at Knossos, which were only published after his death. Evans controlled Minoan writing, and to cross him or his ideas could be professionally disastrous.[4]

Evans was neither the first to dig at Knossos nor the first to tie it to myths, such as Theseus and the Minotaur's labyrinth. In the time of Nero the discovery of ancient writing at Knossos caused a sensation, and it was linked to mythic Troy.[5] Evans created a Minoan Empire composed of people from the south and east who had established a peaceful world protected by navies, a fairly obvious mirror of the imperial British self-image. The peaceful element was inspired by Evans's witnessing the Greco-Turkish War of 1897, and he designed the Knossos excavation itself as a way to peaceably bring the warring factions together. He routinely linked pacifism, modern politics, and archaeology throughout his life, and in the aftermath of the First World War, Evans's archaeology helped influence the creation of Yugoslavia as an independent state.[6]

The blank historical space created by the undecipherable Linear A and Linear B allowed others to project Atlantis onto the Bronze Age Aegean. Excavations on the island of Thera as early as 1866 uncovered evidence that a volcanic eruption had buried a Bronze Age settlement. The 1883 Krakatoa eruption inspired in 1885 the idea that Thera may have been Atlantis, and others eventually tied Evans's Minoan discoveries to Atlantis.[7] Evans did not make the Atlantis connection per se, but his construction of a powerful Minoan Empire sounds eerily like both Plato's parable and the contemporary British Empire.[8]

With the decipherment of Linear B, the language of at least late Knossos was revealed to be Greek. The Mycenaeans had conquered Crete and left palatial inventories. Once the presence of the Greek language weakened the old interpretations, recognition of the evidence of militarism, human sacrifice, and possible cannibalism doomed Evans's peaceful Minoan Crete.[9] Even trickier connections between language, nationality, and ideology can be found in the reconstructions and fantasies surrounding the undeciphered Indus script.[10]

Sylvanus Morley and Sir J. Eric Thompson, both considered the premier experts of their day on Mayan inscriptions, transformed the meaning and character of ancient writing not through what they could read, but through what they were unable to read. Morley wrote an early guide to Mayan writing despite an inability to read beyond calendrical glyphs. He did not even record noncalendrical inscriptions because he could not read them. Thompson likewise wrote a calendar-focused volume that was supposed to be a comprehensive overview of the system, as well as a glyph catalog that was instrumental to later decipherment. An earlier catalog by William E. Gates, the first director of Tulane University's Middle American Research Institute and a seeker of Atlantis, likewise emphasized ideographical and mythological connotations in Mayan writing.[11]

One example of where authority grew from this selective ignorance is an unusual vase that was excavated by the Carnegie Project at the Mayan site of Waxaktun in 1932. It was dubbed the Vase of the Initial Series on account of the unusually full Long Count date statement. The Long Count keeps track of the days since the beginning of the world and is the most famous part of the Mayan calendar. Morley insisted that the vase must have been inscribed inaccurately because it did not match what was known of Mayan historicity or calendrical structure. Thompson went further and assumed the author of the vase texts was poorly educated. Remember, neither of these men could read much more than the basics of the Mayan calendar when they made these statements. The vase turned out to be part of a series of vessels with supernaturally themed iconography made by specialists at the site of El Zotz, and it is a cacao drinking vessel that portrays mythical events meant to justify later royal actions. The vessel may be a form of propaganda for the hegemonic Snake dynasty's attempts to use myth to justify its transformation of the Classic Maya political order.[12] The issue here isn't that Morley and Thompson were wrong, or even forcefully wrong. The real issue is that their statements carried greater interpretive authority because the text could not be independently read. Morley's and Thompson's expertise was enhanced by their special access to the secrets of Mayan hieroglyphs, access that turned out to be illusory. Copán villagers called Morley a "sorcerer" living among the ruins for unknown purposes, a description that is not entirely inapt.[13]

Outside of technical scholarly works, Thompson speculated on a priestly Mayan society of devout aristocratic astronomers who would never erect gaudy monuments to the deeds of kings and would never record the names of individuals.[14] We now know these were the most common kinds of Maya texts. Thompson imagined that the great cities were vacant ceremonial centers, the intellectual playgrounds of these priests. Morley, Thompson's contemporary and collaborator, also believed this and focused on his calendrical glyphs even when confronted with evidence of dense residential settlement.[15] Thompson's priest-astronomers weren't just a projection of himself into the past. They also arose out of the limitations of early Mayan epigraphy. The initial breakthroughs in calendrics, the almanac nature of the surviving Maya books, and the failures of eccentric phonetic researchers like Charles Étienne Brasseur de Bourbourg and Benjamin Lee Whorf meant that scholars like Thompson could justify wearing blinders that focused all attention on a time-obsessed Mayan people.[16] In his influential examination of archaeological practice, W. W. Taylor criticized Middle American archaeology generally and the Carnegie Project explicitly for relying too heavily on "ready-to-hand" epigraphy and iconography.[17] Thompson authoritatively described a script he could barely read and posited a peaceful Mayan priesthood from texts we can now read, which are full of ego and war.[18]

Thompson compared the Mayas to a decadent modern Britain or the West and believed that his priest class was overthrown by a popular revolutionary mob, which at times he explicitly referred to as a proletariat influenced by outside ideologies.[19] These "red scare" and Cold War themes combined with Thompson's disbelief that the Mayas recorded historical texts, part of his decades-long struggle to keep Soviet scholar Yuri Knorozov's phonetic decipherment out of Maya studies. Thompson's undeciphered texts could be filled with the mystical, which in turn made his Mayas a wonderfully unique, peaceful, and learned people of gentlemen-scholars, a respite from Thompson's body and world, both of which were ravaged by war and threatened by communists.[20]

Mystical Egypt

Like the situation with the Mayas, fantasies about Egyptian hieroglyphs long predated their modern decipherment. The use of Egyptian imagery in Greek and Roman magical amulets illustrates the mystical importance of Egyptian writing and lore in the classical world.[21] The most influential collision between Greece and Egypt was the transformation of Thoth, the Egyptian god of writing, into the magical author Hermes Trismegistus, who gave his name to the Hermetic tradition, a major part of Western occultism that emphasizes knowledge through revelation instead of empirical examination. Many classical Greeks believed (at times erroneously) that their knowledge and even their gods derived from Egypt. The revival of classical texts in the Renaissance bound Egypt to scholarly and popular ideas of ancient wisdom and magic. Copernicus cited Hermes Trismegistus as having already placed the sun as a central entity in the universe. The Hermetic tradition came to adopt Moses and kabalistic mysticism, which persists outside of mainstream archaeology in the speculation that Moses was Akhenaten or followed his teachings.[22] Akhenaten was a New Kingdom pharaoh who emphasized the divine Aten sun disk over the other gods of Egypt and built a new capital focused on this religious leaning. The impact and scope of these activities are still debated in Egyptology, but in the popular mind-set Akhenaten was erased from history for being the world's first monotheist, a notion promoted by Sigmund Freud. Despite this belief, Akhenaten's abandoned city has been the scene of extensive archaeology; his wife, Nefertiti, is famous due to the marvelous bust of her found at the site; and their son became the boy king Tutankhamun.

Alchemy was claimed to originate in Egypt and can be traced in classical and early medieval Egyptian texts; its name may derive from a name for Egypt, Kemet. Arab alchemical texts were said to have been excavated from Egyptian temples and tombs in the ninth century CE. Recorded on golden tablets hidden in a tomb or on ancient subterranean statues or walls, these discoveries echo the appropriation of the Pyramid Texts into the Coffin Texts, the more mythical discovery of the Book of Thoth by Naneferkaptah and Setne Khamwas (see below), and other Egyptian tales of discovering magic in ancient places. Actual Arab exploration of Egyptian temples informed alchemical texts as did European Hermetic occult practices. In the tenth century Ibn Wahshiyya included hieroglyphs among the scripts in his book *The Long-Desired Fulfilled Knowledge of Occult Alphabets.* The primacy of the Bible for most Europeans in understanding Egypt likewise points to magic and a supernatural atmosphere with its sorcerous duels, curses, and prophetic dreams.[23]

The classical notion of Egypt as the source of esoteric wisdom was a charter myth for the explosion of Rosicrucian, Masonic, and other secret societies beginning in the seventeenth century and for occultists and magicians ever since, a tradition Erik Hornung dubs "Egyptosophy." The stereotypical fortune-telling "gypsy" derives its name from the supposed Egyptian roots of the Romany and the Hermetic influences that became associated with the tarot. The more high-minded theosophists of the nineteenth century initially claimed an Egyptian legacy. H. P. Blavatsky's Theosophical Society succeeded the Hermetic Brotherhood of Luxor, blending aspects of Freemasons' lodges into spiritualism and using scientific Egyptological texts.[24] Expanding European imperialism in Asia eventually increased the prestige of Hindu, Buddhist, and Taoist philosophies in theosophy and the broader Western occult community.

The new emphasis on Asia did not end the occult interest in Egypt, which can be detected at the beginning of the twentieth century in Rudolf Steiner's secession of anthroposophy from theosophy and in Aleister Crowley's travels in Egypt. The "Great Beast" of "magick" undertook secret rituals at Giza on his honeymoon (as one does) and was gifted in return by being the channel for *The Book of the Law*. Crowley would later write a Book of Thoth guide to the tarot, following in the footsteps of Antoine Court de Gébelin, who claimed in 1781 that the tarot encoded secrets of the Book of Thoth.[25]

Crowley came to believe that he was a reincarnation of Ankh-af-na-khonsu, a scribe mentioned on what he called the Stela of Revealing. The stela is a relatively unremarkable funerary monument, but Crowley became obsessed with it when he saw it in the Cairo Museum in 1904 during his honeymoon. The key was the museum accession number: 666. Crowley fashioned himself as the Great Beast and took the number, that of the beast of the biblical book of Revelation, as a sign. Crowley was able to turn to the museum's keeper who was also a friend and fellow occultist, the Egyptologist Battiscombe George Gunn. Into his thirties Gunn was involved with various theosophical activities, with members of the Order of the Golden Dawn, and with Crowley himself, as revealed in personal correspondence. Gunn later discarded the occult and became known as an expert on Egyptian writing, particularly for his book *Studies in Egyptian Syntax* (1924).[26]

Crowley's mystical revelation at Giza resembles the infamous Masonic wizard Alessandro di Cagliostro's initiation into Egyptian secrets under the pyramids more than a century earlier, which continue to inform secret occult initiations.[27] A secular version is reflected in the 1994 science fiction film *Stargate* in which the royal sarcophagus of an extraterrestrial pharaoh acts as a regeneration and resurrection chamber. The Egyptian linchpin in occultism continues in the present with the importance of paranormal and conspiracy theory mythology about hidden Halls of Records under a pre-pharaonic Sphinx and secret tunnels under Giza, claims that the global elite of the New World Order were going to usher in the millennium at Giza, and belief in the popular version of mystical Egypt in the form of

FIGURE 4.3. The hieroglyphs on this obelisk follow the symbolic model for hieroglyphics used by European scholars of the time. From Horapollo, *Hieroglyphica* (1556), 221.

ancient extraterrestrials building the pyramids. Present-day visitors to the Petrie Museum at University College London see Egypt as a "magic terrain where myths may be real."[28]

The Egyptians themselves thought of hieroglyphic writing as *medunetjer* ("words of the gods"), so it is unsurprising that classical authors considered hieroglyphs to be mystical and metaphorical symbols of the divine essence of things, even when the phonetic system of Egyptian writing was explained to them.[29] This reached a climax with Horapollo's *Hieroglyphica*, a purported translation of an Egyptian book perhaps from the fourth century CE, which was rediscovered on the Greek island of Andros in 1419. The rediscovered book inspired Pierio Valeriano's *Hieroglyphica* (1556), the authoritative work on the subject until the end of the seventeenth century. Even the infamous prophet Nostradamus took a crack at interpreting Horapollo's *Hieroglyphica*.[30] Most glyphs in the *Hieroglyphica* were erroneously explained as profound symbols, but some had their correct phonetic or semantic meanings, such as the ouroboros (a snake eating its own tail) and its meaning of eternal renewal (figure 4.3).[31]

The Greek mystification of Egyptian hieroglyphs is just the biggest example of populating blank textual spaces with esoteric philosophy and profound secrets about the true nature of the universe, just as archaeological artifacts are routinely interpreted as the remnants of supernatural or legendary people with a more direct connection to the origin and sources of creation. The two strategies were combined by Giovanni Nanni, who attempted to please his dangerous patrons the Borgias by claiming they were descended from the ancient Egyptian king Osiris (who was not a human king but actually the lord of the underworld). Luckily Nanni was able to find or make ancient lost texts and a monument in his hometown of Viterbo, a move that also gave Italians a direct line to Egyptian wisdom over the Greeks.[32] A seventeenth-century Italian alabaster urn ended up in Sweden, where its unusual text was interpreted as a mix of ancient Greek letters and hieroglyphics. The text urged its owner to drink and feast in the manner of a German, or at least of a German stereotype found in classical texts. The urn's presence in Sweden surely meant that the Swedes were actually Gothic Germans. (I return to archaeology constructed in the service of nationalism in the next chapter.) By this time pan-European interest in hieroglyphs had fused with Northern European interest in the esoteric and in the magical properties of runes.[33]

It is not surprising that interest in hieroglyphics grew alongside literacy in the wake of the printing press. Mass production made text common, but hieroglyphs were esoteric to all but the initiated. These divinely inspired symbols transcended time and language. Today hieroglyphs are routinely and erroneously compared with emoji icons and described in the popular press as primitive "picture writing" with less nuance than more abstract alphabetic writing. Some of these discussions use the same logic suggested by Leon Battista Alberti in the fifteenth century, that common letters would be unintelligible in the future, but the universal symbols of hieroglyphs (or, apparently, emojis) would be timeless.[34]

Egyptian and Mayan scripts, both described as hieroglyphic, primarily and phonetically represent speech. However, Egyptian writing could be used in purposely vague or enigmatic ways through the careful use or omission of determinatives and other elements.[35] The ancient age and the seemingly less-abstract stick figure and animal signs of Egyptian writing led Europeans to believe that the script did not communicate sound or even a specific language and was therefore closer to the origin of language itself, a symmetrical opposite of the allegedly futuristic, nonlinguistic nature of emojis.

The Renaissance interest in Egyptian hieroglyphs led to widespread use of pseudoglyphs and spurious translations in European products, including the creation of a pseudo-obelisk in Paris in 1549 and faux hieroglyphic inscriptions in Leonardo da Vinci's paintings. For something to be "hieroglyphic" came to mean that it contained a secret allegory or was weird enough to look like it might. Even in the Enlightenment, when scientific and philological approaches were being applied to ancient Egypt and its writings, the old symbolic hieroglyphics inspired Napoleon's choice of a bee as the new emblem of France and informed both Romantic art and idealism.[36]

Early modern Europeans grouped two other writing traditions with Egyptian hieroglyphs as primitive and magical in nature. The first description of Mesoamerican writing in 1520, as the Spanish war against the Aztec Empire raged, compared Mexican books to Egyptian, and by 1563 Mesoamerican writing was called hieroglyphic. Chinese writing was first described in Europe in 1569, and it too was compared to Egyptian and Mesoamerican writing by 1590. Eighteenth-century historians linked Egypt and China based on the supposed similarity between the scripts, a form of hyperdiffusionism (the explanation of cultures' changes through the spread of important innovations long distances from a more "civilized" source) still practiced by pseudoarchaeologists today. Vague linguistic similarities were seized upon, such as the "similarity" between Thoth in Egypt, the Tao of China, and the teotl of Nahuatl in Mesoamerica. While this notion was completely wrong, it did lead to the suggestion, based on a similar delineation of names in Chinese texts, that cartouches in Egyptian texts might contain names, the insight that would lead to the decipherment of the Rosetta Stone decades later.[37]

Many scholars believed Egyptian, Chinese, and Mayan writing to be evidence of the prior existence of a universal language, which inspired utopian projects to once again create a single tongue.[38] As the chair of mathematics at Jesuit College in Rome, Athanasius Kircher was the most influential of these scholars. Kircher directed the archaeological excavation of an obelisk in Rome in 1650 and wrote *Oedipus Aegyptiacus* between 1652 and 1654. His recording of Egyptian monuments remained an important source until Napoleon's scholars created *Description de l'Égypte*, and Kircher was one of several citizens of Rome who created museums of Egyptian materials in the seventeenth century. Kircher's alchemical pursuits led him to seek the presence of God in the concepts behind all things, and he believed that the Egyptians had done this in hieroglyphs and then spread this wisdom around the world. As artists had in the previous century, in 1669 Kircher created his own modern hieroglyphs in *The Great Art of Knowing* (Ars Magna Sciendi). Yet Kircher was one of the first serious scholars of Coptic, which is descended from the ancient language of Egypt. He suspected that hieroglyphs could have been used for alphabetical purposes, but he spuriously saw them as the basis, via Coptic, for Greek letters.[39]

After Kircher, more grounded scholars began to suspect that Egyptian hieroglyphs recorded mundane topics, such as human history, in the spoken Egyptian language. Hermes Trismegistus was recognized as a concoction of the classical era and not a source of ancient wisdom, marking the beginning of the split between Egyptology and Hermetic magic.[40] It is in the popular and occult realms that the idea of hieroglyphs as magical, nonlinguistic symbols encoding universal truths has persisted as "picture writings" and symbolic teachings. Enlightenment era magicians and Freemasons reveled in Egyptian imagery and hieroglyphs. One of the most famous of these, Cagliostro, wore robes emblazoned with Egyptian hieroglyphs during his rituals.[41] The Mormon prophet Joseph Smith collected and exhibited mummies and other Egyptian relics, and he claimed to have deciphered Egyptian papyruses.[42] Autodidact Daniel Smith believed he had found the common alphabet underlying all ancient languages, and he harassed the British Museum keeper Samuel Birch. Like any number of subsequent pseudoscientists, Smith raged that the officials of the museum were willfully ignorant.[43] Theosophical leader H. P. Blavatsky wrote that skeptical scientists had missed symbolic truths in "the secret language of picture writing" of Egypt, Asia, and Mesoamerica.[44]

Extraterrestrial Hieroglyphs

Hieroglyphs have continued to be symbols of otherworldly secret knowledge. Reports, in some cases clear hoaxes, of aerolites inscribed with hieroglyphs or containing objects or bodies from other worlds (especially Mars) occurred throughout the nineteenth century and early twentieth alongside tales of alien spaceships and other artifacts. A likely inspiration for many of these tales was a fictional story run as fact in the French newspaper *Le Pays* in 1864, which reported a calcified Martian mummy and images of alien creatures discovered in Colorado, though the location of the story would be modified as it spread throughout Latin America in the 1870s. In 1865 descriptions of the surface of meteorites being like hieroglyphics or covered with hieroglyphs alongside apparent machinery appeared in news accounts, including a discovery in Montana.[45]

One heavily reported case occurred in Binghamton, New York, on 13 November 1897. Numerous newspapers, including the *New York Times*, carried the story of Professor Jeremiah MacDonald's discovery of an aerolite bearing a message from Mars in characters resembling Egyptian hieroglyphs.[46] Professor Wiggins of Ottawa, whose full name was not provided, declared it a Martian message, the latest of thousands of written messages that had fallen to earth since ancient times, inspiring ancient civilizations and religions: "The ancient Jews and other nations speak of their sacred books as having fallen from heaven. As the earliest important records were preserved in stone, it seems probable that the idea originated with aerolites like that of Binghamton."[47] A drawing of the aerolite in the 21 November edition of the *New York World* resembles the bottom of a steam iron more than a hieroglyphic tablet (figure 4.4), though the presence of a cross "shows that religion exists in other planets."[48]

The "aerolite" was apparently a piece of sandstone, a material with "almost no resemblance to meteorites."[49] The episode was a piece of self-promotion by a printer turned astrologer and patent medicine purveyor, who called himself "Professor" MacDonald.[50] As early as 1885 he had begun writing bizarre mystical material, such as the essay "The Earth Is Flat." Once he moved to Binghamton in 1895 MacDonald must have noticed that Dr. Kilmer's Swamp Root Cure had made the Kilmers the richest family in the city.[51] MacDonald jumped into the patent medicine market with the Atlas Compound, "The King of All Cures." When the federal government cracked down on his compound, *MacDonald's Farmer's Almanac* and its astrological forecasts and prophecies became the family business; it is still published today.[52]

FIGURE 4.4. Article from the *New York World* (1897) about Jeremiah MacDonald's aerolite, showing the alleged Martian inscription. The original of the medallion with MacDonald's face is among his personal papers at Binghamton University, suggesting collaboration between the newspaper and the astrologer.

Perhaps in order to compete with Dr. Kilmer, MacDonald began procuring diplomas in 1899 from medical schools in Chicago, Philadelphia, Pittsburgh, and West Virginia as well as supportive notes from officials in Kansas, Michigan, and Texas.[53] His son's biographical sketch mentions none of these places, and a later owner of MacDonald's Atlas publishing company suggested that MacDonald had probably not traveled to these places, but they were sufficiently far away to make checking his background difficult.[54] Even more ridiculous, MacDonald's earliest "degree" was from a school of astrology he himself founded; he signed the diploma twice, as both school founder and student. These tactics got MacDonald memberships in the American Association of Physicians and Surgeons of America and the New York Society of Osteotherapeutic Physicians; he finally registered as a doctor of osteopathy in New York state.

All of this followed MacDonald's aerolite claims, which appear to have been part of an attempt to associate the MacDonald name with cutting-edge science. He abused the credibility of the only local science teacher, Professor Eddy R. Whitney, who was selectively quoted to appear to be in support of the aerolite.[55] The ancient extraterrestrials authority Professor Wiggins was an eccentric prophet of weather and earthquakes and a recurring *New York Times* character—more valued for his entertainment factor than his scientific eminence and mocked by Mark Twain.[56] The late Victorian imagination was fascinated by the idea of life on Mars, fired by astronomer Percival Lowell's publication of "canals" on Mars in 1895, and one contemporary press account suggested that the aerolite was a hoax inspired by H. G. Wells's *The War of the Worlds* (1897). The astrology connection fit a popular link between Mars and spiritualism and psychical research.[57]

The MacDonald hoax was committed after the 1896–1897 wave of sightings across America of the "Great Airship," which was supposedly equipped with propellers, wings, fins, and spotlights. Most of the accounts described human pilots working on secret aircraft, some of which were to be used to fight Spaniards in Cuba. However, on 19 April 1897, the *Dallas Morning News* reported that a small ship had crashed into a windmill in Aurora, Texas, and that the townsfolk had buried the ship, which contained undecipherable "hieroglyphics," and its dead Martian pilot. Some UFO researchers later found the crash to be a hoax intended to bring some notoriety to an economically depressed small town.[58]

The association of "hieroglyphics" and alien spacecraft has continued into the present. Initial reports of the 1947 crash outside of Roswell, New Mexico, described a "flying disc" only two weeks after that concept had emerged, and the case was largely forgotten. Much of the subsequent Roswell story resembles a prototype, the Aztec, New Mexico, UFO crash hoax described in the first book on UFOs, *Behind the Flying Saucers*. That book portrayed the alien writing as a "pictorial script,"[59] an idea popularly synonymous with hieroglyphs. When the Roswell tale resurfaced thirty years later, the wreckage now contained "hieroglyphs" explicitly compared with Egyptian hieroglyphs and archaeology and even containing symbolic "pyramids."[60] Later Roswell investigators suggested that these may have been misidentifications of decorative tape used to create secret US Army Air Force balloon trains,[61] but they fit into a century-old idea of extraterrestrial hieroglyphs.

The 1980 fictional film *Hangar 18*, loosely based on the Roswell story, continued this notion by depicting control surfaces of a downed UFO nearly identical to ancient, albeit fictional, pre-Columbian Mexican writing that, like the Nazca geoglyphs, can be read from the sky. The film was released by Sunn Classic Pictures, the studio famous for 1970s documentaries about topics such as UFOs, ancient extraterrestrials, Noah's ark, and

Bigfoot (the famous Patterson-Gimlin film of a creature loping through the northern California forest was first featured in a Sunn production). *Hangar 18* opens with a title card suggesting that the story is based on secret events and closes by thanking NASA and various UFO investigation groups. Control-panel hieroglyphics had already been introduced by the 1978 ancient extraterrestrials and Mormonism mash-up *Battlestar Galactica* in which Mayan bar-and-dot numerals were used on an elevator control panel, and pilots wore helmets fashioned after the *nemes* headcloths of Egyptian pharaohs.

A reported UFO crash outside Kecksburg, Pennsylvania, in 1965, which gained media attention and new eyewitnesses after the Roswell incident's resurfacing in the 1980s, also featured hieroglyphics. Subsequent claims of UFO crashes in the mode of the Roswell legend have carried on the tradition of hieroglyphic-like writing.[62] The circle back to Hermetic constructions of hieroglyphs closed in the early twenty-first century with the Chad drone or CARET hoax.[63] In May 2007 the first of a series of high-resolution photos of drone-like UFOs spread virally across UFO and paranormal websites. Initially called the "Chad drone" due to the name of an alleged eyewitness, the images came to be associated with supposedly secret documents about a project to reverse-engineer the drone's technology. When inscribed on specific material and exposed to specific energy, the glyphs were said to produce seemingly magical results, such as antigravity. Symbolic, exotic, and sacred hieroglyphs persist in the mythological world of the extraterrestrial.

The Mummy

Universal Pictures' 1932 movie *The Mummy* is popularly considered to be the beginning of archaeology stereotypes in film, especially the horror tropes of curses and awakening preternatural terrors (figure 4.5). The film was strongly influenced by ancient Egyptian history and legend as well as by contemporary archaeological practices. *The Mummy* opens in 1921 at the camp of the British Museum's field expedition to Egypt. The archaeologists are elated at having discovered the unique mummy of the high priest Imhotep. The real, historical Imhotep designed the first Egyptian pyramid when tasked with creating a grand mastaba funerary monument for the

Third Dynasty king Djoser. This fame resulted in Imhotep becoming the only nonroyal Egyptian to be deified—as the god of medicine, the model for all sages. Later he was associated with the Greek Asclepius.[64] It is noteworthy that Imhotep's hieroglyphic name and title were (mostly) written correctly on the movie props. On the prop sarcophagus physically in the scene with the actors, the name is poorly written but recognizable. Almost as if the filmmakers expected the audience to be literate in hieroglyphs, a close-up shot with a clearer version of the name was edited into the scene. The early 1920s date, the discovery of a mummy, and a curse resulting in tragedy all evoke the Tutankhamun discovery, itself referenced later in the film as a fabulous discovery. The emphasis on text is echoed in the major plot device of the film: the mummy is resurrected by reading ancient inscriptions and is destroyed by ancient prayer.

In *The Mummy* the curse begins when the experienced archaeologist Sir Joseph Whemple fails to stop the young Oxford man Frank Norton from reading the scroll of Thoth buried with Imhotep. The shock of the revived Imhotep drives Norton mad, and he dies in an asylum shortly thereafter. The three archetypes of the archaeologist on display in this memorable scene are interesting. Sir Joseph is a disciplined and cautious scientist who praises the knowledge that can be gained from the tedious study of broken potsherds over the discovery of sensational treasures. Young Norton is an undisciplined student in search of excitement and fame. Sir Joseph is also aided by an old friend, Dr. Muller, a believing expert in the ancient Egyptian occult. He warns Sir Joseph that while the power of the Egyptian gods has faded, it has not disappeared, and that the scroll should be reburied. When Sir Joseph doubts him, Muller asks why he was invited onto the project, since his expertise in the occult is not being heeded. Dr. Muller is a carbon copy, down to his vaguely Germanic name, of Van Helsing from the 1931 film *Dracula* (the same actor played both roles).

If Sir Joseph had been up on his Egyptian literature, perhaps he would have listened to Dr. Muller, for an extremely similar story, *Setne Khamwas and Naneferkaptah*, had been found in 1864.[65] The story is contained on papyruses from the third century BCE in the Ptolemaic period but features a legendary version of an actual New Kingdom royal prince, Khaemweset (ca. 1279–1224 BCE). The real prince, a son of Ramesses II, lived during the Nineteenth Dynasty and was a *sem* priest of Ptah, which is reflected in the

FIGURE 4.5. Movie poster for *The Mummy* (1932).

FIGURE 4.6. The tomb of Unas, housing the oldest Pyramid Texts. This building was later repaired by Khaemweset, the model for Setne Khamwas and by extension the archaeologists in *The Mummy*.

fictional character's name, Setne, and responsible for studying and restoring ancient temples and tombs. In addition to directing major royal building projects, Khaemweset restored ancient ruins, including a pyramid at Saqqara that contained the tomb of Unas, the last king of the Fifth Dynasty. This was the first pyramid to contain the Pyramid Texts (figure 4.6), which are a collection of magical spells that guide the spirit of the king through the dangers of the underworld. These texts are the oldest known examples of Egyptian funerary magic, though the concepts were likely centuries older.[66]

Khaemweset's particular interest in these activities has led him to be called the first archaeologist.[67] He was remembered in Egypt as a legendary magician who sought ancient lore. In the story *Setne Khamwas and Naneferkaptah*, the character Setne Khamwas is a magician and student of ancient monuments and lore who learns of the book of magic personally written by Thoth, the divine inventor of writing and the patron god of scribes.[68] A Book of Thoth appears in supernatural fiction in 1914 in Sax Rohmer's *Brood of the Witch-Queen* (often suggested as a source of inspiration for *The Mummy*), and given Rohmer's use of Egyptian details in various stories, he may have been aware of the legendary volume.[69] A text called the Book of Thoth is discussed at least as far back as the Middle Kingdom in the Coffin Texts, which are funerary magical instructions in the tradition that includes the Pyramid Texts and the Book of the Dead. Thoth had long been a figure of magic, and by the Late Period he was considered the deity of magic (figure 4.7). A demotic script version of a Book of Thoth dating to Egypt's Late Period appears to be an initiation text for a scribal-training institution or school, alternately known as the House of Life or the Chamber of Darkness, and may be related to the blended Greek-Egyptian Hermetic tradition.[70]

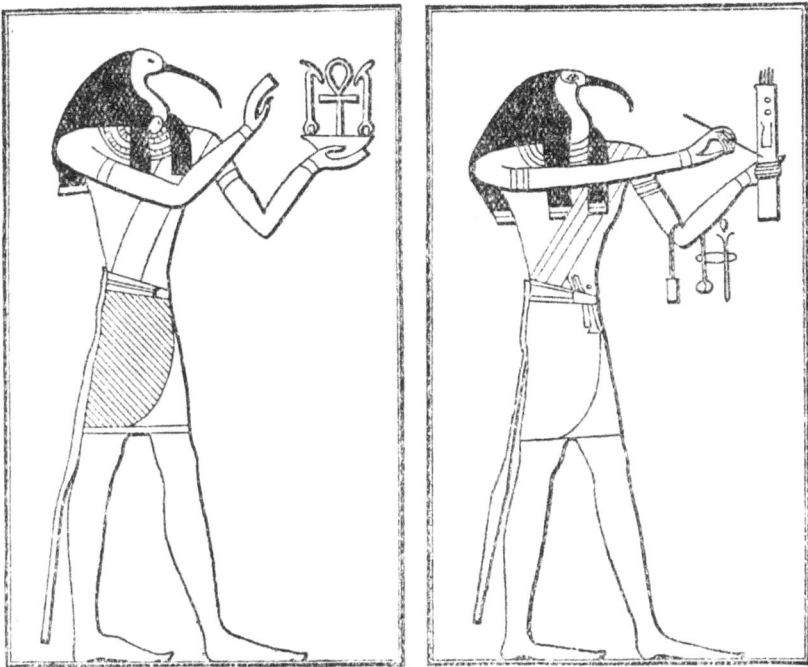

FIGURE 4.7. Thoth the divine scribe. From E. A. Wallis Budge, *Osiris and the Egyptian Resurrection* (New York: Putnam's, 1911), 10.

The other half of the story's title is Naneferkaptah, an ancient priest buried with the book in his tomb in Memphis. Setne Khamwas and his brother Inaros discover the tomb and open it with magical rituals, an act similar to the real Khaemweset's discovery of funerary texts on artifacts in tombs. Before the fictional brothers are able to seize the book, they are confronted by the reanimated Naneferkaptah and the *ka* spirit of his wife, Ahwere. She is incorporeal, since her body lies buried where she died in Coptos.[71] The appearance of the dead in this fashion was not a common feature of earlier Egyptian magic.[72] The model for Setne Khamwas and the Book of Thoth may be ancient, but the undead portion of this story is more of the Hellenistic period.

Ahwere relates how the quest for the Book of Thoth brought doom to their family. Naneferkaptah had, like Setne Khamwas, been a seeker of ancient knowledge, spending his days reading ancient monumental inscriptions. Intriguingly, Naneferkaptah's name and nature in the story reflect the ties the real Khaemweset had to Ptah and the Apis bull, suggesting that both Setne and Naneferkaptah were modeled on the real New Kingdom royal priest.[73] An old priest had mocked Naneferkaptah, telling him where to find true knowledge: a book written by the god Thoth himself. The book contains two spells, one for controlling everything in nature and the other revealing the true nature of the gods and the afterlife. It was hidden in a nested series of boxes on an island at Coptos, guarded by snakes and scorpions.

Despite his wife's warnings about the dangers, Naneferkaptah was obsessed with obtaining the book.[74] After killing a supernatural snake, Naneferkaptah retrieved the book, and he and Ahwere read the spells, learning all of nature. The actual demotic Book of Thoth includes discussions of birds and other animals and their relation to hieroglyphs as sacred objects.[75] Back in the *Setne* story, the seizure of his book angered Thoth, and the gods decreed that the thief and his people would be destroyed. One by one the family died by drowning in the Nile. Naneferkaptah bound the book to himself with linen before he died, and it was buried with him.[76] In *Setne Khamwas and Naneferkaptah*, the ambitious Naneferkaptah is treated well upon his death, being properly interred despite his crime against the gods. The priest Imhotep in the film *The Mummy*, however, is mummified alive for attempting to steal the scroll of Thoth. This memorable scene is reminiscent of the punishment of a palace conspiracy against Ramesses III in which one of the pharaoh's own sons may have been buried alive in an unmarked coffin.[77]

The fictional Setne Khamwas is unmoved by this warning and uses superior magic to defeat the mummified priest, who curses that Setne will eventually return the book in defeat. Nor does Setne heed the entreaty of his father, the pharaoh, to put the book back. Soon Setne is beguiled by a monstrous woman who seduces him to give up his possessions and his family, comparable to Naneferkaptah losing his family.[78] In *The Mummy*, the young and ambitious Norton is warned to leave the scroll of Thoth alone, but he cannot resist the temptation to read it and is driven mad by the reanimated Imhotep. Setne is not as harshly punished, for the destruction of his family is only a hallucination, though he shamefully wakes up naked in the desert where he is found by his father, the pharaoh. The scholar rightfully interprets his experience as a message from Naneferkaptah and returns the book to the tomb.

As part of his penance, Setne goes to Coptos to retrieve the bodies of Ahwere and her son Merib. He is unsuccessful in his search of ancient funerary monuments until an old man, who is the mummy Naneferkaptah in disguise, appears and points the way. The ancient priest's family is excavated and reunited in the Memphis tomb.[79] A disguised ancient priest guiding an archaeologist to the tomb of his wife is also found in *The Mummy*. After the disastrous discovery of Imhotep and his scroll, the film advances to contemporary 1932 and another British Museum expedition. It is explicitly stated in the film that Tutmania has increased competition between diggers and made it more difficult to make significant finds. The expedition's luck changes with the arrival of Egyptian scholar Ardeth Bey, in reality the disguised Imhotep searching for the tomb of his beloved Ankh-es-en-amon. Bey tells the archaeologists he found inscribed pottery associated with the tomb, but as a native Egyptian he is not allowed to dig the tombs of his ancestors.

This scene is doubly interesting. It draws clear inspiration from the end of *Setne Khamwas and Naneferkaptah*.[80] The film takes a plot device from the original story, that Naneferkaptah cannot excavate the tomb of his wife because he is a spirit, and turns it into what appears to be a critique of colonialism, given the awkward body language and pause during Bey's statement on why he cannot excavate. This interpretation is also suggested some scenes later when archaeologist Frank Whemple, the son of the more scientific Sir Joseph, complains that his expedition must give all of Ankh-es-en-amon's treasures (several of the props are modeled on objects found in Tutankhamun's tomb) to the Cairo Museum rather than shipping them to Britain. He is reminded by his father that this arrangement is in accordance with the expedition's contract with the Egyptian government and that the expedition has not come to Egypt for loot. The Cairo Museum is run in the film by European colonists, and Egyptian characters only appear in servile or villainous roles, yet this is a significant statement on the changing state of archaeological practice. This issue was not raised in the film's prologue, which is set in 1921. In the real-world 1920s, Egypt began to seriously enforce laws forbidding expeditions to follow the older custom of partitioning the loot, an ongoing struggle inflamed by the Tut excavations and the displaying of the Nefertiti bust, excavated at Amarna, in Berlin.[81]

Such familiarity with the practice of contemporary Egyptology makes sense in light of screenwriter John Balderston's experience as a journalist covering the Tutankhamun excavations.[82] Notes in the script make it clear that Balderston was familiar with Egyptological lore, and he referred to Nefertiti not only in the script of *The Mummy* but in dictating the famous towering hair of *The Bride of Frankenstein* (1935). Balderston may have gotten Dr. Muller's name from the English translation of Setne Khamwas. The design of Boris Karloff's mummy makeup appears to have been inspired by actual mummies in the Cairo Museum, especially Seti I.[83]

Balderston's background may also explain a bit of archaeological practice incorporated but left unexplained in the film. Upon the discovery of Ankh-es-en-amon's tomb, the excited European archaeologists leap from their seats and rush past Egyptian laborers passing dirt out of the pit in woven baskets. Realizing the importance of the find, one of the archaeologists barks "Double baksheesh!" upon which the workers step up their efforts. The payment of baksheesh, a monetary bounty, for intact artifacts was extensively promoted by Sir Leonard Woolley, whose excavations at Ur were major news in the years leading up to the filming of *The Mummy*. Woolley also authored popular books and presentations on archaeology and describes baksheesh in his 1930 *Digging Up the Past*. A worker could additionally be honored by a volley of gunfire. Baksheesh encouraged good morale and rewarded careful excavation. But its primary purpose was to prevent the disappearance of finds into the robes of excavators. Large-scale archaeological teams could involve dozens or even hundreds of workers supervised by a small number of experienced foremen and diggers and an even smaller number of archaeologists. Baksheesh would vary depending on the context, but was meant to match what an antiquities-buying mid-dleman would pay local diggers for looted artifacts.[84] In 1932 *The Mummy* attempted to reasonably represent contemporary archaeological practice. Present-day museum practice returns the favor by crafting exhibits to resemble mummy movies, such as displaying coffins upright.[85]

The Mummy's Curse

The 1999 remake of *The Mummy* follows the plot of the original film but ignores virtually all the semirealistic elements of setting and atmosphere, inventing or mangling Egyptian conventions. Whole scenes are spoken in Egyptian, however, and aspects of ancient Egyptian culture are referenced, such as the perhaps outdated notion of the *medjay* as a Nubian mercenary or police force.[86] The film is set in 1923, evoking Tutankhamun and Howard Carter, but never presents anything like the Tut excavation. Unlike in the original film, the only significant authorities are Egyptian, but they are orientalist tropes. One is a fat and corrupt government official. Another is Terrence Bey, the museum director hiding his secret membership in the ancient mystical society of the medjay. The tomb raiders in the film are a cartoonish mix of American cowboys, British fops, and noble savage med-jay, who are part Bedouin and part ninja. The other scholarly figure in the film is Evie Carnahan (shades of Lady Evelyn Carnarvon), a clumsy female descendant of an ancient Egyptian line (she is revealed in the sequel, *The Mummy Returns*, to be the reincarnation of the daughter of Pharaoh Seti I). Evie's character arc tempers her pride in her academic skills as she becomes a better sword fighter and more worldly figure (her first experience with alcohol and romance unleashes unholy evil). Other than some of the ancient Egyptian technical details, the archaeology in the film derives more from the pistol-packing video game *Tomb Raider* and the retro-pulp films of the 1970s and 1980s that inspired the game, most obviously *Raiders of the Lost Ark* and its sequels. In the 1932 movie, most of the protagonists are scientific archaeologists, the events are squarely in the frame of archaeological discovery, and the undead mummy masquerades as a scholar. In the 1999 version, the action revolves around treasure-grabbing gunfighters and secret mystical societies. Keep this in mind for the last chapter of this book.

Both the 1932 *Mummy* and the 2001 *Mummy Returns* heavily feature reincarnation. In the original film, the sole female character is a reincarnation of Imhotep's lost love, Ankh-es-en-amon, who ultimately destroys Imhotep by appealing to Isis, the goddess of magic. The 2001 film treats reincarnation as a form of character development while the 1932 movie depicts it as a primal occult mystery, a theme common in earlier mummy stories and films. This emphasis on reincarnation does not derive from Egyptological scholarship but more from the blending of European beliefs about Egyptian Hermetic magic with new developments in the Western occult tradition, particularly the impact of Hinduism-influenced theosophy.[87]

Mummy stories as allegory or farce emerged with Jane Webb Loudon's *The Mummy! A Tale of the Twenty-Second Century* in 1827.[88] More serious tales of the mummy as an immortal character who may either bring enlightened knowledge to the present or threaten it with destruction become popular after the invention of spiritualism: Theo Douglas's *Iras: A Mystery* (1896), Clive Holland's *An Egyptian Coquette* (1898), and Guy Boothby's *Pharos the Egyptian* (1899). The occult idea of immortals, similar in some respects to theosophy's ascended masters, was a staple of adventure romances, most famously H. Rider Haggard's 1886 novel, *She*. The story hook of this influential tale is a map inscribed on a potsherd, a representation of which was created to illustrate the novel.[89] Haggard notably wrote the story in a study containing a mummy he had recently acquired, a souvenir of his brother's military service in Egypt. Haggard had a significant Egyptian artifact collection that included a ring allegedly looted from the tomb of Akhenaten. Another of his Egyptian rings became a prominent plot device in *She*.[90]

Marie Corelli's occult-influenced novel *Ziska, the Problem of a Wicked Soul* (1897) sets the pattern for later tales of moderns doomed to relive past Egyptian loves and rivalries. The story climaxes in hidden chambers under the pyramids, echoing the Hermetic-inspired lore of hidden magical chambers at Giza.[91] Bram Stoker's reincarnation tale *The Jewel of Seven Stars* (1903) was based in part on Howard Carter's discovery of the tomb of Queen Hatshepsut earlier that year and reflects a broader interest in Egyptology.[92] Other examples include Guy Boothby's "A Professor of Egyptology" (1904), the film *When Soul Meets Soul* (1913), Burt Stevenson's *A King in Babylon* (1917), and Lily Adams Beck's *The Way of Stars: A Romance of Reincarnation* (1925).[93] The concept of a reincarnated Egyptian princess acting out past traumas also survives in such unusual places as the 1987 comedy *Mannequin*, in which embalming a human body into a lifeless object is reversed by the *Pygmalion*-esque creation of a woman from a lifeless store mannequin, resurrecting the early fantasy of lonely men reviving women from mummies.

The 1932 *Mummy* originally featured a sequence of flashbacks in which the heroine remembered numerous past lives. The sequence was censored due to its occult nature, much to the consternation of Zita Johann, the film's female star, an adherent of reincarnation and occult themes. Nevertheless, this "unusual picture" was advertised with the endorsement of the Ancient and Mystical Order Rosae Crucis. The AMORC, part of the legacy of Rosicrucianism, was founded in 1915, and by the time of *The Mummy* was centered in San Jose, California. The organization's Egyptian-themed headquarters is billed as the largest collection of Egyptian artifacts on exhibit in the western United States. The *Mummy* endorsement was in tune with a larger AMORC campaign of advertising in pulp magazines.[94]

Marie Corelli's other lasting impact on Egyptological lore is her role in creating the "Tut curse." Curses did exist in Egyptian magic. One spell in chapter 163 of the Book of the Dead protects the tomb and the body of the deceased with flame and fire, which will be raised against those who would harm the tomb. Other tomb-protecting magic spells invoke dangerous ghosts who haunt the land of the dead because they have not successfully passed on to existence with the gods, or they invoke the spirit of the deceased, who is in preparation for that journey.[95]

Beyond actual Egyptian curses, the Tut curse had decades of precedent. Roger Luckhurst suspects that this tradition, at odds with earlier satirical or mystical tropes in fiction, reflected a growing British unease with Egypt during a period of military defeats. The initial British attitude toward Egypt was largely indifferent or disdainful on the surface, though there were hints of interest in ancient secret knowledge. This changed with the 1882 British occupation of Egypt and its all-important Suez Canal, a costly move many observers predicted would come to destroy the British imperial project. Luckhurst particularly notes two previous models for Tut's curse: the "unlucky mummy" case of the British Museum and the first cursed mummy in the unfortunate case of Walter Herbert Ingram.[96] Both incidents had strong ties to British military exploits and setbacks in North Africa, particularly the highly publicized destruction of General Charles Gordon and his troops in Khartoum. Gordon himself was something of an archaeological mystic, and when he visited Jerusalem two years before Khartoum he believed that he had used ancient Aramaic and biblical clues to discover the tomb of Jesus Christ on a skull-shaped hill he believed to be Golgotha, the Place of the Skull. After Gordon's death, the tomb he had designated became a shrine to Christian imperialism.[97] The sins of empire and the execution of revenge against colonialism began to manifest in folklore and fiction through guilt-laden looted treasures and human remains.[98] A possible early model for this equation was the cursed life of Lord Elgin after his removal of the Parthenon sculptures that would come to bear his name.[99] Mummy curse stories appear in fiction as early as 1862.[100] The "Indian burial ground" curse in North America also reflects imperial fears and guilt more than it reflects any older beliefs by colonized peoples.

The immediate cause of the Tut curse was poor media management. Reporters frustrated by Lord Carnarvon's sale of exclusive Tut coverage rights to the *Illustrated Times* of London printed anything that fed the public hunger for Tut.[101] More than a month before Carnarvon's death, novelist Marie Corelli suggested that he had taken ill because of poison.[102] Two weeks later she revealed her source as a book "translated from the Arabic by a professor to Louis Xvi [*sic*], which states that Egyptian tombs contained boxes of secret poison, presumably put there to harm those who should venture to invade the tomb." She also provided some of the text from that book, the now infamous "Death comes on wings to he who enters the tomb of a pharaoh." This fictional curse was transferred by reporters to the door of the tomb (a practice replicated by *The Mummy*, which fixed the notion in the popular consciousness). Corelli's book does appear to have existed as *Egyptian History*, based on an Arabic volume written around

1200 CE, which in turn was based on the twelfth-century *Akhbār al-zamān*, a key repository of Hermetic lore about ancient Egypt.[103]

After Carnarvon's death, Sherlock Holmes's creator and spiritualist Arthur Conan Doyle, endorsed the existence of a curse. Conan Doyle blamed the death on "elementals," the spiritualist conceptualization of ghosts, just as he had when his friend Bertram Fletcher Robinson died in 1907 after reporting on the "unlucky mummy" housed in the British Museum.[104] Conan Doyle was not the only writer to make a connection between the two cases. In the supernaturally themed, Tut-inspired short story "The Adventure of the Egyptian Tomb" (1924), up-and-coming mystery author and soon-to-be archaeologist Agatha Christie specifically cited the unlucky mummy as a parallel to a Tut-like set of deaths.[105]

Matters were made worse when Egyptologist and journalist Arthur Weigall decided to settle old scores. Carter had gotten Weigall drummed out of Egyptology over rumors that Weigall was selling artifacts, though the same accusation dogged Carter throughout his career. Weigall dismissed the idea of curses in one breath, was purposely vague on the topic in another, and in a third spun ghoulish stories about the spooky nature of Egypt and its mummies. He claimed to have had something of a premonition of Carnarvon's death at the moment he entered Tutankhamun's tomb. Weigall also told a now infamous tale of how his wife and friends were struck by bizarre illnesses while attempting to produce a play about Akhenaten.[106] In reality, there was no significant correlation between excavating Tutankhamun's tomb and an investigator's age of death.[107] Yet with archaeologists like Weigall, public figures like Conan Doyle, and media outlets like the *New York Times* collaborating to produce Tut's curse, it is difficult to blame Hollywood for this trope. The mummy's curse is less a silver screen fantasy than a reflection of the practices and public image of contemporary real-world archaeology.

5

Myth and Protohistory

IN 1899 CHARLES Eliot Norton gave a mission statement at the first general meeting of the Archaeological Institute of America. The institute is America's oldest extant society for archaeology, the publisher of *Archaeology* magazine, and America's primary organization for classical archaeology. Norton stated that archaeology covers the "full circle of human affairs and interest" and seeks an understanding of "the origins and goals of our own civilization." Further, archaeology provides "a juster appreciation of the ways and works of man, and of man's relation to that inconceivable universe, in the vast and mysterious order of which he feels himself an infinitesimally small object."[1]

This mission statement encapsulates a persistent tension in archaeology between the scientific study of past humans and the mythic resonance of origins. Archaeology maps mythic territory and materializes the literal stuff of legend. The most famous archaeologist other than perhaps Howard Carter is Heinrich Schliemann, the creator/discoverer of the material treasures of the Homeric epics. Among the most electrifying discoveries contemporary with Schliemann were Near Eastern texts regarding the biblical deluge, which were followed by the alleged physical identification of the deluge and other biblical landmarks by Sir Leonard Woolley, the greatest popular voice for archaeology in the first half of the twentieth century.[2] Archaeology charts a mythic past, a human past welcome in contrast with Charles Norton's "inconceivable universe" that makes humanity "an infinitesimally small object."

The archaeological exploration of mythic time has been particularly vital in the creation of modern legends. Nationalists have exploited protohistory, a glitch of archaeological technique. In the previous chapter, I explored the mythic power granted to early writing, especially the "sacred symbols" of hieroglyphs. A related phenomenon is found in the collapsing of origins into the boundary between the "historic" and the "prehistoric," the edge of mythic time and the realm of heroic or supernatural actors. National, ethnic, and religious labels and ideas found in the earliest documentary records of a place take on a primordial cast and act as charter myths.

The effect is exacerbated by the nature of early states, the creators of sacred hieroglyphic scripts. Supernatural appeals to power and legitimation of authority are particularly important to the political practices and strategies of early states. These states spent massive amounts of resources on monumental imagery in order to legitimate their existence by tying elites and institutions to the larger cosmos in ways labeled as religious or supernatural.[3] Rulers were glorified with myth and legend, and their monuments were captioned with magical hieroglyphic writing intended to be an esoteric mystery to all but the literate few. Early states quickly became a focus of early archaeology. Investigators from modern nation-states constructing identities around the notion of civilization sought charters in the origins of civilization. Archaeology became synonymous with the elite and most visible remnants of such societies: monumental pyramids, statues, temples, palaces, and richly stocked tombs.

All of these aspects came together in the late nineteenth century to create nationalist and global charter myths. The greatest of all pseudoarchaeological myths, Atlantis, emerged at that time as one of those global charter myths of human civilization. This myth was never accepted by mainstream archaeology, but some members of the archaeological community were intrigued by its explanatory power to fill the gaps left by earlier archaeological methods and theories. The two most striking forms of "evidence" for Atlantis and its successors (such as the ancient extraterrestrials genre of charter myth) have been the reinterpretation of monumental buildings and artwork, and the alleged discovery of technologies "out of place," mirroring the techniques of early diffusionist archaeology. As diffusion was replaced by more scientific theory, Atlantis became a rallying symbol for resistance against the influence and power of a professional, materialist, and secular science of archaeology.

Early Supernatural States

Many early archaeologists focused on the 1 percent of society who claimed divine ancestry and depicted in art and iconography their ability to touch other worlds. An emphasis on the theatrical display of elite supernatural authority or ancestry reached its height in early states, exploding in scale when authority and wealth were concentrated in a single, centralized authority. Many of the massive monumental structures built by preindustrial societies were constructed by the earliest states in the region. The Great Pyramids and the Sphinx were built in Egypt's Old Kingdom and are far larger than anything that followed.[4] Teotihuacan was considered the "city of the gods" by later Mesoamericans. The massive pyramids and monuments of the city were built in the second or third century CE, relatively early in its history.[5] El Mirador, the greatest of all Mayan cities, was contemporary with early Teotihuacan, centuries before the more famous Classic Maya cities. Mayan institutions that would last for a thousand years were likely developed there. The most powerful dynasty of the Classic era, the Snake kings, claimed El Mirador as their origin. The city is dominated by El Tigre and La Danta, two massive pyramid complexes that could each engulf the core of the largest Classic Maya cities. The first North American polity of the Mississippian tradition in North America was Cahokia, the largest pre-Columbian settlement north of Mexico. Cahokia boasted the largest earthen monumental construction in Monks Mound and vast displays of wealth and power in the sacrificial deposits under Mound 72. It is no surprise that it was the first emperor of unified China, Qin Shi Huang, who was buried amid the almost unimaginable amount of resources of the terra-cotta army, a vast earthen pyramid, and rumored treasures yet to be uncovered.

None of these constructions are palaces, granaries, aqueducts, or other forms of infrastructure. They feature in public religious ritual or mortuary rites. In life, early Egyptian rulers embodied Thoth, the god of civilization and the inventor of writing. In death, they became star gods. As the power of the Egyptian state declined in later centuries, magical books and protections independent of the king's favor, such as images of the grotesque dwarf and magical protector Bes, became more prominent in Egyptian temples.[6]

David Wengrow argues that monstrous images like Bes or other composite creatures are particularly associated with the social conditions in early states. Stereotypes of nonstate "primitive" art emphasize monsters and other exotic images, but in reality monsters that combine natural elements in unnatural ways are relatively rare in Paleolithic art. There are exceptions, however, such as the Lion Man of the Hohlenstein Stadel. A famous example, the French cave painting of the Sorcerer in the Trois Frères Cave, is often used as evidence of shamanic transformation but may have been overenthusiastically interpreted by Henri Breuil. This interpretation was significantly inspired by Margaret Murray's discussion of the Sorcerer as the horned god of her witch cult, a topic I address in chapter 9. Composite creatures make up only 3–4 percent of the corpus of more recent southern African rock art. Natural creatures are the norm in the wall art of Near Eastern Neolithic sites, such as Çatalhöyük, and on Neolithic Yangshao pottery in China.[7]

Monsters lurk in the political and commercial networks of socially disruptive emerging elites in periods often labeled "proto-," "archaic," or "formative," before states solidified artistic canons or styles. Images proliferated in these social contexts as ways of expressing power relationships. Mesopotamian serpent-necked felines quickly spread on objects, such as cylinder seals, and were incorporated in Egyptian predynastic elite tokens of the unifying Egyptian state, including the Narmer Palette.[8] Composite creatures, such as the taotie, appear on cast bronze vessels used by Shang Chinese elites to communicate with spirits, and later records claimed serpent or dragon origins for early kings.[9]

Most Classic Maya texts relate events in the lives of lords and nobles, many structured by a series of specific dates in the repeating fifty-two-year Calendar Round and the Long Count of thousands or even millions of years. Classic Maya texts can include retrospectives, describing events of the long past with political relevance to the present. The acts of human or human-like figures in retrospective Mayan texts provide symbolic or supernatural charters for later royal activities. Retrospective texts include anomalistic elements, such as vast periods of time or calendar calculations that would not function properly in the present-day interlocking Mayan calendrical cycles of "historic" time. The effect is as if a serious historical account described an event as occurring on 30 February, or if the longest day of the year was on the autumn solstice or the winter equinox. Like the two suns setting on the horizon of Tatooine in *Star Wars*, the time anomalies in Mayan retrospective texts reinforce that these events took place a long time ago, though perhaps not far, far away. Furthermore, like the space pilot Luke Skywalker; his dark father, Darth Vader; or the roguishly independent Han Solo, the names of mythohistoric figures in Classic Maya retrospective texts can be transparently symbolic of elements of rulership.[10] Mythic resonance in naming is shown in the practice of naming nations after mythical founders. Medieval European accounts of ancient heroes, such as Albina or Brutus or Francus, echo the story of Romulus of Rome and distinctly act in a mythological time and manner that recalls the book of Genesis as well as classical models.[11]

Chasing Legends

The quest for these god-kings was a key element of the emergence of European colonial empires. Napoleon brought hundreds of scholars in his invasion of Egypt, and it is nearly impossible to find the line separating the early archaeologists from the colonial officials and imperial spies (see chapter 8). Europeans and Americans wanted to control and possess the origins of civilization to justify their own emerging nations. These activities echoed the Roman pilgrimages to Egypt after its conquest by Augustus. Romans visited the Valley of the Kings and the pyramids, collected Egyptian relics to fit out temples to Isis and Sarapis, and built Egyptian-inspired structures in Europe. Several emperors played with being depicted as pharaohs or enacted other Egyptian-themed rituals.[12]

Heinrich Schliemann became famous by excavating the mythic city of Troy into a real place. Historical traditions in the Troad of Anatolia had preserved the memory of Troy for centuries, and Schliemann was not the first to suggest that Troy might be located at the site of Hisarlik, a solution first offered by Charles Maclaren in 1822.[13] Yet by and large the rationalism of the Enlightenment had led European intellectuals to abandon the Trojan War and its tales of gods and immortals as myth. The revival of a "real" Troy created an archaeology able to project a human mythic past beyond the security of "historical" text.[14] Schliemann built a fortune as a bookkeeper, gold trader, and arms merchant during the Crimean War and used it to investigate sites mentioned in *The Odyssey*. Following the advice of archaeologist Frank Calvert, who owned part of the site, Schliemann began excavations at Hisarlik in 1871.[15]

Schliemann's greatest "find" was Priam's Treasure, an assortment of precious objects cobbled together in 1873 from several contexts. Like Frankenstein, Schliemann resurrected the mythic hero from parts illicitly robbed from multiple graves. After being convicted of smuggling his treasure out of Turkey, Schliemann settled on paying five times the smuggling fine, and the government dropped its claim to the treasure.[16] In reality Schliemann created his Troy with objects a thousand years older than the Late Bronze Age. Troy was the mythic bedrock of European civilization, so Schliemann dug to the subsoil predating human occupation. Schliemann had criticized archaeologists for wasting time and money by digging with a careful stratigraphic approach, though he eventually hired more skilled excavators.

When he dug in Greece, Schliemann stopped excavation once he had found a number of skeletons equal to the number of heroes of Mycenae, and he may have cobbled together treasures from several unauthorized digs.[17] Another forgery tied to Schliemann was a lead figurine recovered from Hisarlik. The problem with the object is a swastika scratched into the vulva of the figurine. Cathy Gere documents the convoluted story of how the swastika migrated along the newly discovered Indo-European language concept, helped create the Aryans, and ended up in Nazi Germany in part due to its alleged importance in German-excavated Mycenaean and Trojan sites.[18]

Some archaeological mythmakers were heads of state themselves. The German kaiser Wilhelm II attempted to create a cult of personality around himself as a divinely anointed monarch. In 1903 he commented on an academic argument over the possible Babylonian roots for the Old Testament by claiming that God had revealed himself to his grandfather Kaiser Wilhelm the Great, as he had to important figures like Moses, Homer, Shakespeare, and Goethe.[19] Wilhelm II had a deep interest in archaeology and admired Heinrich Schliemann. In the 1870s Wilhelm II and his father began excavations of the Saalburg, a Roman castle in Germany ascribed to Roman emperor Antoninus Pius, and in 1900 he restored the site and made speeches comparing the Roman and German Empires. He also undertook excavations at Corfu from 1911 to 1914, which sparked a lifelong interest in the sun cult and gorgons, a topic about which he wrote a treatise in 1936. After the First World War, the exiled kaiser hosted an annual archaeology conference in the Dutch city of Doorn and continued publishing on the cult of the sun and sacred kingship.[20]

Wilhelm II had expanded German academic and political influence in the Middle East, sponsoring the Deutsche Orient-Gesellschaft (German Orient Society) and undertaking a six-week tour of the region in 1898. The imperial caravan was compared to the military campaigns of crusader kings to much British and French alarm. Wilhelm visited the Temple of Jupiter at Baalbek, Lebanon, which was constructed by his divine king, Roman emperor Antoninus Pius. Wilhelm was so amazed by the vast structures of the site that he ordered four years of German excavation. Germany offered the Ottoman Empire a powerful ally against British and French imperial efforts to partition the region.[21] As I show in chapter 8, archaeological espionage surrounded the German effort to build the Baghdad railway, which was central to their imperial plans for the region, and the attacks against the Ottoman Empire in the First World War.

Collapsed Protohistory

In a continuous cultural and historical tradition, relatively recent objects and sites might gain legendary aspects, but they are often interpreted within a historical framework of earlier known periods or dynasties. Chinese, Near Eastern, Egyptian, and Mesoamerican scholars can identify archaic texts and objects from earlier dynasties, and artisans can create purposeful archaisms, stylistically "old" objects meant to evoke ancient times for political or aesthetic messages. These practices need not be historically accurate by modern archaeological standards. In fourteenth-century Padua a gravestone labeled "T. Livius" was hailed as that of the famous historian and a point of civic pride, though the rest of the inscription identified the man as a freed slave.[22] Classical Greeks left offerings at Mycenaean tombs and created fictive ancestors from the heroes of the Homeric epics.[23] The Bronze Age heroes they created had supernatural entanglements with the Olympic pantheon but were considered named individuals with largely human concerns.

A legendary blend of the human, the supernatural, and the prehistoric is found in the twelfth-century writings by Geoffrey of Monmouth, who assigned King Arthur as a historical Roman figure and claimed that an ancient monument was built to honor those who died fighting the Saxons. The reassignment of ancient sites to more recent historical times, such as the belief that ancient earthen constructions are recent burial places or military fortifications, is not unusual.[24] In Mexico, Mixtec books placed named historic figures in mythic rituals as part of stories of the founding of dynasties. Today, the first of four Mixtec historical periods is the period of the stone men. I noted in chapter 2 that these appear to be extrahumans, though they may preserve some memory of the collapse of the Zapotec state around 750 CE. The stone men were followed by the organization of the recent world, which set up the third time, that of the named legendary dynastic heroes of the pre-Columbian Mixtec books. These figures enact mythic narratives but also interact with real places and are considered by indigenous and non-indigenous scholars to be historical figures. Finally, the most recent ancestors are those who lived and died after the arrival of Christianity.[25]

As discussed in chapter 2, a significant break in historical tradition, such as colonialism or religious conversion, is more likely to produce supernatural and nonhuman interpretations of the archaeological. In colonial contexts, archaeological artifacts are typically assigned to the societies first historically documented by the colonizers. For example, European artifacts and sites were assigned to the "barbarians" surrounding Rome during its initial expansion: Celts, Picts, druids, Germans, Scythians. The boundary between "barbarian" Europe and Roman "civilization" was particularly alluring to the first generations of professional British archaeologists, and even Paleolithic remains were compressed into protohistory.[26]

The Inka and Aztec Empires were founded in the fifteenth century but became the prism through which American prehistory and indigeneity were reconstructed. Unprovenanced artifacts were attributed to these identities almost randomly.[27] Early Mesoamerican archaeology categorized most artifacts as either Aztec or Toltec, the two main historical labels recorded in sixteenth-century chronicles of the contact period. Teotihuacan was persistently identified with the "civilized Toltecs." The sixteenth-century Mexicas spoke of the Toltec capital of Tollan as a fabulous city of artisans. Archaeologists and historians saw Tollan in the massive city of Teotihuacan, but ethnohistoric research made a compelling case that the Tollan visited by the Mexicas on their journey through Mexico must have been the smaller Early Postclassic site of Tula, Hidalgo. Ironically, as discussed in chapter 2, while the Mexicas were remembering Tula and its contemporaries, the memory of a great Tollan may be the shadow of Classic Teotihuacan, Mesoamerica's first great empire. Only scientific excavations based in the stratigraphic exploration of mundane potsherds, supplemented later with radiocarbon dating, finally brought pre-Hispanic Mesoamerican chronology into some kind of order.[28]

Precontact North Americans were stereotyped through the most iconic images of the eighteenth and nineteenth centuries as the United States surged west. Indigenous identity and legal rights have become frozen at the time of European contact and historical documentation. In archaeology, these protohistoric labels became the basis of "culture history" in the direct historical approach. There is a clear logical line one can take by starting with the historically known and then moving into the less well-known archaeological. Following this method, one might take a seventeenth-century historical document of people in eastern North America (or first century BCE France) and make ties between the sites and material culture of those people and that which is chronologically slightly older and stylistically similar. One then builds a cultural history further into the past. For much of the twentieth century, this was the main business of archaeology. However, the events at historical contact between indigenous peoples and colonial empires almost certainly are not representative of what came before. Historically known hostility between groups may be sparked by foreign invasion, masking longer-term unity and social affinity.[29] Freezing today's identities and the relationship to the past on that moment has real scientific, historical, and political ramifications for colonized peoples and their descendants. Furthermore, foreign colonizers, such as European settlers in the Americas or Romans in Northern Europe, constructed indigenous people as barbarians and by doing so created themselves as civilized. This process of difference produces a "weirdness" that in turn makes indigenous symbols ripe for adoption by countercultural scholars, nationalists, and the public.[30]

Early archaeology's dependence on text as a handmaiden to history distorted archaeological interpretations in ways that directly relate to later alternative archaeology. Prior to the discovery of radiocarbon dating in the late 1940s, centers of early literacy, the hearths of civilization, would by the presence of early records be assigned the oldest archaeological monuments. Egypt had the oldest written records, and therefore its impressive stone monuments would be older than those associated with nonliterate peoples in Eurasia or Africa, who were in contact with the later Greeks and Romans. This dating technique—archaeological relics being associated with peoples on the spreading boundaries of historical texts—logically produced diffusion. "History" would begin in the "hearths of civilization," and then superior technology and culture would diffuse to less developed lands. Egypt and Babylon (and Sumer after its discovery) were the origin of all important things. From the European perspective, technology, language, and religion were a light shining out of the east, *ex oriente lux*. The greatest of the academic hyperdiffusionists, the anatomist Grafton Elliot Smith, founded the diffusionist paradigm on the assumption that megalithic architecture and embalming were too complex to have been independently invented and must have come from Egypt.[31] The influential scientific Egyptologist Flinders Petrie disagreed with the extreme form of diffusion promoted by Smith, though he did agree with some diffusionist ideas in part due to the collision between his notions of an Egyptian race and his support for eugenics. His student and colleague Margaret Murray, who is discussed in more detail in chapter 9, was more open to diffusionist ideas.[32] Diffusion made history into a series of cultural conquests of the less civilized, which pushed civilization forward.[33] The appeal of diffusion during the height of European imperialism is obvious.

It would be hard to find a greater emotional champion of the modern and Classic Maya than Sir J. Eric Thompson. Yet even Thompson, considered during his lifetime to be one of the greatest scholars of the pre-Columbian Mayas, suggested that most of the complex aspects of Mayan civilization may have arrived relatively late, along with "Hinduism and debased Buddhism" from Asia, perhaps carried by a population somewhat racially distinct as per the research of the now notorious Earnest A. Hooton.[34] Thompson wasn't alone in casting the Mayas through the lens of diffusion. The first serious exploration of a Classic Maya city, by Captain Antonio del Río at Palenque in 1787, was also the first in a long line of observers seeing sophisticated foreigners as responsible for Mayan art, architecture, and sciences.[35] In the next chapter I examine how some of the more extreme ideas about the Mayas birthed a new, imaginary continent.

Primordial and Supernatural Protohistory

The flip side of collapsed protohistory is that relatively recent societies are made primordial. At first, antiquarians assumed that any ancient artifacts or structures must have been built by the Greeks and Romans.[36] However, the search for coherence with classical texts could turn the arrow of time. The English medieval Bradbourne cross was destroyed by iconoclasts during the Reformation. Its fragments then were erroneously thrown backward in time by antiquarians who transformed it into a "Roman" monument.[37] As antiquarian pursuits expanded, "barbarian" labels from classical texts, such as Celt or druid, were applied to megalithic standing stones and artifacts from widely separated times and places.

The belief in ley lines preserves the antiquarian collapsing of protohistory. As discussed in chapter 3, Alfred Watkins proposed that lines could be drawn through monuments or other markers and that they possibly represented ancient pathways, though followers of Watkins tied the leys into earth energies and UFOs. Ley line enthusiasts primarily consider the system to be a relic of the Neolithic, but virtually all ley lines are dependent on the inclusion of more recent monuments. None of the 350 ley lines tested, according to rules created by ley line authors, works with just Neolithic sites, and the vast majority of the lines incorporate post-Roman stones and buildings, some nearly modern in age. By creating an "ancient" period composed of everything before the industrial era, the antiquarian preference for the historical edge of protohistory over object-based prehistory is made apparent. The conflation of the medieval, the Roman, the Bronze Age, and the Neolithic becomes a testament to continuity in the face of the scientific archaeological dismemberment of a dead temporal landscape. The mania for survivals and the idealization of a single paganism is reinforced by the alleged continuity of place in which medieval structures continue to mark sacred Neolithic sites.[38]

The same phenomenon of making societies on the edge of history "primordial" has occurred in many parts of the world, such as the labeling of numerous sites in both Mesoamerica and North America as "Aztec." This term is problematic enough in a Mexican context, since it can at best be tied to certain kinds of societies in Central Mexico from 1200 to 1600 CE. But numerous North American indigenous sites and artifacts became tied by nineteenth-century Anglophone colonists to the "Aztecs," "Toltecs," or "Aztlan" because of the importance of these terms in the ethnohistorically focused scholarship on pre-Hispanic Mexico. These sites include Montezuma Castle, Arizona; Aztec, New Mexico; the Toltec Mounds in Arkansas; and the Aztalan Mounds in Wisconsin. One notorious case was showman P. T. Barnum's exhibition of two small and possibly microcephalic El Salvadoran children named Maximo and Bartola as "Aztec children" of the lost city of Iximaya. The exhibit was a parody of the popular travel writings about the Mayan region by John Lloyd Stephens and Frederick Catherwood and part of a larger midwestern and southern American belief in Aztec migrations and/or a race of pygmies reminiscent of the fairy races proposed in Europe.[39]

Glyn Daniel suggested that the popularity of Phoenicians, Trojans, druids, Egyptians, and Atlanteans—each as the sole font of civilization—is due to their perceived simplicity contra complex prehistory.[40] Two characteristics suggest another motivation. First, the mythical histories associated with these ideas, while not based on legitimate interpretations of the evidence, can be arcane and convoluted in detail. Second, all of these sources are named in written texts from the past. Confronted with a yawning abyss of deep time, many Romantics, including archaeologists, retreated to the nameable and knowable historical recent past rather than address the unstable past deduced from fragmentary evidence. Terms like "Aztec," "Inkan," and "Celtic" became regional generic labels for anything old. These terms came to be signified by material culture and imagery from a wide array of anachronistic places and times. European medieval and "Celtic" elements of all sorts were collapsed by antiquarians and Romantics into a fantastical Celtic identity that included a newly constructed and idealized druidic religious movement.[41] The collapsing of human protohistory mirrors the catastrophist notion that geological processes must have acted with greater rapidity in the distant past.[42] The key element here isn't simplicity, but a preference for the literal certainty of historical or sacred texts over the uncertainty and questioning inherent in scientific investigation.

The collapsing of tremendous amounts of time into labels perched at the edge of history has made these labels seem primeval and "primitive." "Celts" became the "noble savages" of Europe, descended from figures of the Old Testament or classical myth and associated with resistance to modernity, including weirdness, monsters, supernatural powers, and mystical knowledge.[43] The "savage" aspect of Celtic nature appears in the ongoing interpretation of "sacrificial altars" at "druid" sites like Stonehenge. Their "noble" nature was equally powerful. The term "Celt" has come to be most prominently associated with Ireland, Scotland, and Wales, yet these nationalist identities are heavily indebted to nineteenth-century linguistic analysis. Archaeological interpretation is still entangled with nationalist and antinationalist politics.[44]

Celtic Revival intellectuals, like W. B. Yeats and George Russell, promoted and elaborated on the folklore of fairies and supernatural heroes. This process blended Celticism with other countercultural elements of Victorian intellectual life, such as theosophy and the magical practices of the Hermetic Order of the Golden Dawn, of which Yeats was an important member. Yeats believed that the Irish, by being left out of the Industrial Revolution, had a stronger connection with the invisible world and that the secrets of the symbols found in ceremonial magic could create a sacred Irish literature.[45] Another major proponent of the Celtic Revival was the Scottish anthropologist and folklorist Andrew Lang. As a member of the Society for Psychical Research, Lang believed that many religious phenomena were the result of psychic abilities, and he urged anthropologists to study the work of psychical researchers.[46]

The protohistoric twilight has made the Celtic chronoscape an ideal home for the mythic and the supernatural.[47] Ley lines became part of a broader conception of "druidic" or "Celtic" megaliths as transcendent icons of continuity and mystical power. A more sensational version of the Celtic supernatural emerged out of a Northumberland garden in 1971. Two boys digging near the surface of their yard in Hexham unearthed two crudely carved heads. Analysis of the Hexham Heads bounced their identity from medieval to Roman to Celtic and back.[48] Almost immediately they became associated with terrifying supernatural events, one of several cases in the later twentieth century of alleged Celtic heads (nearly impossible to date) attached to paranormal curses. One "Celtic head" found in the floor of an English political club in the wake of the Hexham Heads was blamed for numerous injuries to and misfortunes for museum staff both before and after the object was determined to be from eighteenth- or nineteenth-century Sierra Leone.[49]

Poltergeist activity was reported in the home where the Hexham Heads were discovered, and a neighbor moved from her home after reporting that she was confronted by a half-man, half-sheep apparition in the night. As amusing as it might be to call this entity a were-sheep, the figure with sheep legs has a more demonic cast to it.[50] Such a tale might have become one more bit of paranormal lore but for the intervention of archaeologist Anne Ross, an influential scholar of Celtic language, folklore, and archaeology who just happened to champion Celtic survivals generally and a Celtic "cult of the head" specifically.[51] Ross proclaimed in the press that she and her daughter on several occasions had seen and heard a werewolf in their house in Southampton subsequent to receiving the Hexham Heads for study. The spectacle of a respected archaeologist talking about curses and werewolves ignited first the local and then national press. Rather than the heads turning Ross into a believer, Ross appears to have enchanted (or cursed) the heads. She claimed to have had childhood experiences with supernatural wolves, and an obsession with werewolves was part of a "second sight" she inherited from her mother.[52] As an archaeologist she had encountered numerous artifacts that emanated unpleasant or even dangerous supernatural power. Getting rid of the Hexham Heads did not end the matter, however, and Ross allegedly came to believe that only disposing of all of her "Celtic heads" would free her from dark mystical forces.[53]

Matters were only made murkier by a former Hexham tenant who claimed that he had made the heads fifteen years earlier out of crude cement, a claim confirmed by geological analysis. The Hexham Heads subsequently disappeared from a Newcastle University museum and entered into mythmaking, paranormal experimentation, and supernatural dread. Although Ross later backtracked on the exact nature of the sculptures, she continued to be a proponent of supernatural and Celtic pagan survivals but rejected claims for Celtic settlements in the Americas.[54]

Political Protohistory

Archaeology and the antique can provide charters for those wishing to overthrow the status quo. The nature of archaeology, of discovery, finding physical incontrovertible truth under one's feet, makes it a powerful symbol for challenging conventional wisdom. Liberal revolutionaries of the Enlightenment questioned the scientific and moral authority of the king and the church. They pointed to the Greeks, reason, and democracy while they built the political and architectural framework of their new states and empires on the model of Rome.[55] One weapon in their arsenal was to use reason in undermining or claiming tradition, resulting in archaeology, paleontology, and other historical sciences. The discovery of deep time and prehistory challenged the religious charters of creationism and catastrophism, embedding the ideals of reason and inquiry into the fabric of nature itself. The quests for the origins of writing, with the important links between language and identity, challenged the accepted status quo.[56] Greek and Egyptian architecture and imagery supported Enlightenment bureaucratic states and new elites in supplanting the old order of the aristocracy and the church. The Hellenic ideal produced a European historical origin, while the creation of Minoan culture as distinctly European provided a prehistory not obviously dependent on Memphis or Ur.[57]

The old European regime's antiquarian pursuits, such as genealogy and documenting continuity in ecclesiastical architecture, were surpassed in the globalized scientific imagination by lost civilizations. Egypt provided a model for a centrally governed hierarchical state of monuments, public works, and an elite rich in personal artworks. The Great Exhibition in London in 1851 showcased an Egypt of monuments and power, inspiring much of the image of Egypt that would be replicated in literature and other media for the next century.[58] In Egypt itself, interest in pre-Islamic antiquities was minimal prior to independence. Ahmed Pasha Kamal, an assistant curator at the Cairo Museum until 1914, was an important advocate for the value of Egypt's pre-Islamic past. The almost simultaneous discovery of the Tutankhamun tomb and Egypt's declaration of independence led to a flowering of Egyptians' interest in the ancient past as a powerful symbol of their national glory. This flowering was diminished, however, as Gamal

Abdel Nasser first promoted a pan-Arab ideology and then returned with Anwar Sadat as a critic of the pan-Arab movement, part of a pattern of Egyptians wielding pharaonic nationalism "oppositionally" in the twentieth century.[59]

Once Europe's Enlightenment rebels became institutional elites, they inspired opposing Romantic rebels. The collapsed protohistory of early archaeology created primordial peoples for Romantic nationalists. Ancient ancestors, created to resist modernity and empire, were modeled on the "noble savages" oppressed by colonialism.[60] Enlightenment imperialists collected treasures from early civilizations while the nationalists recovered the lost lore of their homelands. French cultural elites had downplayed the importance of material remains for understanding the past and creating modern identity. But in the later nineteenth century French Republicans used the Celts and Gauls conquered by Rome to unify a French identity against an aristocracy justified by Germanic origins and affiliation with the church, though Germanic elements could be appreciated for their military contribution to French national identity. The site of Alésia, where Caesar defeated Vercingetorix and the Gauls, became an archaeological monument personally funded by Emperor Napoleon III, complete with a massive statue of Vercingetorix carved in the emperor's likeness. Napoleon III wrote two volumes on Caesar, which recorded his history and his conquest of the Gauls. The site became a potent symbol of both the Gallic nation and the Roman mission of bringing civilization to the world through empire. As Franco-German tensions increased between the Franco-Prussian War and the First World War, Alésia became a distinctly nationalist site. The journal that reported on excavations at Alésia was filled with pro-Gallic jingoism, and a statue of Joan of Arc, who had no historical connection to the site, was erected at Alésia. More recent political acts and the sponsorship of archaeological exhibitions have emphasized the parallels between a pan-European Celtic nation and the European Union.[61]

Mexican nationalists likewise drew imagery and ideology from the contact period Aztec Empire and its legendary Toltec ancestors. Despite the work of Manuel Gamio at Teotihuacan in creating a national identity, the archaeological Classic metropolis was relegated as a prelude to the historically documented Aztec Tenochtitlan.[62] The limited knowledge about the pre-Columbian and the demand for local symbols fed the market for

"Aztec" fake objects, which continue to complicate archaeological understanding to the present day.[63] The mutable fantastic past was also a factor in the friendly relations between Mexican liberals desirous of casting off ties to Europe and Mormons establishing their church in Mexico, who took Nahuatl-ish names, such as "Aztecas" or "Netzahualcoyotl," from popular histories.[64]

New racial hierarchies, scientific racism, and settler colonialism spawned mystical fantasies that appropriated the archaeological ruins of early states, removing them from association with the ancestors of the colonized. Lost white races were alleged to have built the mounds of North America and the masonry of Great Zimbabwe. Allegedly white Egyptians or Near Eastern colonists were initially credited with building Mayan cities.[65] Subtler colonial myths, such as those created by British agents around the Bigo earthworks in Uganda, provided charters for colonial allies.[66]

The mix of nationalism and protohistoric mysticism reached its lowest points with Nazi Germany. Heinrich Himmler's Schutzstaffel (SS) and the Ahnenerbe, an institute for "ancestral research," justified German imperialism and racial hygiene through the attempted resurrection of an imagined German culture and religion. One of the most influential of Germany's nationalist and racist prehistorians was not a professional academic, and he gained much of his prominence from an antimainstream stance that invited the esoteric. Gustaf Kossinna completed a thesis on German language and ancestry in 1881 and subsequently worked as a librarian at the University of Berlin; the university would eventually title him an "extraordinary professor." Following the racial culture ideas of Rudolf Virchow, Kossinna developed "residence archaeology," which identified archaeological sites by culture and race.[67] Using protohistoric identity as a justification for conquest was not new. Napoleon had created the Académie Celtique in 1805 for similar reasons.[68] In 1912 Kossinna's *German Prehistory, an Extraordinary National Science* claimed the ancient German people to be the cultural and biological pinnacle of civilization, having invented bronze and the alphabet. Kossinna called for archaeology to be weaponized and in 1919 urged German negotiators at Versailles to not give up the Danzig corridor due to prehistoric "German" sites in the area.[69]

After Kossinna's death the Nazi state adopted his racial archaeology and supported research into Germany's "eminence at the dawn of civilization," as Himmler put it. Racial and *völkisch* ideology grew in importance, though many professional German archaeologists resisted and excluded the "Germanomaniacs," such as Himmler's Holy Grail-seeking protégé Otto Rahn.[70] Himmler instead employed them in the Ahnenerbe, a bizarre research institute and action group that conducted "ancestral" research around the world and distorted and looted the archaeological records and treasures of Europe. The organization has become an infamous fixture of fiction, pseudoarchaeology, and conspiracy theory. The *Indiana Jones* movies popularized the supernatural Nazi archaeology trope, and elements of the Ahnenerbe were at least as sensational as the movie and comic book versions. Rune magic, superscience weapons, mystical artifacts, the Holy Grail, and Atlantis helped direct and justify mass murder.

Karl Maria Wiligut, a deeply disturbed and disturbing channeler, German pagan occultist, and self-proclaimed avatar of the god Thor, had been involuntarily committed to an asylum prior to becoming a chief advisor to Himmler. Wiligut fed Himmler's obsession with Nordic myth and magic, including his belief that he might re-create Thor's hammer, Mjolnir, as an electrical superweapon. Wiligut claimed he had access to ancestral race memories and prophesied a climactic battle to save the world for Aryan supremacy. Himmler tasked him with finding a literal black castle to be a magical academy, ancestral shrine, and stronghold for the SS. In response, archaeologist Wilhelm Jordan stocked Wewelsburg Castle with artifacts and fossils.[71]

Today "Celtic," "Nordic," and "Germanic" icons and, to a lesser extent, classical Greek and Roman mythology are once again countercultural in Europe-focused neo-paganism. Druids and neo-pagans who hold Stonehenge to be sacred paint themselves (at times, literally with paint) as "noble savages" possessing wisdom fated to be swept away by rationalist materialism. French druids hold fire festivals at Bibracte, the site associated with Vercingetorix unifying the Gallic tribes against Rome.[72] From an American perspective, which dominates media portrayals, neo-paganism is often associated with the political left and feminism due to the arrival of Wicca and related religious movements in the United States in the 1960s. By contrast, many of Britain's early neo-pagans emerged from an anti-modern right-wing occult underground with fascist overtones, splintering from a broader antiquarian movement in conflict with left-leaning professional dirt archaeologists.[73] Both forms of neo-paganism cohere with the countercultural themes of their context, the same dynamic found in nationalist archaeology. All dig to undermine existing structures.

Others who claim the druid title and hold rites at Stonehenge heavily draw on various strands of Asian spirituality.[74] As I discussed in chapter 3, antiquarian occulted archaeologists followed in the footsteps of anthropologists and folklorists, like Frazer, in constructing global myths out of components of the late Victorian academic culture and the occult counterculture. This same mix can be seen in the witch cult (chapter 9). More broadly, the pseudoarchaeology discussed in chapter 11 continues the practices of collapsed protohistory, including a dependence on text and hyperdiffusion. Another Victorian survival is the rejection of progress in Mayan and Egyptian epigraphy and iconography, continuing to treat these well-understood writing systems as mystical symbolic codes. Myths are treated as historical text and preferred over the scientific study of artifacts.[75]

Aliens, Nationalism, and the Nazi Kiss of Doom at Tiwanaku

The ruins of Tiwanaku in Bolivia are perhaps the least understood major culture in the pre-Hispanic Andean region and demonstrate the trajectory of archaeological mythmaking through collapsed protohistory and nationalist archaeology. The city rests high in the mountain plains, the altiplano, at nearly 3,900 meters above sea level. From about 400 to 1000 CE, the city culturally dominated much of the Andes. It was fed by a system of raised fields along the shores of Lake Titicaca. The large andesite monuments at the site inspired later Inkan architecture. The Inkas claimed it as the mythic origin spot of their gods and civilization, though many of the imperial practices of the Inkas can actually be traced back to Tiwanaku's imperial rivals, the Wari. By the sixteenth century Tiwanaku had long been an abandoned mythic place. Chroniclers took note of its architecture, including the famous monolithic, carved Gateway of the Sun, but the city was downplayed by colonial elites disinterested in past indigenous glories. Liberal revolutionaries then attempted to use the site as a national symbol. In 1825 Bolivia's second president, Antonio José de Sucre, had the Gateway of the Sun excavated as a symbol of the nation. But for most of the nineteenth and twentieth centuries the continuing disdain for the Bolivian indigenous majority led non-indigenous elites to discard Tiwanaku in the dustbin of history.[76]

Foreign archaeologists, such as Ephraim Squier and Max Uhle, took an interest in Tiwanaku, and it was the Austrian-born naval engineer, warrior, adventurer, and entrepreneur Arthur "Arturo" Posnansky who turned Tiwanaku into a world-famous mystical center. He thought it was the "cradle of American man" and the heart of civilization and began surveying and digging in 1904.[77] In the introduction to his grand volume on Tiwanaku, Posnansky describes himself with a number of titles, including president of the Archaeological Society of Bolivia and commander of the Royal Order of Wasa, as well as his officer status and membership in organizations such as the New York Academy of Sciences and the International Congress of Americanists. The volume's glowing prologue is by Bruno Oetteking, who retired from Columbia University and in 1945 was employed by George Heye's Museum of the American Indian.[78]

Posnansky did important work by recording the fine sculptures of Tiwanaku's gateways, monoliths, and carved walls. But he has largely been forgotten due to his more extreme ideas, the crankish way in which he promoted them, and some of his more dubious connections. At every turn Posnansky raged against mainstream archaeology for denying his geological and racial claims. He also criticized "animalistic" and "half-breed" indigenous people who, cooperating with the Catholic Church, attacked the ruins.[79]

Posnansky's tensions with the rest of Bolivian society crystallized when a massive carved monolith was discovered by the American archaeologist Wendell C. Bennett in 1932. Nationalist newspapers attacked Bennett as a foreigner, and political tension between Bolivia and Paraguay halted further excavation. Fearing that locals and tourists would destroy the Bennett monolith, Posnansky paid to have it moved to the capital in La Paz, seventy kilometers distant. White Bolivian elites hated the monolith as a primitive reminder of the past while mestizo[80] and indigenous Aymara residents of La Paz believed it was cursed and blamed it for mishaps. Yet with time the monolith influenced both Bolivian artists and indigenous nationalists. In 2002 a festive procession returned the monolith to Tiwanaku, though subsequent rains were interpreted as anger of the sacred ancestor. In 2006 Evo Morales, Bolivia's first indigenous president, held his inauguration at the site.[81]

Tiwanaku is an indigenous symbol inside Bolivia, but globally it is more famous for Pumapunku, one of the monumental structures at the site, which is a fixture of books and television programs on alternative archaeology and especially ancient extraterrestrials. Atlantis and aliens enthusiasts point to the fine-cut masonry and the high altitude of Pumapunku as mysteries. Posnansky's solution to these mysteries was claiming that Tiwanaku had once been at a lower altitude, but geological changes involving sunken continents thrust it into the mountains and forced the Aztlan people to flee and spread their high civilization throughout the Americas. The term "Aztlan" is protohistoric, derived from sixteenth-century Mexican chroniclers, but Posnansky used it for an ancient Atlantis-like civilization. He used other protohistoric names, such as Arawaks and Khollas, for ancient "races," and his entire scheme is racial, describing the distinct creations of Negroes, Mongoloids, and Middle Easterners. Posnansky derided European science for denying his notion that humans in their modern form have been around for millions of years after evolving in the Arctic regions.[82] He reconstructed all of this through elaborate and dodgy geological calculations and through a sloppy brand of archaeoastronomy. According to his methods, artwork on the Gateway of the Sun and other Tiwanaku monuments, combined with astronomical alignments, dated the site back to the Pleistocene. He also cited as "evidence" the presence of early "subterranean" buildings, in other words covered buildings made of stone, which allegedly demonstrate evolution from cave-dwelling troglodytes to civilized people.[83]

Posnansky defended his work by emphasizing the many papers he gave at German conferences and his collaboration with German scholars.[84] One of these scholars was Edmund Kiss, an architect who surveyed the site with Posnansky. Posnansky's (very) big book was originally published in Spanish and posthumously translated into English in New York in 1945. The English translation describes Kiss as a state architect and mentions his 1937 book, *The Sun Gate of Tiwanaku*, in a footnote. In the original Spanish, Kiss is "our appreciated friend," his ideas are more prominently supported, and it is made clear that Kiss was not just a state architect. Kiss was the architectural consultant for the German government, a man Posnansky housed in his home and described as having good intentions but also a wild imagination in regard to concepts like the world ice theory.[85]

In reality, Edmund Kiss was an explorer for the SS and a proponent of the world ice theory, a catastrophist history of cosmic collisions and geological upheaval that the math-hating Austrian engineer Hanns Hörbiger claimed appeared to him in a dream. Several points of the world ice theory, including humans dating back to the Tertiary and diffusion to and from Mexico and the Andes are very similar to Posnansky's ideas. The world ice theory was supported by Adolf Hitler as an alternative to "Jewish physics" and was official dogma in the SS. Kiss was drawn to Tiwanaku by Posnansky's ideas, many of which are found in Kiss's four bestselling novels about the Nordic Atlantean master race. In these novels, humans originated in the Arctic, as in Posnansky's writings. After the destruction of Atlantis, survivors of the Nordic master race conquered the plateau of Aztlan in South America before colonizing classical Greece. Kiss's more "serious" book, *The Sun Gate of Tiwanaku*, inspired popular scientific articles in Nazi publications, including the official magazine of the Hitler Youth, and Heinrich Himmler gave a custom leather-bound copy to Hitler as a Christmas present. Kiss intended to continue research about the world ice theory in Peru with a twenty-scientist Ahnenerbe team, but the invasion of Poland brought other priorities, and Kiss joined the Waffen-SS, eventually becoming commandant of the guard at Hitler's headquarters at Wolfschanze.[86]

Global Protohistory: Atlantis

An increasingly professional archaeology with more data and better techniques grew wary of more extreme diffusionism. Prehistorians like V. Gordon Childe constructed diffusionary regional culture histories based on careful comparisons of pottery, weapons, and other physical evidence rather than broad (and often erroneous) similarities in monuments, iconography, and hieroglyphs.[87] Global hyperdiffusion was increasingly ruled out. Too many aspects of technology and daily life were sufficiently different between ancient Egypt, China, and Mesoamerica to be credibly linked in the way that Balkan Neolithic pottery might be tied to slightly later German Neolithic pottery. The introduction of radiocarbon dating in the late 1940s largely ended the importance of diffusionism and culture history as significant topics of archaeological research. Archaeological theory moved on to questions of process, of epistemology, and of the role of archaeology in society.

Yet hyperdiffusion continues as a key framework of alternative archaeology. Alternative theorist Robert Bauval identifies the 1940s as the breakpoint when archaeology abandoned magic and myth and rejected its proper place as a "sacred science."[88] The split began with the subdued version of diffusion found in culture history. This diffusion did not answer the big questions of human origin and nature, and was simply too unsexy to hold the attention of all but the most dedicated students of mainstream archaeology. After the First World War, hyperdiffusion had promised an ancient golden age, a lost civilization that could stand for benevolent colonization, religious unity, and ancient wisdom.[89] If scientific authority would not critique the new bureaucratic world, then the malcontents of industrialization and materialism would challenge scientific authority itself. Gaps in scientific knowledge hid the evidence of the world's primordial truth: not a soulless prehistory created by professional scientists and supporting the secular material society of the present, but a golden age found just at the edge of recorded history, in the legends of kings, gods, and monsters.

The homeland of this golden age is Atlantis, or at least the Atlantis constructed in the nineteenth century to defy elite science. The origin of Atlantis is in text, a fictive discussion written by Plato in which his students Timaeus and Critias cited Atlantis during a seminar on the ideal political state. Plato invented or modified myths to communicate an idea, as he did with the allegory of the cave in *The Republic*.[90] Plato sourced his Atlantis in ancient Egyptian lore, which the Greeks imagined as an idealized alternative to Greek society. Timaeus and Critias told of Solon's research in Egypt, which found knowledge of past cataclysms lost to history. One of these lost stories was of the powerful empire of Atlantis, founded by Poseidon and his children and rich in mineral resources.[91] Atlantis grew decadent and greedy, forcing an ancient and noble version of Athens to destroy both Atlantis and itself 9,000 years ago. Plato's Atlantis was an allegory for the Athenian politics of his own day. The next major use of Atlantis, Sir Francis Bacon's *New Atlantis* in 1627, was also a utopian allegory. Nonetheless, Atlantis started to be "remembered" as more than just allegory. Some classical authors understood Plato's motivations, but others took him at face value and placed Atlantis in their histories.[92]

With the European discovery of the Americas, Atlantis was revived as early as 1535 as a possible record of these continents or a source for indigenous Americans, with a recognizable form of Atlantean hyperdiffusion suggested by the Mexican scholar Don Carlos de Sigüenza y Góngora in the late seventeenth century.[93] Also in the seventeenth century, the Swedish scholar Olaus Rudbeck suggested that Atlantis was the key to understanding how Scandinavia fit into world history.[94] By 1787 the Azores and Canary Islands were suggested as possible Atlantean mountaintops.[95] In fiction, the submarine explorer Captain Nemo visited the ruins of the city in Jules Verne's 1870 novel, *Twenty Thousand Leagues under the Sea*.

Today's hyperdiffusionist Atlantis is that of Ignatius Loyola Donnelly (figure 5.1), a populist politician who campaigned against railroad tycoons and other monopolists at the end of the nineteenth century. During a low point in his political and financial life, Donnelly wrote on several topics, including the conspiracy theory that Sir Francis Bacon (author of *New Atlantis*) had written the works of several contemporaries, including Shakespeare, and a pseudoscientific catastrophist novel, *Ragnarok: The Age of Fire and Gravel*, about an ancient destructive comet. His 1882 book, *Atlantis: The Antediluvian World*, was wildly popular.[96] Donnelly transformed the myth by emphasizing quasi-scientific lines of evidence for a sunken continent and suggesting that Atlantis was not Plato's evil empire but the origin of civilization. In a list of thirteen propositions Donnelly claimed that Atlantis was the antediluvian paradise of Eden, the Elysian Fields of the Greeks, and the Norse sacred realm of Asgard.[97] Its kings and heroes were euhemerized into the gods of the Greeks and Hindus while its religion of sun worship was preserved in ancient Egypt and among the Inkas of Peru (note the collapsed protohistory). Egypt's pyramids, the European Bronze Age, and the alphabets of the Phoenicians and Mayas all descended from Atlantis. A catastrophe destroyed the continent, and its survivors spread to what were to be the civilized places of the world, bringing their deluge tales as a misremembering of the physical, real Atlantis.

The popularity of Donnelly's Atlantis lies in its syncretic explanation of the fragments of prehistory and being named in texts. Blavatsky described Atlantis as the "first historical land."[98] An origin for humans had not yet been identified in 1882, and what little was known did not easily correlate with biblical scripture or other ancient works. Pyramids, hieroglyphs, and bronze were found in various parts of the world that otherwise did not seem connected. Nineteenth-century historians and anthropologists found (or imposed) folklore motifs, creation stories, and other legends too similar

FIGURE 5.1. Ignatius Donnelly, the master of Atlantis, in 1890. From *American Monthly Review of Reviews* 21 (1900):647.

to be coincidence. If mundane archaeological diffusion could not directly link Egyptian and Aztec pyramids, then perhaps they both shared a more ancient source. Atlantis became the archaeological equivalent of the missing link, a popular and easily digestible Holy Grail that would sort out the fragmentary puzzle pieces of prehistory. But researchers increasingly found gaps in time and space that made hyperdiffusion impossible. Donnelly suggested they hadn't looked back far enough. Atlantis provided a common-sense answer for the diversity of the past by creating a fictional super-empire reflecting the height of European imperialism and racial obsession.[99]

Donnelly simultaneously answered these questions while also solving the biggest problem of interest to his audience: the authority of text in the face of scientific and materialist assault. Donnelly was a founder of the Populist Party, but one of its great champions was William Jennings Bryan, today perhaps most famous for his role in the Scopes "monkey trial" as a defender of literal biblical creationism. The professionalization of science took historical identity out of the hands of common people during the construction of nationalism. It limited scientific inquiry to a largely elite professional class at a time when growing literacy and publishing provided greater access to historical writings and scientific evidence. A resistance to mainstream scientific authority was the first of two general characteristics of early alternative archaeologists, like ley line hunters. The second was a belief in Atlantis as the source of ancient wisdom.[100] But Atlantis was not the only sunken continent.

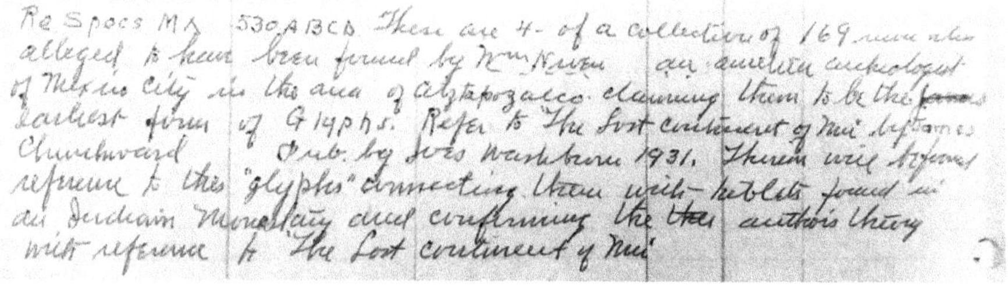

FIGURE 6.1. Original notes on the Mu stones in Miami University's collection. The card reads: "Re specs MX 530 ABCD. These are 4 of a collection of 169 river/rare[?] stones alleged to have been found by Wm Niven an amateur archaeologist of Mexico City in the area of Aztapozalco [sic] claiming them to be the earliest form of Glyphs. Refer to 'The Lost Continent of Mu' by James Churchward pub. by Joes[?] Washboro[?] 1931. Ther[e]in will be found reference to the 'glyphs' connecting these with—tablets found in an Indian Monastery and confirming the author's theory with reference to 'The Lost Continent of Mu.'" Image by author, used with permission of Miami University.

6

The Creation of a Lost Continent

Discovering a Lost Continent in the Basement

In February 2014, I was teaching for the first time a course on art, archaeology, and the impact of private collections and museums on the looting of
archaeological resources. For decades Miami University in Ohio had an
anthropology museum based in large part on alumni donations, especially
the local resident and Colgate-Palmolive vice president James A. Coulter.
Fascinated by archaeological and ethnographic artifacts, Coulter was an
active collector during the first half of the twentieth century and traveled
the world in search of antiquities. He also bought and traded substantial
collections. Even after two and a half years on the job I was still exploring
my university's museum collections. I tasked my students with helping to
reconstruct the life and times of James Coulter in order to better understand our collections.

To prep a course exercise, I began examining the original documentation
of the Coulter collection. One Saturday evening, I read an entry scribbled on
some old notebook paper (figure 6.1), jumped out of my chair, bolted from
my office, and ran down to the subbasement storage area. On a metal shelf
lay four lumps of light, fragile volcanic tuff (deposits or rocks composed of
consolidated volcanic ash), which were marked by shallow incisions of geometric designs, sloppily filled in with red pigment (figures 6.2, 6.3). I stayed
long into the night doing three-dimensional scans of the objects, almost
afraid I would somehow lose the lumps to a mysterious fate.

The origins of the stones are shrouded in doubt, and the ones I locked

FIGURE 6.2. Miami University's Mu stones. Image by author,
used with permission of Miami University.

away in my laboratory are some of the only examples still known to exist
of a collection originally 2,600 items strong. They almost certainly have no
purchase on antiquity and are a perfect example of the collision among
museums, shadowy collectors and diggers, and sensational claims about
the past. These stones are said to be fragments of the lost continent of Mu
and are part of a complex case study of the people and ideas that have
helped make archaeology spooky.

The Prehistory of Mu

Mu springs directly from the origins of Mayan archaeology and epigraphy.
The name was coined by Abbé Charles-Étienne Brasseur de Bourbourg, a key
figure in Mayan studies. During his research in Spanish colonial archives
Brasseur uncovered one of the first copies of the Popol Vuh, the sacred book
of the K'iche' Mayas and the greatest of indigenous American texts, written
in K'iche' Maya using Spanish letters. In Madrid he also discovered a fragment of one of the few remaining pre-Hispanic Maya books, which was eventually joined with other fragments and named the Madrid Codex.

Perhaps Brasseur's most important discovery was a seventeenth-century
copy of the legal defense of Diego de Landa, the archbishop of Yucatán at

FIGURE 6.3. The most intricate of Miami University's Mu stones. Image by author, used with permission of Miami University.

the end of the sixteenth century. Spanish culture during its imperial expansion in the sixteenth century was heavily based on legal proceedings, and colonial authorities were legally investigated at the end of their tenure in office on the presumption that corruption or abuses were likely. Archbishop de Landa's defense was *Relación de las Cosas de Yucatán* (ca. 1566), a major work providing details of the pre-Hispanic Mayan culture, including its

FIGURE 6.4. Archbishop Diego de Landa's "alphabet." From his *Relación de las Cosas de Yucatán* (ca. 1566).

social structure, calendars, mathematics, and writing. One section in particular attracted Brasseur's attention, a bilingual "alphabet" of Maya hieroglyphs that could serve as a New World Rosetta Stone (figure 6.4). Prior to Brasseur's discovery of de Landa's alphabet, the linguistic and historical affiliation of "Mexican" writing with the Mayas was still tenuous at best. Mayan texts were previously attributed to the Toltecs of early colonial Mexica (Aztec) legend.[1]

Brasseur did not realize that de Landa had not understood the nature of Mayan writing. When he demanded the "letters" of the Mayan system in correspondence to Spanish *letras*, de Landa received the syllables used to spell out the names of the Spanish letras. For example, the Maya glyphs spelling *ah* and *che* are correlated with *h* in de Landa's alphabet, since the name of this letra spoken aloud is "ah-che." De Landa's alphabet would ultimately prove to be the Rosetta-like key to the Maya script. In the 1950s the Soviet linguist Yuri Knorozov realized de Landa's errors, but Knorozov's decipherment was not broadly accepted in the West for another twenty years due to professional rivalries and Cold War tensions.[2]

Using this alphabet Brasseur tried to read parts of the Madrid Codex and found evidence supporting his belief in a fiery destruction of Atlantis and the diffusion of high civilization to Mesoamerica. He later realized that he had been reading the text backward, though this would not have made much difference. Brasseur was obsessed with ideas such as Atlantis, Phoenicians in Brazil, and Mayas at the Temple of Solomon, perhaps driven by the same imagination that also produced thirteen novels. Inspired by Alexander von Humboldt, Brasseur began interpreting American myths as encoding real history, and he found secret meanings in mundane colonial era documents, driving him to ill-fated forays into archaeological work. In 1868, Brasseur was one of the first to propose the conspiracy theory that an archaeology museum was hiding the truth, declaring that the Louvre refused to buy pre-Hispanic golden artifacts to cover up the "fact" that the greatest goldsmiths of the ancient world were American.[3] Brasseur was neither the first nor the last Maya scholar to mix hyperdiffusion with the publication of valuable manuscripts and codices. Lord Kingsborough, for example, published several important Mesoamerican codices and also believed that the Lost Tribes of Israel had settled Mesoamerica.[4]

Brasseur's attempts at a phonetic decipherment of Mayan writing led to decades of scholars holding any phonetic approach in disrepute. His Madrid Codex translation was based on the belief that all glyphs have a secret meaning tied to the volcanic destruction of Atlantis.[5] While this may seem, and frankly is, a bit unhinged, Brasseur' s secret symbolic meanings differed little from the pre-Enlightenment European fixation on Egyptian hieroglyphs as sacred mystical symbols.

In his "translations" Brasseur deciphered "Mu" as the name of a sunken continent destroyed in a fiery cataclysm. Brasseur's "discovery" influenced the theosophical pair Augustus and Alice Le Plongeon, who pioneered some of the first archaeological excavations in the Mayan region. Their chief rival was the photographic pioneer Désiré Charnay, who entertained theories involving the recent arrival of white Toltecs and Atlantean refugees in Mexico. The Le Plongeons dug at Chichén Itzá in the 1870s despite fear of attack by antigovernment Mayan followers of the "talking cross" oracle, coming to a tacit alliance with the rebels.[6] The Le Plongeons were constantly guided in their investigations by prophecy and mysticism, including tales of mysterious Mayan books. Augustus claimed that his

Yukatek workers at one point took the similarity between his bearded profile and that of a figure on a Chichén Itzá bas-relief as proof of reincarnation.[7] Whether a misunderstanding, the purposeful embodiment by Augustus of the colonialist legend of being considered a white god by swarthy natives, or a pure invention, it fit the colonial, mystical, and theosophical themes of exploration, hidden global knowledge, and reincarnation that were expected in early archaeology.

The Le Plongeons believed that Alice was the reincarnation of an ancient Mayan queen named Moo, and, possibly directly inspired by photographs of Heinrich's wife, Sophie, wearing part of the treasure of Priam, Augustus outfitted a jadeite tube from the Platform of the Eagles and Jaguars on a gold brooch for Alice to wear. The Freemasonry-littered story of Queen Moo/Alice was outlined in Augustus Le Plongeon's *Sacred Mysteries among the Mayas and Quiches, 11,500 Years Ago* (1886) and a decade later in his *Queen Móo and the Egyptian Sphinx*. After her beloved Prince Coh (an earlier incarnation of Augustus) was murdered and buried alongside the chacmool sculpture later excavated by the Le Plongeons, Moo fled to Egypt to become the goddess Isis, build the Sphinx, and establish Freemasonry as part of her grief over Coh/Osiris.[8] The Le Plongeons had been promoting the idea of ties between Egypt, Japan, and other parts of the world and the "Mayax" for years, including in the pages of *Scientific American*.[9] These stories also included the destruction of Atlantis, as revealed in the murals and hieroglyphs of Chichén Itzá. The ancient Mayan source of spiritual wisdom survived even in Christ's last words on the cross, which were "actually" in Yukatek Maya, not Aramaic.[10]

The Le Plongeons came to be shunned by the academic establishment but embraced by the theosophists. Alice published in *Theosophical Siftings* and in the Theosophical Society's magazine the *Word*.[11] The theosophical leader H. P. Blavatsky referenced their work several times in *The Secret Doctrine*, yet gave it a less than positive review.[12] Alice left their photographs, notes, and artifacts to a theosophical follower, Maude Blackwell, who also made fraudulent claims that the Le Plongeons had discovered Mayan books. After Charles Lindbergh grabbed headlines by leading an archaeological aerial survey over Mayan land in 1929, Blackwell negotiated over the Le Plongeon materials with Maya archaeologists Sylvanus Morley of the Carnegie project and Frans Blom of the Middle American Research

Institute at Tulane University. Morley was extremely dismissive of the Le Plongeons' and Blackwell's occult ideas. Blom was courteous. Neither got the Le Plongeons' materials because Blackwell sold the archives to the alternative author and speaker Manly P. Hall and the Philosophical Research Society in Los Angeles, though some of the materials arrived at the American Museum of Natural History in the 1950s.[13]

In 1912, an author claiming to be Paul Schliemann, Heinrich Schliemann's grandson, followed in the footsteps of the Le Plongeons and proclaimed "How I Found the Lost Atlantis, the Source of All Civilization."[14] The story was likely the invention of a staffer at William Randolph Hearst's *New York American*. Heinrich's son, Agamemnon Schliemann, was a diplomat from Greece to America and had no children.[15] Paul Schliemann's article described an English expedition to the Bay of Campeche in search of sunken cities and their treasures and how Heinrich Schliemann had left a sealed envelope upon his death for a family member worthy of taking up the quest for Atlantis (something the real Schliemann had no interest in). The letter directed the "grandson" to break open an owl-headed vase to find documents about Atlantis along with artifacts, such as fossilized bone, pottery sherds, and weirdly alloyed coins. The alleged notes of the elder Schliemann compared these to artifacts from "Tihuanaca" (a misspelling of Tiahuanaco or Tiwanaku) and to a Maya document transcribed by Aztec and Spanish priests. "Paul" went on to tell a racist tale of Atlantis and doomed love. In his subsequent globe-trotting research, he found more coins and different writing in Egypt, West Africa, Peru, and Mexico, all leading to the location of Atlantis. He then specifically cited Augustus Le Plongeon and reproduced a "Maya" text discussing the "Land of Mu," which was corroborated by the fictional "Lhasa text," a Chaldean document in a Tibetan monastery. Mu refers here to a high priest of Ra who predicted the destruction of Atlantis.

There are two clear influences on this story, the first being the Le Plongeons doomed romance of Queen Moo in the lands of Atlantis, Egypt, and Yucatán. "Schliemann" masculinized Queen Moo into Priest Mu. The piece also strongly resembles the opening of H. Rider Haggard's massively popular 1886–1887 serial adventure romance novel *She*. Among fans of the novel was Sigmund Freud, who had a private artifact collection and extensively used archaeological metaphors in his writing, though he believed psychology to be superior to archaeology in understanding the human past.[16] The theosophical themes in *She* would have appealed to someone familiar with the Le Plongeons. *She* begins with an aged professor near death leaving notes to his son, just like Schliemann supposedly did. In *She*, these are contained in a box rather than an owl vase, but in both cases the instructions detail how to find a lost city and include records and strange artifacts from various ages, most famously a potsherd that Haggard had commissioned to illustrate the novel. Egypt and the priests of Ra are prominent in both tales.

Haggard's use of artifacts to drive the plot of *She* is not surprising because he owned a significant collection of artifacts and wrote often about Egypt and immortality. The novelist was a friend of the British Museum's Egyptian keeper Wallis Budge and dedicated his novel *Morning Star* to him. Howard Carter gave the novelist a heart scarab and a tour; they were the first white men to enter the tomb of Queen Nefertari.[17] Unsurprisingly, Haggard also was interested in psychical research, the occult, and paganism.[18]

How Artifacts from the Lost Continent of Mu Ended Up in the Basement

Like other cases in this volume where mistaken or esoteric archaeology by real scholars fueled fiction and hoaxes, Mu was returned to the material realm with questionable artifacts from Mexico and was transformed in the process. Those four stones in our museum were collected by Scottish American geologist William Niven (figure 6.5). Museums and collectors supported Niven as an obtainer of unusual things. He forged a long-term relationship with the American Museum of Natural History after finding a massive garnet stone in a New York construction project and was twice made a lifetime member of the museum, though this affiliation is minimized today.[19]

Geological prospecting led Niven to Mexico, but he soon became interested in archaeology. Museum support, particularly for the colonial extraction of artifacts, helped differentiate archaeology from antiquarianism. In Victorian Britain the members of antiquarian, archaeological, and historical societies were largely university educated, many were clergy, and most undertook their studies as leisure hobbies separate from their jobs as

FIGURE 6.5. William Niven digging at Azcapotzalco. This photo, from the Middle American Research Institute archives, may date to Morley, Blom, and Gann's visit. Used with permission of the Middle American Research Institute, Tulane University.

Wm. NIEVEN . Atzcapazalco

lawyers or merchants. By contrast, archaeologists were increasingly distinguished as romantic travelers to exotic lands, especially the Near East. Few were university educated, but many were employed as full-time field archaeologists, sponsored by museums in exchange for the sensational artifacts they could obtain.[20] Niven began collecting artifacts in Guerrero, Mexico, with the support of the American Museum of Natural History. His first excavations at Omitlán produced 400 artifacts that became the Jesup Collection of Mexican Antiquities, named after Morris K. Jesup, the president of the museum. Niven suggested that jade and other items at Omitlán pointed to contact with China, a recurring theme in Niven's career.[21] Decades later, the source of Mesoamerican jadeite was found in the Motagua River valley in Guatemala.[22]

Stories of mysterious treasure lights led Niven to find a "vein of death," a thick layer of bones accumulated by seasonal flooding, at Zumpango.

Niven suggested that the phosphorus from this deposit created the lights in the dampness of the rainy season.[23] Perhaps Niven's material explanation was right, but treasure light folklore is found throughout Latin America and resembles the European association of spirits and fairies with tombs as well as rural Mexican stories of witches that move as balls of light.[24] Niven heard similar stories at Chalchiutepetl, "the hill of precious stones," of hilltop fires that were the spirits marking treasure, and he found evidence for recent burnt offerings.[25] Burnt and other offerings at preconquest sites continue in Mesoamerica to the present day.

The American Museum of Natural History reported on Niven's work in Guerrero for years.[26] Among his Guerrero finds were numerous examples of minimalist sculpture that came to be representative of the Mezcala culture. Most examples of Mezcala material have no documentation or were recovered from caches outside of Guerrero. The minimalist and pseudo-modernist aesthetic of Mezcala sculptures made them particularly popular in the twentieth century, a phenomenon also seen with the moai of Easter Island and Cycladic sculptures in the Aegean, which has led to suggestions that many Mezcala sculptures are forgeries.[27]

Niven opened a combined gallery, museum, and store in Mexico City, reputed at 15,000–20,000 pieces to be the largest private artifact collection in Mexico. The museum notes at my university suggest that this store was the primary source for the four glyph stones owned by James Coulter and eventually donated to Miami University along with more traditional Mesoamerican artifacts. Niven ceded much of his collection to the American Museum of Natural History in New York, Yale's Peabody Museum of Natural History, Harvard's Peabody Museum of Archaeology and Ethnology, and others. After Niven returned to the United States he donated part of his collection to the Houston Museum of Natural Science, where he was an early member of the board of directors.[28]

Despite these respectable museum affiliations, Niven's work increasingly contained sensational claims. In 1911 he claimed to have uncovered a vast and ancient civilization on the outskirts of Mexico City. Digging under a volcanic ash layer, Niven claimed to have found petrified wooden arches, evidence of a workshop for gold and silver working, and a dramatic scene of a burial with a copper ax stuck in the head of a poor individual—all of which turned to dust upon exposure to air (a common trope in early archaeological narratives). It is possible these accounts are garbled or fanciful descriptions of actual archaeological deposits, but they do not sound like the types of sites subsequently found in decades of archaeology in Mexico, and the technology and architecture sound more like Victorian stereotypes of classical ancient civilizations than anything typically found in Mesoamerica. There are numerous photographs of Niven digging, but no pictures or drawings of these fabulous finds.

I cannot securely place the original source for that article, but it seems to date to 1911 and was in the scrapbook of the occultist and later Niven collaborator James Churchward. His great-grandson Jack Churchward published a transcript of this article as found in his ancestor's scrapbook, and he kindly sent me images of the original pages.[29] Jack Churchward runs a website examining the legacy of his famous ancestor, making material available, and setting facts straight when possible.[30] Jack Churchward has examined his great-grandfather's works and generally finds himself skeptical of James Churchward's conclusions, as I found out during an interview on his podcast.[31]

The article is not dated nor does it contain a source, but it is on newsprint and the byline is William Niven, CE, MA, member of the New York Academy of Sciences, and mineralogist of Mexico. A theosophical newsletter repeated the core of this story in 1911, attributing it to a *Los Angeles Times* article in May 1911, but that article does not contain most of the details of interest and instead only discusses a stamp seal.[32] Perhaps Churchward's scrapbook article is an article that was in the *Mexican Herald* in September of that year.[33] Even if this story was a theosophical invention, which it does not appear to be, it predates James Churchward's interest in Niven and suggests that Niven was more than willing to find a lost civilization no one else could subsequently locate.

Niven's museum-store set the stage for a larger dispute between him and the influential Mexican archaeologist Manuel Gamio, a student of Columbia University's Franz Boas. Gamio's multidisciplinary Teotihuacan project and the San Miguel Amantla sequence, the first stratigraphic excavation in North America, established the basics of Mexican pre-Hispanic chronology and is often cited as the origin of scientific archaeology in the New World.[34] Gamio was increasingly dismayed by Niven's Mexico City store, its display of human remains, and its stream of non-Mexican customers. In 1916 he obliquely criticized the store in the press and referred to archaeological charlatans in regard to a supposedly extremely ancient skull in Niven's shop.[35] Niven collaborated with Professor L. H. Dudley Buxton of the University of Oxford, who presented a paper on twenty-six of Niven's "partitioned skulls" at the 1924 annual meeting of the British Association for the Advancement of Science in Toronto. Buxton's analysis focused on ethnic distinctions between Mayas and Nahuas in the "Toltec" skulls, a reflection of the protohistory and race-focused practices of the day.[36]

The antiquity of humans in the Americas was perhaps the most contentious question of early American archaeology and had political ramifications for the politics of colonialism and indigeneity. Gamio believed the Archaic "mother culture" to be at least 4,000 years old and perhaps older, followed by Teotihuacan, and then the Mayas and Aztecs. This contrasted with the assumption by non-Mexicans that the Mayan cities to the south were the base of Mesoamerican civilization.[37] Since Gamio's time, the depth of human settlement in the Americas has been extended to perhaps 20,000 years. Increasingly robust archaeological and especially genetic evidence supports the idea held by Gamio and others that northeastern Asia was the source of human colonization of the Americas. Gamio explicitly criticized the belief in a complex civilization 30,000 years old or older based on faulty geological evidence, which may refer to Niven. The mound-builder myth had been official American history in living memory, and hyperdiffusionists continued to suggest colonization by Phoenicians, Khmers, or other sources. While Niven sometimes downplayed such ideas, at other times he described the figurines from his excavation as being Phoenician, Egyptian, Mongolian, or Ethiopian, and he divided the prehistory of the Basin of Mexico with catastrophic destructions by flood and volcano. Long before the glyph stones were discovered, Niven's work was being cited for all sorts of hyperdiffusionist ideas ranging from Chinese settlers of Mexico to the sunken continents of Atlantis and Lemuria.[38]

Niven believed that Gamio orchestrated his arrest in 1913 on suspicion of allegiance to the revolutionary Emiliano Zapata. Niven was working during the height of the Mexican Revolution and was at times interrupted in the field by random hostilities and gunfire. Another reason for Gamio's annoyance was Niven's close relationship with the national museum, to which Niven had donated many artifacts, and its rivalry with the Dirección de Antropología, which Gamio founded in 1917. Gamio eventually lowered his rhetoric and in 1920 even asked Niven for advice on acquiring some artifacts for a gift.[39] It seems more than coincidental that Niven's discoveries would soon produce evidence of an ancient literate civilization, the exact sort of evidence to prove himself right and Gamio wrong.

In October 1921, Niven began uncovering "glyph stones" or "tablets" from the outskirts of Mexico City. After the first tablets appeared at San Miguel Amantla, Niven expanded his operations, although a 1923 news account describes the excavations as "creeping along" due to lack of funds.[40] On small slabs or boulders of soft andesite or other volcanic rock, lightly engraved simplistic designs were filled in with red or other pigment. Niven described the stones as ranging from a few inches across to thirty inches; they were covered in strange symbols that differed with every stone.[41] The soft material, crude painting, and unbroken status of the stones do not inspire confidence. Any archaeologist with excavation experience will tell you that with rare exceptions the vast majority of artifacts are fragmentary with breaks in any painted or engraved designs. Yet in every example or depiction of the Niven stones, be it a photograph, drawing, or the rare surviving example, the inscribed designs always fit within, and often conform to, the contours of the largest and flattest surface on each rock.

Niven claimed that the stones were part of an organized library of books of an ancient city 7,000–10,000 years old. He again prompted press speculation about Chinese, Egyptian, and African influences.[42] The stones' discovery under a volcanic layer was presumably inspired by the discussion of the subpedregal in contemporary archaeology.[43] We now recognize this layer as dating to the early first millennium CE, derived from a volcanic eruption that covered important Preclassic sites like Copilco and Cuicuilco. When I show my students these stones after they have worked with real archaeological artifacts, they are instantly incredulous about their supposed origin under a volcanic layer thousands of years old.

Anomalous Collections

The nature and context of these finds scream hoax. Similar massive collections of anomalous modern artifacts from the Americas, only found in one place or by one person, include the Acambaro figurines of western Mexico and the Ica Stones of Peru. Both depict humans interacting with prehistoric creatures, such as dinosaurs, as they appeared in earlier twentieth-century reconstructions now considered inaccurate, or in the presence of advanced technology. Waldemar Julsrud purchased thousands of crude and ropey clay figurines from villagers in Acambaro, Guanajuato. In Peru Javier Cabrera ultimately gave up his medical practice to collect thousands of Ica Stones in his Museo de Piedras Grabadas (Museum of Carved Stones). Ancient extraterrestrials promoters embraced the stones, which in some accounts were carved a million years ago by "gliptolithic" travelers from the Pleiades, who landed at the Nazca lines "spaceport." In the Acambaro and Ica cases, investigators found physical evidence of fraud or even got the creators to confess. Investigation by researchers at the University of Pennsylvania discovered direct evidence of the modern manufacture of the Acambaro figurines, including thermoluminescent dating of their recent construction. Basilo Uschuya admitted making most of the Ica Stones, "aging" them by baking them in animal dung, a practice also utilized by the Acambaro villagers.[44] In both of these cases, rural artisans created and sold the strange figurines or stones by the thousand to a hopeful but uncritical outsider, obtaining a steady stream of income. Despite their authors' confessions, both the Acambaro figurines and the Ica Stones have been adopted by biblical creationists and alternative archaeologists for their depiction of human-dinosaur interaction.

An even closer model for the Niven stones is the nearly contemporary Glozel affair. In March 1924 a young farmer, Emile Fradin, found some bricks in a field in Vichy, France. Local schoolteachers and an amateur archaeologist visited the site and interpreted it as a kiln for making glass. One of the teachers also began discussing archaeology with Fradin and gave him books on the subject, which may have been the inspiration for the subsequent "artifacts" found at the site, including an inscribed ax similar to one presented in a 1917 *Bulletin* of France's Prehistoric Society. The catalyst for the Glozel phenomenon was the arrival of a medical doctor named Antonin Morlet, an amateur archaeologist who bought exclusive rights to the site and paid by the piece. The first fragments sold to Morlet were of unbaked clay, but over time the 3,500 artifacts would improve in manufacture to match the needs of Glozel supporters. The scale is comparable to the

Ica Stones, the Acambaro figurines, and Niven's glyph stones. Morlet and most subsequent supporters interpreted the site as a "missing link bridging the Paleolithic and Neolithic."[45]

The Glozel "alphabet" described by Morlet drew the most attention. Some of the inscriptions contained eastern and especially Phoenician elements, but the alleged continuity with the Paleolithic and with pre-Indo-European Basque allowed supporters such as Salomon Reinach, the keeper of the Museum of National Antiquities in Saint-Germain, to suggest that civilization began in France rather than in the East.[46] Echoing the tradition of magical hieroglyphs, historian Camille Jullian believed that a Roman era sorcerer inscribed the Glozel artifacts with a form of cursive Latin believed to have magical powers.[47]

Reinach's assistant believed the objects to be fakes, but after Reinach himself excavated a tablet he and others were convinced of their authenticity. Unlike Niven's case, professional archaeologists from France and other nations, as well as interested laypeople, descended on Glozel to investigate and found evidence of hoaxing. Marcellin Boule, an anatomist and the creator of the erroneous caveman stereotype (due to his study of Neanderthals), sent André Vayson de Pradenne to the site. Vayson de Pradenne became convinced that someone in the Fradin family was seeding the site, and Boule found a supposedly Paleolithic depiction of a reindeer to have no patina over the incisions, evidence of recent carving. Morlet angrily denounced the skeptics as being "Sherlock Holmeses," an inversion of the usually positive association of archaeologists with detectives.[48]

An entire panel of Sherlocks was convened by the International Anthropological Congress and France's Ministry of Fine Arts in November 1927, including the influential archaeologist Dorothy Garrod. The local authorities in Vichy, interested in promoting the region, provided lodgings, banquets, and other logistics while the team dug for five days. The team quickly concluded that the site was rife with hoaxing. The corkscrews included in the gift baskets were subsequently found in a "prehistoric" context by the Glozel excavators, demonstrating their inability to detect disturbance of the site or fraud. The government removed the protection it had given Glozel as a site of scientific interest. Despite this and other findings that the objects were fraudulent, incised pebbles using the Glozel alphabet began appearing in other corners of France in support of the Glozelians.

The case ended in legal investigations of fraud against unknown persons—Fradin was never conclusively proven to be the forger—and a libel lawsuit against the anti-Glozelian René Dussaud, the curator of the Louvre.[49]

Niven and the Scientists

William Niven had previously admitted to falling prey to such a seeding hoax. Niven's earlier finds were used by Ramón Mena and geologist George E. Hyde to create a chronology of the Valley of Mexico. While there were some similarities to the chronology Gamio was creating, the Niven-based chronology included Chinese, Egyptian, and Hindu origins and migrations in its Tlachichique (2000–1500 BCE) and Mongoloide (2500–2000 BCE) periods.[50] When communicating in private with American museums, Niven downplayed these suggestions of Chinese origin as nothing more than press sensationalism. Yet the "apparently" Asian nature of the artifacts led the secretary of the Chinese legation to Mexico to declare, after visiting Niven's shop in 1921, that the Mongol Empire had once controlled Mexico.[51] Many of the figurines in photos of Niven's collections are actually in the Classic Teotihuacan styles of the first millennium CE, while Niven's supposedly 9,000-year-old Archaic figurines are from the Preclassic, primarily the first millennium BCE.[52] Even worse, some of the artifacts in the Mena and Hyde chronology were examples of Tlatelolco ware, a common forgery in nineteenth-century Mexico. The black ware was made in the Tlatelolco section of Mexico City and is characterized by baroque designs that can incorporate Classic Teotihuacan adorno fragments from incense burners.[53] Figures 3, 4, and 5 in Mena's report are good examples, and the ropey mother-and-child figurines in figure 6 do not inspire much confidence. The artifacts were clearly frauds, and Niven agreed to destroy them.[54] A precedent for fraud, even if Niven was not a party to it, had been set.

Excitement greeted the news that Niven had potentially found the origins of Mesoamerican writing. The museums Niven worked with wanted to examine the stones for themselves, and Niven sent drawings, photos, and samples. According to Niven the British Museum examined one of the stones at the microscopic level and subsequently placed it on display in the Department of Ceramics and Ethnography. At the request of the American Museum of Natural History's president, Henry Fairfield Osborn, Niven sent 5 stones and 110 photos, drawings, and rubbings to the museum.[55] Like my students, archaeologists soon questioned the recently carved and fragile appearance of the stones. Niven's self-appointed representative in the United States, George R. Fox (who praised Niven by saying he knew even more than the "so-called expert archaeologist"),[56] presented a paper for Niven at the American Anthropological Association Central Section Meetings. Audience members, like Ralph Linton of the Field Museum, suggested that Niven's workers had provided him with fake artifacts.[57]

Some samples went quietly into collections without any significant analytical remark. One example survives in New Orleans. As part of the research discussed in chapter 4, I returned to my alma mater of Tulane University and its Middle American Research Institute to research the original records of the excavation of an inscribed vessel in El Salvador. While there, I found several photographs of William Niven and his artifacts and a catalog entry for one of his stones. This stone is labeled M.19.2 40-1652 by the institute, but was Niven's Tablet No. 1154. Measuring 12 × 9 × 8 centimeters, the volcanic tuff resembles the others with red pigment filling incisions that conform to the shape of the stone. The notes say it was found at Chimalpa, six miles northwest of Mexico City, on 27 March 1924.[58]

Several papers accompanied the stone. On 28 October 1925, institute director Frans Blom responded to a previous letter from Niven, the contents of which are not known.[59] Blom wrote that he might visit Niven's home in Tampico if his upcoming travel to Mexico made it convenient. He also asked for a clipping of a newspaper article describing Niven's work. This may have been from the *Dearborn Independent*'s coverage of Niven. Images from that article appear in James Churchward's scrapbook and may have first led to Churchward's interest. The *Independent* was Henry Ford's newspaper, and it was already embroiled in controversy and legal action over its anti-Semitic content. It would close in 1927. Niven's "library," described as "Chinese," was given prominent coverage by the *Los Angeles Times*, and one of the tablets was illustrated and potentially dated to 10,000 years ago.[60]

Niven replied a few days later (3 November 1925) on stationery depicting Teotihuacan-style incense burners found by Niven, one of which was donated to the national museum.[61] In this letter Niven mentioned that "our old friends" Professor Mena and Director Luis Castillo Ledón had been reinstated at the museum. This passage alludes to the political struggle that colored Niven's friendship with the museum's staff and the problems they had with Gamio and his archaeology department. Niven's disenchantment with Mexico City was indirectly on display as he described moving the remainder of his private museum collection to Tampico by the end of 1925. On the topic of the tablets, Niven included a copy of a *Dearborn Independent* article from 25 July, though this is only attested in the letter and is not in the collection in the institute today. One line reveals an important sense of Niven's operations. The day prior to writing the letter (2 November), Niven had received 182 carved tablets, bringing the total to 2,041. In the notes accompanying the Coulter stones at Miami University, they are described as being part of a collection of 169. Niven generally visited his excavations on Sundays, and 2 November was a Monday. This suggests that Niven was minimally present at the dig site, and he was receiving periodic shipments.

A year later, Niven sent the stone to Tulane.[62] By October 1926, Niven's stationery only listed an address in Tampico and not the Mexico City store. The collection of tablets had grown by this time to 2,166. Tulane received the stone on 6 December 1926.[63] In thanking Niven for the stone, Blom stated that the museum was financially unable to purchase collections, but donations were appreciated.[64] This statement could lead one to believe that Niven had been trying to sell some part of his collection to Tulane and was sending the stone as a "free sample." In a letter to Tulane on 15 December 1926, however, Niven included a forceful postscript that his collection was not for sale, but he could provide photographs and drawings for study (figure 6.6).[65] Yet we know that at other times Niven did try to sell or trade his collection.

What did Blom and the Tulane scholars think of Niven's stones? Blom had already visited Niven's excavations in June 1923 along with archaeologists Sylvanus Morley and Thomas Gann during negotiations in Mexico City between the Carnegie Institution and the Mexican government over excavating Chichén Itzá. The archaeologists found the stones to be crude hoaxes at first, and Blom suggested that the paint on the stones was fresh. They assumed that Niven's workers had seeded the stones. When Morley and Gann accompanied Niven to his excavations one Sunday, they saw incised slabs being pulled out of excavations and concluded (somewhat

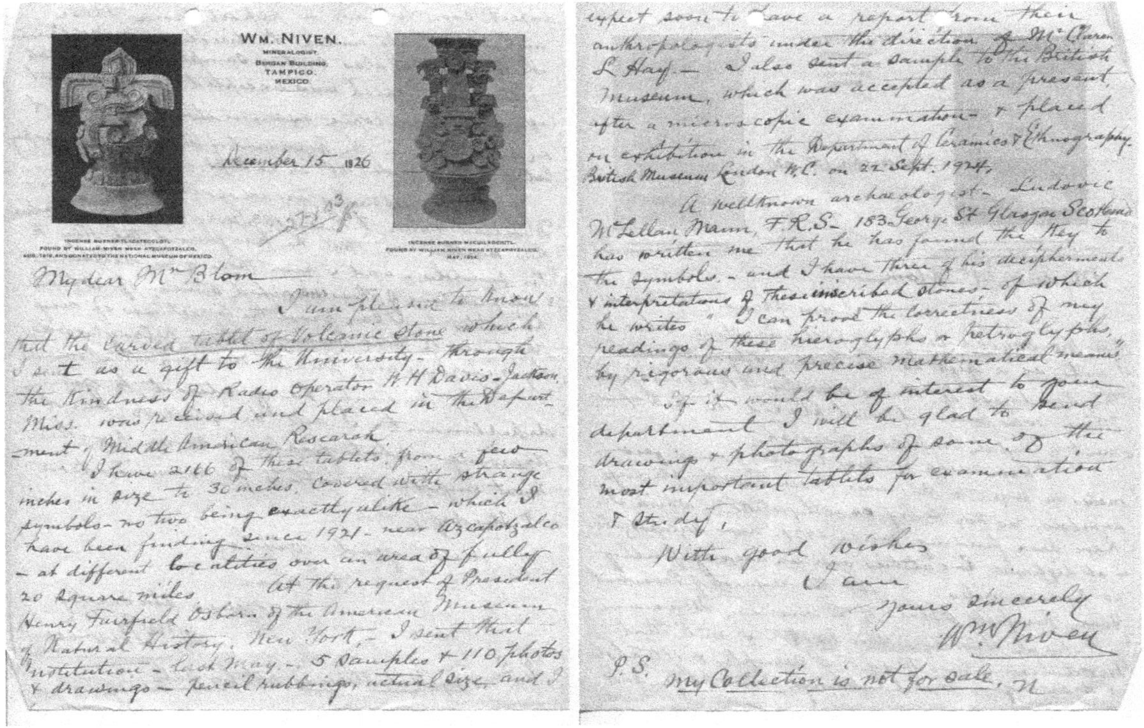

WM. NIVEN.
MINERALOGIST.
BURGAN BUILDING
TAMPICO.
MEXICO.

December 15 1926

My dear Mr Blom

I am pleased to know that the carved tablet of Volcanic Stone which I sent as a gift to the University – through the kindness of Radio Operator H. H. Davis-Jackson Miss. was received and placed in the Department, Middle American Research.

I have 2166 of these tablets from a few inches in size to 30 inches, covered with strange symbols – no two being exactly alike – which I have been finding since 1921 – near Azcapotzalco – at different localities over an area of fully 20 square miles. At the request of President Henry Fairfield Osborn of the American Museum of Natural History, New York, – I sent that institution – last May – 5 samples & 110 photos & drawings – pencil rubbings, actual size, and I expect soon to have a report from their anthropologists under the direction of Mr Clarence L Hay. – I also sent a sample to the British Museum, which was accepted as a present after a microscopic examination – & placed on exhibition in the Department of Ceramics & Ethnography British Museum London W.C. on 22 Sept. 1924.

A wellknown archaeologist – Ludovic McLellan Mann, F.R.S. 183 George St Glasgow Scotland has written me that he has found the key to the symbols – and I have three of his decipherments & interpretations of these inscribed stones – of which he writes "I can prove the correctness of my readings of these hieroglyphs or petroglyphs, by rigorous and precise mathematical means"

If it would be of interest to your department I will be glad to send drawings & photographs of some of the most important tablets for examination & study.

With good wishes
I am
Yours sincerely
Wm Niven

P.S. My Collection is not for sale. N

FIGURE 6.6. Letter from William Niven to Frans Blom, the director of the Middle American Research Institute, 15 December 1926. Used with permission of the Middle American Research Institute, Tulane University.

paradoxically) that the conditions were so perfect for a hoax that a hoaxer wouldn't create such a scenario. I suspect they overestimated the hoaxers, or Niven, or both. Morley also suggested that since Niven's workers were not paid by the find, they had no financial reason to create fake artifacts. However, Niven's excavations in the Valley of Mexico over fifteen years paid rent to landowners on fourteen farms and employed their family members, and the sales from Niven's store funded the work.[66]

I revisit Gann a bit later due to his collaboration with F. A. Mitchell-Hedges, another archaeological explorer accused of fraud, and due to Gann's spying activities and disgrace over antiquities smuggling. Gann wrote of the stones in the *Illustrated London News* on 6 October 1923 in an article titled "The Oldest Civilization on the American Continent," dating them to 3000–1000 BCE under a volcanic layer.[67] Gann included Niven's stones in a synthesis of Mexican archaeology but did not put much importance on them; they only merited part of a paragraph in an entire book. He did not think they were examples of writing but a picture gallery.[68] Morley, possibly the leading Maya hieroglyph expert in the world as well as one of Gann's spymasters, never wrote about the Niven stones in any significant way. He was much more excited by the new Maya glyphs he saw at the national museum during the trip.[69]

Despite Blom's initial skepticism he continued to deal with Niven as an artifact source. In January 1928 Blom obtained a small collection of figurines, molds, and spindle whorls and a stone bark beater from Niven in Tampico. Some of the objects were from Veracruz, while others were from the Basin of Mexico and presumably were excavated before Niven left Mexico City. Perhaps due to Niven's problems with the Mexican government, the artifacts were provided to Tulane without any government knowledge, prompting Tulane to refrain from any press publicity.[70] Blom himself called Tablet No. 1154 a "small volcanic rock on which is an ancient carving."[71] This cannot be taken as a firm statement of support for Niven's geology or archaeology. Blom had a tempestuous career at Tulane, and one can imagine that a letter to the university president proclaiming the acceptance of a fraud would not have gone over well. On the other hand, Blom did not condemn the stone, and he continued friendly relations with Niven. Was Niven's large collection of for-sale artifacts, especially after the Mexican government had begun to crack down on antiquities trafficking, sufficient motivation to politely ignore some eccentric tablets?

Artifact seeding by workers or colleagues happens. In 1997 I was directing the excavation of a modest masonry platform at Campana San Andres, El Salvador. One of the excavators called my attention to a crude cross incised on a stone, which had cut marks about the same width as the blade of the excavator's sharp steel trowel. This issue was quickly dropped and appeared to be an expression of evangelical Christian religiosity, boredom, and play. On this same excavation, religious and supernatural topics were a common theme of discussions between workers and the site management staff, including arguments about giants in the book of Genesis, sightings of UFOs at the archaeological site of Tazumal, and conspiracy theories imported from North America about the New World Order and the mark of the beast.

When academic attention had previously been drawn to Mena's chronology based on Niven's excavations, critics had revealed fraudulent artifacts allegedly seeded by his workers. The same reaction greeted the glyph stones. Perhaps Niven's workers fooled him. He was usually only present at his excavations on Sundays, making oversight of the industrial-scale work (removing more than 100,000 tons of earth at multiple sites) difficult.[72] In 1922 Niven described his work schedule. Over the course of the week he would hire four or five men to dig a trench about ten square meters in area and about two to three meters deep. Niven would then arrive on Sunday and supervise twice as many workers in personally excavating ash and gravel pits of interest.[73] It seems unlikely that Niven had much control over excavations of this scale. The Field Museum's Ralph Linton also noted that the associated figurines were from a mélange of time periods.[74]

A case can also be made for Niven the hoaxer. Manuel Gamio called Niven a charlatan for promoting hyperdiffusionist fantasies and criticized his store, the source of Niven's wealth and the funding for his excavations. Niven's work underpinned a chronology to rival Gamio's but had only resulted in exposing some of Niven's artifacts as fakes. The glyph stones, if genuine, would have supported Niven's claims in his dispute with Gamio. Niven spent some of his last years fighting for money to export the large "altar" that Morley and Gann had seen excavated at Azcapotzalco. Niven tried to get Morley's Carnegie Institution to provide $6,000 to move the stone (the equivalent of close to $100,000 today). Niven offered the Mexican government all of his glyph stones in exchange for exporting this one altar. When permission was denied Niven angrily claimed that the great altar had recently eroded beyond repair.[75] This suspicious story, the carving and pigment style that followed Niven, and the motives of reputation and money are concerning.

In 2015 I brought the four stones to Miami University's Center for Advanced Microscopy and Imaging. I was hoping that an obvious industrial additive might appear in the pigment. This was not to test whether the stones were modern hoaxes; all of the other contextual data supported that conclusion. However, I hypothesized that if Niven had commissioned the creation of the stones, it was possible he would have been expected to supply the paint. The X-ray diffraction spectroscopy performed by Matthew Duley and Richard Edelmann of the microscopy center found no such obvious additive in the pigment, just extra potassium, sulfur, and iron in comparison with the stones themselves, which are largely silicon and aluminum. Examination of Niven's notes show no documentary evidence of hoaxing.[76] It is still possible that Niven commissioned the stones for his own reasons, but these lines of evidence make me wonder, like his contemporaries, if he was fooled by locally made forgeries that gave Niven exactly what he wanted.

The Creation of Mu

Niven felt betrayed by the museums that purchased his other artifacts but politely ignored or returned his stones. After the discovery of the glyph stones, Niven began to be refused excavation and export permits from the Mexican government.[77] Today, the American Museum of Natural History briefly mentions Niven in its history.[78] Only Harvard's Peabody presents its Niven stones, with minimal comment, in its online museum.[79] Tulane University's Middle American Research Institute director Frans Blom was skeptical of the glyph stones, but the institution continued to obtain real artifacts from Niven.

A few scholars were interested in the stones. Archaeologist J. E. Pearce of the University of Texas wanted to acquire the stones because he thought the designs were similar to those on local pottery, but Niven refused when his price of $500 was not met.[80] Niven was pleased with Scottish scholar Ludovic McLellan Mann's comparison of the stones to Scandinavian petroglyphs as part of a sun cult honoring Jupiter. Niven referred to Mann as "a well known archaeologist" and provided Tulane with his address, presumably to compare notes.[81] In this description for Tulane, Niven did not mention any of Mann's specific ideas, just that Mann had provided him with three decipherments based on a "key" derived from "rigorous and precise mathematical means." Mann provided similar Maya-influenced readings to F. A. Mitchell-Hedges and Lady Richmond Brown when they presented ethnographic textiles from Panama to the Royal Society (see chapter 7).[82] I suspect that Mann would have been able to read any pattern of images in his "system."

One man took great sympathetic interest in the stones and made them part of Western occult lore. James Churchward wrote a number of theosophical books detailing the legacy of the ancient lost continent of Mu. Churchward was a friend of the Le Plongeons and heavily based his writings on the sagas of Queen Moo and sunken continents.[83] He substantially quoted Brasseur and drew a line of inference through Brasseur, Le Plongeon, the almost certainly fictitious Paul Schliemann, and Niven to his own discoveries. Churchward took the name Mu from Brasseur and used it for the lost continent he "discovered" in the Pacific Ocean and introduced in his *The Lost Continent of Mu* (1926). Mu bears some resemblance to the sunken continent of Lemuria, invented in 1864 by zoologist Philip Sclater to explain the biogeographical distribution of lemurs, a puzzle now explained by continental drift. Theosophists embraced Lemuria as home to one of the earlier root races of humanity before Atlantis.[84] By giving his Pacific continent a new name and tying it to other sources of evidence, Churchward successfully made Mu his own.

Humans had been created with a soul, rather than having evolved, in the garden of Eden on Mu at least as early as the Oligocene (Churchward used vastly shorter spans of time for geological epochs than do geologists). Though housed within the larger tradition of theosophy and its distorted Victorian conceptions of ancient Egypt and of Hinduism, Churchward's research supports a quasi-Christian belief system and white supremacy. Churchward denounced modern science as pure speculation that mistook degenerate idiots like Neanderthal and Piltdown for human ancestors and ignored the pure white Mu, Naacal, and Mayan races of the Americas. Christ was a perfect figure, and only Moses had successfully preserved ancient Muvian teachings, copying this wisdom in symbolic hieroglyphs in Egypt that modern Jews could not understand.[85]

Ten racial tribes inhabited Mu, led by a dominant white Aryan race (Churchward made a distinction between Northern European Aryans and less perfect Mediterranean white people) and ruled by the emperor of the sun, the Ra Mu. The Muvian imperial navies sailed around the world and built colonies, leaving behind huge statues, monoliths, and roofless temples for sun worship, not unlike the massive open temple at Akhenaten's Amarna. The continent sank 12,000 years ago, killing 64 million people and leaving above water only the mountaintops, which became the Pacific islands. The survivors turned to cannibalism before establishing a savage way of life still followed in the Pacific today.[86] Churchward bragged of using ghosts to find the ruined cities of Mu. He alleged that since native guides believed such ruins to be haunted, Churchward needed only to insist on going the opposite way his guides suggested. When they ran away Churchward knew he had found a haunted ruin.[87]

All of this was based on Churchward's later claims of having read mystical tablets in an Indian monastery while providing famine relief in the 1870s. He claimed to have apprenticed himself to one of only three priests who could read the ancient form of a Mayan language called Naacal (a word borrowed from the Le Plongeons). After months of persuasion, the priest, who had never dared to gaze upon the sacred tablets, agreed to study them with Churchward.[88] Churchward followed Brasseur by suggesting that entire languages symbolically encoded memories of the ancient deluge and destruction in their "vocables" and writing systems. He explicitly used Brasseur's translation of the Popol Vuh into French, and Augustus Le Plongeon's translation of that into English, as the allegorical basis of Muvian secret initiatory rites encoded in the Egyptian Book of the Dead and the architecture of the Great Pyramid.[89]

The discovery of tablets in a monastery is just like the tale of the alleged Paul Schliemann, which likely copied H. Rider Haggard's novel *She*, which in turn resembles a number of revealed-knowledge narratives of the time, including Blavatsky's meetings with the ascended masters and her mystical *Book of Dzyan*. Blavatsky suspected that Haggard had channeled theosophical truth in a dream before writing *She*, whereas Churchward explicitly cited "Schliemann" and his Atlanteans.[90]

When Churchward saw press reports of Niven's excavations, he apparently recognized the glyph stones as Naacal, just as the supposed Paul Schliemann had found proof all around the world for the strange artifacts in his "grandfather's" possession. Churchward republished some of the images of Niven's stones that had appeared in the *Dearborn Independent* and praised Niven's work as some of the most valuable geological and archaeological discoveries ever made. He combined Niven's stratigraphic suggestions with his own beliefs about the age and nature of the world's landforms and mountains (pushed up by cataclysmic movements of underground gas belts) to date the height of Muvian civilization to 50,000 years ago.[91]

Churchward also reproduced Niven's discussion of a "little Chinaman" figurine found in his excavations and Niven's interpretations of the "Mongoloide" roots of civilization in Mexico. Churchward's Muvian colonists were white Aryans at first, who built the ruined cities of Yucatán during numerous dynasties, including the Can dynasty of Queen Moo. Churchward claimed that his Mayan history was based on notes received personally from the Le Plongeons. The white Mayas were destroyed 11,500 years ago when the cataclysms that destroyed Atlantis depopulated Yucatán with earthquakes and tsunamis.[92] Churchward claimed to have heard tales in Honduras and Guatemala of the Quetzals, white Indians with blond hair. He also described the descendants of later races, such as three-foot-tall, dark-skinned pygmies with long hair supposedly still living in British Honduras and speaking fluent Maya.[93] Churchward believed that the subsequent Mongoloide Nahuatls emerged in South America and conquered the region after 1000 CE.[94] This racial sequence, along with prophecies of a return of white colonists in the future, makes Churchward's writing one more manifestation of the colonial myth of an ancient white race, like the moundbuilder myth in North America, the Spanish colonial legends of Quetzalcoatl and Cortés, and the racist fantasies surrounding Great Zimbabwe. Just as Blavatsky believed that fiction writers were channeling secret knowledge, Churchward believed that the racial history in H. Rider Haggard's novel *Montezuma's Daughter* must have relied on secret lore.[95]

Churchward ignored scientific work in the region, mocking the Carnegie excavators as "picnicking" at Chichén Itzá and underestimating the age of the ruins by millennia.[96] Yet much of the structure of *The Lost Continent of Mu* can be found in the obsessive symbolic interpretations of Brasseur, the romantic fantasies of Augustus and Alice Le Plongeon, the fraudulent use of Schliemann's name in a newspaper story likely based on the novel *She*, and the hyperdiffusionist search by William Niven for deeply ancient civilization in Mexico. If, as I suspect, Churchward did not understand that the Schliemann article was a hoax, his "research" was based on occult-minded archaeologists and historians who were considered eccentric but valued for their ability to find lost cities and obtain rare antiquities for museums.

Happy to have an interested party who might help promote the stones and his planned book, Niven gave Churchward illustrations of the glyph designs. Since most of the stones have disappeared, the line drawings in Churchward's Mu books are the best record of the variety of designs etched into Niven's stones. In his 1931 book, *The Children of Mu*, Churchward described these as recording an alphabet of sixteen letters and many diphthongs. Each letter contained three glyphs, including a hieratic letter with a hidden meaning, just like Brasseur's Maya or the Hermetic reading of Egyptian.[97]

Two papers, handwritten and illustrated by Churchward, are in the Tulane archive. One is about Tablet No. 1154, the Tulane stone. It does not provide much information other than to speculate that the image may be of a dragon, that it belonged to a primitive level of civilization, and that it had been found four meters below the ground surface.[98] The second paper is an interpretation of Tablet No. 339 and is marked "This copy for William Niven" (figure 6.7). There is no indication as to why Niven sent this additional interpretation to Tulane. The contemporary notes by Blom suggest that only one stone was donated to the university. According to the archived paper, Niven found stone 339 (measuring 16 × 10 × 3 centimeters) at Hacienda de Leon in sand five meters below the ground surface. Churchward interpreted it as symbolizing law and order evolving out of chaos. A butterfly head, four dots in a circle, represents the "Godhead of Five, the Creator and his Four Great Commandments" emerging from an empty chrysalis of chaos.

When the Aztec literature scholar J. H. Cornyn, who had visited Niven's

FIGURE 6.7. Undated letter from James Churchward, interpreting the Muvian iconography on stone 339. This letter was found at the Middle American Research Institute with one of the stones and letters from William Niven. Used with permission of the Middle American Research Institute, Tulane University.

excavations and took Niven's discoveries seriously as possibly being Aztec, warned Niven of Churchward's unscientific manner, Niven was disappointed in Cornyn. Over time, Niven and Churchward routinely corresponded, and in 1931 *The Children of Mu*, a revision of *The Lost Continent of Mu*, was dedicated to Niven.[99] Churchward not only gave Niven the attention no one else would in the 1920s, but the notion that North America was the first colony of Mu and that the civilizations of Europe, Egypt, and the Near East were "tailenders" could have resonated with Niven in light of his dispute with Manuel Gamio.[100]

Relic Hunters and Haunted Museums

THE SMITHSONIAN INSTITUTION is not only "America's attic" but an important resource for American science, especially archaeology. Yet even the august Smithsonian has a dark side and a weird side. The massive collections of indigenous human remains, some very recent when they were collected in the nineteenth century, made the Smithsonian exhibit A of the case to give such remains the same legal protections given to the ancestors of other communities. This struggle became federal law with the 1990 passage of the Native American Graves Protection and Repatriation Act.

In contrast with the legally problematic collection of indigenous remains, conspiracy theorists have accused the Smithsonian of being the center of a vast plot to seize, hide, destroy, or otherwise cover up the remains of giants. Creationists and others point to hundreds of newspaper articles from the nineteenth and early twentieth centuries about the discovery of supposed giants' bones, which sometimes resembled folk or religious descriptions of the semiangelic Nephilim of the Old Testament in having horns or extra fingers or teeth. By the late twentieth century, these claims morphed into a conspiracy legend of Smithsonian archaeologists collecting and hiding or destroying such bones, presumably as the arm of a devilish (possibly literally Satanic) plot to hide the sacred "truth" about the past. The collection of plenty of real human remains by the Smithsonian seems to have fueled this belief. The role of the Smithsonian in debunking folk archaeology claims was also to blame. The Smithsonian was the principal investigating institution that declared the moundbuilder idea of an ancient white race in North America to be a myth. Statements by the Smithsonian physical anthropologist Aleš Hrdlička in 1934 debunking giant skeleton claims are also routinely cited as evidence of the conspiracy.[1]

Public exhibitions and a distrust of expert institutions are integral to the giant skeletons myth. The interpretation of large bones as being from giant humanoids was not new in the nineteenth century, but such accounts became very popular as a biblical literalist reaction to discoveries in geology, paleontology, archaeology, and evolutionary biology. It was these attitudes that George Hull wished to mock with his "Cardiff giant" archaeological hoax. Hull was an outspoken atheist, and after an argument with a Methodist preacher in 1867, Hull was inspired to create a fake giant.[2] The Cardiff giant drew enormous attention and crowds and inspired sensation exhibitor P. T. Barnum to create his own giant when his bid for the original was rejected. The Cardiff giant is still on display today in the Farmers' Museum in Cooperstown, New York.

As weird as conspiracy claims about a vast warehouse of giants' bones may sound, the origins of the Smithsonian contain an even stranger story. In 1818, John Cleves Symmes Jr., a former naval officer from a prominent Ohio family, wrote "Circular Number 1" and mailed it to as many important figures as he could. It detailed a hollow earth of concentric spheres that could be entered at the poles, and he urged America to boldly claim this chance for exploration. Some scholarly figures supported a hollow earth theory. The astronomer Edmond Halley, for example, had proposed in 1692 that the earth contained a set of concentric spheres. This in turn influenced witch hunter Cotton Mather, who propagated the notion in America. Along with symbolic hieroglyphs, the popularity of the idea of a physically hollow earth may be the fault of Athanasius Kircher.[3]

One of the more vigorous proponents of Symmes's theory was the pioneering Ohio archaeologist James McBride, who published plans in 1826 for reaching the hollow earth. Another of Symmes's followers, Jeremiah Reynolds, advocated for the US Exploring Expedition, a research tour of the southern Atlantic sponsored by the US federal government. Edgar Allan Poe was a fan of Reynolds, whose address to Congress may have inspired Poe's hollow earth tale, *The Narrative of Arthur Gordon Pym of Nantucket*. The 1838–1842 Exploring Expedition collected some 50,000 specimens, and the need to store the objects helped propel the creation of a national natural history museum, the Smithsonian.[4]

FIGURE 7.1. Monument to John Symmes and his hollow earth theory, Hamilton, Ohio. Image by author.

A monument to Symmes was built by his son Americus, and today it stands in the corner of an unassuming public park in Hamilton, Ohio. The monument is fenced off and a bit difficult to see through the bars and tree cover, but a three-dimensional schematic of the hollow earth is visible on its crown (figure 7.1).

The Haunted Museum of Wonders

Why are museums, especially archaeological museums and displays, so readily associated with paranormal themes? We have already seen the supernaturalization of the archaeological and the mythic and mystical qualities attributed to ancient writing. Museums are warehouses of such objects. Hauntings and magical powers might be expected, prompting the practice of women visiting the Cairo Museum in the twentieth century to take advantage of the fertility powers of ancient artifacts, a practice also found at certain megalithic sites in Europe.⁵ The museum as a stage for the artistic representation of the human form only makes matters worse. The classical Greeks saw objects as empty and the Old Testament describes pagan idols as false and therefore powerless, but in Christianity idols became potential houses for demonic spirits and were beyond human control.⁶

Perhaps it should not surprise us that the British Museum became the geographic center of the influential London occult underground. Beginning in 1863 spiritualists, the paranormal investigators of the Society for Psychical Research, and the magicians of the Hermetic Order of the Golden Dawn all moved into the Bloomsbury neighborhood around the museum. I prefer not to provide the location, but I can personally attest that Egyptian-influenced relics of the Isis-Urania Temple, the first center for the Golden Dawn, are still quietly guarded in the vicinity of the museum today. In his classic curse tale "Casting the Runes," M. R. James depicted the British Library, then located inside the museum, as haunted by dueling occultists and as the site of at least one cursing.⁷

One of the key leaders of the Golden Dawn was Samuel Mathers, who described himself as, among other things, a student of occultism, archaeology, and Egyptology. Under the influence of Mathers and others, the Golden Dawn incorporated the discoveries of nineteenth-century Egyptology and Near Eastern archaeology. Mathers was briefly the curator of the Horniman Museum, where he substantially increased the Egyptian holdings, and he was supported in the Golden Dawn for a time by Annie Horniman. She was a champion for Egyptian Hermetic secrets as the key focus of the Golden Dawn and was dismayed when Yeats and his Celtic mystics caused rifts in the order.⁸ In chapter 2, I discussed the strange death of Netta Fornario on a fairy mound in Scotland. The novelist and magician Dion Fortune blamed the death on a psychic attack by Moira Mathers, who had conveniently died eighteen months earlier.⁹

The ghosts haunting museums are those of the stories lost through obtaining antiquities. Collections are still the main public meaning of museums despite efforts to recast museums as places of education or community engagement.¹⁰ Archaeological looting causes a tremendous loss of information from museum pieces, but even the very notion of display and preservation can sever important memories and continuity. The severance of history from mummies, for example, and the inability to touch them makes many museum visitors believe that the displayed mummies are no more real than movie versions.[11] These processes not only destroy original information but also create new meanings tying the present to a mythic past. Roman artifacts found in Anglo-Saxon burials do not appear to be heirlooms from the end of the empire but a mix of objects valued more for their general relation to antiquity and the dead than to any actual connection to Rome.[12] An allegedly devilish-looking stone figurine, Little Mannie, haunts a local museum in northwestern England. Some staff members and archaeologists refuse to work with the object, in part due to its discovery in the basement of a seventeenth-century house, surrounded by candleholders and chicken bones. Like witches and ancient Celts, the figure exudes mystic potency. The problem is that Little Mannie may be a curio from eighteenth-century Africa.[13] The reinscription of new myths in the empty historical spaces of looted objects creates museums full of the curious and exotic,[14] just as colonialism and similar disruptions demonized ancient remains, as discussed in chapter 2.

Loss of information is not always accidental. Antiquarian diggers for museums in nineteenth-century France would occasionally blur or falsify provenance in order to protect rich find spots.[15] Collectors and dealers today may provide only vague provenances for artifacts. Some are sourced to "old collections" that predate international legal agreements. These blank spaces not only aid looting but encourage forgeries. In other cases, such as in the Mayan region encompassing Mexico, Guatemala, Belize, Honduras, and El Salvador, an object may be designated as belonging to a broad area covering multiple possible countries of origin.[16] Just as a hopeful child might play one parent off another in attempting to obtain permission to attend a party, the holder of a collection can answer a claim from one nation by suggesting that an object might have been found across a border drawn in colonial times. Scholars working at the Heye Museum of the American Indian in the early twentieth century guessed at provenances when writing official catalogs.[17] Agatha Christie's firsthand account of baksheesh and artifact collection in 1930s Syria—in which workers held onto objects until they were paid a bonus, "worthless" bits were tossed away on-site, and gangs of workers died in wall collapses trying to beat each other to rich finds—is terrifying.[18] Even if information is not lost, it might be minimized in display, as in the case of two Congolese carvings captured as war trophies by Belgian lieutenant Emile Storms in the defeat of Chief Lusinga in Mpala. The carvings were initially displayed in public in ethnographic cases honoring Storms's collection before becoming more anonymous "Tabwa artworks." The later display of these objects as part of a discussion on the making of Belgium and Congo through colonialism was not well received by collectors and critics.[19]

Sketchy appropriation is compounded by the motivations for collecting. In the early eighteenth century a split developed between artifacts intended for scientific research and those driven by the aesthetic priorities of collectors and institutions. Antiquarians were portrayed as Professors Dryasdust for their interest in Roman spoons and other bits of everyday life.[20] Horace Walpole, widely credited as the inventor of the Gothic novel, strongly opposed sullying artistic appreciation with the archaeological study of common objects.[21] By the 1970s, university-housed American anthropological archaeology came to view museum collections as embarrassments from the bad old days, and scientific journals refused to publish unprovenanced artifacts.[22] We can see the split in the case of a looted Sicilian gold phiale, which was returned to Italy in 2000. During the appeals process, multiple museum organizations led by the American Association of Museums (now the American Alliance of Museums) issued a legal brief against the repatriation while the Archaeological Institute of America responded with a brief supporting the repatriation. While a cynical interpretation might focus on the financial interests of museums in limiting international heritage law and subsequent repatriation, a deeper ideological conflict between art- and science-driven perspectives may be at play.[23]

Today the Egyptian collection is the most popular part of the British Museum. The first Egyptian materials in the museum, captured from Napoleon, were displayed so that their supposedly ugly and primitive nature in comparison with later European classical works could demonstrate the core message of nineteenth-century museums: the progress of civilization.[24] Sir Flinders Petrie is widely considered to be the first scientific Egyptologist, and he created the technique of seriation in order to study the pottery of predynastic Egypt. The British Museum at one point rejected the "worthless" potsherds and fragmentary artifacts from Petrie's scientific excavations.[25] Decades later, the New York museum owner and expedition backer George

Heye had seventy barrels of potsherds thrown away, including some from unpublished stratigraphic excavations.[26] The British Museum rejected another Petrie find, a valuable wall relief of the sexually aroused Egyptian god Min, because it was "unhistoric rather than prehistoric."[27]

The battle of the sexy wall relief was part of a lifelong war between Petrie and the British Museum keeper Sir E. A. Wallis Budge, whom Petrie privately referred to as "Bugbear." Petrie was dedicated to protecting Egyptian archaeological heritage. Wallis Budge was a skillful artifact smuggler who tripled the size of the British Museum's Egyptian collection between 1883 and 1924. Egyptian police surveilled Wallis Budge's contacts because it was assumed they were criminals. He personally smuggled pieces out of Egypt by quietly traveling via mail boats and military transports, despite the rage his actions provoked in British imperial officials concerned about calming Egyptian public attitudes. Human skulls were declared to be "bone manure."[28] Accusations of the same tactic emerged in 2015 and were confirmed in a 2017 settlement between Hobby Lobby and the U.S. Department of Justice over a shipment labeled as containing $300 in "hand-crafted clay tiles" turned out to be cuneiform tablets destined for the Museum of the Bible in Washington, DC.[29]

The philosophical difference survives today in the Petrie Museum at University College London, a short walk from the British Museum. Fragments of monuments and sculptures can be found on display, but the true strength of the museum lies in its learning galleries, vast arrays of cases and drawers full of potsherds, ushabtis (figurines with incantations powering them to serve their owner in the afterlife), and other small artifacts organized by either object type or time period. The Petrie has for most of its existence been a specialist museum for training experts. It was part of Amelia Edwards's gift to the University College London in 1892, but only started actively appealing to the general public in the 1970s. From an annual visitorship of 200 in 1970, the museum grew to nearly 9,000 annual visitors by 2000.[30] On a visit in 2015, I found students hard at work at desks and tables, examining specific collections while their children played with Egyptian-themed toys and participated in Egyptian-themed activities. By contrast the British Museum was choked with great crowds moving without care for chronology or context through beautiful sculpture galleries and displays of mummy cases.

Museums can tend to emphasize funerary objects as representations of daily life. Egyptian displays routinely feature coffins or mummified remains as centerpieces, and visitors demand mummies as standards of museum displays.[31] In addition to the attraction toward such items because of the Western fascination with Egyptians and death, mortuary objects are far more likely to have been deposited intact in contrast with the fragmentary artifacts found in trash middens or construction fill. Museum displays of beautiful and informative artworks and artifacts thus drift toward the dead.

The antiquarian and archaeological fixation on objects of the dead forms the main theme in the tales by Edwardian author and Cambridge scholar M. R. James, often considered to be the master of the classic ghost tale in which ancient wrongs are brought to light after uncanny events and entities manifest. James's antiquarian background is evident in almost every story. Many of his protagonists are proxies for James, the solitary antiquarian in pursuit of unusual information from the past who disturbs the dead before finding himself in over his head in unknown environs. This literary model influenced the American horror and science fiction author Howard Phillips Lovecraft, who is the subject of chapter 10. James's stories are primarily not about characters but about haunted antiquities, such as cursed spyglasses, whistles, paintings, scrapbooks, and other artifacts that refuse to be owned.[32] Most of James's medieval scholarship was historical, but he participated in two archaeological excavations. One of these, in which James identified the graves of six historically attested abbots and enabled their proper reburial, resembled one of his ghost stories come to life.[33]

The incautious protagonists of James or Lovecraft may seem like fictional extremes, but the disruption of the dead and the erasure of history for the sake of aesthetic pleasure or morbid curiosity makes hauntings inevitable. As the American Museum of Natural History in New York began the process of cataloging its Native American objects for possible repatriation, security guards reported the voices of the dead, the sound of moccasined feet, and ghostly apparitions.[34] Employees of the Institute of Texan Cultures in San Antonio have described ghostly occurrences inside their museum either "because of the land it was built on or because spirits became attached to the artifacts inside." The most involved haunting is a "full-body apparition" of an apparently Native American woman in "the cave," an exhibit with Native American artifacts. Employees investigated and recorded "electronic voice phenomena."[35] These phenomena, furtive whispered sounds parsed out of the background of audio recordings, are a staple of ghost hunting. Two skulls accompanied by an apotropaic Bible were a carefully guarded and taboo subject in Turton Tower, a Lancashire museum, on account of hauntings and prurient occult interest from visitors. Despite these concerns, the museum has opened to ghost-hunting tours.[36]

The film versions of the mummy's curse owe a great deal to Khaemweset and the tale of Setne Khamwas, but the broader idea of a mummy's curse can be best tied to the unlucky mummy case, exhibit number EA22542 at the British Museum. Sir E. A. Wallis Budge was not only responsible for accessioning the case for the museum, he was also primarily responsible for propagating the curse story. Wallis Budge first told the story to the *Daily Express* reporter Bertram Fletcher Robinson in 1904. Five Englishmen had purchased the case lid in Egypt and then began to suffer misfortune and death. Robinson himself died a few years later at the age of thirty-seven and was said to be another victim of the curse. Sir Arthur Conan Doyle blamed the death of his friend Robinson on elemental spirits guarding the mummy, just as he would in the case of Carnarvon and Tutankhamun. Media-driven panic over the unlucky mummy led to collectors ridding themselves of artifacts, donating them as "scare gifts" to the British Museum to avoid supernatural destruction, a phenomenon that repeated during the Tutankhamun media frenzy. This was not a new practice according to the former inspector general of antiquities in Egypt, Arthur Weigall, a significant promoter of the Tut curse legend.[37]

Just as Weigall positioned himself as a passive-aggressive skeptical promoter of the Tut curse two decades later, Wallis Budge found himself torn between the need to maintain his scientific credibility and the benefits that come from being a good storyteller. The unlucky mummy lid had been purchased by Thomas Douglas Murray, a wealthy spiritualist and colonial adventurer. Wallis Budge accepted Douglas Murray's invitation in 1904 to attend a dinner at the private Ghost Club, where Britain's elite met on the condition they would share a ghost story. The membership of the Ghost Club significantly overlapped with London's occult scene, including the Society for Psychical Research and the Hermetic Order of the Golden

Dawn.[38] Wallis Budge's *Book of the Dead* was a major influence on occult practices and occult-themed pulp fiction.[39] Wallis Budge told the Ghost Club of working on the translation of British Museum exhibit number 24402, a cursed mummy mask. The mask had been owned by Valerie Susan, Lady Meux, a close friend who had helped Wallis Budge purchase a home and defend himself against a slander lawsuit.[40]

Psychical researchers and occultists routinely confronted Wallis Budge as the (gate)keeper of the Egyptian halls of the British Museum, a space haunted by spirits and elementals according to at least one ghost hunter.[41] Wallis Budge refused to allow Douglas Murray and reporter W. T. Stead to hold a séance there. Stead was the most famous Englishman to die on the *Titanic*, and his involvement in the unlucky mummy case meant that with time the mummy was blamed for sinking the *Titanic*.[42] Archaeologist Margaret Murray, whose witchcraft investigations are the subject of chapter 9, claimed to have invented the connection between the *Titanic* and the mummy case as a practical joke.

Adventure and Intrigue at the Museum

In late October 2011, the University of Pennsylvania Museum of Archaeology and Anthropology hosted a "once-in-a-lifetime paranormal investigation of the galleries and their ghostly inhabitants" in the event "We See Dead People." The occasion included the Free Spirit Paranormal Investigators group and promised the use of "ghost-hunting" equipment and the participation of psychics. The event was marketed by a video teaser resembling the security camera "found footage" in the horror movie *Paranormal Activity* (2007), and promotional material discussed the ghost of a deceased director who supposedly haunts the building.[43] The advertising suggested a more cultured version of a haunted house attraction or Halloween party for the museum's target audience of young adults, something not unknown in other museums.[44] Ghost stories continue to be part of museum exhibits on Egypt. Undead mummies, ghosts, and invitations to pretend to be scared are meant to engage young visitors, though often by the end the exhibit has been designed to humanize its subjects.[45] Ghosts have become common in official National Trust and English Heritage presentations of UK heritage sites.[46]

Creative forms of outreach are to be expected in an environment of austerity policies that defund educational and scientific institutions.[47] There is also a growing recognition that "an overbearing appeal to notions of expertise or exclusivity can alienate potential visitors."[48] In September 2012, the National Atomic Testing Museum hosted a mix of historians and paranormal authors for a public symposium on military UFO secrets.[49] The American Museum of Natural History was the first to host the traveling exhibit *Mythic Creatures*, an exploration of science and folklore through the lens of cryptozoology, the hunt for hidden legendary animals. The exhibit featured the yeti, unicorn, and kraken, among other mythical beasts.[50] The traveling exhibit *Indiana Jones and the Adventure of Archaeology* combined the spooky themes of archaeology, props from the popular films, and actual artifacts.[51] It was one example of a popular blockbuster exhibit strategy: displaying movie props along with real-world influences or ephemera from major film franchises. When I visited the traveling exhibit *Tutankhamun and the Golden Age of the Pharaohs* in 2009, the narration was performed by Harrison Ford (the actor who portrayed Indiana Jones), who was also elected to the board of the Archaeological Institute of America and presented with the Bandelier Award for positive contributions to the profession.[52] The focus on pop culture is not exclusive to archaeology. The National Air and Space Museum has hosted exhibits of props and wardrobe from both *Star Trek* and *Star Wars*. The private International Spy Museum in Washington, DC, places significant emphasis on fictional superspies, such as James Bond. A traveling *Harry Potter* exhibit drew criticism for being a synergistic advertisement for the films and books still in production at the time.[53]

Television documentaries demonstrate similar trends. In the 2000s loosely veiled advertisements for movies were framed as documentaries telling the "real story." The documentary *Quest for King Arthur* featured archaeologists discussing whether the big-budget movie *King Arthur* might resemble real events.[54] Some suggest that if pop bands and athletes promote themselves in carnivalesque ways, why should scientists demur?[55] By 2010 even the pretense of including legitimate material disappeared from many cable television "documentaries" and "reality" shows. The Animal Planet and Discovery television channels have aired "mockumentaries" about fictional sharks and mermaids as if they were real creatures, with only a brief on-screen disclaimer that the viewer was watching fiction. Promotional websites have used faked images and video to further the deception, a strategy pioneered by the 1999 horror movie *The Blair Witch Project*. In July 2014, publicists for Discovery created a viral video (without disclaimer) using a robotic shark, sparking fears of sharks in Lake Ontario and prompting government reaction and subsequent condemnation.[56] The impact of sensational fiction on science knowledge isn't clear-cut. At least one study suggests that consumers of science fiction learn some legitimate scientific information while paranormal-themed entertainment does not inherently increase paranormal belief.[57]

Museums and the Crystal Skulls

In the *Indiana Jones* exhibit, movie props of fictional artifacts were intermingled with real archaeological artifacts provided by the University of Pennsylvania Museum of Archaeology and Anthropology. The exhibition invited visitors to "discover the steps archaeologists take to uncover real-world artefacts [*sic*] and their meaning."[58] It "shed light on how archaeologists really work on projects such as deciphering ancient scripts and discovering the true origins of the mysterious Nasca [*sic*] lines in southern Peru."[59] The Nazca lines are famous because of their appropriation by ancient extraterrestrials promoters and were included in *Indiana Jones and the Kingdom of the Crystal Skull*. The crystal skull headlined in the movie title is entirely based on late nineteenth-century or early twentieth-century hoaxed artifacts made infamous by famous museums and their dubious agents.

The most famous of all crystal skulls is the Mitchell-Hedges skull, named after its "discoverers," F. A. Mitchell-Hedges and his adopted daughter, Anna, who claimed she found it on her birthday during the 1926–1927 excavation of Lubaantun in southern Belize. This story eventually led to a controversial lawsuit against the Disney corporation over exploitation of the Belizean cultural patrimony in *Indiana Jones and the Kingdom of the Crystal Skull*. However, all evidence suggests that the crystal skull has never actually been in Belize.[60]

The first mention by F. A. Mitchell-Hedges about the skull is in his autobiography, *Danger My Ally*, and notably only in the 1954 edition of this book. There is no mention of Lubaantun nor excavation, but a simple statement that Mitchell-Hedges has a "reason for not revealing" how he obtained it. He claims that "much" has been written about it and that "it has been described as the embodiment of all evil." It is "at least 3,600 years old," and according to legend the "high priest of the Maya" could use it in "esoteric rites" to will the death of others. Unnamed "scientists" say it must have taken more than 150 years to polish the skull to perfection.[61]

Anna provided the Lubaantun origin story in a book she commissioned.[62] The story spread via speculative programs such as *In Search of...* alongside mysteries like ancient extraterrestrials. The Heye Museum of the American Indian displayed the crystal skull in an exhibit of Native American skull masks.[63] It is unsurprising that the crystal skull was displayed at the Heye. Founder George Heye put his inherited petroleum fortune to solving "the great mystery of the origin of the prehistoric races of the Western Hemisphere" and in 1904 started funding expeditions, at times joining in fieldwork. Franz Boas and Aleš Hrdlička had hoped to bring Heye's collections to their institutions, but Heye preferred retaining control and founded his own Museum of the American Indian. The museum was initially an organized private collection for Heye and invited scholars, not the public. He hired scientists and explorers ranging from the sensationalist Mitchell-Hedges to solid scholars like Marshall Saville, M. R. Harrington, Jesse Nusbaum, and Samuel K. Lothrop to collect vast quantities of archaeological and ethnographic materials from the Americas. Controversy plagued the Heye, including indictments in the 1970s over trustees buying museum artifacts at deflated prices.[64]

Despite Mitchell-Hedges's claims, in 1933 the London art dealer Sydney Burney wrote in a letter to George Vaillant of the American Museum of Natural History that he had obtained the crystal skull from an unnamed collector, and Burney was credited as the owner in a 1936 article in the British Museum's journal *Man*. The article suggested that the skull was stylistically related to the crystal skull owned by the British Museum. In the same issue Adrian Digby denied any link, making bizarre claims about the presumed sex and age of the skull in craniometric techniques and whether it could be the symbol of a "deathgod."[65] Digby's conclusion that the British Museum skull was more likely to be Aztec versus the recently created Burney skull became the conventional wisdom for decades. The

Burney/Mitchell-Hedges skull has mechanical grinding marks and apparently metal-drilled holes in the base for support pegs.[66] Traces of a mechanical rotary wheel were found on the teeth in the 1960s and later confirmed with scanning electron microscopy. The British Museum's skull had been owned by the archaeological entrepreneur and enthusiast Eugène Boban, who may have acquired it in Germany. Boban owned an antiquities store and museum in Mexico City and with the aid of the Mexican archaeologist Leopoldo Batres had tried to sell the skull to Mexico's Museo Nacional de Antropología. Boban eventually sold it to Tiffany and Company, which sold it to the British Museum. At least two other crystal skulls now residing in museums likely passed through Boban's shop. Burney put his skull up for auction in 1943, and Mitchell-Hedges bought it in 1944, beating the British Museum to the punch.[67]

Anna Mitchell-Hedges claimed that her father had previously owned the skull but had put it up as collateral when obtaining a loan for expedition funds from Burney. All the evidence for this was supposedly destroyed during her father's globe-trotting adventures. Mitchell-Hedges left a long history of sensational and outright fantastical accounts of his archaeological explorations, deep-sea fishing, and other adventures in the Caribbean and Latin America. Mitchell-Hedges claimed to have been kidnapped by Pancho Villa and to have subsequently ridden in Villa's revolutionary forces. This episode forms much of the basis of a convoluted conspiracy theory about Mitchell-Hedges, Mexican archaeology, British Intelligence, the crystal skull, and the disappearance of author Ambrose Bierce.[68] The claims in this theory entirely rely on trying to understand what motivations Mitchell-Hedges might have had for lying in his autobiography, presuming shadowy occult intelligence activities as a more likely rationale than simple egotistical mythmaking. This story seems particularly unlikely following the description by Thomas Gann that Mitchell-Hedges had such poor command of Spanish that he could not hire archaeological laborers without help.[69]

Mitchell-Hedges was a fantasist, but like Indiana Jones he was an "obtainer of rare antiquities" that belong in a museum. In the 1920s Mitchell-Hedges and his partner in exploration Lady Richmond Brown obtained a collection of Muisca artifacts from Colombia and excavated at the Mayan city of Lubaantun, Belize, based on the encouragement of

British Museum director Frederic Kenyon. Mitchell-Hedges claimed that his party first discovered Lubaantun in early 1925. These excavations were headlined as being of "the greatest importance" by Kenyon, suggesting that the site represented the origins of Mayan civilization.[70] Yet despite statements by the British Museum's T. A. Joyce, Mitchell-Hedges's digging partner Gann had worked at Lubaantun since 1903, as had R. E. Merwin of the Peabody Museum at Harvard. Mitchell-Hedges also described the Santa Cruz people as bloodthirsty and living in a land "no white man has ever yet been able to penetrate." But rather than being primordial natives, the Santa Cruz got their name from the role of a "talking cross" in the Caste War in Yucatán in the mid-nineteenth century. They were Yukatek Mayas who had fled to British Honduras as refugees, and the white Gann had reported on the everyday life of the Santa Cruz years earlier.[71] These supposedly bloodthirsty people not only allowed Gann to visit, but he measured their heads and took their photos without becoming a human sacrifice.

After the media splash, the British Museum continued excavating Lubaantun under the more professional direction of Joyce, J. Cooper Clark, and the young Mayanist J. Eric Thompson.[72] Thompson suggested that Mitchell-Hedges had bought the crystal skull in a shop in London.[73] While the actual archaeological work remained unpublished for decades, Gann and Mitchell-Hedges did produce lurid adventure books about Lubaantun. These books present death, sacrifice, and cannibalism but no crystal skull and no Anna Mitchell-Hedges accompanying her father.[74] One of Gann's adventure books opens with the discovery of a corpse and a battle with a sawfish before turning to news of a lost Mayan city.[75] Gann had a reputation as a sketchy teller of tall tales and a notoriously destructive digger. But he parlayed his collection of more than 1,000 Mayan artifacts into a semi-honorary lecturer position at the University of Liverpool, which funded additional excavations in return for materials for the university and its backers. The collection was destroyed by heavy German bombing in 1941.[76]

Major museums relied on Mitchell-Hedges to fill their displays and storerooms despite his credibility issues. A strange incident on an English road led to him being branded a charlatan in a court of law. On 15 January 1927 (note that Anna Mitchell-Hedges claimed that she and her father were digging in Belize in early 1927 when they found the crystal skull), Mitchell-Hedges was traveling by car after having dropped off a male companion when he apparently was attacked by an armed gang of thieves. The ruffians beat the explorer, bound and gagged him, and left him in the mud by the side of the road as they made off with a valuable suitcase. The entire affair was initially "surrounded by an air of gruesome mystery," heightened by Mitchell-Hedges's statements that he had been targeted for the suitcase but could not reveal its contents. Media reports suggested that the case contained documents from the explorer's recent trip to Honduras and six shrunken heads. Mitchell-Hedges said the stolen goods were very valuable and that he "would give £5,000 to undo what happened."[77]

Questions soon appeared, including how the robbers had found Mitchell-Hedges after he had made an unforeseen detour to take his friend home. Mitchell-Hedges produced a new motive, suggesting that he had been attacked by young men offended by a speech in which he had chastised the youth of England for not having the "old spirit of adventure" and telling them that "life would be very gray without excitement." Mitchell-Hedges claimed that one of the perpetrators had sent him a letter confirming this reason and offering the contents of the suitcase, "a document affecting prominent financial houses which would have had serious results to the people concerned had it been discovered," in return for a retraction of Mitchell-Hedges's statements.[78] After several reporters stated the obvious, that this was a publicity stunt, the explorer sued London's *Daily Express* for libel. Counsel for the *Daily Express* convinced the judge and jury that Mitchell-Hedges and his explorations were fraudulent.[79]

The explorer had been found a fraud, but museums supported Mitchell-Hedges and his ability to obtain artifacts. In December 1929, more than a year after the libel case, the Heye Museum and museums at Oxford and Cambridge accepted portions of an ethnographic collection from Panama. Mitchell-Hedges and Lady Lillian "Mabs" Richmond Brown, his traveling companion and co-explorer, allegedly were able to befriend indigenous people based on their reputation of treating diseases plaguing other Central American tribes. The artifacts given to the Heye in 1929 came from indigenous villagers along the Chucunaque River in Panama, who were described as a fallen people, the degenerate descendants of a higher culture.[80] Mitchell-Hedges routinely called them degenerate, animalistic, and inferior. He was just as mean-spirited to other indigenous peoples of Central America.[81] He claimed that he and Lady Richmond Brown were treated as spirits delivering the commandments of gods in the subtly titled chapter "We Became Gods." Richmond Brown said that she came up with the "esoteric" approach of posing as magically powerful divine messengers.[82] She had taken up the adventuring life after being given an erroneous terminal diagnosis and became a fixture in Mitchell-Hedges's adventures, even helping him wrestle an eighteen-foot boa constrictor when it escaped at Paddington Station in London.[83]

Mitchell-Hedges described himself in *Land of Wonder and Fear* as a "Member of the Maya Committee of the British Museum." One of the many artifacts that Mitchell-Hedges collected for the British Museum was a Chucunaque "fetish" to be used as a last-resort healing tool. This object was a human fetus that was allegedly preserved by some unknown technique.[84] The fetish was examined by Sir Arthur Keith, the conservator of the museum of the Royal College of Surgeons and one of the most influential physical anthropologists of his day. Keith was the chief supporter of Piltdown man because it supported his notions about a Pliocene "dawn man" and the multiregional evolution of separate human "races." This theory was compatible with Keith's eugenics sympathies.[85]

The Heye Foundation and its museum continued to benefit from Mitchell-Hedges, who called George Heye a friend who had backed his work in "many ways."[86] In January 1931, Mitchell-Hedges announced plans for an expedition to La Mosquitia in northern Honduras, backed by the Heye and the British Museum to an eye-popping alleged total of $250,000.[87] The expedition, allegedly the first to combine American and British cooperation, would traverse "almost impenetrable jungles, guarded by well-nigh inaccessible mountain ranges" to a "secret region" unexplorable by air. This likely referred to the recent, highly publicized first aerial survey of the Mayan region by Charles Lindbergh and a team of archaeologists.[88] Mitchell-Hedges and Richmond Brown had visited the region the previous year, returning with pottery and figurines for their backers at the Heye. They allegedly obtained these from caves and a cenote (a collapsed sinkhole), described by archaeologist William Duncan Strong as "The Sacrificial Spring," on Guanaja.[89] Artifacts from the Sacred Cenote at Chichén Itzá had been revealed to the public in 1923, informing Mitchell-Hedges's exploration on Guanaja.

Mitchell-Hedges eyed a bigger prize than ceramic fragments, however.

He was going to find the cradle of humanity, a culture at least as old as "Ur of the Chaldees." Ur had recently made headlines due to spectacular finds but also sensational claims about Old Testament events, including Sir Leonard Woolley's reports of finding physical traces of the biblical deluge.[90] Mitchell-Hedges claimed that his discoveries could "change the entire scientific conception of the aboriginal races of Central and South America." He also painted the region in mysterious and ominous hues, beset by a "cruel jungle" that is still the subject of legends about the disappearance of conquistador Cristóbal de Olid and Ciudad Blanca (see below). The "lost legions" of Olid weren't lost. Olid had been sent by Hernán Cortés to conquer Honduras, but he rebelled and planned to keep the province for himself. Supporters of Cortés murdered Olid during a dinner, and his men joined other factions squabbling for control of the region before Cortés arrived and imposed order.[91]

No matter his faults, Mitchell-Hedges could score headlines like "Museum Endorses F. A. Mitchell-Hedges."[92] While noting that Mitchell-Hedges was not a scholar, British Museum director Sir Frederic Kenyon gave him the museum's "blessing" because he had "already done excellent work and produced valuable material for the museum." The same article quoted a curator and trustee at the American Museum of Natural History who refused to support Mitchell-Hedges's claims and activities. In 1933, the Heye exhibited materials that Mitchell-Hedges had recently obtained from the Bay Islands of Barbareta, Helene, Roatan, and Morat,[93] off the coast of Honduras. The Heye received half of the nearly 5,000 objects Mitchell-Hedges brought back, and the other half went to the British Museum.[94] In the field Mitchell-Hedges upbraided his secretary, who wanted to keep some artifacts, telling her, "That belongs to the Museum, like all the others, and isn't yours at all."[95] Mitchell-Hedges claimed that these artifacts were evidence for an outpost of the lost Atlantis, and he went on radio programs to promote the idea.[96] Lady Richmond Brown suspected that the wide variety of physical types, cultural practices, and artifacts they encountered could be evidence of a lost Pacific continent.[97]

When I saw the Honduran materials in storage at the British Museum, they were typical of later pre-Hispanic Pech and Tawahka materials from the region, not terribly rare, and certainly not related to Atlantis (figure 7.2). The ceramics include a number of handles and hollow vessel supports. The elaborately carved handles depict local animals and are examples of a common pottery type known as San Antonio Carved made during the transitional Selín phase of 800–1000 CE. This was during the decline of the Classic Maya cities to the west and their trade routes. The last inscribed monument at Copán in western Honduras was left unfinished in 822 CE, with evidence of a handful of settlers reoccupying the once royal capital and reusing carved monumental stone blocks they either didn't understand or didn't care to understand. A few modeled hollow supports in the Mitchell-Hedges material belong to the ceramic type Dorina Abstract Incised Punctate, dating to the early Cocal phase comparable with the Early Postclassic of Mesoamerica.[98] The patterns of Central American cultural, economic, and technological exchange (including metallurgy like the little copper bell found in the British Museum's Mitchell-Hedges collection) intensified as Mesoamerican society oriented itself more toward maritime exchange and moved to a less centralized political structure. Some notes accompanying the Mitchell-Hedges materials describe vessels with a line of circular impressions. While these may be Dorina Abstract, they also sound like Tegucigalpa Punctated Raised Band, an early Selín type contemporary with the rise of Copán in the west.[99]

None of this has anything to do with Atlantis or any weird mystery. To be somewhat fair to Mitchell-Hedges, the first archaeological typology of the region appeared the same year he presented his materials to the British Museum. This work, by William Duncan Strong, incorporated Mitchell-Hedges's "very striking" collection at the Heye.[100] Strong and his team explored several of the same sites encountered by Mitchell-Hedges, whom Strong described as "under the auspices" of the Heye. Strong politely noted that their maps were very different. He mentioned but did not comment on comparisons to Chichén Itzá and Stonehenge.

While the expeditions of Strong and others were defining the first serious archaeology in the region, Mitchell-Hedges painted a picture of danger. He survived standoffs with armed and violent locals, who then came to accept him as a fast friend, and he traveled with a crew of hardened killers.[101] Excavations were quick and dirty, emptying burial sites in an afternoon of pickaxes and ticks. At rich sites, machetes replaced the pickaxes—not to better record the context but to ensure that any museum-quality whole pieces were not damaged. One excavation pit in a cave on the

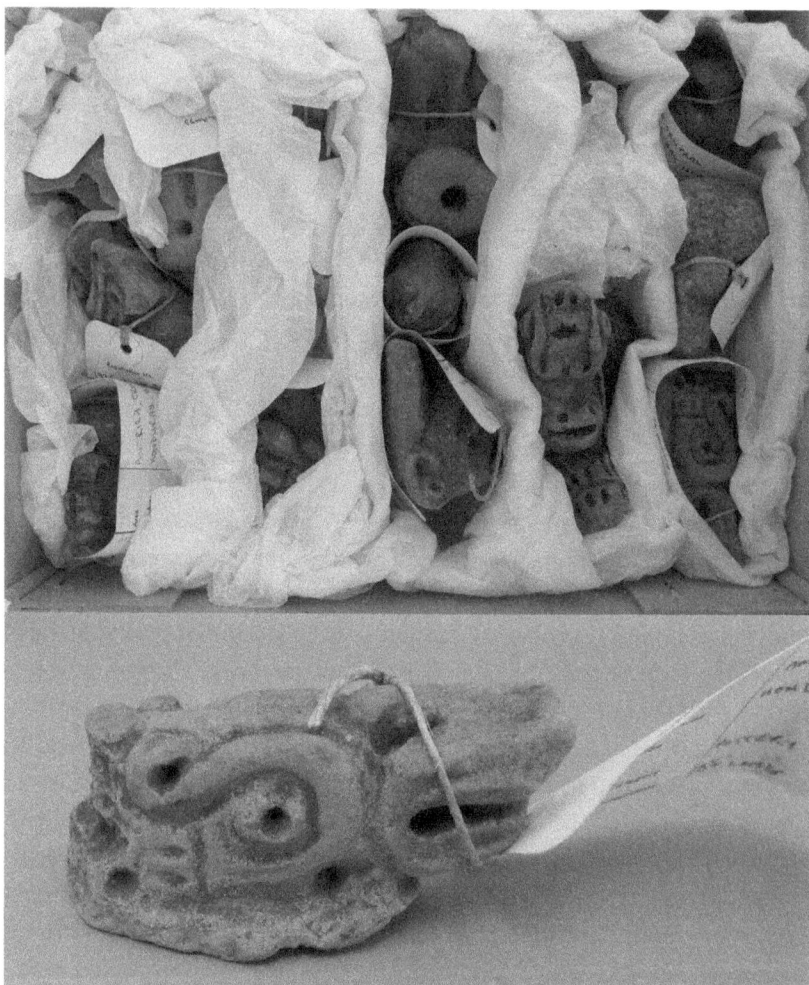

FIGURE 7.2. Mitchell-Hedges artifacts from the Bay Islands, Honduras, in the collection of the British Museum. Image by author. Courtesy of the Trustees of the British Museum. *Top*, box 3, America Central, Honduras Bay Islands, Pottery Lugs, Museum Numbers 1935.12.16. for all with last number sections 176, 180, 186, 195–197, 199, 204, 205, 207, 209, 210, 218, 222. *Bottom*, British Museum Number Am1935.1216.195.

island of Barbareta allegedly produced more than 2,000 pieces, with 120 vases in varying states of completeness pulled from an excavation slightly bigger than one by two meters.[102] Rumors about Mitchell-Hedges and hidden treasure persisted in the Bay Islands decades later.[103]

In his autobiography Mitchell-Hedges reprinted letters from George Heye in his capacity as the chair and director of his museum and from T. A. Joyce as the director of the Department of Oriental Antiquities and of Ethnography at the British Museum, both proclaiming the importance of his Bay Islands discoveries. Mitchell-Hedges carried a similar letter from Heye about earlier discoveries when he arrived in New York in 1931.[104]

The Lost City of La Mosquitia

Mitchell-Hedges was not the only colorful explorer of Honduras supported by the Heye and other major museums. The Heye Foundation sponsored collecting activities in the Ulua Valley of western Honduras in 1915, and the explorers, as always, returned with material from a "lost city."[105] Interest in the eastern part of the country grew after Herbert Spinden, a well-known scholar of the Peabody Museum, led a 1923 Harvard expedition into the Mosquitia wetlands to the east. This period was a major escalation in North American archaeological interest in the Mayan region. The Carnegie Institution of Washington funded a multidecade project at several Mayan sites after the First World War, led by the archaeologist and spymaster Sylvanus Morley (who had previously worked with Spinden), while Tulane University inaugurated its Middle American Research Institute with an expedition to Mexico in 1925. Spinden, a scholar of Mayan art and writing, was less than impressed with the petroglyphs of the region, but nonetheless believed they formed a "missing link" between cultures in Central America.[106]

Spinden proposed a softer version of the moundbuilder myth, suggesting that the ruins of Honduras were of an ancient culture destroyed just prior to the Spanish conquest by the indigenous peoples living in the region today; the surviving "civilized" inhabitants fled north into Mesoamerica. The utility of disenfranchising the indigenous peoples of this region with a long history of conflict with Hispanic authorities is clear.[107] Spinden's public reporting emphasized the importance of the United Fruit Company's infrastructure in exploring archaeological ruins. Spinden had been one of Morley's Office of Naval Intelligence agents during the First World War, and all of those men had connections to the United Fruit Company and other American interests in the region. United Fruit also supported Mitchell-Hedges in his exploration and tourism of eastern Guatemala.[108] Spinden did not sensationalize the mound architecture and corn-grinding metates he found. As the curator of primitive art for the Brooklyn Museum, he and his wife, Ellen, also an anthropologist, continued in the region and led an expedition to the Nicaraguan Mosquitia in 1936.[109]

Such mixed-gender fraternization in the jungle did not go over well with Captain R. Stuart Murray, an explorer who forbade women from accompanying him on archaeological adventures. The pith-helmeted manly man preferred the company of a loyal dog in the bush. Perhaps Murray was referring obliquely to Mitchell-Hedges's traveling companion Lady Richmond Brown and her divorce proceedings. Maybe he alluded to Jane Harvey Houlson, a secretary and traveling companion to Mitchell-Hedges ("My Chief," she called him) on his 1932 trip to Honduras. Murray chased the sensational, starring in a Camel cigarettes advertising campaign. But this didn't stop him from working for Heye and his museum, the US State Department, the American Museum of Natural History, and Spinden's Brooklyn Museum. Murray produced ethnographic observations and films for the Honduran government, documenting the "disappearing" indigenous lifeways in La Mosquitia in the face of development. Like a comic book character, he adopted an orphaned indigenous Honduran boy as a sidekick, educating him to act as a cultural interpreter.[110]

Murray claimed to have found a piece of slate with alleged unidentifiable writing "resembling cuneiform," but his real goal was the "City of the Monkey God."[111] This is what Murray called the legendary lost city of the Mosquito Coast, better known as Ciudad Blanca for its location near white cliff faces and/or its construction in white stone. The first account of this lost city, recorded by Bishop Cristóbal de Pedraza in 1544, resembled the El Dorado legends, which always seemed to direct the gold-hungry Spaniards toward a city anywhere but where the teller lived, in this case the city of Tagusgualpa, where people ate from golden goblets and plates.[112] Mitchell-Hedges described it as a place the native people would not go or discuss, a place of the dead, ghouls, and vampires, a place from which people did not return alive.[113]

The most "successful" explorer of Ciudad Blanca was Theodore Morde. A dropout from Brown University, Morde went to sea and circled the world five times while he wrote news pieces, including on the Spanish Civil War. Rumors of espionage followed Morde, who was one of the first agents in William J. "Wild Bill" Donovan's Office of Strategic Services, the forerunner to the CIA. George Heye's connections to US government interests may have facilitated Morde's place in the OSS. When Morde was found hanged in his parents' bathroom in 1954, family members suggested that one of Morde's espionage enemies, or the lost city's curse, was responsible for his death, rather than bouts with alcoholism, which had resulted in the desertion of his wife and children.[114]

After Murray could not find Ciudad Blanca, in 1940 Morde had become Heye's newest agent in La Mosquitia. Like previous Heye-backed explorers, Morde emphasized the economic potential of gold, silver, and oil in the region, and during his first press conference after the expedition he showed off gold he had collected by hand. Morde's journals and public statements focused on the hardships and dangers of the expedition, which though a small operation was equipped with more than 1,000 pounds of gear, dynamite, a Luger pistol, a rifle, and two men with murderous pasts.[115]

The idea that a monkey god was central to a lost Mosquitia city may have originated with Murray, but Morde enthusiastically embraced the notion. He wrote of a lurid Tawahka ritual, the "dance of the dead monkeys." Hunted spider monkeys were allegedly impaled on spears and tossed in a bonfire in revenge against the Ulaks, which were half-man half-monkey spirits that walked upright and kidnapped women.[116] Morde was not the only explorer looking for fantastical apes in Honduras in the 1930s. In 1933 professor Gregory Mason of the Penn Museum was preparing to research sightings of anthropoid apes in Honduras in search of the origins of humanity.[117] While modern cryptozoologists might invoke this tale as evidence of Bigfoot-like creatures, the source was almost certainly Western obsessions with evolution. The Darwinian revolution had transformed the legendary wild man or werewolf of European nightmares into a racially coded ape or ape man, a potent symbol of savagery in an age of racial hierarchy and unease with the idea of human evolution.[118] Morde's journals tell of squalor and sickness in indigenous villages, but his most complete account of the lost city focuses on the incredibly stereotypical dance, complete with drums, a bonfire, an animalistic medicine man, bronzed bodies, and symbolic cannibalism.[119]

When Morde returned to New York, he donated several hundred artifacts to the Heye museum and told an eager press that he had found the lost city and its monkey-like carvings. Journals and press statements mentioned stone masonry and twelve-foot-high walls, but these received much less attention from Morde than the collection of rare birds and Asian monkey lore. Morde suggested ties between the city and the worship of the Hindu monkey god Hanuman, and he detected "Chinese and Hindu" or stereotypical "Oriental" features in the local people.[120] Morde's ancient Chorotega civilization was cut from the same hyperdiffusionist cloth as Niven's Asian influence on archaic Mexico and Churchward's Muvian Pacific civilization.

Morde's description of a legend he heard of a great statue of the monkey god in the center of the city, combined with accounts of great stone walls, gave the renowned pulp illustrator Virgil Finlay license to create fantastical images extremely similar to those seen in *King Kong*. The success of the *Kong* movie in 1933 and the subsequent sequels and knockoffs emphasized the racially coded obsession with apes menacing nubile white women and produced the filmic iconography of lost cities and the exploration of ancient ruins. *Kong* may also have inspired the creation of the Loch Ness and Cadborosaurus sea serpent legends, both of which emerged in 1933.[121]

Perhaps we should not blame museums for working hand in glove with eccentric peddlers of tall tales. Professional journalists were no better. When Mitchell-Hedges arrived in New York in June 1931 on the White Star liner *Adriatic*, he declared that his explorations had served as the "vanguard of a trade army which must follow." Although the same report also noted another passenger on the ship—John Maynard Keynes, who was to lecture at the University of Chicago—the *Times* reporter did not ask Keynes his opinion on economic matters.[122] Despite lacking academic training Mitchell-Hedges claimed membership in the American Geographical Society and the Committee of the British Museum on Maya Exploration, and being a Fellow of the Royal Geographical Society, the Linnaean Society, the Zoological Society, the Entomological Society, the Royal Anthropological Society, and the Royal Scottish Geographical Society.[123] Fellow museum agent Captain Murray had similar credentials.[124]

Ciudad Blanca reemerged in the twenty-first century in a cloud of controversy. Since Morde's expedition, others had sought the city.[125] I personally remember receiving an email around 1995, looking for archaeologists interested in investigating the myth. In 2012 a team using satellite imagery, three-dimensional scanning technology, and light detection and ranging (LiDAR) announced they had found something.[126] Opinions differed among the team members as to whether the sites had anything to do with Ciudad Blanca or the monkey god, though these elements were included alongside discussions of Atlantis and El Dorado in subsequent print, television, and Internet media products by *National Geographic*.

The turning point came with the discovery of a cache of carved metates, corn-grinding stones, on the surface at one of the sites. Statements by project members described the area as free of human presence and larger than other sites in the region. The images of carved jaguars emerging from the tropical vegetation and soil fed an international media frenzy. The site became a political issue, with the Honduran president providing military security for the newly dubbed City of the Jaguar and vowing to protect the region from ecological damage. The *National Geographic* article that presented the project ended by noting the importance of the sites to Honduran national pride in the face of social unrest, and suggested that if the sites could protect La Mosquitia from logging, then it did not really matter if the legends were real or myth.[127]

Many Honduran and international archaeologists greeted these developments with skepticism. After the initial 2012 announcement of the LiDAR finds and the subsequent 2015 expedition, archaeologist Rosemary Joyce cautioned that more was known about the region than was being represented in the popular media and that Ciudad Blanca is a legend. Soon, other archaeologists joined the conversation in the press, and an open letter to *National Geographic* protested some of the project's practices.[128]

I signed that letter because I had known about similar sites in La Mosquitia for years. In 1997 I worked on an archaeological project in El Salvador directed by Christopher Begley, who surveyed and excavated in La Mosquitia as part of his doctoral research at the University of Chicago. Over cold beers in a cantina in Santa Tecla, which had been home a year earlier to United Nations officials working on the postwar peace in El Salvador, Begley described finding numerous large settlements in La Mosquitia with stone mounds, Mesoamerican ballcourts, and—the detail I remembered most of all—lots of stone metates lying all over the surface. The *National Geographic* reports were just like the sites Begley described.

Begley had gone on to become a *National Geographic* explorer, was featured in an article for the *New Yorker* by Douglas Preston, was quoted in the 2015 *National Geographic* piece, and was the main character in Chris Stewart's book *Jungleland*, which followed Morde's expedition in search of the "city of the monkey god." In 2012, prior to any of the *National Geographic* announcements, I had asked Chris to present his work on Ciudad Blanca at the Society for American Archaeology meetings. This presentation subsequently became a book chapter in which Begley found that the legend preserves old ideas of discovery and that high technology like LiDAR can obscure long-term local knowledge. He detailed how important the indigenous Pech and Tawahka have been in understanding the archaeology of La Mosquitia. Their indigenous history views archaeological remains as the place of the ancestors, known as the White House. The White House is not any one set of ruins, but reflects a broader ancestral past of mythic protohistory. The legend of Ciudad Blanca is a malformation of indigenous history pushed into a European mold, the fantasy of the lost city.[129]

Time Detectives and International Intrigue

The Not-So-Great Archaeological Caper

Even a quaint college town has a dark underbelly. I found that out the hard way. I got a call that no archaeologist wants to get, and I got it at the worst time. The smartphone screamed at me to wake up, echoing across the dingy room full of weird books and bad taste. A break-in. Artifacts gone. I was needed.

Half an hour later, I was staring at a forced door, cut latches, and other evidence I can't reveal. I photographed it all. Two cabinets had been busted into. One that had been full of ethnographic materials was completely bare. The archaeology display told me more. My students had studied these former museum objects. An Egyptian predynastic crescent knife. A Neolithic Danish dagger. Aztec plates. A Costa Rican effigy vessel. All these and more, gone. The thief had left some good stuff, including a Nicoya Polychrome and some Andean vessels. He took some cheap stuff, including a mass-produced Civil War era pipe so bent out of shape it had been tossed out in Point Pleasant, Ohio, unsalable 160 years ago. It was likely still unsalable.

The thief had been in a hurry. The artifacts he left were in the left back corner of the case, farthest from the opening. Running out of patience or time, he had filled a bag with the closest objects. He didn't know what he was targeting, so he took the display captions. My students had sweated over getting these cards right, with all the details of time, place, and cultural attribution, along with bits of intriguing information. I had cut the printed captions to the right size, glued them to index cards, and carefully placed them on display. I had taken a photo because I was so proud of my students. That photo was now evidence.

If the thief wanted to sell the pieces, we probably stopped that. News bulletins had quickly followed the police investigation. I had been in the midst of negotiating a temporary international loan of artifacts for study, and now my name was blasted across news media. Archaeology. Break-in. Missing artifacts. Priceless.

They weren't priceless, however. A day on eBay, Craigslist, and the websites of art and antiquities galleries taught me that everything has a price. Over the coming months I obsessively revisited these sites looking for "Neolithic dagger" or "Aztec knife" or "Civil War pipe" hoping that someone would slip up for a quick buck. I also wore out shoe leather in antique stores in the area, although I had no idea how I'd play it cool if I got lucky. Now that the heat was on, the thief had probably ditched the pieces or buried them in a backyard. Two weeks after the robbery, I sat in an oppressively hot room in San Salvador, tapping out emails to Interpol, giving them catalog numbers and descriptions for an international watch list. Bigwigs compared to a small-town private dick. Um, I mean archaeologist.

Excuse my stylistic excursion. We did have a break-in. I prepared a report and conducted my own investigation. No one was surprised that I'd taken photos, mapped the stolen artifacts, or investigated local leads. I was an archaeologist, so of course I would. Because we're detectives.

Detectives and Archaeologists

My brief and unsuccessful experience with detective work pales in comparison to that of Ian Graham, the man behind Harvard's Corpus of Maya Hieroglyphic Inscriptions project. Graham has won numerous accolades, including a MacArthur Foundation genius grant, for trekking through the forests of the Mayan region recording Mayan monuments and texts. This work put Graham squarely in the path of looters who carved up monuments for sale to collectors, who would in turn donate the scarred objects to museums in exchange for tax breaks. Graham took up this part of his work with gusto. In 1971 he tracked the movements of dealers in the United States and got a friend to pose as an interested buyer, all to get enough material for the FBI and the Department of Justice to successfully prosecute dealers.[1] Graham also aided in a case where an expert on Olmec art took an immunity deal in exchange for information on a shady dealing network.[2] Archaeologists continue to take part in investigations and even antitrafficking raids.[3]

Ian Graham didn't always get his man. In another case a mailing sticker on a copy of the *New Yorker*, obtained by an acquaintance, put Graham on the track of a dealer alleged to be involved in the sale of a Mayan wall panel to a major museum. In order to gain access to the dealer's house, Graham disguised himself as an interviewer with the Canadian Broadcasting Corporation. His fake moustache came partially unglued during the interview, however, and Graham later discovered that his nemesis already knew who he was.[4] Not exactly the epic struggle of Sherlock Holmes and Professor James Moriarty over Reichenbach Falls, but nonetheless a game of cat and mouse.

Other than Holmes and his creator, Sir Arthur Conan Doyle, one of the names most associated with the detective story is Agatha Christie. The celebrated author became a mystery herself when she disappeared for eleven days in 1926, sparking a police investigation and a media frenzy. After this breakdown Christie rebuilt her life in no small part by marrying the young archaeologist Max E. L. Mallowan. Christie had volunteered at Sir Leonard Woolley's excavations at Ur and was accepted due to his wife, Katharine Woolley's, appreciation of Christie's mysteries. The feeling was not mutual. Christie found Katharine Woolley so overbearing that she was the inspiration for the murdered Louise Leidner in the 1936 novel *Murder in Mesopotamia*, though Katharine never realized this. The novel was based on not only the Ur dig but also other expeditions and travelers Mallowan and Christie had encountered doing archaeology.[5]

Max, with Agatha at his side, dug at numerous sites, including Ur, Nineveh, and Nimrud (recently plagued by Islamic State militants). Christie photographed the sites, developed film, conserved artifacts, and became enough of an expert on Mesopotamian pottery that she incorporated it into her mystery writing.[6] The complex, entwined characters, objects, and detailed locations of a Christie story can resemble an archaeological monograph, and the mystery may require maps, lists, and tables in order to be solved.[7] Much of the 1944 novel *Death Comes as the End*, a murder mystery set in ancient Egypt, was based on unpublished Middle Kingdom papyruses. In 1937 Christie wrote a play about the Amarna period in New Kingdom Egypt, *Akhnaton*, though it was not published until 1973 during the Tutmania inspired by the traveling Tutankhamun exhibition. The play focuses on the historical characters of Amarna and takes inspiration from numerous archaeological texts and objects.[8] Other archaeological adventures in the Christie canon include *Appointment with Death* (1938), set at Petra, and *Death on the Nile* (1937).[9] In the latter novel, detective Hercule Poirot explicitly describes his crime-solving methods through the analogy of archaeology: he methodically clears away extraneous matter to reveal the truth.[10]

The appeal of the science-based detective has not been lost on archaeologists. The fragments of evidence, the exotic but macroscopic and intelligible nature of most archaeological techniques, as Glyn Daniel described archaeology, as well as the morbid subject matter of graves and bones and mummies make the comparison between the detective and the archaeologist inescapable. Daniel knew a thing or two about detective stories since he wrote two examples of "donnish mysteries" (*The Cambridge Murders* and *Welcome Death*), a midcentury tradition of British academics writing humorous detective stories, typically under pseudonyms. Both of Daniel's novels, like several others in the genre, feature an archaeologist-detective.[11] Archaeologists and researchers in related fields (especially those who work with bones, such as forensic anthropologists) cast themselves or find themselves cast as one of the most persistent figures of modern popular culture: the detective, an integral part of supernatural fiction and folklore.

When archaeologists popularize or explain their work, the detective is a commonly chosen archetype.[12] The sometimes fuddy-duddy detective persona is usually contrasted with the colonial adventurer to illustrate how we've moved from reckless explorers to careful scientists.[13] Both the archaeologist and the detective reconstruct past events through carefully collecting and analyzing physical trace evidence and building from the ethnographic or historical testimony of eyewitnesses.[14] Wearing a jacket, a tie, and glasses Professor Henry Jones Jr. follows clues as the detective until

X marks the spot, when like any other superhero he changes into his distinctive costume and becomes Indiana Jones the adventurer. This dichotomy is not new. In 1949 A. V. Kidder, a leader of the profession, a technical innovator in the American Southwest, and an explorer who flew across Yucatán with Charles Lindbergh in the first aerial survey of the Mayan region, wrote of the "hairy-chested" adventurer and the "hairy-chinned" Professor Fuddy-Duddy.[15] When archaeologists wish to flatter themselves for leaving behind their dubious colonialist origins, the detective archetype grounds the archaeologist as an intelligent and useful problem solver rather than as a racist international exploiter and thief. Publications and museums typically display archaeological treasures in whole or restored condition. They present the broken and dirty bits of recovered materials to illustrate the archaeologist-detectives following clues.[16]

Variations on the theme have emerged with new popular media constructions of technology. The media described the identification of English king Richard III's remains as being like "CSI," a generic term for crime scene investigation but associated with the popular television franchise *CSI*.[17] Though this television show was not the first to feature forensic analysis, it paved the way for numerous television series featuring eccentric, nerdy police investigators. The franchise has spawned many imitators, including museums. The American Museum of Natural History offers a teen educational experience, "Crime Scene Neanderthal," which mixes paleoanthropology and forensic investigation.[18]

The Smithsonian showcased forensics in a National Museum of Natural History exhibit, *Written in Bone: Forensic Files of the Seventeenth-Century Chesapeake*. The Smithsonian's Jamestown exhibit website emphasizes participation and encourages visitors to be future forensic anthropologists. The exhibit began in 2009 but became particularly relevant in 2012 when evidence of cannibalism was found on the skeletal remains of a young English colonist nicknamed "Jane," a development that was explicitly covered in the press as "CSI: Jamestown."[19] One cannot help but think of the popular television show *Bones*, a forensic anthropology-focused crime procedural that features a Smithsonian doppelgänger, a Washington, DC, public museum called the Jeffersonian. Early in the show's run the cast included an archaeologist as the museum director, and a number of story lines revolved around the archaeological. My students commonly reference

Bones, and the show inspired several of them to investigate anthropology as a career.

The title gives away the theme of *Mysteries of Çatalhöyük*, an exhibit funded by the National Science Foundation at the Science Museum of Minnesota about the famous Neolithic site in Turkey. The sections aimed at children feature mystery and investigation, including "mystery cards" inviting visitors to interpret the use or meaning of artifacts. The long-term nature of the Çatalhöyük archaeological project allows for a focus on the process of investigation "in the throes of uncertainty."[20]

Mystery and intrigue are not new to Çatalhöyük. Archaeologist James Mellaart is the name most associated with the initial discovery of the site, but within a few years he ran afoul of the Turkish press and was banned from working in Turkey. Journalists Kenneth Pearson and Patricia Connor atmospherically captured the intrigues of the case in their book, *The Dorak Affair*. The story began in 1958 when the recently married Mellaart allegedly met a beautiful young Greek woman on a train in Turkey who, after the archaeologist inquired about her gold bracelet, showed him a fabulous treasure that had been excavated decades earlier. The pieces from Egypt and elsewhere confirmed Mellaart's theories, and he spent several days at the young Anna Papastrati's home recording the treasures. He never saw Papastrati or the artifacts again and had not been allowed to photograph them, frustrating any attempt at academic publication.[21] His sketches illustrated an article in 1958 in the *Illustrated London News*, long a source for archaeology news, including the exclusive deal with Lord Carnarvon over Tutankhamun.

The fallout from the article, including baseless accusations that Mellaart was a looter, worsened when no one could find Anna Papastrati or her treasure. Pearson and Connor suspected that Mellaart (whom they described as being able to read "signs like a Sherlock Holmes") had been conned by Papastrati and possibly a criminal gang into unknowingly authenticating an unlikely mix of frauds.[22] More recent allegations have suggested that Mellaart concocted a hoax. An unusual date format in several letters typed by Mellaart or his wife, Arlette, also appears in the only physical evidence for Papastrati's existence: a single, intimate goodbye letter to the archaeologist. The date coincidence is not definitively conclusive, but some of Mellaart's friends and colleagues have revealed their doubts about the Dorak treasure.[23] A mysterious treasure, a femme fatale in a suspicious meeting on a train, allegations of Turkish covert agents planted in archaeological excavations, shadowy smugglers, a potential damning clue, and a disgraced archaeologist. It might seem the stuff of cloak and dagger, or an Agatha Christie story. Perhaps we should not be surprised that Mellaart and his wife were friends with Agatha Christie and Max Mallowan.[24]

A salient point of the Dorak affair is not whether it was a hoax but that the subterfuge surrounding it might have been acceptable if it were not a hoax. Had Anna Papastrati and her treasure been located, would Mellaart have received such scorn for clandestine meetings and shadowy informants? The Grolier Codex case suggests no. Three Maya hieroglyphic books were discovered in the nineteenth century in Dresden, Madrid, and Paris, and they now bear the names of those cities. In 1971, the Grolier book club in New York displayed a fourth book. The Grolier Codex has prompted questions about its authenticity ever since. The pages are pre-Hispanic in age, but in the years prior to the Grolier's appearance there were reports of caches of ancient paper being found in caves in Mexico. The story of the purchase of the codex involves a Mexican doctor flying to a remote secret location with bandits, haggling with the thieves who were demanding a higher price due to their possession of an antiquities auction catalog, and writing a check on the spot.[25] Twenty-first-century reanalysis of the case has strengthened the argument that it is a real Maya book.[26] Whether or not the Grolier is authentic, that the story is the stuff of potboiler thrillers gives some archaeologists pause.

Archaeologists, Intrigue, and Espionage

There are methodological similarities between the archaeologist and the detective, but there is an even stronger connection between the archaeologist and the intrigue-cloaked world of the spy. Arguably the highest-profile archaeological project since Tutankhamun was the search for the *RMS Titanic* led by Robert Ballard. The world was stunned by the news of the wreck's discovery in 1985, and the project has gotten massive media attention ever since. In 2008, a *National Geographic* television program revealed that the project was part of a secret US Navy search for two missing submarines. The *Titanic* project was legitimate, but it provided cover for the increased naval presence in the Atlantic, not unlike the plot of the technothriller *The Hunt for Red October,* at a time when the Cold War was still quite active.[27] The relationship between military high-technology mapping and reconnaissance and archaeological surveying is an obvious one, and aerial archaeology largely grew out of the First World War. The dramatic increase in aerial and orbital surveillance of the earth and the declassification of older imagery have given archaeologists a wealth of data.[28]

However, it is the long history of archaeologists acting as intelligence agents that has contributed intrigue to the profession's profile. The stereotypical spy is international in scope. Fictional spies, especially in the wake of the James Bond novels and films, have become guides to an exotic world of international adventure and sophisticated tastes and trappings.[29] After director Steven Spielberg was denied a James Bond film, his friend George Lucas said that he had a much better idea for a character. The planning sessions for creating Indiana Jones contained numerous explicit references to spies and private detectives.[30] Even Agatha Christie's fictional fuddy-duddy archaeologists were unflappable in the face of danger and made unpretentious and skilled cultural mediators.[31]

Anthropologists and archaeologists combine the international expertise, the local knowledge, the training to piece together disparate bits of data in the face of mystery, and the skills needed to survive in rough conditions that make for good intelligence agents.[32] The Swiss adventurer Johann Ludwig Burckhardt traveled in the early nineteenth-century Middle East under the cover name of Ibrahim Ibn Abdallah and, like Sir Richard Burton, "infiltrated" Mecca and Medina in disguise. Upon "discovering" Abu Simbel near the second cataract of the Nile, Burckhardt/Abdallah alerted the British consul general Henry Salt to take action.[33] Abu Simbel became even more famous as the focus of immense international effort when the damming of the Nile threatened the site. The need for foreign expertise led to the return of European scholars after decades of mistrust following Egyptian independence and the Tutankhamun sensation.

Not all archaeologists who have worked as spies combined the two fields simultaneously. Michael Coe described his recruitment for the CIA by the Harvard anthropology professor Clyde Kluckhohn. Coe supported anticommunist forces in China during the Korean War before returning to Mayan studies.[34]

The Mayan Spy Ring

Sylvanus Griswold Morley's passion for documenting Maya hieroglyphic inscriptions made him an influential Maya scholar. His proposal and organization of the Carnegie Institution of Washington's investigations of the Mayan region formed the backbone of Mayan archaeology. His popular lectures and writing helped create the notion of the Mayas as the "Greeks of the New World."[35] His synthetic work *The Ancient Maya* (1946) was the first comprehensive volume on the pre-Columbian Mayan civilization, and with subsequent editions by different authors it is still the primary textbook on the pre-Columbian Mayas. Less public was Morley's role as a spy and spymaster for the US Office of Naval Intelligence; he was the best intelligence asset in Latin America during the First World War.

Adventure fiction, specifically Lew Wallace's *The Fair God* and H. Rider Haggard's *Heart of the World*, inspired Morley to pursue Central American archaeology.[36] Morley was also a devotee of detective stories, and he has been called "one of the world's most fascinating detectives," having spent "a lifetime of distinguished sleuthing on the greatest Whodunit of all time—the Mystery of the Mayas."[37] Morley wanted to study Egyptian hieroglyphs due to their lingering mysterious reputation, but Charles Bowditch, a patron of early Mayan archaeology at Harvard, and Peabody Museum director Frederic Ward Putnam influenced Morley to study Maya rather than Egyptian hieroglyphs. Morley would continue to equate Maya and Egyptian epigraphy and archaeology, reflecting the sixteenth-century conception of the "hieroglyphic."[38]

Morley's Harvard roommate was John Wetherill who, with his brother Richard, recorded Mesa Verde and conducted other important archaeological work in the American Southwest. Their activities shaded into cowboy stereotypes. Richard Wetherill homesteaded in the ruins of Pueblo Bonito before being shot to death in an argument over a horse. His sale of artifacts and his involvement with expeditions plundering Chaco Canyon for eastern collectors and museums ultimately provoked the passage of the federal Antiquities Act in 1906, the first US law protecting archaeological resources.[39]

In 1904 Morley wrote a paper on deluge myths in Central America. After he graduated, the Archaeological Institute of America sent Morley to Yucatán to study linguistics. On this trip he visited Edward Thompson at Chichén Itzá. Like Morley, Thompson had benefited from attention by Bowditch. As an engineering student at Worcester Polytechnic Institute, Thompson had written an article entitled "Atlantis Not a Myth," describing a peninsula jutting into the Atlantic and a hearth of diffusion of civilization to Eurasia. He cited Plato as "almost authentic history" and Brasseur de Bourbourg as an expert. Even after working in the region, Thompson suggested that the ancestors of the Mayas were a blue-eyed and light-skinned people who brought their civilization to Mesoamerica over the sea.[40]

Thompson's article prompted Bowditch, along with the vice president of the American Antiquarian Society, Stephen Salisbury (who had supported Augustus Le Plongeon and in return received artifacts from the Le Plongeons), to introduce Thompson to Senator George Frisbie Hoar. They arranged for President Grover Cleveland to appoint Thompson as a "consul archaeologist" to Yucatán and Campeche, at twenty-five the youngest member of the consulate service and tasked primarily with archaeological goals.[41] After purchasing Chichén Itzá, Thompson dredged treasures from the sacred Well of Sacrifice, a collapsed sinkhole or cenote that gives the site its identification as the "mouth of the well of the Itzás." Morley was impressed by Thompson and took up archaeology. In 1907 he began working alongside Kidder on a Southwest US survey project directed by Edgar Lee Hewett (who had fought to stop the eastern museum expeditions aided by the likes of the Wetherill brothers).[42]

In 1912, Morley used his personal charm and enthusiasm (he was known for excitedly tripping over himself at archaeological sites and was praised by his friends for his boundless energy) to successfully propose a twenty-five-year Mayan archaeology program for the Carnegie Institution of Washington.[43] Morley's plan divided Mayan history into two periods based on monumental inscriptions. To investigate the "Old Empire" (today known as the Classic period of competing city-states and noble houses) in the southern lowlands of the Petén forest, the Carnegie excavated at

Waxaktun, Guatemala, from 1926 to 1937. These excavations produced the ceramic sequences still used in much of Mayan archaeology, early evidence for the astronomical architecture in Mayan cities, and other major breakthroughs. We now know that the roots of Mayan civilization are much older than Waxaktun or the early calendrical dates that were so important to Morley. His "New Empire" has not fared well either, with sites like Chichén Itzá demonstrating northern contemporaneity and continuity with the end of the Classic order in the south.[44] Nevertheless, Morley's historical scheme was the scholarly and popular view of the ancient Mayas for decades.

The Carnegie's Mayan project stood apart from its contemporaries by not engaging in museum collecting and by exporting only information and copies rather than actual antiquities, leaving behind restorations at excavated sites.[45] From the Mexican government's perspective, granting the Carnegie permission to dig at Chichén Itzá aided diplomatic relations between Mexico and the United States and reinforced internal control. A virtual state of war had followed a US gunboat attack on Veracruz in 1914, and Yucatán had been in rebellion for decades.[46]

While the Mexican Revolution ran its course, Morley surveyed Guatemala, Belize, and the Usumacinta border region for monuments.[47] Though he lived a life of adventure, Morley was not a macho figure. The small, bespectacled man who favored oversized, floppy straw hats was often gravely ill with tropical diseases and stated that "anyone who says he likes the bush is either a bloody fool or a bloody liar."[48] Expeditions were a series of hardships along muddy trails plagued by ticks and flies. Rainwater would quickly disappear down into the karst (limestone) geology. Morley and a colleague once quenched their thirst during a rainstorm by drinking water leaking through the roof of a thousand-year-old temple.[49] Morley complained about suppers of cheese, crackers, sardines, and canned pineapple, which were supplemented only by the occasional roasted animal obtained by hunting.[50]

Morley's 1916 expedition to the newly discovered site of Waxaktun ventured into a war between Mexican chicleros and Guatemalan soldiers and ended in lethal chaos.[51] Many of Morley's discoveries relied on collaborations with chicleros, the backwoodsmen who tapped chicle trees to supply the international gum market. These rough men knew the forests better than anyone, and Morley offered a bounty of twenty-five dollars for a solid lead on a new site or monument.[52] Before leaving British Honduras, the expedition had armed itself with two shotguns, two Winchester rifles, a Lee rifle, a Luger pistol, and Morley's .38 Colt automatic.[53] This kind of weaponry seems typical of Mayan exploratory expeditions in the early twentieth century. A British Museum expedition carried rifles, pistols, and a rifled shotgun designed to stop any creature in its tracks.[54] Mitchell-Hedges and Lady "Mabs" Richmond Brown used their .45s to lay down suppressive fire against suspected bandits in highland Guatemala, and rifles and shotguns were standard gear on their adventures.[55] By contrast the Tulane expedition of 1925 was unarmed during the first half of its travel through Mexico and Guatemala, though at Palenque the members obtained a .22 rifle for subsistence hunting.[56]

On 17 May 1916, as his expedition was heading home, Morley dropped his glasses and dismounted to retrieve them. Moments later, hidden Guatemalan soldiers, allegedly mistaking the party for guerrillas, opened fire. The medical doctor Moise Lafleur of New Orleans, who had taken Morley's position in the caravan as Morley retrieved his glasses, was killed. Another casualty was the Mexican chiclero Ladislao Romero, who had obtained permission for safe passage through the revolutionary lines (Morley was also carrying letters of passage from the Guatemalan governor of Petén). After a brief firefight, the expedition survivors fled through the bush, losing their scientific equipment and weapons. The same military unit was also involved in a deadly skirmish with British colonial troops, and despite a truce to retrieve the mutilated body of Lafleur, the Guatemalan government never admitted any responsibility for the incident.[57]

Despite Morley's disinterest in adventure and his harrowing encounters with death, he offered his services to US Naval Intelligence prior to American entry into the First World War. While in the United States, Morley openly wore his uniform and hid neither his military appointment nor his activities. He began as an ensign in the Naval Coast Defense Reserve and retired in 1919 as a lieutenant, junior grade. Outside the United States, Morley traveled as an archaeologist, which was his cover for searching coastal areas of Central America for German submarine bases, but he only discovered treasure hunters searching for pirate gold.[58] Morley and his colleagues also reported on possible German sympathizers in Latin America and worked to influence Central American governments. He recruited archaeologists and anthropologists into a spy ring.[59] One of the archaeologists, Samuel K. Lothrop, encoded his notes in an alphabetic code based on Egyptian hieroglyphs and Mesoamerican bar and dot numerals. Lothrop returned to service in Peru as an agent for the FBI during the Second World War.[60] Other wartime FBI archaeologists were not as dedicated. A couple of amateur archaeologists, Dana and Ginger Lamb, appear to have been more interested in obtaining artifacts for Nelson Rockefeller during their travels in Central America, and the FBI terminated any collaboration with the couple in October 1943.[61]

As part of a larger mission to sway El Salvador away from German sympathies, Morley helped write a press release for the US State Department absolving El Salvadoran president Carlos Meléndez Ramirez from blame for an earthquake and volcanic eruption in 1917. Many Salvadorans believed that Meléndez's construction of a dam on Lake Ilopango somehow caused these disasters. Morley's public statements predicting better coffee crops after the eruption caused outrage, and he fled when a band of farmers showed up with weapons. The predictions turned out to be accurate.[62] This meddling in local politics by foreign archaeologists may seem strange, but even Mitchell-Hedges bragged (but do remember that he lost a libel suit regarding his adventures) about supping with the Nicaraguan president during the height of César Augusto Sandino's revolution and hobnobbing with politicians during the ensuing civil war.[63]

After the First World War Morley continued his intelligence work and urged the United States to control Central America as a series of protectorates, agitating for a permanent US intelligence network in the region.[64] The American intelligence infrastructure was somewhat dismantled in the interwar period, but Morley's vision came to fruition during the Cold War and even more openly in the "war on drugs." El Salvador went from a possible German ally in Morley's day to having US military reconnaissance aircraft and personnel stationed at the international airport at the end of the twentieth century.

When the prominent anthropologist Franz Boas of Columbia University discovered a spy ring through the trail of two failed American agents in Mexico known to his former student Manuel Gamio, he was outraged. Without naming names, Boas published "Scientists as Spies" in the *Nation* after *Science* rejected it. He protested that politics should be kept out of science and that the use of scientific investigation as a cover for spying would put all field researchers under suspicion.[65] Indeed, by the time of the Second World War the archaeological expedition was such a common cover for spies that it had become a cliché and had lost much of its value. A biographical history of Harvard's anthropologists found that most of those active in the middle of the twentieth century worked in military intelligence during the Second World War.[66]

Boas was a political progressive and conducted research to debunk the popular racist notions of the day. He was also against the war, and he was German (Morley strongly disliked Germans for years after the war), though ironically Boas had come to the United States because he opposed German imperialism. These facts created significant problems for Boas, leading the American Anthropological Association to censure him. Morley and several members of his spy ring voted against Boas, who also had to resign from the National Research Council.[67] The American Anthropological Association eventually moved to repudiate its condemnation of Boas—eighty-six years later.[68]

Morley's espionage was not publicly known during his lifetime, though his cell members and their activities were openly discussed by 1950.[69] His reputation was based on his research into Maya epigraphy and his writing for popular publications, such as *National Geographic*. These works reflected the obsession Morley and other early Mayanists had for the Mayan calendar, and their inability to read virtually any other part of the script prior to the 1950s. Morley's fixation on finding new calendrical inscriptions led him to neglect his leadership in Carnegie excavations, and he was frozen out. Morley's old coworker A. V. Kidder was put in charge of Carnegie's archaeology division in 1926.[70]

Another stain on Morley's reputation resulted from project member Thomas Gann smuggling a piece of looted jade out of Mexico. Gann, the chief medical officer for the colony of British Honduras (Belize), was already in his fifties when he joined Morley's spy ring as agent 242 for the Office of Naval Intelligence, and he was the chief British intelligence officer in British Honduras.[71] Gann was not one to slow down, getting married at the age of sixty-six and taking his bride, Mary Wheeler, into "the wilds of Guatemala . . . to search for buried treasure."[72] As I already mentioned,

Gann worked with the crystal skull "discoverer" F. A. Mitchell-Hedges in the 1920s at Lubaantun, though he had visited the site in 1903. Gann left his imprint on the exploration of the Mayan region by excavating numerous sites and writing half a dozen popular books on his exploits. Gann filled these books with the lurid, including murders, dangerous creatures, ghost stories, and tales of mysterious disappearances.[73] His destructive excavation techniques, including the use of dynamite, coupled with a fixation on aesthetically pleasing objects gave Gann a notorious reputation.[74]

One of these aesthetically pleasing objects was a large jade plaque depicting a seated Mayan-style lord. Such plaques are generally found outside the Mayan region and appear to be interregional gifts between elites. Such objects would have been exotic and even supernatural due to their distant origin, just as archaeological objects became exotic and supernatural with the rise of the Western museum. Gann's plaque was found at Teotihuacan when Leopoldo Batres controlled Mexican archaeology at the beginning of the twentieth century. Batres gave it to Mexico's finance minister, and it eventually ended up in the hands of a curio dealer. The plaque was offered to Morley for $500 during his 1923 visit to Mexico City, the same trip in which he visited William Niven and his excavations. After Manuel Gamio had the piece authenticated, Gann purchased it for $250. Gann believed that the piece was from Palenque due to the material and style, but all similar plaques have derived from Central Mexico and not the Mayan lowlands. Gann sewed the plaque into his coat and smuggled it into the United States, infuriating Gamio. Gann's notoriety led to his removal from Morley's Carnegie Project. The affair also scotched cooperation between the British Museum and Tulane University in excavations at Copán, though Director Frans Blom later made Gann an honorary associate at the Middle American Research Institute at Tulane.[75] Today the plaque is on display at the British Museum.

Spies in the Desert

Morley's more famous contemporary, T. E. Lawrence ("of Arabia"), is better known for his wartime exploits than his archaeology. At the age of twenty-one Lawrence surveyed the Crusader fortresses of Palestine for his thesis at Oxford, and his knowledge of military history in the region and the detailed maps made by the British Royal Engineers and the Palestine Exploration Fund informed the guerrilla war he waged against the Ottoman Empire during the First World War. The British government classified these maps during the war.[76] Lawrence was one of the last in a century-old combination of archaeology and European influence in the dying Ottoman Empire, and it is fitting that the most flamboyant architect of the empire's final demise was an archaeologist.

Before the war, Lawrence smuggled weapons to the British consulate at Aleppo and assisted Sir Leonard Woolley in excavations at Carchemish, a project teamed with a rough-and-tumble local staff of outlaws and murderers.[77] Woolley himself could be a rough character. During excavations in Italy, an exasperated local government guard began waving his pistol around and threatening to arrest everyone involved in Woolley's excavations. Woolley drew his own revolver, held the guard in a standoff, and then with the help of his organized crime connections made sure that the guard's superiors put him at Woolley's disposal.[78] Woolley later held his pistol to the ear of a Turkish governor and successfully demanded permission to dig at Carchemish. To gain local respect in the Middle East, Woolley held himself out as a sort of armed desert chieftain. During some court proceedings, Woolley and Lawrence drew their guns and forced their way to freedom with the help of Woolley's well-armed bodyguard.[79]

The Carchemish project was nominally working for the British Museum but had shadowy anonymous funding and ties to British intelligence. It was involved with scouting and espionage against German efforts to build the Berlin-Baghdad rail line. Woolley and Lawrence used false names to gain access to the railway, and Lawrence may have used a lens from within the Carchemish field house to spy on German activities. Woolley and Lawrence gave Roman stones from their excavations to the rail project and watched as the Germans added the materials to the construction. Despite these activities on the eve of the war, Lawrence's and Woolley's formal participation in intelligence activities seems to have been relatively minimal.[80]

With the outbreak of war, Woolley and Lawrence joined the archaeologist and intelligence operative D. G. Hogarth, the keeper of the Ashmolean Museum, as part of the Arab Bureau, the British Empire's intelligence-gathering and analysis center in Cairo. When the archaeologist and explorer Captain Gertrude Bell joined them at the end of 1915, they became known as the Oxford Four, although other archaeologists worked in the larger British network in the Mediterranean. Bell was a key expert on the Arab world, and with her contacts and knowledge the group pushed for action against the Ottoman Empire, a course Bell had advocated before the war. Lawrence was dispatched on his famous mission to organize Arab guerrilla activities against the Ottomans in 1916. Woolley directed intelligence operations out of Port Said until his active participation in reconnaissance boat missions led to his capture by Ottoman forces in August 1916 and his imprisonment until the end of the war.[81]

After the war Gertrude Bell became the first director of antiquities in Iraq, founding the National Museum of Iraq in Baghdad as well as laying the ground for the creation of the Iraqi state and the postwar political framework in the Middle East. Her obituaries called her the "Uncrowned Queen of Mesopotamia" and the "Mystery Woman of the Near East."[82] Lawrence's war exploits combined with his status as an adventurous archaeologist. But as Boas warned, the romantic legend of archaeological spies endangered others, as in the case of a German journalist jailed in Iran in 1930, mistaken for the mythic Lawrence of Arabia.[83] The accusation of being a spy is a common one against archaeologists and anthropologists, and professional rivals have fostered such rumors despite the potentially lethal consequences.[84]

Such dangers did not stop archaeologists from playing the spy game in the Second World War or the Cold War, however. As the Americans replaced the British as the dominant power in the Middle East, archaeologists continued to have key roles. Joseph Upton conducted excavations at Nishapur in Iran for the Metropolitan Museum of Art. He continued this work during the Second World War as cover for his Office of Strategic Services (OSS) activities. He was joined by the Persian language expert and later chair of Princeton's Oriental Studies Department T. Cuyler Young, while the missionary and archaeologist Edwin Wright worked for military intelligence in Cairo.[85]

The OSS included luminaries from across the elite spectrum of American society. The OSS mastermind "Wild Bill" Donovan called it a "league of gentlemen," and it included future Supreme Court justice Arthur Goldberg, film director John Ford, and celebrity chef Julia Child. It is conventional wisdom within anthropology that Ruth Benedict's military intelligence report on Japanese culture, later released in civilian form as *The Chrysanthemum and the Sword* (1946), influenced the course of postwar Japan. Benedict's emphasis on the emperor's role in modern Shinto allegedly helped convince US commander General Douglas MacArthur to leave the emperor as a figurehead in Japan's new constitutional republic, though Benedict's influence has been disputed.[86]

After Germany and Japan surrendered, the OSS became the foundation for building in 1947 the Central Intelligence Agency, which continued to employ anthropologists and archaeologists. In the early years after the Second World War, such work was viewed as patriotic and was at times discussed openly in mass media.[87] Other scholars cooperated with the army in intelligence gathering. Project Camelot began paying anthropologists in 1964 to monitor and protect against potential insurrections across the globe. Camelot fell within a year when the Chilean press exposed anthropologist Hugo Nutini's work with the program. The resulting anti-American backlash in South America helped close similar programs by 1966.[88] When I sat as a student in one of Nutini's classes thirty years later, I was not aware of this history.

Donald Wilber was one of the more influential OSS archaeologists who continued in the CIA. He credited his "unusual interests" to youthful reading of adventure stories by the Tarzan creator, Edgar Rice Burroughs, and fascination with a neighbor's collection of books on astrology and spiritualism.[89] He later got the opportunity to indulge his occult interests as part of a CIA project, learning from a stage hypnotist how to produce trances. Wilber came to believe that Christian and Muslim mystics placed themselves into trances, and he wrote an article on this topic for the occult magazine *Fate*, a publication born out of the early controversy over UFOs and related paranormal topics.[90] Starting in 1930 Wilber worked for a series of archaeological projects in Egypt, Greece, Syria, and Iran. His boss, Charles Breasted of the Oriental Institute at the University of Chicago, had to talk Wilber out of bringing a revolver with him for protection against Egyptian "natives."[91] Wilber's attitude changed for the positive, and his proficiency in languages allowed him to cultivate keen on-the-ground diplomatic skills.

Five months after Pearl Harbor the young assistant professor was secretly tapped for the OSS and received training in espionage tradecraft.[92] Allied forces occupied Iran to keep oil deposits out of German hands and to ensure a supply route for the embattled Soviet Union. While Wilber surveyed medieval Persian architecture, he also searched for German agents. However, Wilber and other OSS agents were more concerned about postwar Soviet influence in the region and began establishing intelligence networks for potential anticommunist efforts.[93] In 1947 Wilber became a half-time contract employee of the newly formed CIA, engaged primarily in the "political action" of supporting anticommunist regimes with psychological warfare or propaganda. One of his campaigns incorporated the discovery of Chinese porcelain in recent archaeological excavations in Africa, which was evidence of Ming dynasty exploration, into propaganda alleging Chinese plans to kill or sterilize Africans.[94]

According to Wilber, prior to his retirement in 1969 he was the CIA expert on Islam, and his CIA work took him to numerous countries in Africa and southern Asia. These travels produced several academic and popular books, including the successful *Iran Past and Present*.[95] The subtitle of the ninth edition of this book was *From Monarchy to Islamic Republic*, referring to the then-recent Iranian Revolution of 1979. The emergence of the Iranian theocracy was widely interpreted as a rejection of the brutal regime of the shah and as the result of anger at the United States for backing that regime.[96] Most contentiously, the shah had come to total power through a coup in 1953 that aligned Iran firmly with the West. In the 1981 *Iran Past and Present*, Wilber wrote that allegations that the coup was engineered by the Americans and British "ha[d] won acceptance" but that the shah credited his Iranian supporters for his victory.[97]

Five years later Wilber wrote in his memoirs of engineering the coup. Confirmation came in 2000 when the secret CIA history of Operation TP-AJAX, written by Wilber, was leaked to the *New York Times*.[98] After Iranian prime minister Mohammad Mosaddeq nationalized the Anglo-Iranian Oil Company, the British Secret Intelligence Service, better known as MI6, convinced the Americans to remove Mosaddeq. Two British professors, a historian and a scholar of religion, hatched the initial idea, and Wilber, the Princeton archaeology professor, plotted the CIA operation in cooperation with MI6. Men like Wilber had been cultivating anticommunist operatives in Iran since the OSS days and used them to organize pro-shah army officers, create and distribute propaganda leaflets, and undertake a false-flag bombing campaign to drive a wedge between religious leaders and Mosaddeq. Pro-shah articles were also placed in American newspapers, primarily for consumption in Iran, and the CIA network helped to protect pro-monarchy officials and to organize street mobs and military units in street fights leading to Mosaddeq's removal.[99]

The Archaeologist-Spies Who Went into the Cold
(to Search for the Abominable Snowman)

George Allen Agogino can perhaps lay claim to being the spookiest of all serious archaeologists in the later twentieth century, a triple threat of archaeological scholar, cryptozoologist, and spy. Agogino was a respected archaeologist who had founded Eastern New Mexico University's Anthropology Department and had extensive experience in the southwestern United States. He collaborated with geologist C. Vance Haynes to examine the controversial Sandia Cave site.[100] Excavations at Sandia Cave in New Mexico had turned up what appeared to be mammoth bones and Paleo-Indian artifacts sealed within a sequence of cemented breccia layers with lower strata under a calcium carbonate deposit thought to be at least 25,000 years old and with a uranium series date of more than 200,000 years ago.[101] For much of the twentieth century, distinctive Clovis projectile points dating to 14,000 years ago were considered the oldest in the Americas, a model generally discarded today. Haynes had been a key critic of pre-Clovis claims, and in the case of Sandia Cave he identified the cause of the stratigraphic problems to be bioturbation, disturbance by burrowing rodents.[102]

Agogino was one of the scientific advisors in the yeti expeditions organized by the Texas oil millionaire Tom Slick and his tycoon friends. The *yeh-teh* has roots in Nepalese culture but was appropriated in the twentieth century and transformed by Westerners into the more ape-like "abominable snowman." That form of the legend leaked into the global imagination in 1920 alongside media coverage of attempts to climb Mount Everest. The climbing expedition led by Eric Shipton in 1951 catapulted the yeti to international fame with photographs of a line of footprints, including one of a footprint and an icepick, a tool of exploration, added for scale. Despite subsequent claims that the footprint was a composite of two mundane prints melted in the sun, or that Shipton had faked the line of tracks, the yeti became the subject of intense interest by real and armchair explorers.[103] Sir Edmund Hillary, the leader of the first Western team to summit Everest, organized an unsuccessful expedition to track the snowman. Slick entered the scene at this point, hiring primarily nonscientist trackers and explorers to hunt the yeti and bring evidence back to specialists working with Slick.

As part of Slick's 1959 expedition, Agogino coordinated a secret network of researchers on yeti fecal material at laboratories in the United States. Agogino's equivalent in the United Kingdom was William Charles Osman Hill, an accomplished primatologist who had also investigated the Nittaewo little people legends of Sri Lanka and, like MacRitchie and others had concluded for Europe half a century earlier, suggested that they might be a relict population of fossil hominins. Agogino and Osman Hill were the tissue connecting other anthropologists and researchers quietly working with Slick's monster hunters. An opinion survey twenty years after Slick's expedition found that one in eight physical anthropologists believed that mystery primates like the yeti might be real.[104]

Agogino was never comfortable with Slick's team of cryptozoologists. He was friendly with the television animal presenter and paranormal author Ivan Sanderson and collaborated with him in various ways but thought that Sanderson's low-quality work was harming the science. While Agogino was involved from the start with Slick's hunt for North America's Bigfoot, he found the unprofessionalism of Slick's yeti hunters had turned more toward fraud. He was increasingly skeptical as each physical sample he analyzed turned out to be fraudulent or mistaken. Yet Agogino continued to work in cryptozoology, including appearing on television.[105]

Slick's most infamous cryptozoology actions involved the Pangboche hand, a skeletal "yeti" relic in a Nepalese lamasery. Cryptozoologist Peter Byrne obtained parts of the hand by swapping them with known human thumb and phalanx bones, unbeknown to the monks of the lamasery. The supposed yeti bones were then passed to the actor Jimmy Stewart and his wife, Gloria, who hid them in her underwear (not while being worn) and smuggled them out of India to England. Both Agogino and physical anthropologist Carleton Coon were skeptical of the hand. Coon, an OSS veteran wounded in North Africa, suggested that the yeti may be related to *Gigantopithecus*, a massive Pliocene-Pleistocene ape of Southeast Asia.

Coon continued his interest in cryptozoology throughout his life and gave the keynote address at the University of British Columbia's "Symposium on Sasquatch and Similar Phenomena" in 1978.[106]

While he truly was interested in the yeti research, Agogino's participation belied the dual purpose of Slick's expeditions. Slick's airline was a front for CIA operations. Agogino, like Coon and many other American anthropologists of the time, had been in the OSS, and he admitted to cryptozoological writer Loren Coleman that he was one of the CIA's anthropologists. It seems that Slick's expeditions were spying on the Chinese repression in Tibet. The yeti and similar creatures, as well as a hunt for Noah's ark near the Soviet-Turkish border, provided ample if less-than-subtle cover for intelligence work.[107] Agogino's undercover CIA work as part of his hunt for the yeti becomes even stranger when one realizes that Agogino's Sandia Cave work was in direct response to archaeologist Frank Hibben, who claimed to have been shot at by Chinese soldiers during work as a CIA field agent in outer Mongolia.[108]

9

Digging Up Witches and Murder

Detectives and the Supernatural

From the beginning of the genre, the detective story featured the struggle between eerie mystery and rational investigation. Both the detective story and the ghost story are rooted in the Gothic world of mystery, danger, and the uncanny.[1] Edgar Allan Poe set the model for the fictional detective with C. Auguste Dupin in "The Murders in the Rue Morgue." Beyond Poe's fame for uncanny horror, this ur-mystery already stretched the boundaries of the nascent genre by featuring a nonhuman killer. Arthur Machen judged Poe's Dupin stories to be the only detective tales worthy of the label "fine art" because of the juxtaposition of the puzzle with a mystical air of ecstasy.[2] Sir Arthur Conan Doyle and his Sherlock Holmes further fixed the detective genre into a materialist form comparable to archaeology. Holmes provides comfort to an anxious middle class by "dispel[ling] magic and mystery" with scientific analysis just as the eccentric forensic specialists of *CSI* or *NCIS* do today.[3] The structural frame of the "explained supernatural," introducing a mystical atmosphere and subsequently explaining it away, became a staple of the detective story with Conan Doyle's *The Hound of the Baskervilles* (1902) but derives from Ann Radcliffe's Gothic novel *The Mysteries of Udolpho* (1794).[4]

The resemblance between the fictional detective and the archaeologist is clear. Most archaeologists have some form of a speech that extols the importance of everyday objects, that explains how a hairpin or a broken piece of crockery is actually more important to understanding the past than all the glittering gold raided from a royal tomb. The fuddy-duddy stereotype of the archaeologist derives from this practice. Our methodological training teaches us to see minute or ephemeral signs (sherd scatters, changes in topography, use wear on stone tools) that may seem invisible or pointless. We then carefully record these clues so that we can then spend our lives explaining their importance to clients, students, and a public that presumably cannot see what we can see. They are our Watsons or, on a bad day, our Inspector Lestrades.

Detection is a major element of stories involving the supernatural, the horrific, and the macabre. At the beginning of the twentieth century, the most popular forms of the horror story in English fiction were the psychic detective story and the antiquarian/academic ghost story.[5] The psychic detective subgenre initially began with the protagonists debunking spiritual mysteries. I have already mentioned the Glozel diggers' dismissal of debunking archaeologists as "Sherlocks," and novelist Dorothy Sayers said that the Glastonbury archaeologist Frederick Bligh Bond's activities in the Society for Psychical Research were "to Sherlock-Holmes about for the haunters!"[6] Fictional psychic detectives stopped being debunkers and, armed with superscience and occult knowledge, became supernatural explorers, mirroring the real-world abandonment of psychic research to believers in the early twentieth century. Flaxman Low, the psychic detective created by Kate and Hesketh Prichard, was an Egyptologist, as was Dr. John Richard Taverner, the psychic detective created by occultist Dion Fortune.[7] Another example is the psychic detective Moris Klaw authored by Sax Rohmer, the creator of Fu Manchu. Many of the "dream detective" Klaw's adventures involved psychically potent Egyptian artifacts.[8] Algernon Blackwood created Dr. John Silence, who investigated crimes and mysteries emanating from powerful psychic forces. Blackwood was a major influence on the cosmic horror author H. P. Lovecraft (see chapter 10). In "The Nemesis of Fire" Silence faces the wrath of a fire elemental protecting the mummy of an Egyptian priest, a curse only ended upon the return of a stolen gem.[9] The repatriation of a looted treasure is a persistent theme in early detective novels.[10]

In pushing back against elemental forces, the psychic detective exposes the invisible underpinnings of reality, expanding knowledge of the unseen and unknown, rather than using Sherlock Holmes's deductive dictum to "eliminate all other factors, and the one which remains must be the truth." Nevertheless, modern psychic detectives, such as FBI special agent Fox Mulder of *The X-Files*, continue to evoke the rationalist Holmes as a model.[11] The hyperrational Holmes is the antithesis of the psychic detective, yet he was created by Sir Arthur Conan Doyle, an avowed spiritualist, promoter of the paranormal, and producer of popular Egyptian mysteries.[12] Conan Doyle's 1892 story "Lot No. 249" introduced the Egyptian mummy as a shambling horror controlled with ancient Egyptian rites, while his story "The Ring of Thoth" (1890) situated eternal love in a blend of ancient alchemy and museum antiquities.[13] I have mentioned that Conan Doyle publicly blamed the 1907 death of his friend Bertram Fletcher Robinson and Lord Carnarvon's death in 1923 on elemental spirits guarding Egyptian mummies. Robinson provided the kernel of the most famous of all Sherlock Holmes stories, *The Hound of the Baskervilles*, a tale steeped in a threat of supernatural terror and peppered with archaeological imagery, including a collection of skulls and a Neolithic ruin. Conan Doyle met Robinson when the latter was a war correspondent in South Africa and in 1901 visited Robinson's home in Devon. Robinson had become an antiquarian authority on the Dartmoor region, had written on its ruins, and collected stories of spectral hounds and an evil squire very similar to the legend of the fictional Sir Hugo Baskerville. The carriage driver who took the spiritualist author and the mummy-cursed reporter across the moors was named Harry Baskerville.[14]

The academic/antiquarian ghost story celebrates the failure of purely materialist scientific techniques in the face of the supernatural.[15] One can detect the simultaneous demand for scientific fact and supernatural mystery in the real-world account of a haunted archaeological excavation in the 1956 *Antiquity* article "St. George the Vampire." The excavation of a Mycenaean tomb becomes the focus of uncanny happenings, which culminate in spooked archaeologists and a local mob convinced of the apparition of a saint. Author A. J. B. Wace penned the article, which is very much like one of the antiquarian ghost tales of M. R. James, beginning with a warning about how few of the witnesses survive to tell the tale.[16] According to Wace the events eventually transformed into the legend of a vampire and a doomed English archaeologist, who died in the First World War.

This tension between rational investigation and the hidden fantastic produces the discovery plot found in most traditional horror stories. A monstrous horror appears, often arisen from the past and hiding among decent people, and threatens civilization. Trace evidence and clues of the monster's crimes lead the protagonists to discover its existence. By collating evidence from current atrocities with fragments of information about similar horrors in the past, the protagonists can combat the monster. This form of the supernatural horror story crystallized in the late Victorian "urban gothic," sometimes specified as "London Gothic."[17] The transition from the multigenerational rural estate ideal to transitory urban life also fed the haunted house genre with its now cliché conceit of the new family occupying a place of ancient secrets, which must be uncovered and resolved through investigation.[18]

Dracula (1897), the story of an illegal immigrant intent on conquering the heart of the British Empire, is one of many examples of the urban gothic that played on concerns about rapid globalization.[19] Dracula arrives from an exotic and archaic Eastern Europe, once under the thumb of the ailing Ottoman Empire. He is a visitor from the past, an abomination that sleeps in the earth and climbs up the ladder of civilization from a medieval backwater to the world's de facto capital. Dracula's creator, Bram Stoker, moved in the same social circles as explorers and Egyptologists, and he visited the same tropes of the threatening past in the Egyptian-themed *The Jewel of Seven Stars.*[20] Rather than arriving in London as a controlled scientific specimen or trophy, like an Egyptian obelisk or a Greek sculpture, Dracula takes over a ship and lands where and when he chooses before disappearing into the population. But even controlled international imports frightened Victorian Londoners. Only a small portion of the visitors to the Great Exhibition of 1851 were foreigners, but the international character of the event heightened fears over an influx of aliens visiting the imperial capital.[21] During miserable years living on Great Russell Street, Arthur Machen came to view London as a "city of nightmares," in which a short walk in any direction would place him in a world as unknown and foreign as the far reaches of Africa.[22] The address Machen cited, 36 Great Russell Street, is directly across from the British Museum, and this general area became a scene of the uncanny in his fairy race story "The Red Hand."

One can detect the dangerous, transgressive, ancient, and hidden supernatural threat in Dracula's contemporary real-life London counterpart,

Jack the Ripper. Social reformers blamed the murders on the squalid condition of London's Whitechapel slums, inspiring action to improve living
conditions.[23] Jewish immigrants in Whitechapel were particularly targeted
for reprisals, and police feared anti-Semitic mobs. Initial public speculation
blamed foreign suspects, such as Russians and Americans, but private letters to the police concentrated on British suspects.[24] The fictional criminals
in the contemporary Sherlock Holmes stories were likewise disproportion-
ately foreign in comparison to those actually imprisoned.[25] The supernatural aspects of the crimes were immediately publicized, and a significant
number of would-be detectives boasted to the police of their psychic abilities.[26] The Masonic royal conspiracy theory for the murders mirrored
archaeological fantasies, turning the victims into human sacrifices by an
ancient secret conspiracy guided by literal touchstones of geomancy and
symbolic architecture, like mysterious druids letting blood on ley-line-
connected megalithic altars. One twenty-first-century theorist suggested
that Tut's curse was actually a string of murders by occultist Aleister
Crowley in an attempt to copy magic rituals supposedly committed by Jack
the Ripper.[27] The nameless killer turned supernatural mystery reflects the
transformation of the nameless prehistoric into the supernatural realm of
myth.

One of the key villains of Ripper conspiracy theories is Sir Charles
Warren, commissioner of the Metropolitan Police at Scotland Yard. Warren
plays his role in Ripper stories through his Masonic status, his personal role
in destroying a mysterious inscription at one of the crime scenes, and his
resignation immediately before the final, "canonical" murder of Mary
Kelly.[28] Amazingly, popular lore generally omits Warren's role as an archaeologist and colonial official in the Holy Land. In 1867 Lieutenant Warren of
the Royal Engineers secretly had dug around the foundations of the Temple
Mount. These secret excavations, involving tunnels more than a hundred
feet below the surface, were incredibly dangerous both politically and physically. In addition to uncovering the first evidence tying archaeological
deposits in Jerusalem to the Bible, Warren was collecting military intelligence for the War Office. Warren returned to service in 1882 to investigate
the disappearance of the Arabic scholar Edward Henry Palmer, who was
on a secret intelligence mission in the Sinai Peninsula. Warren followed the
trail, discovered that Palmer and his men had been robbed and murdered,

and supervised a criminal investigation and subsequent executions, which demonstrated British control over the peninsula.[29] I am honestly shocked that Warren's digging has not featured more in the Templar/Freemason conspiracy theories about Jack the Ripper.

Outside of cities, horror may hide in a haunted house or a remote village with a terrible past. The investigation of a haunted house and its secrets provides clear comparisons with archaeology.[30] The rambling Victorian haunted house reflects the Romantic fixation on a past giving way to urbanization and reason. The turrets and crenellations are neo-Gothic architectural evocations of castles and medieval ruins and are of a piece with the artificial ruins built as follies by the most affluent. As industrialization transformed the European landscape, these faux antiquities became symbols of the preindustrial, prescientific order, including threats from the past.[31] In an era of typewriters, train schedules, and blood transfusions, the medieval monster Dracula moves from his crumbling castle to the old Carfax Abbey, a once-powerful place in the English landscape but now just a property handled by clerks.

Experts in the Occult

Uncovering hidden monsters and their ancient secrets is the work of a horror expert, a special type of detective, "that characteristically Victorian discoverer of secrets," a person of any profession who is "accustomed to gathering data, weighing evidence, and drawing conclusions."[32] Detective work was the "defining epistemology" of the Victorian era.[33] The detective is often an amateur but brings an array of scientific techniques and aptitudes to crime solving.[34] During the bulk of a horror story, the monster lurks offstage. Tension builds through uncovering clues about the horror. The monster's true nature is not shown in action until it is interpreted from clues about its past. More than other literary genres, horror stories try to align the emotions or perspective of a character with those of the audience. This close alignment between the audience and the protagonist in horror stories makes a voice of reason and knowledge particularly powerful and the science detective a common horror character.[35]

One effective method is to lead the audience through the discovery process of the detective-protagonist. In no genre is the sequential narrative of unfolding information more important than in horror, though the detective story follows close behind. Both audience and characters learn of the nature of the horror simultaneously. This building of tension through knowledge is an integral part of the experience of horror. By discussing the awful nature of the monster, the horror tale involves the audience in "the drama of proof," just as in a detective story. In these discussions, the expert may provide exposition, as archaeologists and anthropologists do in many horror movies.[36]

A key difference between supernatural horror stories and mundane tales of mystery or suspense makes the antiquarian or the archaeologist a particularly common horror character.[37] Horror antagonists are not just threatening; they are inherently uncanny and not of the normal world. The danger in a horror tale comes from the fringes of the world of science or from the world of the supernatural beyond mundane reality. In the discovery plot, skeptical authorities force the protagonists to defeat the threat themselves by invoking information from the outside or even becoming part of the outside themselves, transcending conventional boundaries and mediating opposing worlds.[38] In *Dracula* the chronological correlation of notes and documents with ancient supernatural lore identifies the anomalous threat.[39] This is a common horror trope, one I examine in depth in the archaeological "The Call of Cthulhu" in chapter 10. Science temporarily halts Dracula's curse through blood transfusions, but only Van Helsing's practical mastery of ancient mystical lore can track and defeat the vampire. It is unsurprising that both Dracula and Van Helsing are old scholars of the supernatural markedly accented as continental Europeans in a story about the invasion of Britain and otherwise populated by native Anglophones.[40]

Despite the danger inherent in monsters, horror tales celebrate unnatural knowledge.[41] The existence of abnormalities outside of scientific knowledge reenchants Max Weber's world shorn of wonder. One of the reasons we love our monsters is that they are evidence of a secret and often ancient world hidden under and around that which science allows us. In virtually all supernatural horror tales, the root of the horror and the source for information on how to stop it are ancient: a primeval curse, an angered pagan god, a centuries-old vampire, an undying member of a lost civilization, a prehistoric survival. In an M. R. James story, the mere existence of an ancient textual object can awaken horror.[42]

The scientific excavator who unearths ancient secrets is the ideal horror detective: a storyteller who examines traces and clues, dredges up the back-story, and collates this into an interpretative narrative. The scientific detective restores the human individual and the quest for knowledge back to importance in the face of geologic time and disinterested uniformitarianism.[43] A need for human importance motivated the eclectic band of hobbyists and enthusiasts who chased ley lines in the 1930s. The ley line literature was routinely framed as mystery and adventure, and in becoming scientific pioneers (as they saw it), ley hunters were restoring an amateur human element to antiquarianism in the face of archaeology's professional development.[44]

The most common genre of fictional movies containing anthropologists is the horror film, and one reason for that is anthropological expertise in supernatural topics, such as vampires, spirit possession, and magic.[45] This is even more true for archaeologists. In *Raiders of the Lost Ark*, an army intelligence agent introduces Indiana Jones as a "professor of archaeology, expert in the occult, and . . . obtainer of rare antiquities." The rupture of memory imbues archaeological objects and sites with supernatural qualities. Museums and archaeological collections that divorce exotic objects from their context envelop them in the fog of mystery. Archaeologists investigate enchanted relics of the past that anomalously and supernaturally persist into the disenchanted present as a violation of the natural order.

Excavating Dark Conspiracies

The expert scientific detective became less common in horror tales after 1970. Parallels can be drawn to the explosion of pseudoscience (discussed in chapter 11). However, given the role of the horror expert-protagonist as a defender of the status quo, and the strong relationship among supernatural horror, the exotic, and colonialism, another possibility suggests itself. The supernatural horror tale after 1970 was typically not about an external threat invading a conservative landscape or finding sanctuary in dangerously culturally diverse cities, but instead the threat was all around us, could not be kept out, and was an inherent part of us. It is not hard to see this shift as a reaction to the collapse of imperial regimes and colonial, race-based, segregationist societies.[46]

One way this reaction manifested was the growth of the anti-cult movement, initially rooted in concerns over Asian religious movements entering the West but eventually spawning the Satanic panic. At the core of the panic was a fear-based subculture driven by pseudoscholarly "occult experts" and "former Satanists" who "trained" concerned law enforcement and parents about ritual occult practices situated within a conspiracy theory of a vast network ritually abusing and murdering people, especially children, in worship of Satan. Joe Laycock argued that proof is inherent to Satanic ritual abuse investigations—not to prove that abuse exists, but to prove the existence of a supernatural world.[47] Brutal fantasies were propagated in order to make a world plagued by demons, and potentially saved by angelic and divine mercy, more credible. This is particularly important in the post-Enlightenment world, in which the authorized way of knowing is through rationality and evidence, which may conflict with a blatantly supernatural worldview.

The most infamous incident in the Satanic panic, the McMartin preschool case, continues to prop up conspiracy theories in no small part due to an archaeological excavation. Accusations of ritualistic sexual abuse at the preschool began in 1983, resulting in a four-year trial that led to the dropping of all charges against the accused in 1990. Critics of the Satanic panic used the case to shame mainstream media allies of the panic into apology and retreat.[48] But the conspiracy theory survived and merged with a belief in the vast experimentation on and abuse of children by elements of the social elite and the intelligence world.[49] Missing children are alleged to have been taken and murdered by methodological descendants of the CIA's MKULTRA mind control experiments, or forced into paranormal experiments and missions at secret underground bases under Montauk Point on the eastern end of Long Island.

During the McMartin investigation, the accounts by children became increasingly wild and physically impossible. Skeptics held such testimony as evidence of confabulation, of priming by one of the parents (who was later diagnosed with paranoid schizophrenia), and of investigators asking leading questions answered by children emotionally needing adult approval.[50] Some people alleged that the school sat atop secret underground tunnels. Two archaeological examinations were conducted at the site of the preschool. The first, contracted by prosecutors, turned up little beyond a mostly undisturbed concrete slab. Unsatisfied parents and private investigators commissioned a second excavation. This project concluded that at least one potentially occult symbol and filled-in tunnels corroborated the stories of ritual activity.[51] Subsequently a clinical psychologist studying the "recovered memories" practices of the sort used in the McMartin case reanalyzed the archaeological report and disagreed with its findings, concluding that the tunnel feature was a series of trash pits dating to a documented mid-twentieth-century family household on the land. Among vast amounts of refuse the only anomalous objects were one 1980s sandwich bag, a kind of object easily moved by taphonomic processes such as rodents, and two pipe elements that might have been introduced during plumbing repairs.[52]

These were not the first archaeologists to dig in search of an occult conspiracy. Elements of the Satanic panic were inspired by a grand conspiracy theory fashioned by romantic folklorists and occultists, including archaeologist Margaret Murray, and the new religious movement they created.

The Archaeologist and the Witch Cult

Archaeologists have been spies and have compared their work to that of detectives, but one of the starkest cases of melding mystery, intrigue, the occult, and archaeology is that of Margaret Murray. Starting as an Egyptologist, Murray's work took her to folklore, to witchcraft and fairies, to murder investigation, to the creation of a major new religious tradition in the form of Wicca, and to the most prominent form of spooky archaeology today, the belief in ancient extraterrestrials.

Margaret Murray grew up near the White Horse, the Dragon Mount, and other points of antiquarian and folkloric interest in a Victorian culture concerned about the loss of rural England. After being recognized as gifted in epigraphy, she studied and worked with the pioneering Egyptologist Sir Flinders Petrie, published several significant archaeological and linguistic books, and received an honorary doctorate. Her research in Egypt belied many of the stereotypes about women and fieldwork as Murray ran a field crew like any other archaeologist and joined with other women in guarding her excavations.[53] Like other fieldworkers past and present Murray became fascinated by modern cultural practices at her site, especially with regard to magical and religious matters. She was treated with a Coptic healing ritual after a bite from a potentially rabid dog.[54] After 1904 her fieldwork was significantly curtailed because she took on the duties of teaching Petrie's students, some of the earliest professionally trained archaeologists.[55] She also promoted the importance of anthropology training for British imperial administrators and colonists.[56]

With travel interrupted by the First World War Murray turned her attention to European folklore, occult beliefs, and archaeology at home. Murray visited Glastonbury after she became ill during her service as a war nurse. The magical lore of Glastonbury has long focused on regeneration with its healing waters, associations with Arthur's Avalon, and rumors of Joseph of Arimathea and the Holy Grail. As Murray recuperated in Glastonbury she attempted to link the grail legend with Egyptian traditions, research that appears to have led to research into a secret witch cult.[57] The mythic resonance of Glastonbury has similarly impacted others, including Frederick Bligh Bond, who could have attended a lecture Murray gave in Glastonbury in 1915.[58]

After the publication of her first witch cult book, Murray excavated the medieval site of Homestead Moat in Whomerley Wood, Hertfordshire, possibly because of her growing belief in the witch cult. Her later excavations of megalithic sites in Malta and Minorca were accompanied by investigations of local folklore, including beliefs regarding spirits and buried treasure, and led Murray to join the Folklore Society and eventually become its president from 1953 to 1955.[59] In 1961 a late medieval intrusive pit into a Neolithic barrow on Galley Hill, Bedfordshire, included a posthole interpreted by excavators as a possible gallows. Murray suggested that an associated horse's skull and chalk dice were related to witchcraft.[60]

Murray consciously linked archaeology and the occult. Of the thirteen chapters of her autobiography, archaeology and the occult get one chapter each, filled with sentiments like "I find that all good archaeologists are expected to have had at least one occult experience either personal or of somebody that he knows."[61] The crystal skull fabulist F. A. Mitchell-Hedges made a similar statement about occult occurrences at excavations all over the world.[62] Murray took paranormal claims seriously, though she found many of them wanting. In one case, she devised a series of experiments to determine why an Egyptian magical scarab amulet was apparently always warm to the touch, even testing it for radiation.[63] Murray's colleagues in the Folklore Society praised this material rationalization of folkloric and paranormal claims.[64] She was an advocate for parapsychology and condemned a Judeo-Christian bias in the archaeology of religion.[65] Her interest in magic was not just academic but practical. Murray saw herself as a witch and apparently successfully cast curses on colleagues, rivals, and, perhaps in jest, her fellow archaeologist Kaiser Wilhelm II.[66] Murray claimed to have invented, as a prank, the persistent legend that the unlucky mummy case lid caused the wreck of the *Titanic*. This story haunts the British Museum to this day.[67]

Murray's most famous legacy was a product of her demystifying and materialist but countercultural approach to the occult. Other approaches to European witchcraft had dismissed it as a torture-induced fantasy or saw it as a Satanic reality. Murray denied a Satanic or supernatural aspect yet affirmed that something extraordinary had been taking place beyond the mass murder of innocents.[68] She expanded on the nineteenth-century argument that early modern witch trials documented a pre-Indo-European religion with roots in the Paleolithic. Murray's witches, routinely identified with fairies and elves in Scotland and elsewhere, inherited the Old Religion from MacRitchie's pygmy fairy races of pre-Indo-European Europe. They shared human sacrifice, the mounds, fairy gold, and a number of names with the devil of the witches.[69]

Murray's witches had magical powers entangled with archaeological remains. She reconstructed flying on a broomstick through a window as a remnant of a fertility ritual designed for ancient barrow mound architecture, the refuge of the fairy/dwarf race when invaders occupied their land. Numerous trial documents considered factual by Murray describe standing stones as the sites of the witches' Sabbath. The elf arrowheads described in chapter 2 were shot and their injuries cured by witches.[70]

Jules Michelet's *La Sorcière* (1862), arguably a social and political work of Romantic Satanism, helped create the idea of the witch cult and argued that the role of neo-paganism, be it the elevation of witches or the British intellectual fad of adoring Pan, was a response to modernity. Alfred Watkins suggested that the secret of his ley lines may have inspired the staves and wands of wizards and witches. Significant parts of Murray's later ideas can be found in an 1897 essay by mathematician Karl Pearson titled "Woman as Witch."[71]

In 1899 folklorist Charles Leland published an alleged firsthand account of the witches' religion in *Aradia; or, The Gospel of the Witches*. *Aradia* is drawn from collaboration with Maddalena, an alleged Italian hereditary witch with whom Leland claimed to have collected a "gospel" of a surviving folk paganism descended from the Etruscans but rapidly disappearing in the face of modernity. Leland's witches and wizards were freethinkers who celebrated the equality of women and resisted medieval Christianity.[72] The idea of witchcraft as the historical root for those disenchanted with both Christianity and authority clearly appealed to many figures in Western occultism, including the suffrage activist and critic of Christianity Margaret Murray.

I have already mentioned Murray supporting T. C. Lethbridge in the Gogmagog affair. Her letter to the *Times* not only held the hill figures to be authentic but also angrily attacked "scientific" archaeology as inferior in technique to antiquarianism.[73] Her witch cult thesis addressed the core idea popular with antiquarians, archaeologists, and folklorists influenced by Edward Burnett Tylor and James George Frazer of a pagan religious survival in European folklore.[74] Murray's tortured leaps of logic in interpreting witch trial documents have been heavily and rightly criticized, including her transformation of the sabbat from an association with anti-Semitic propaganda to *s'ébattre*, meaning "to frolic."[75] The most widely accepted historical evidence for pagan survivals being recorded in witch trials is radically different from Murray's claims and does not support the existence of a witch cult.[76]

Murray presented her Old Religion findings in archaeological and folklore journals, followed by *The Witch-Cult in Western Europe* in 1921 and *The God of the Witches* in 1933.[77] Though initially criticized or ignored by other historians (whom Murray believed to be biased by their adherence to Christianity), by the end of her lifetime, Murray's witch cult had become conventional wisdom. This was in no small part due to her authorship of the entry "Witchcraft" in the *Encyclopedia Britannica* from 1929 to 1969 and her ascension to the presidency of the Folklore Society in 1953.[78] An even greater legacy was her lionization by the emerging neo-pagan movement. The earliest leaders of the movement considered Murray to be "where the Wicca revival really began," and the *Occult Review* featured her findings. Murray wrote the introduction to Gerald Gardner's foundational Wiccan text, *Witchcraft Today*, and Gardner considered her to be the "godmother" of the witches.[79]

Gerald Gardner identified as an anthropologist, published on archaeology, and was a council member of the Folklore Society alongside Margaret Murray.[80] While working on plantations in the British colonies around the Indian Ocean, Gardner's contact with foreign cultures sparked his interest in anthropology and magic. Tellingly, he referred to Dayak divination as "séances."[81] Gardner published on archaeological matters, including the metallurgy of ancient Cyprus, and was an authority on traditional Malaysian weapons. His fascination with such weapons, particularly the kris dagger, may be one of the reasons that the athame ritual dagger gained such prominence in modern Wicca.[82]

Gardner's "discovery" of the "authentically" pre-Christian New Forest coven in the English countryside resembles Leland's discovery of Maddalena and must be taken with several cauldrons of salt. Much of Gardner's Wicca resembles Victorian occult constructions, including Hermetic ceremonial magic, the Order of the Golden Dawn, and Buddhist and Hindu influences on theosophy. Gardner himself noted some of these similarities before dismissing any direct connections. These influences should be no surprise since Gardner was a Freemason, a member of the Rosicrucians, a priest of the Ancient British Church, and a leading figure in Aleister Crowley's Ordo Templi Orientis, an offshoot of the Golden Dawn. Like other members of these groups, Gardner tied his Wicca to the occult underdogs of Western imagination, such as the druids and the Knights Templar, and replicated MacRitchie's and Murray's suggestions of the Old Religion originating with a race of little people remembered as fairies.[83] Even if Gardner discovered an already existing magical group, the influence of Murray's *Witch-Cult* on Wicca is clear. Before the discovery, Gardner had already been consulting with Murray on apparent early modern witchcraft relics.[84]

Ronald Hutton argued that the transgressive nature of Gardner's religion, the combination of all the secret society lore with the forbidden image of the witch and the primordial countercultural witch cult, was the key to Wicca's success.[85] Outside of the occult underground a British witchcraft panic began in the 1920s and grew in intensity after the war and the repeal of Britain's Witchcraft Act. The catalyst may have been the Murray-inspired *Witches Still Live* (1929) by the American author Theda Kenyon. Another major inspiration for the British concerns over Satanism was the occult fiction of Dennis Wheatley, itself inspired by the less-than-credible lore promoted by Montague Summers and Aleister Crowley, the latter an influence on Gerald Gardner's Wicca movement.[86] Police and the public had come to believe in a secret underground of witch cults, orgy sects, and blackmail gangs operating at all levels of society.[87]

Witches, Conspiracy, and Murder

Margaret Murray fanned the flames. As early as 1929, Murray was proclaiming in the press that the witch cult was still active in Britain and France.[88] By the 1940s Murray was alleging a modern conspiracy that included ritual human sacrifice.[89] In *The Divine King in England* (1954), Murray proposed that a number of British royals had been not only members of the witch cult but human sacrifices in the mold of the ritual murder of the king in Frazer's *The Golden Bough*. Criticism of her book did not stop Murray, who seems to have seriously considered the possibility that witchcraft practices or fears were behind at least one murder in the 1940s. On 14 February 1945, someone murdered the elderly farmworker Charles Walton as he trimmed hedges in Lower Quinton, outside of Birmingham. Walton's throat was slashed, and he was pinned to the ground with a pitchfork through his neck. Scores of Italian prisoners of war from a nearby camp were interrogated without success. Walton's employer was unable to stick to one story about the events prior to the murder, though police were never able to bring charges against him.

Five years later the case took an occult turn that attracted Murray's attention. Investigation by Detective Superintendent Alec Spooner, the chief of the Warwickshire Criminal Investigation Department, and a letter by a local woman suggested similarities to a murder in 1875. On 4 April 1950, Agnes Pullinger testified that in 1875 a madman fatally stabbed her grandmother with a pitchfork. Police withheld from the eighty-year-old Agnes that the killer had believed Pullinger's grandmother was a witch who had put the evil eye on him. According to a memorandum on 30 March

1950 from the assistant chief constable of Warwickshire to the commissioner of Scotland Yard, Pullinger's testimony was prompted by the intense media coverage of the alleged ritual elements of Walton's murder.[90]

This development gave the Walton murder an occult shadow of witchcraft, and within a few months Margaret Murray investigated the case firsthand. Several sources have suggested that the media attention was a result of Murray's witchcraft investigation in Lower Quinton.[91] However, Pullinger contacted the Warwickshire County constabulary early in 1950, while Murray seems to have timed her investigation of the Walton murder to coincide with her presentation for the Folklore Society at the meetings of the British Association for the Advancement of Science. The British Association meetings were a week of presentations by scientists and researchers in late August to early September 1950 in Birmingham. For a week Murray carried a sketchbook and pencils, posing as an artist so that she could discreetly question locals about the murder of Charles Walton and perhaps find her witch cult.[92] Contemporary and later sources have suggested that she consulted with Colonel Geoffrey White, the chief constable of Warwickshire, who allowed her to examine the case file of Walton's murder, though there is no explicit mention of Murray in the Metropolitan Police file.[93]

This was no private eccentricity. Murray was the author of the *Encyclopedia Britannica*'s authoritative entry on witchcraft, she was soon to be president of the Folklore Society, and she was openly sharing her investigations in the press. After she was interviewed by reporter Alan Dick of the *Daily Herald*, several newspaper articles quoted Murray regarding the case, though these were not picked up by the *Birmingham Post* or the *Birmingham Evening Post*.[94] Murray believed that Walton might have been murdered as part of an agricultural fertility ritual, and she later cited the importance of spilling blood on the earth in *The Divine King in England*.[95] She also suggested that the 14 February date of the murder was really the ritual date of 2 February (Imbolc in the pre-Christian calendar). The suspected similarity to the 1875 murder was mentioned in interviews with Murray, as was police interest in the witchcraft theory.[96] However, Murray also left open the possibility that the pitchfork could have been an Italian signature, suggesting that one of the Italian prisoners of war could have committed the murder.[97]

Murray's role in the case was revived by the tabloid *Reveille* on 1 June 1956 in a story that also included the Rollright Stones archaeological site, even illustrating them at the bottom of the article.[98] Scotland Yard chief inspector Robert Fabian had first connected the archaeological site to the case in a January 1950 news article, and he repeated the allegation in his 1953 memoir and subsequent writings. Fabian claimed that local police immediately raised the similarities to the 1875 "witch" murder.[99] "Fabian of the Yard" became a publishing and television celebrity who later spun tales of the witchcraft rumors surrounding the stones. Fabian's publicity campaign revived interest in the case and in supposed witchcraft. Yet Fabian's official reports mentioned nothing of the Rollright Stones, and they are twelve miles from the murder site. A circle of stones appeared in supposed testimony about the case by an anonymous cultist, published in the *News Chronicle* in 1956.[100]

Reveille was full of weird news, pinups, and humor. The Walton story was the second in a series of three articles on "grey magic." The overall tone of the series is panicked, with the first story suggesting that there was widespread involvement in sex, cults, and blackmail. The author of the three articles cited a rector, an unnamed police officer, and the founder of a metaphysical society who all claimed that hundreds of Satanists, including prominent businessmen and "high-ups," were conducting African voodoo-like rituals in the Midlands. The third story, "Underworld of Black Mass Maniacs," cited a former vicar's claims that there were covens brought by Celtic immigrants in cities across England.[101]

The public was afraid of and fascinated with witchcraft, and stories about it were not restricted to tabloids.[102] Margaret Murray was even called on to promote *Night of the Demon* (1957), the film adaptation of M. R. James's story "Casting the Runes." At a 1956 event promoting the upcoming film, the same year as the *Reveille* series on magical cults, the film's star, Dana Andrews, appeared with Murray and drunkenly gave the archaeologist a kiss on the cheek and the greeting "You old son of a witch."[103] The film incorporated Murray's and Gardner's theme of surviving ancient rural sects and modeled the sorcerous villain on Aleister Crowley. *Night of the Demon* begins with a serious narration about ancient black magic laid over film of Stonehenge. Archaeology was a common aspect in James's stories but not in "Casting the Runes." The opening with Stonehenge mirrors the incorporation of the Rollright Stones into the Walton murder.

Robert Fabian, the chief inspector in the Walton case, claimed in his popular writing that the Kensington, Paddington, and Bloomsbury areas of London were full of secret Satanic temples and that the gateway to this world was "two or three dusty little London bookshops that specialize in volumes on the occult, diabolism, alchemy." Victims of Satanic orgies were selected from "likely-looking students at lectures on spiritualism, necromancy, tribal rites."[104] I visited several occult bookshops in Bloomsbury while researching this book, and I attended a lecture on Egyptian magic at one of them. I may be in some peril.

Donald McCormick promoted, and perhaps exaggerated, the occult angle of the Walton case in *Murder by Witchcraft: A Study of the Lower Quinton and Hagley Wood Murders*. A number of McCormick's "facts" about Walton and his murder do not hold up.[105] McCormick claimed to have interviewed Murray (who was deceased by the time of publication) and reported her conclusion that Walton's murderer was a local who had come to fear Walton's reputation for witchcraft. McCormick called Murray "somewhat of a detective herself: she reveled in unravelling mysteries, whether they were archaeological or occult."[106] McCormick quoted Murray that "a number of unsolved crimes . . . that have been regarded as ordinary murders should have been treated as witchcraft crimes. This certainly applies to some forms of child murders, especially those with a sexual connotation."[107] Shades of the McMartin case. The web of hearsay grew when McCormick quoted an anonymous witch priestess of a coven in the area as also having met Murray. According to McCormick's witch priestess, Murray discovered that a suspect in the murder had checked *The Witch-Cult in Western Europe* out of the local library, had underlined a section on witches causing impotence, and had scribbled in the margin, "it happens today."[108] Without any names for the source or the library, it is impossible to determine if the high priestess existed, if she met Murray, if Murray examined a copy of her own book from a nearby library, if that copy was annotated, and if the annotation had anything to do with the murder. But it makes for a great urban legend.

McCormick tied the Walton murder, and Murray's interest in it, to another murder in the Birmingham area. I have not been able to find any evidence predating McCormick's book that ties Murray to this second case. In 1943 the bones and clothing of a woman were found inside of a wych elm tree in Hagley Wood. Graffiti soon began appearing locally asking variations on the question "Who put Bella in the wych elm?" According to McCormick, Murray believed that the finding of "Bella's" scattered finger bones may have been evidence of a "hand of glory," a magical artifact created from the hand of a convicted criminal. The name Bella was found to be a "witch name" in Murray's decades-old analysis of witch-trial records, and Murray allegedly associated the location of the graffiti with a nearby haunted golf course.[109] It is possible that McCormick was simply using Murray's published material after her death, but the focus on "witch names" is definitely a feature of Murray's work.

Whether or not Murray investigated the Hagley Wood case, she did investigate the Walton murder. Here is the archaeologist not only playing detective but uncovering deep hidden truths that led to ritual cult murder. Even McCormick, selling a book on occult murder, reported that the people of Lower Quinton did not see witchcraft in the murder of Charles Walton and did not enjoy Murray's statements to the press.[110] Between the press interviews, the alleged consultation with police investigators, and McCormick's possibly exaggerated recounting, Murray had transformed from an archaeologist to an occult investigator of lurid mysteries akin to pulp fiction. Unbeknown to her, Murray had already inspired an occult pulp fiction that would dramatically transform modern engagement with the human past.

Cthulhu and Cosmic Mythology

EVERY SINGLE ONE of my students recognizes the Internet meme of Giorgio Tsoukalos, the host of the History Channel's *Ancient Aliens*, with the word ALIENS under his outrageous hair and between his outstretched hands. It's a good icebreaker at the beginning of any introductory course to anthropology. *Because all of my students know who he is and what he's teaching.*

How did we come to a place where the most recognizable explanation for the human past is space aliens? My students are in for a shock when they learn that we can directly trace the concept of ancient extraterrestrials back to fiction, and that fiction mirrored the practices and products of early twentieth-century archaeology. Different strands of archaeology combined to produce new religions and a new form of archaeological science fiction. This new science fiction mythology reentered the "real world" as the ancient extraterrestrial "theory" or myth, shaping some of the most popular pseudoscientific and conspiracy theory ideas of our age.

The Archaeology and Pseudoarchaeology of Cthulhu

Howard Phillips Lovecraft's short story "The Call of Cthulhu (Found among the Papers of the Late Francis Wayland Thurston, of Boston)" is the testimony of the dead anthropologist Francis Wayland Thurston, who worked from the notes of a dead archaeologist (George Gammell Angell, a professor emeritus of Semitic languages at Brown University).[1] The story has three sections, each with an archaeological component. In the first part, "The Horror in Clay," an artist consults the archaeologist Angell to understand some strange dreams that drove the artist to sculpt an ancient-looking bas-relief inscribed with undecipherable writing. The archaeologist collects press clippings of others who suffered from similar dreams from 28 February to 2 April 1925.

In the second part, "The Tale of Inspector Legrasse," we discover that the same archaeologist, Angell, had previously encountered the details of these dreams when Inspector Legrasse of the New Orleans police traveled to a meeting of the American Archaeological Society.[2] His men had seized a statuette from a murderous cult in the Louisiana swamps, and he had needed help identifying the artifact. A cult member claimed that the figure represented extradimensional aliens who colonized earth eons ago and inspired a religion among the first humans, one that persists as a secret global cult centered at the archaeological ruins of the legendary city of Irem of the Pillars in Arabia. Another archaeologist (William Channing Webb, a professor of anthropology at Princeton University) recognizes this religion from his archaeological exploration of Greenland.

The events in the third section, "The Madness from the Sea," spring from a chance discovery of a newspaper in a museum, which leads to another image (safeguarded in an Australian museum) of the ancient extraterrestrial Cthulhu and ultimately to its tomb in an ancient ruined city risen from the sea floor. This last act of "The Call of Cthulhu" resembles Lovecraft's earlier "Dagon," in which a traveler escapes from a German U-boat attack only to end up driven mad on a recently risen island, where he discovers archaeological bas-reliefs of monstrous fishmen and evidence that the images may be carved from life. An unnamed anthropologist in "Dagon" dismisses comparisons to Dagon, a Philistine fertility god (erroneously) believed to have a fishman appearance. The narrator is fatally sure that these creatures will soon rise and destroy humanity.[3]

The first two acts of "The Call of Cthulhu" are primarily about the people and places of archaeology, do not resemble earlier Lovecraft works, and set the standard for most of Lovecraft's "Cthulhu mythos." Lovecraft himself did not refer to these tales by that name, nor were they planned as a whole. Beginning with "The Call of Cthulhu," Lovecraft began linking names, places, characters, and concepts in his own short stories, dropped references to the works of authors he admired into his writing, and encouraged his friends to borrow his creations. The collaborative nature of his

"Yog-Sothothery" captured the imagination of readers and authors alike, dramatically influenced other popular works of fantasy and horror, and created a devoted fan community that continues to create Cthulhu mythos fiction and art. The Lovecraft circle's collaborative approach has more broadly inspired similar activities, such as fantasy role-playing games and folkloric collaborative fiction, such as the infamous "creepypasta" character Slenderman.

To be considered part of the Cthulhu mythos, a story typically contains two basic criteria.[4] The first is the use of one of the creations (or a recognizable parody or pastiche of same) introduced by Lovecraft or his followers, such as the fictional grimoire *Necronomicon*, the imagined New England town Arkham and its Miskatonic University, or his aliens/gods, such as Cthulhu and Yog-Sothoth. The second criterion, vital to Lovecraft's impact on popular archaeology, is that the story should at least somewhat engage with Lovecraft's ideals of "cosmic horror," in which horror is rooted in the implications of scientific discovery. Spatial and temporal scale is particularly important in Lovecraft stories, with vast gulfs of space and time being more horrifying than a gruesome monster or grisly murder. Lovecraft's lifelong love of astronomy informed his spatial terror, and his work injected the extraterrestrial into the previously supernatural horror genre. Time inspired even more fascination and dread for Lovecraft and his followers, and he most commonly expressed this through the imagery and concepts of archaeology. Lovecraft first fused all these aspects together in "The Call of Cthulhu."

The Prehistory of Cthulhu

Lovecraft's earlier writing, like "Dagon" (1917), resembles the weird discovery tales of William Hope Hodgson and the stories of suffocating doom by Edgar Allan Poe. Lovecraft found his voice with "The Call of Cthulhu" (1926) through an investigatory and mystery angle that he subsequently explored through archaeological sites, artifacts, and anthropological and folklorist academic protagonists.[5] In "Dagon," an anthropologist is mentioned in only one sentence because he is too "hopelessly conventional" to believe the narrator's tale. "The Call of Cthulhu" consists of the posthumous research notes of three generations of anthropologists and archaeologists piecing together the global clues, like detectives, about Cthulhu and its cult. Their quest begins at an archaeological conference, and they visit or allude to numerous locations of academic archaeology, including several universities and museums, before the climax in an ancient ruined city.

A key element of the first act of "Cthulhu" appeared to Lovecraft in a dream in 1920 that featured a ruined city thrust up from the ocean, an image he had already created in "Dagon" and one found in several later Lovecraft stories.[6] In the same dream, Lovecraft shaped a clay bas-relief depicting Egyptian priests, inspired by a world of dreams older than "brooding Egypt or the contemplative Sphinx or garden-girdled Babylon."[7] In the story, the artist's skill and uncanny link to the past shock a skeptical museum curator. The nucleus of the second act of "Cthulhu" first appeared in Lovecraft's commonplace book, a journal of ideas, many used in later published stories.[8] A 1923 note reads, "Antediluvian-cyclopean ruins on lonely Pacific island. Centre of earthwide subterranean witch cult." The first sentence is the recurring Lovecraftian island of ancient "cyclopean" ruins in the Pacific. The term derives from Mycenaean archaeology, but Lovecraft used it numerous times to refer to ancient, large, rough-hewn stone architecture. The second sentence alludes to archaeologist Margaret Murray's powerful influence over Lovecraft, his mythos, and broader perceptions of the mythic past.

Lovecraft and the Witch Cult

Margaret Murray's *The Witch-Cult in Western Europe* is named in "The Call of Cthulhu" and clearly influenced Lovecraft's fiction, his understanding of prehistory, and virtually every story that follows in the Cthulhu mythos. Murray's basic conceit, that occult beliefs are a euhemerized memory of prehistory, fascinated Lovecraft.[9] Lovecraft combined this notion with his interests in science and astronomy to form the foundation of his Cthulhu mythos and, inadvertently, the later pseudoarchaeological belief in ancient extraterrestrials.

Lovecraft was primarily self-educated and read and wrote extensively on topics that fascinated him, such as classical studies and astronomy.[10] Classical studies in particular inspired a number of his early Dreamlands stories, such as the classical Greek weird tale "Hypnos" and "The Cats of Ulthar," which is heavily based on the Roman historian Diodorus's personal experience with the execution of a Roman soldier who had killed a cat in Egypt.[11] This autodidactism led Lovecraft to selectively adopt anthropological ideas about prehistory or race that fit his personal tastes and biases. Murray's witch cult fit perfectly into Lovecraft's taste for the weird, hidden, and mysterious and may have matched his class biases.[12] He likely read *The Witch-Cult in Western Europe* in 1923 before writing "The Festival" in October. The story reveals a hidden ancestral sect of "pre-Aryan" sorcerers or witches who congregate in the fictional town of Kingsport, Massachusetts, on the winter solstice.[13] The nucleus of this tale is found in a 1923 commonplace book entry: "Hideous secret society—widespread—horrible rites in caverns under familiar scenes—one's own neighbour may belong."[14]

In the 1930s Lovecraft wrote of the witch cult to the pulp author Robert E. Howard, creator of Conan the Barbarian. Lovecraft tied the cult to "The Festival" and described it as "fact, now widely emphasized by anthropologists." By examining trial records, these "scholars now recognise [sic] that all through history a secret cult of degenerate orgiastic nature-worshippers, furtively recruited from the peasantry and sometimes from decadent characters of more select origin, has existed throughout northwestern Europe" as well as in New England during the Salem witch panic.[15] Lovecraft took pagan survivals as fact, such as his citation of Sir Rennell Rodd's folkloric work on pagan survivals in Greece.[16] The infamously racist Lovecraft saw the witch cult through the prism of a race-based prehistory that incorporated the Piltdown man hoax and notions of an Aryan Eurasian "dawn man" championed by Sir Arthur Keith, the president of the Royal Anthropological Institute.[17] Lovecraft built on Murray's inclusion of fairy races in the witch cult, seeing it as the religion of prehistoric "squat Mongoloids."[18] Lovecraft pulled all of these ideas from respected contemporary anthropologists.

Once Lovecraft read *The Witch-Cult in Western Europe*, his tales prominently featured anthropological or archaeological evidence of an ancient hidden religion, especially practiced by racial others. A few months prior to the likely period when he read Murray, Lovecraft included archaeological evidence of a localized British pagan cult, investigated with the help of an archaeologist and an anthropologist as minor characters, in the Poe-like "The Rats in the Walls."[19] Some of these tropes parallel those of Arthur Machen, himself inspired by MacRitchie's fairy race. Lovecraft had recently discovered Machen and would write several Machen-like stories, but Murray's influence on "The Festival" is unmistakable, and ancient non-Aryan cults increasingly appeared in his tales. The antagonist of "The Horror at Red Hook" is a debased but sympathetic anthropologist ensnared in ancient pagan and Satanic rituals practiced in the hidden warrens of an immigrant community.[20] "Red Hook" targets Yezidis, a Kurdish minority who are widely and incorrectly labeled as Satanists, a belief Lovecraft got from the Asian peril fiction of Robert Chambers.[21] These beliefs have inspired attempted genocide in the twenty-first century by the Islamic State. Some accounts of Kurdish origins hold that they are the offspring of jinn and European women abducted for King Solomon's harem.[22]

The Archaeologists and the Cthulhu Cult

In "The Call of Cthulhu" Lovecraft for the first time featured archaeologist protagonists and archaeological museums, conferences, and ruins as primary settings. Previous Lovecraft protagonists were more like the neurotics of Poe or the unlucky travelers of William Hope Hodgson, but after "Cthulhu" the academic protagonist became a Lovecraftian cliché.[23] Even the geological and mathematical faculty and students of Lovecraft's fictional Miskatonic University are well versed in anthropology, history, and folklore à la Murray and her inspiration, Sir J. G. Frazer, who is also referenced in Lovecraft's tales.

The archaeologist makes an excellent detective protagonist, and archaeological trappings effectively communicate deep cosmic time. The Old Ones were billions of years old, but Lovecraft signified their antiquity with exotic cities explicitly compared to Machu Picchu or Nan Madol (both medieval in age) and with alien jewelry and statuettes likely to end up in museums. In depicting incredibly ancient time and utterly alien civilizations with the trappings of human societies of the last five thousand years, Lovecraft was collapsing protohistory and antiquity. He simultaneously communicated age and kept his fictional creations on a recognizable human level, materializing myth across the expanse of deep geological time. Tim Murray argued that the first theoretical framework of scientific anthropology and archaeology—the evolution from simpler societies similar to small-scale societies of the present—served much the same purpose. Ethnographic models provided a comprehensible human past when archaeological methods could not (and perhaps still cannot) intelligibly represent human origins in deep time. Much of Lovecraft's fiction was inspired by the abyss of deep time that science revealed in the nineteenth century, and archaeology was one of the main symbolic and scientific fields that confronted this abyss. Victorian conceptions of this abyss, including the sweep of human existence and fears of degeneration, are common Lovecraftian themes.[24]

Lovecraft used the witch cult as cutting-edge anthropology and archaeology in the same way he fictionalized contemporary science, such as the physics of relativity, tectonic plate theory, Antarctic exploration, and the discovery of Pluto. The notes in "The Call of Cthulhu" explicitly state that the witch cult is distinct from the Cthulhu cult, but as I already mentioned one of the commonplace book entries centers the witch cult on a Cthulhuesque Pacific island. This entry is between two others about voodoo and possession that show clear similarities to the possession-like dream state and swamp rituals in "Cthulhu." The importance of dreams in this story is echoed by Margaret Murray's discussion of dream visions being a key to not only the witch cult, but all religions.[25]

When Lovecraft wrote "Cthulhu," he expanded the southern voodoo of his 1923 commonplace book entry into a secret, global, and ancient non-Aryan cult—like Murray's witch cult. In "Cthulhu" archaeologists and anthropologists discover the cult through broad cultural comparisons and through seeing hidden history where others see myth and superstition—like Murray. Virtually every subsequent mythos story by Lovecraft presents science fiction, such as an ancient extraterrestrial civilization or the warping of space-time, through a scholarly protagonist and his discovery that myth and folklore euhemeristically preserve historical reality ignored by conventional wisdom but kept alive by a secret cult of eccentrics or degenerates. *The Witch-Cult in Western Europe* is explicitly mentioned in "The Horror at Red Hook," "The Call of Cthulhu," and "The Whisperer in Darkness."[26]

The swamp cult ritual in "The Call of Cthulhu" strongly resembles the sacrificial rituals of Murray's witches, who kidnapped and sacrificed children. Celebrants joyously (a descriptor provided by Murray and used twice in "The Call of Cthulhu" to describe the cult) dance in a ring around a bonfire, pretending to be animals in a ritual dating back to the origins of human religious practice in the Paleolithic. The object of worship inside of the ring was either an imitator of the god/devil, an inanimate image of the same, or a standing stone.[27] The Cthulhu cult's Halloween bonfire rites in the Louisiana bayou are indistinguishable from Murray's witch cult celebrants except for the image of Cthulhu atop a standing stone rather than the horned or black man.

The Witch-Cult in Western Europe seems to have significantly inspired "The Dreams in the Witch House," Lovecraft's story most directly based on witch lore and the Salem trials.[28] Specific details include a ritual site marked by standing stones, the importance of infanticide, the use of secret witch names such as Naip in Murray and Nahab in Lovecraft, and witches' familiars that suckle and drink blood from their masters.[29] The religion of the dark, squat, ancient non-Indo-European Basques appeared in detail in Lovecraft's dreams on Halloween 1927, in which Roman soldiers met their doom at the hands of a Basque cult, leaving relics that were discovered by modern archaeologists in Spain.[30]

A 1925 note in Lovecraft's commonplace book ties the witch cult to Native American prehistory with "rumours of witches' sabbaths and Indian powwows on a broad mound rising out of the level where some old hemlocks and beeches formed a dark grove or daemon-temple."[31] Lovecraft placed ancient pre-indigenous hilltop megalithic ruins in western Massachusetts in "The Dunwich Horror" and a secret megalithic chamber somewhere in New England in "The Thing on the Doorstep."[32] The mix of Puritan, indigenous, and demonic evildoings in "The Dunwich Horror" may have influenced the backstory assembled for the supposedly real *Amityville Horror*, including claims of an indigenous burial ground and a space for the insane. There are some strikingly Lovecraftian overtones in the tale.[33]

Darryl Caterine lays much of the cursed Indian burial ground myth at Lovecraft's feet because of stories such as "He."[34] Lovecraft spent several unhappy years in New York City during a brief and unsuccessful marriage, and this tale records his hatred for New York and its diverse population. In

"He," an antiquarian (a proxy for Lovecraft) meets a mysterious man in Greenwich Village who magically shows him the horrible secrets of past and future New York. The display ends when a protoplasmic mass with stereotypical Native American tropes, such as a tomahawk, appears and murders the sorcerer in revenge for his poisoning a tribe to steal their land and their secret to immortality. "He" bridges two distinct versions of the Indian curse, the generalized Indian curse and the cursed Indian burial ground. The destruction of the treacherous sorcerer strongly resembles the nineteenth-century literary and folkloric trope of the broader Indian curse against immoral white men.[35] However, Lovecraft specifies the address of the horror as 93 Perry Street, located in a section of New York that in Lovecraft's time was considered to have been particularly settled by indigenous people in the past, something Lovecraft likely knew,[36] presaging the localized cursed Indian burial ground. Lovecraft also hinted at the idea of a sacred or cursed ground that must not be built upon in his commonplace book, though as seen in the story "The Shunned House" this need not refer to an indigenous curse.[37]

With the exception of "He," Lovecraft's use of indigenous North Americans in his stories is minimal and feels like a relocation of the anthropological folklore of Celtic Britain, as expressed in the horror fiction of Arthur Machen. Invented native Penacook lore provides a deeper history to the horrors in "The Whisperer in Darkness," but this tale is Lovecraft's version of Machen's "The Novel of the Black Seal." Lovecraft set "Whisperer" in Vermont, where he had recently visited, explicitly used an approach similar to that of Charles Fort, and showcased his beloved astronomy. Native "conclaves" are rumored to have occurred among the megalithic ruins of New England in "The Dunwich Horror" (a clear pastiche of Machen's *The Great God Pan*), but the presence of European-like skulls and other evidence suggests a deeper hidden history to these ruins. Even in "He," part of the secret to immortality was borrowed by the indigenous New Yorkers from an old Dutch colonist. Early European colonists, especially the Puritans, were a more potent source of horror and wonder for Lovecraft, who marveled, "Can you imagine anything more magnificent than the wholesale slaughter of Indians—a very epick [*sic*]—by our New-England ancestors in the name of the lamb?"[38] On the other hand, in an unpublished fragment intended to be a quote from the fictional colonial book of wonders *Thaumaturgical Prodigies in the New-English Canaan*, Lovecraft spins a tale of standing stones erected by Wampanoag wise men to contain an evil demon called up by a white settler.[39] He also appreciated news of archaeological discoveries in North America and suggested that someone could put indigenous folklore to use in creating weird fiction.[40]

Lovecraft instead preferred hyperdiffusionist ideas, suggesting that Phoenicians may have visited and intermingled with Native Americans in classical times and that the idea of non-indigenous "stocks" in prehistoric America "is an open question."[41] In his youth, Lovecraft wrote unpublished stories of Romans colonizing Providence and the modern discovery of their ruins.[42] He was very taken with the Newport "tower," to which I return below, due to the idea of it predating indigenous Americans, and he wrote notes on it that were incorporated into a "posthumous collaboration" with publisher August Derleth.[43] Lovecraft was familiar with Dighton Rock, Massachusetts, and its alleged engraved text, a favorite of hyperdiffusionists, but apparently not so familiar with it that he could spell its name right, calling it Brighton Rock. He found the "text" to be "uncertain," and he was also uncertain about the Kensington Runestone in Minnesota.[44] He noted news stories about southwestern hidden cities, including a Roman artifact hoax in Arizona.[45]

The tales Lovecraft ghostwrote for Zealia Bishop, "The Curse of Yig" and "The Mound," underline Lovecraft's general disinterest in indigenous North America.[46] In "The Curse of Yig," a pair of Euro-American settlers run afoul of the native snake god Yig and look for guidance to Native American specialists, but Lovecraft's conception of this deity was more influenced by what little he knew of the importance of snakes in Mesoamerican culture, particularly the myth of Quetzalcoatl.[47] Zealia Bishop wanted "The Mound" to elaborate on local Oklahoma legends of a headless ghost, sometimes of a woman, on top of a mound, but Lovecraft thought a story about a native ghost would be boring.[48] He delivered an elaborate lost world tale (like *The Coming Race*) of a preindigenous race that lived below North America, had become decadent and depraved, and used psychic powers to torment interlopers. Lovecraft had created a science fiction horror version of the moundbuilder myth. Rather than populate the dark prehistory of North America with native ghosts, Lovecraft expressed the still popular notion that Native Americans were relatively recent arrivals from Asia, and in his fiction suggested that an eldritch race akin to or even connected with Murray's, Machen's, and MacRitchie's witch cult pygmy race was the reality hidden below America.

Howard Carter and Cthulhu's Curse

Was Murray's *The Witch-Cult in Western Europe* the sole source for Lovecraft's occult archaeologists and ruins? The first Lovecraft tales showing Murray's influence were only halting steps in her direction. The timeline of the creation of "The Call of Cthulhu" is important. "Dagon" in 1917 and a 1920 dream both contain elements of the story. The impact of Murray's *Witch-Cult* appears in "Cthulhu" plot seeds in Lovecraft's commonplace book in 1923. The story itself is mostly set from 28 February to early April 1925 based on Lovecraft's use of current events, such as a real-world earthquake and a massive police crackdown in New York.[49] Lovecraft plotted out the story's basics in mid-August 1925 and completed it in August 1926.[50]

Lovecraft personally felt that earthquake, but he also sought inspiration in press clippings, which he called his "weird data" or "weird files" "on weird topics—reports of monsters, lost races, excavated cities of antiquity, sunken islands, etc.—for possible future use in fiction."[51] "The Call of Cthulhu" is composed of such notes and newspaper clippings, with the final part of the story triggered by a random piece of newspaper. Lovecraft had read *Dracula*, the first half of which depends on the collation by Mina Harker of the notes of the other characters; it is an immersive narrative punctuated with newspaper stories of strange events. Even more relevant to "Cthulhu" is Arthur Machen's use of a similar technique in "The Novel of the Black Seal" and "The Great Return."

"The Call of Cthulhu" marks Lovecraft's first and most thorough use of this document-driven technique of journals and notes, specific dates, and a heavy emphasis on fictional newspaper tales, though such devices would continue throughout Lovecraft's fiction, especially in his mythos stories. Another likely influence was the weird "nonfiction" of Charles Fort, the inventor of the modern paranormal or conspiracy theory style. Fort spent his days in libraries combing newspapers and scientific journals for strange events, such as sea monster sightings, animals appearing where they should not (Fort invented the word "teleport"), and bizarre meteorological events, including falls of frogs, fish, meat, or jelly from the sky. Fort wanted to demonstrate that the scientific establishment ignored inconvenient information, hence the title of his *Book of the Damned* (1919). At the most charitable, Fort was an early critic of positivist science, presaging Thomas Kuhn's suggestion that anomalous data demonstrate the weaknesses of accepted scientific paradigms. Less charitably, Fort collated absurdist nonsense. It is impossible to separate the fictional from the factual in Fort's work. He suggested that our reality is the fantasy of a consciousness outside of our experience.[52] Fort's attack on scientific authority and his love for anomalous animals and strange events in the sky were tremendous influences on the paranormal style that would emerge in the 1950s, which simultaneously claimed to be a truer form of science (despite its obvious ties to older forms of mysticism) than institutional science and authority. Fort's most famous quote, from *The Book of the Damned*, "I think we're property," forms the core ethos of both Lovecraft's mythos and subsequent UFO lore.[53] Its resemblance to religious cosmology, particularly the gnosticism that inspires much of occultism and the paranormal, is difficult to ignore. Fort thought religion to be false and possibly a tool for the suprahuman forces that "own" us.[54]

Lovecraft read *The Book of the Damned* around the time he discovered Murray's *Witch-Cult* and the stories of Arthur Machen. He read Fort's second book, *New Lands* (1923), by October 1927, noting Fort's method of weaving paranormal stories out of odd news accounts.[55] Lovecraft mentions Fort along with *The Witch-Cult in Western Europe* in "The Whisperer in Darkness," a story with numerous similarities to "The Novel of the Black Seal," Machen's most extensive exploration of the fairy race idea. "Whisperer" was a possible influence on the development of UFO lore, particularly the tales of alien abduction and the men in black. These parts of UFO legends in particular have often been compared to fairy lore, just in case you weren't already confused.

Lovecraft had a Sunday subscription to the *New York Times*, advertised in the *Times* to seek employment, and was inspired by a *Times* editorial to travel to Elizabeth, New Jersey, in search of colonial antiquities.[56] He seems to have directly incorporated a *Times* piece into at least one of his stories. The ethnologist narrator of his ghostwritten "The Mound" cites the work

Archaeologists

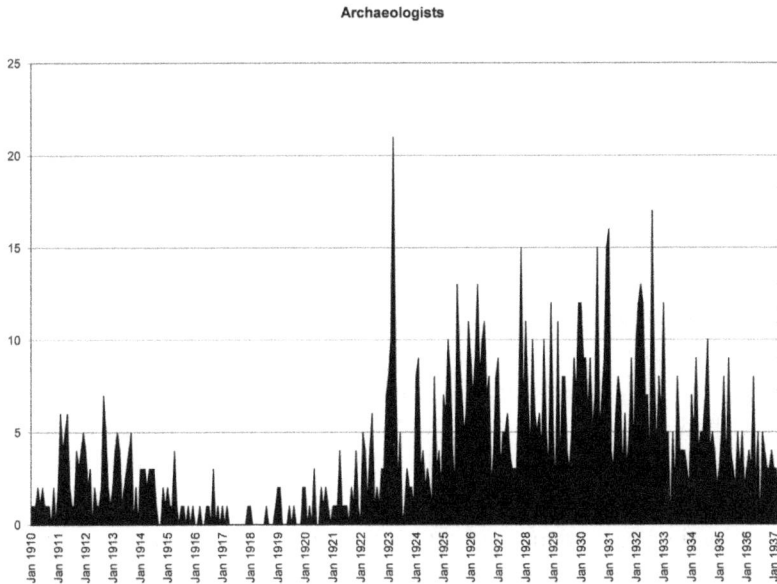

FIGURE 10.1. The number of stories mentioning the word "archaeologist[s]" in the *New York Times* (excluding obituaries and society pages) from January 1910 until Lovecraft's death in March 1937. Image by author.

of anthropologist Frederick Webb Hodge in tracing the explorer Francisco de Coronado's route. This had been reported in September 1929, several months before Lovecraft wrote "The Mound."[57] In 1935, well after he had left New York, Lovecraft transcribed a *Times* article about a mysterious island so that he could use it in a later tale.[58]

What news clippings might Lovecraft have saved from 1923 to August 1926, the creative period that produced "The Call of Cthulhu"? That Lovecraft would adopt the trope of the archaeologist in exotic and supernatural danger is unsurprising in the context of the tremendous interest in archaeology and archaeologists after the discovery of Tutankhamun's tomb and its "curse" in late 1922. The quarter century prior to Tutankhamun has been called a heroic age of discovery in archaeology,[59] but it was not until Tutankhamun that emphasis was placed more on the archaeologists than the discoveries they made. Figure 10.1 depicts the frequency of stories (sans obituaries and society pages) about archaeologists in the *New York Times* during Lovecraft's adult life (1910–1937). After the obvious Tutankhamun spike from December 1922 to April 1923, stories about archaeologists became generally more common, only declining in the late 1930s to levels like those before the First World War. This period dominates media depictions of archaeologists (*Indiana Jones, The Mummy, Stargate*), and Howard Carter is still one of the most famous of all archaeologists.

As discussed previously, frustrated reporters, rival archaeologists, and opportunistic occultists collaborated to create King Tut's curse after Lord Carnarvon, the financial backer of the Tutankhamun excavations, died on 5 April 1923. As I explained in chapter 4, novelist Marie Corelli had warned of the curse before Carnarvon's death with the help of what she described as a medieval Arab book of occult knowledge about the past, later translated by an early modern advisor to European royalty. This is very similar to Lovecraft's fictional history of the *Necronomicon* as translated by the Elizabethan royal astrologer John Dee through a Latin version derived from the medieval Arabic *Al Azif*.[60] The Tut concoction of superstitious natives, poisonous objects (most early speculation about the Tut curse blamed poisons or other physical agents), the vengeance of a slumbering undead god/king in his tomb, and an old mysterious book are all found in the pages of "Cthulhu." It is worth noting that Algernon Blackwood, a member of the Theosophical Society and the Order of the Golden Dawn, wrote a piece in the *Daily Express* at the height of the Tut curse media frenzy that credited the reality of curses, but he suspected that no magic could be powerful enough to reach across the centuries.[61] Blackwood was one of Lovecraft's favorite authors, and "The Call of Cthulhu" opens with an epigraph by Blackwood about prehistoric survivals and myth.

There is no evidence that Lovecraft attended Howard Carter's lectures in New York, but, after Lovecraft's first visit in 1922, Lovecraft repeatedly visited the mummies at "Tut-ankha-men's tomb" (as his ex-wife phrased it) in the Metropolitan Museum of Art despite an allergic reaction to the spices used to embalm the mummies.[62] Lovecraft alluded to Tutankhamun in the 1926 tale "Cool Air" in which a doctor uses Egyptian secrets to cheat death.[63] Magician Harry Houdini hired Lovecraft to ghostwrite "Under the Pyramids," a pulp adventure piece exploiting the Tut craze by purporting to recount Houdini's brush with an ancient Egyptian cult and dark magic. Lovecraft likely did a significant amount of his Egyptian research using a

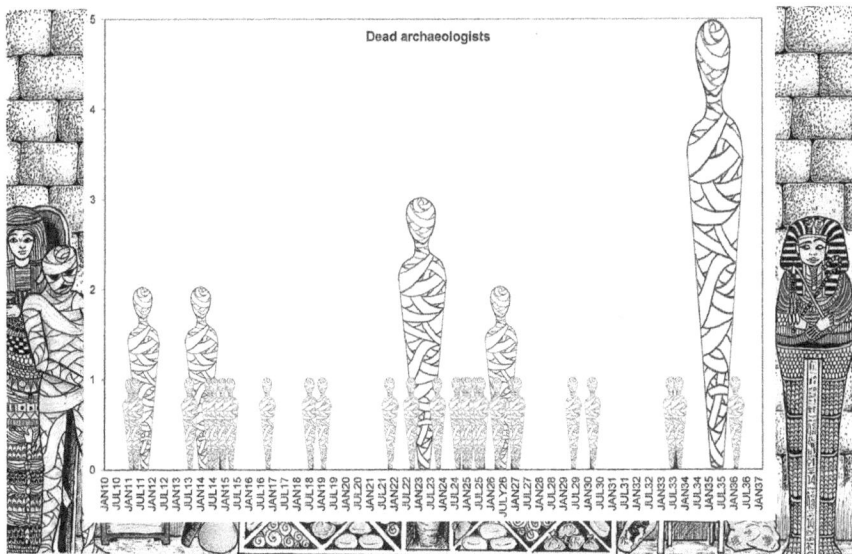

FIGURE 10.2. The number of stories mentioning the word "archaeologist[s]" in the *New York Times* (excluding obituaries and society pages) that are about an archaeologist near death or dying, from January 1910 to March 1937. Image by Emily Ratvasky.

1916 volume, *The Tomb of Perneb*, which was published to accompany the installation of the tomb at the Metropolitan Museum.[64]

The Curse of Cthulhu

The golden treasures of Tutankhamun, the curse, Carnarvon's death, and the squabbling between Carter and the Egyptian government all made archaeologists an intriguing media subject (figure 10.1), especially if they were dying or in mortal danger (figure 10.2). News stories of dead archaeologists are of particular interest since "The Call of Cthulhu" consists of the notes of archaeologists who died under mysterious circumstances after meddling in the affairs of an entombed undead god/alien. Such news stories excited Lovecraft, including the suicide of Lord Westbury, which Lovecraft called in 1930 "as good as any weird fictional plot yet written." Lovecraft noted that Westbury's father worked on Tutankhamun's tomb and that his home was "full of strange Egyptian objects." Lovecraft emphasized that the suicide note—"I really cannot stand any more hor-rors"—was "no product of imagination, but a literal bit of fact from the day's news!"[65] Lord Westbury's suicide has been incorporated into an ever-growing occult ideology of secret societies, magical rituals, Jack the Ripper, and Aleister Crowley.[66]

The increase in news accounts about dead or endangered archaeologists after Carnarvon's death coincided with Lovecraft's writing of "Cthulhu." In 1923, the only *New York Times* article about a dead archaeologist was about Carnarvon. In 1924, the *Times* reported on the possibly scandal-related suicide of the British archaeologist H. G. Evelyn-White and on the expedi-tionary plans of archaeologist Adolph Bandelier's widow to search for Inkan cities, both suggestive of mystery and exploration.[67]

However, in 1925, the year in which "Cthulhu" was conceived, dead archaeologist stories abounded, especially during the early part of the year when "Cthulhu" is set. On 1 February, the *Times* ran an obituary for the Egyptologist and Greek vase expert Joseph C. Hoppin, a Providence native.[68] Lovecraft was living in New York in 1925, a city he hated because of his racist attitudes regarding immigrants. He idolized Providence, later declaring in his epitaph, "I am Providence." News of Hoppin's death was buried on page E7, but the Providence connection may have caught Lovecraft's eye. Hoppin died in Boston, like Thurston does in "Cthulhu."

The following day the death of David B. Spooner in India was a more prominent news story. His widow was an expert in languages (like Angell in "Cthulhu") and religion (like Thurston in "Cthulhu"), and Spooner had achieved fame the previous year by allegedly discovering the bones of the Buddha.[69] Such a find echoes the discovery in "Cthulhu" of an ancient priest/deity. Equating Buddha and Cthulhu was in the atheistic Lovecraft's character since he later burlesqued the crucifixion of Christ in "The Dunwich Horror," in which the offspring of a virgin mortal woman and a god cries out for his divine father to help him as three men kill him on a hilltop. One day after news of Spooner's death, another article described the death of the Boston Egyptologist William Copley Winslow.[70] This string of archaeologist deaths was followed, during the time period in which "The Call of Cthulhu" is set, by the 19 March 1925 death of H. V. Hilprecht. The *Times* ran a major news story about Hilprecht, the translator of the Nippur tablets, which include a 4,000-year-old account of the deluge.[71] The first act of "Cthulhu" involves a well-known expert in epigraphy being consulted about an inscribed clay tablet, created in dreams older than Tyre and Babylon and depicting an ancient epic of a city that sank beneath the waves.

Perhaps it is coincidence that the death of the Minoan archaeologist Richard Seager during a voyage between Crete and Egypt, reported on 14 May 1925, foreshadowed the sea voyage death of the anthropologist Robert Suydam in "The Horror at Red Hook," a story Lovecraft wrote less than three months later on 1–2 August 1925.[72] Lovecraft was fascinated by classical Mediterranean myths (sections of "Cthulhu" allude to *The Odyssey*) and considered the discovery of the historically unattested Minoans and similar scientific finds as one reason to not commit suicide during a low period in his teenage years.[73]

Less prominent stories or obituaries on the deaths of three other archaeologists appeared in the *Times* that summer before Lovecraft started plotting out "Cthulhu."[74] No other such stories appeared for the rest of 1925 or early 1926, until a piece on 11 April was triggered by the death of Professor Georges Aaron Bénédite, the director of the Egyptian section of the Louvre, an alleged victim of the Tut curse.[75] The last major story of a dying archaeologist during this period was that of Gertrude Bell in July 1926, a few weeks before Lovecraft completed "Cthulhu." As a major player in both the archaeology and the politics of the Middle East, Bell's death was major news; there was even a substantial illustrated article in the Sunday *Times*.[76]

"The Sunken-Land Thing": Lovecraft and Atlantis

Shortly after "The Call of Cthulhu" was completed, Lovecraft referred to it as "the sunken-land thing," even though he had already visited the topic in "Dagon" and "The Temple" (1920), in which a U-boat crew encounters Atlantis.[77] He kept news clippings of sunken islands and in November 1925 specifically compared the in-progress "The Call of Cthulhu" to a sunken city discovered in October in the Caspian Sea.[78] Sunken continents no longer had mainstream archaeological cachet but could be found on the edges of the discipline and in the writings of the theosophists from whom Lovecraft was borrowing. During the time frame in which Lovecraft wrote "The Call of Cthulhu," he read the basics of theosophy and sunken continents in *The Story of Atlantis and the Lost Lemuria* (1925) by W. Scott Elliot, and found it to be "something of vast interest as background or source material."[79]

The notion of a sunken continent in the Pacific continued to appear in Lovecraft's work and personal correspondence. Churchward's Mu appears in "Out of the Aeons," a story Lovecraft ghostwrote in 1933.[80] Lovecraft did not read Churchward but cited him, Mu, and Naacal apparently based on reading book reviews. In "Out of the Aeons," a mummy and an ancient text have been thrust up from the Pacific Ocean floor and are determined by Dr. Richard H. Johnson, the curator of the fictional Cabot Museum of Archaeology in Boston, Massachusetts, to derive from Mu, an ancient land inhabited at times by fungal aliens, at other times by depraved humans worshipping inhuman god-things. This story is one of several in Lovecraft's theosophical cycle of ghostwritten or cowritten stories. Lovecraft first used theosophical material in "Through the Gates of the Silver Key," cowritten with E. Hoffmann Price. Price and Lovecraft met in New Orleans in 1933, and during a marathon conversation Lovecraft got his first serious introduction to theosophy.[81]

Lovecraft was skeptical of sunken continents in the Atlantic but found the idea plausible for the Pacific, and in one letter he suggested sympathy for the idea that much more land was above water in the past (i.e., a sunken continent like Lemuria or Mu).[82] In his letters about archaeology Lovecraft was very taken with the idea that there might have been a transpacific civilization and was convinced of hyperdiffusion across the Pacific, including the likelihood of a connection between Indus writing and the *rongorongo* of Easter Island.[83] The hyperdiffusion theory could be found in popular accounts by archaeologists, such as Stanley Casson's *Progress of Archaeology*, a book recommended by Lovecraft.[84]

Media stories related to archaeological sunken lands, like stories of dead archaeologists, also spiked during the "Cthulhu" time frame (figure 10.3). Several of these stories were commissioned by the *New York Times* from "Count" Byron Khun de Prorok, who provided the *Times* with years of exclusive accounts of derring-do and astounding discoveries. Khun de Prorok, an American who claimed a Polish noble title, exemplifies the sensational quasi-archaeological explorers who freely mixed actual discoveries and occult-tinged flights of fancy. He appeared in several public shows in

FIGURE 10.3. The number of stories mentioning the word "archaeologist[s]" in the *New York Times* (excluding obituaries and society pages) that are about a sunken land (e.g., Atlantis), a site found underwater, or related topics from January 1910 to March 1937. Image by Emily Ratvasky.

New York in November 1924 in support of his upcoming expedition to North Africa in search of Atlantis. His expedition included the archaeologist and reporter Alma Reed from the *Times*, and coverage of his activities appeared repeatedly in the paper during 1925, especially in March and April. Reed dug on land with Khun de Prorok's expedition and dived off the coast of Djerba in search of signs of Atlantis. Reed's story on the prior Atlantis seeker Edward Thompson had triggered the controversy over the treasures of the Sacred Cenote at Chichén Itzá.[85]

Khun de Prorok mixed Atlantis together with Carthage, the Hoggar and Tuareg people, and sunken ruins off the North African coast. His 1925 expedition is recounted in his *Mysterious Sahara: The Land of Gold, of Sand, and of Ruin*. The book reads like pulp fiction: full of death, swarthy and cruel fiends, and fabulous discoveries that are often given a feminine cast, a common trope of adventure romance fiction, such as that of

Haggard. Khun de Prorok also tied his expedition to recent sensations, including claiming to have found inscriptions similar to the Glozel alphabet.[86] Yet Khun de Prorok worked with many government, academic, and corporate institutions even though he had no training and no real concern for scientific methods. One of these was the Logan Museum of Anthropology at Beloit University, which obtained specimens and data from an expedition member, the archaeologist Alonzo W. Pond. Khun de Prorok caused considerable diplomatic problems due to the unauthorized removal of skeletal remains and artifacts from Algeria.[87]

Placing Atlantis in North Africa—taking inspiration from selected classical sources—was popular in the early twentieth century.[88] Two months before Lovecraft finished "Cthulhu," the *New York Times* printed discussions on the assertions of geologist Paul Borchardt that Atlantis was off the coast of Tunisia or Morocco.[89] Lovecraft found a North African Atlantis plausible, and he used the concept in the ghostwritten stories "The Last Test" and "Medusa's Coil," in both cases referencing the Hoggars and Tuaregs.[90] It seems almost certain that Lovecraft obtained at least some of his North African inspiration from Khun de Prorok. In a 1927 letter to Zealia Bishop, the titular author of "Medusa's Coil," Lovecraft mentioned "the recent explorer Count de Prorok" and cited eloquent praise of Gustave Flaubert's novel of ancient Carthage, *Salammbô* (1862), which is mentioned in Khun de Prorok's 1926 book, *Digging for Lost African Gods*.[91] Khun de Prorok's writing would have delighted Lovecraft because it shares tropes now considered Lovecraftian, including ancient cults, witches of degenerate races dedicated to dead gods, unspeakable rites involving diabolical orgies of hysterical dancers and inhuman screaming in the eerie light of leaping flames, and the shadows of antediluvian monsters.[92] Much of the 1925 expedition centered around the supposed discovery of the tomb of the legendary queen Tin Hinan, although the tomb's occupant was more likely a later Berber noblewoman, and the expedition archaeologist Alonzo Pond admitted that the tomb was "a well-known landmark."[93] At first glance, the parallels with Lovecraft's ghostwritten "Medusa's Coil," which is about a female noble survivor of the ancient civilization of a Saharan Atlantis, might suggest the Khun de Prorok expedition as a model. However, Lovecraft also read Pierre Benoit's popular novel *L'Atlantide* (1919), which features Hoggars and a Saharan Atlantis, before writing "The Last Test." Khun de Prorok himself admitted the influence of the novel on his work.[94]

Khun de Prorok's expedition took place nearly simultaneously with the rash of dead archaeologist stories in early 1925, during the "Cthulhu" time frame (figure 10.4). If Lovecraft was clipping newspaper accounts, as he later stated was part of his writing method, it seems unlikely he would have missed it.[95] Perhaps driven by the Khun de Prorok expedition, other news items on sunken sites appeared in short order, including one about Roosevelt Lake temporarily exposing the "biggest ancient city of America," the discussion of the North African Atlantis, and three weeks before Lovecraft first plotted "Cthulhu," a report on ancient granite blocks believed to be part of an underwater building off the coast of Estonia, which spawned an editorial a week later about Atlantis and archaeological treasures dredged from the sea. Finally, in the same month Lovecraft finished "Cthulhu," a short column by archaeologist George F. Murrell utilized Neolithic and Roman ruins to calculate that the city of London would sink completely underwater in 75,000 years.[96] This would have tickled both Lovecraft's Anglophilia and his interest in deep time and sunken cities or, as he put it in "The Call of Cthulhu," "What has risen may sink, and what has sunk may rise." This was the last of any significant *Times* coverage of archaeological interest in sunken lands during Lovecraft's lifetime.

"The Authorities at Tulane University Could Shed No Light upon Either Cult or Image"

One additional aspect of this story is notable. The second part of "The Call of Cthulhu" names Tulane University as an authority stumped by the Cthulhu idol obtained from the cult south of New Orleans. In 1924, Tulane's Department of Middle American Research (later the Middle American Research Institute, or MARI), a major seat of Mesoamerican and Central American archaeological exploration and study, was endowed by the United Fruit mogul Samuel Zemurray after he bought the substantial Mesoamerican library of William E. Gates. The self-taught Gates had conducted significant scholarly work on Maya and Mesoamerican writing, helped create the first catalog of Maya glyphs, and was the director general of archaeology for the government of Guatemala, though he had resigned

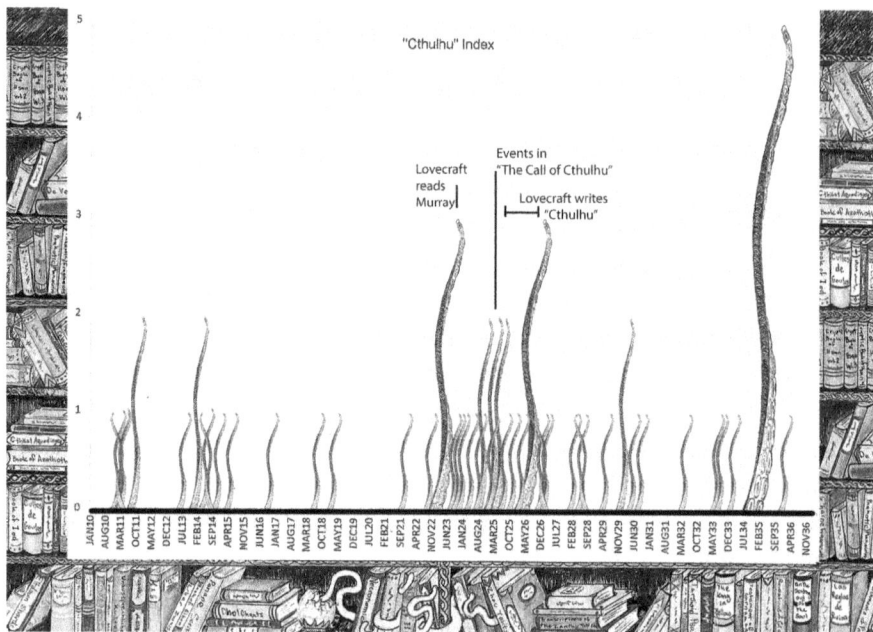

FIGURE 10.4. The "Cthulhu" index. The number of stories mentioning the word "archaeologist[s]" in the *New York Times* (excluding obituaries and society pages) that are about either sunken lands or dead archaeologists from January 1910 to March 1937. Image by Emily Ratvasky and author.

in anger when the government let Morley's Carnegie Institution project dig at Waxaktun.[97]

Gates was named the first director of MARI, an institute modeled on the recently founded Oriental Institute at the University of Chicago. He oversaw Tulane's first Central American expedition, led in 1925 by archaeologist Frans Blom and ethnographer Oliver La Farge and chronicled in the first MARI publication *Tribes and Temples*.[98] Blom subsequently forced Gates out of the MARI directorship and further shamed him by exposing a forged colonial Maya codex published by Gates.[99] La Farge would later write supernatural fiction, including "The Resting Place" (1956), in which a respectful archaeologist finds Pueblo remains with the aid of an indigenous ghost.[100]

The first MARI expedition was reported in the national media repeatedly in the "Cthulhu" time frame, including *New York Times* articles on 29 March and 2 April 1925. At the same time that seismic activity brought the island of R'lyeh to the surface in "Cthulhu," the Tulane expedition was uncovering ancient relics on the sacred island in Catemaco lagoon in Veracruz, Mexico, and documenting a nearby stone idol on the rim of an extinct volcanic caldera.[101] The expedition hit the front page of the *Times* in August 1925, a week after Lovecraft initially plotted "Cthulhu." The newspaper described how the modern Mayas continued to worship their "pagan" idols and how the exhausted explorers had hallucinated a landscape that took a "weird and unearthly shape and the bushes became monsters." Blom was quoted as suggesting that Mayan settlements were purposely placed near freakishly unusual natural spots, which acted as theaters for human sacrifice to "evil gods."[102] The Tulane expedition appeared in the *Times* again in November, when the leaders of the expedition visited New York.[103]

Lovecraft may have been inspired by the archaeological news coming from Tulane, but he likely was not aware that MARI director William Gates was a theosophist who sought Atlantis.[104] Gates lived and taught for a number of years at the Aryan Theosophical Institute, the headquarters for the American Theosophical Society in Point Loma in San Diego, California. The institute included the School for the Revival of the Lost Mysteries of Antiquity, and the architecture blended Eastern, Moorish, and Egyptian elements into an orientalist fantasy. The countercultural beliefs of the theosophists are reflected in archaeological analysis of refuse from the institute. True to their anti-materialist outlook, the theosophists used inexpensive consumer goods sparingly. Fresh meat was rarely consumed at Point Loma, and the institute used a lot of homeopathic remedies.[105]

In Point Loma, Gates ran a publishing operation and learned the skills needed to create a stylized font for printing Maya glyphs.[106] Gates presented a lecture in 1915 titled "H. P. Blavatsky and Archaeology" at the Panama-California Exposition in San Diego. In *The Spirit of the Hour in Archaeology*, the title under which it was subsequently published, Gates presaged much of the argument of Thomas Kuhn about the changing paradigms of science, describing how neglected fields of study can become the new status quo. He then attacked materialist science for being narrow-minded in its dogma, pointing out many recent errors in geology and paleontology. As did many of the figures discussed in this volume, Gates complained that professional scientific archaeology had stripped away its rightful partners of mythology, symbolism, and astronomy. He argued that a spiritual or philosophical form of linguistics is at least as important as archaeology for studying the human past. According to Gates, mainstream science refuses to acknowledge that civilizations such as Egypt are far older than a few thousand years or that the archaeology of Central and South America will expose the ancient influence of Atlantis.[107] As I discuss in chapter 11, all of these are still the primary fixations of alternative archaeologists today.

Gates saw ties between Maya hieroglyphs and the modern Maya language but shared the common view that Maya writing was largely nonphonetic.[108] More unusually, despite the correlations of the Maya Long Count with the Gregorian calendar in 1905, demonstrating that Maya writing was less than 3,000 years old, Gates followed the old notions about hieroglyphs and believed that the allegedly nonphonetic Maya writing was older than Egyptian, which is more than 5,000 years old.[109] Gates rejected much of the archaeological research of his contemporaries, including the mental evolution of humans from apes and the migration of Native Americans via the Bering Strait, a theory that "ignores too much, takes too many unknown things for granted, and tries to explain too much with too little."[110] Gates cited Blavatsky's *Secret Doctrine* and its "root races" in his Mayan scholarship, and he believed that human civilization and advanced technology were older than archaeologists thought and could be traced to Atlantis.[111] Lovecraft's theosophical nightmare of Cthulhu wouldn't have baffled the expert at Tulane; Gates would have recognized the cyclopean relic.

"What Has Risen May Sink, and What Has Sunk May Rise":
Lovecraftian Pseudoarchaeology

While the case is partially circumstantial (the Murray witch cult angle is explicit, the Khun de Prorok element suggestive), the short story "The Call of Cthulhu" bears a striking resemblance to the contemporary media's take on archaeology. The story was conceived, set, and written within a narrow window of time featuring concurrent outbreaks of media interest in themes found in the story: archaeology in general, dead archaeologists in particular, and evidence of sunken cities (figure 10.4). The catalyst for all of this was the tidal wave of popular interest in the sensational Tut tomb and the alleged curse. This real-world narrative of weird deaths visiting those who meddled in the tomb of an undead god-king made archaeologists into media figures and specifically resembles Cthulhu, who kills those that disturb him as he lies "dead but dreaming" in his tomb.

If "The Call of Cthulhu" was the beginning and the end of this real-world archaeological impact, it would be an interesting chapter in the history of fantastical literature. But "The Call of Cthulhu" marks the beginning of the Cthulhu mythos,[112] a subgenre that continues in literature, games, and film to the present and inspires real-world beliefs. The core concept of the mythos is that extraterrestrial intelligent life colonized the ancient earth and is today dimly remembered in ancient esoteric traditions of gods and demons.[113] The aliens left behind ruined cities or tombs in Australia, Arabia, Antarctica, and the Pacific Ocean; stone formations and chambers in New England and the American Southwest; and unusual artifacts in museum archives and scientific collections. Many of these tales, including "Cthulhu," implicitly or explicitly hint that these aliens created life on earth and impacted the course of human civilization, particularly in creating religion as the gods and titans of old. This is the ancient extraterrestrials concept that dominates popular representations of archaeology.[114] Both the Cthulhu mythos and the ancient extraterrestrials ideology are hidden histories of aliens' visitation of earth, rediscovered by eccentric scholars who have pieced together seemingly unrelated clues from ancient sites and texts and who are suppressed by organizations dedicated to keeping such secrets.

In order to understand how pulp fiction became popular pseudoscience, we must examine Lovecraft's literary methods. "The Call of Cthulhu" is a scholar's notes based heavily on news stories of the day. Beginning with "Cthulhu," Lovecraft interlinked many of his tales. Lovecraft's aim, beyond amusing himself with what he called "Yog-Sothothery," was to immerse the reader in a "real" world of wonder and horror. He believed that such stories only produced true terror if they were "devised with all the care and verisimilitude of an actual *hoax*."[115] To this end, Lovecraft borrowed creations from friends who also wrote in the pulp magazine *Weird Tales*, where "The Call of Cthulhu" was published in February 1928. Some names were modified to suggest linguistic drift over time, and some background elements contradicted each other. All of this mirrored the mythology-intensive anthropology and history Lovecraft was drawing from, such as Frazer's *The Golden Bough* and Murray's *Witch-Cult in Western Europe*. As a ghost-writer for a number of *Weird Tales* authors, Lovecraft was able to seed his creations into other works in preparation for his own stories, which mentioned fictional gods, places, and grimoires alongside real-world analogues, leading the reader to treat them all as background reality. In "Cthulhu," Lovecraft mentions Murray's *Witch-Cult*, specifically says that what he is describing is similar but separate from the religion described in Murray's real-world book, and then makes his cult a virtual copy of Murray's creation. Lovecraft used the letter columns and interactive fan communities of proto-science fiction to deepen the appeal of his horror in the same way that the Internet is used to mask the fictional component of works like *The Blair Witch Project* or the shared Slenderman mythos.[116]

Like the authors of these works, Lovecraft had to explain to fans that his work was fiction. Lovecraft felt "quite guilty every time I hear[d] of someone's having spent valuable time looking up the *Necronomicon* at public libraries," and he "was opposed to *serious* hoaxes."[117] After his death Lovecraft's fictional grimoire, *Necronomicon*, began appearing in library catalogs and book dealer advertisements and was eventually published in several versions.[118] During his lifetime some fans believed that Lovecraft and his circle had unknowing psychic access to forbidden knowledge and were channeling nonhuman entities.[119] Subsequently this belief grew among naïve occult dabblers, the Church of Satan, and postmodern chaos magicians who believe in the magical power of belief, even in the fictional, over traditional lore.[120]

Lovecraft borrowed the notion of ancient extraterrestrials from, as he put it in private correspondence, theosophical "charlatans" who engaged in "conscious fakery," but his hoax-like presentation, his use of Fortean style, and his grounding of the concept in a materialist science-fiction frame advanced the idea.[121] He specifically references the theosophists in "The Call of Cthulhu" as having a dimly incomplete and optimistic understanding of the earth's past. Theosophy's acceptance in intellectual circles had declined by the 1920s, but it still had an impact on anthropologists and archaeologists, including the archaeological explorer Nicholas Roerich, whose paintings of Tibet inspired the alien civilization in Lovecraft's *At the*

Mountains of Madness.[122] Lovecraft also was familiar with the exploits of Augustus Le Plongeon, writing that he was either a "plain faker" or a "self-deluded nut."[123]

Lovecraft's more material and "scientific" version of the theosophical root races and ascended masters, now ancient extraterrestrial civilizations, flowed back into the occult underground, where it was explicitly cited as an expression of occult knowledge in the conspiracy theory and counterculture opus *The Morning of the Magicians*. As science fiction fans and publishers, the authors Pauwels and Bergier praised Lovecraft as the father of science fiction and the "greatest poet and champion of the theory of parallel universes," and they translated his works into French. Jacques Bergier claimed to have corresponded with Lovecraft and made it clear that Lovecraft's fiction, Fort's "anomalies," and ideas about extraterrestrial visitation cannot be disentangled. *The Morning of the Magicians* in turn was an admitted source for the ancient extraterrestrials breakthrough a few years later.[124]

Since that time Lovecraft has directly and indirectly inspired UFO, paranormal, and ancient extraterrestrials ideas.[125] Arguably the premier conspiracy theorist in the early twenty-first century is Alex Jones, who rose from community access television in Austin, Texas, in the 1990s to become a significant media and political figure. Jones became the loudest voice of the 9/11 truther movement, but his conspiracy theories have had supernatural and almost Lovecraftian elements. Perhaps the strongest example was an infamous rant in which Jones linked Terence McKenna's extradimensional "elves" (see below) with a cult attempting to bring demonic alien forces into our world through advanced technology.[126] This is basically the plot of every Cthulhu mythos story. Another prominent Texan conspiracy theorist is Jim Marrs, most famous for providing the basis for Oliver Stone's conspiracy film *JFK*. Marrs began his book on the ancient extraterrestrials conspiracy by quoting the opening paragraph of "The Call of Cthulhu."[127]

"Fact-fiction reversals" are inherent to conspiracy theories and pseudoscience.[128] Mainstream knowledge is suspect from this perspective, while works of fiction are reinterpreted as coded versions of reality. Because they are not considered to be true, they are lumped in with other stigmatized knowledge shunned by the mainstream. Fictional presentations remove the rough edges that can be found in folklore, providing a narrative framework for disjointed "real" tales. Examples of fiction inspiring paranormal ideas include early flying saucers, alien contactees, the chupacabra, and the Loch Ness monster.[129] Pseudoarchaeological examples include *The Stargate Conspiracy*.[130] The tangled mess of Templars, holy bloodlines, and *The Da Vinci Code* is a fact-fiction reversal deconstructed in Umberto Eco's novel *Foucault's Pendulum* (1988).

One of these reversals in the ancient extraterrestrials myth, the Reptilians, can be traced directly to Lovecraft and his correspondent Robert E. Howard. After Blavatsky, members of mystical lodges and channelers continued to modify theosophy into new religious movements. In 1931 Maurice Doreal, also known as Claude Doggins, claimed to have met two Atlanteans in caverns below Mount Shasta. Doreal founded the Brotherhood of the White Temple, located in Denver, and continued to be a figure in the occult and subsequent UFO community, prophesizing nuclear war in 1953.[131] Many of the early flying saucer "contactees" in the 1940s and 1950s had previously been in the theosophical and occult communities.

One of Doreal's works was a pamphlet published in the mid-1940s as *Mysteries of the Gobi*, which described an ancient war between humans and a race with serpent heads atop human bodies. These Reptilians, as they would come to be known in UFO lore, had hypnotic powers and could create the illusion that they were human. During that same era, Doreal claimed in *Flying Saucers: An Occult Viewpoint* that these creatures were extraterrestrials that would be revived from suspended animation later in the twentieth century to aid the Antichrist. In the mid-1940s Doreal also produced *Emerald Tablets of Thoth the Atlantean*, about a mystical text from the Great Pyramid of Giza. Doreal claimed at that time that he was given access to it in 1925, yet sections about the Reptilians show clear similarities to and the lifting of phrases from two Cthulhu mythos stories published after that date: Lovecraft's "The Dunwich Horror" (1928) and Frank Belknap Long's "The Hounds of Tindalos" (1929).[132]

Doreal didn't lift just these poetic passages from Lovecraft and his friends; he took the entire concept of a hidden ancient race of serpent people. Lovecraft's career included many tales of lost races in suspended animation or hiding in the dark corners of the earth, such as the fish people of "Dagon" and "The Shadow over Innsmouth," the amphibious lizard race of

"The Doom That Came to Sarnath," [133] and Cthulhu and his kind waiting for R'lyeh to rise. Two in particular, the changeling ghouls of "Pickman's Model" and the Mi-Go of "The Whisperer in Darkness," are Lovecraft's take on a hidden fairy race, with the extraterrestrial Mi-Go a direct homage to Machen's adaptation of MacRitchie's pygmy fairy race. [134] But the parents of Doreal's Reptilians were the mummified reptilians buried in Lovecraft's "The Nameless City," written in 1921, and the serpent men of Valusia in Robert E. Howard's "The Shadow Kingdom" (1929). [135] Lovecraft's crocodilian reptile men were discovered in the present, entombed in their ancient underground city in Arabia, perhaps the same city that is at the center of the Cthulhu cult in "The Call of Cthulhu." Like *Al Azif*, also known as the *Necronomicon*, and its author, Abdul Alhazred, Lovecraft's recurring use of an ancient Arabian city inspired by the legends of the lost city of Irem derives from his youthful love of *The Arabian Nights*. Howard's serpent men could disguise themselves as human and had infiltrated the ancient Valusian society (until they were destroyed by the Atlantean barbarian Kull the Conqueror). Lovecraft borrowed elements from Howard in his ghostwritten tale "Medusa's Coil," which features human-reptilian hybrids and ruined Atlantean cities in the Sahara Desert (echoing Khun de Prorok's explorations in search of Atlantis), though the notion of reptilian hybrid refugees from Atlantis goes back to E. T. A. Hoffmann's 1814 story "The Golden Pot." [136] Soon others in the Lovecraft circle began borrowing these ideas, including Robert Bloch and Clark Ashton Smith. [137]

Doreal's pulp fiction Reptilian pseudohistory must be understood in the larger context of similar conspiracy theories and fiction-inspired shared fantasies of hidden races. As noted in the beginning of this volume, Edward Bulwer-Lytton's *The Coming Race*, a tale of underground dwellers descended from frogs and able to control mystical powers, was influential on both theosophy and fiction, including Lovecraft's ghostwritten "The Mound" (1930), which was not published until 1940, right around the time Doreal began warning the world about serpent people. "The Mound" describes a branch of humans who have fled the surface and remember their extraterrestrial origin, brought to earth by alien gods. These humans have preserved powerful telepathic powers and scientific knowledge but are morally degenerate and amuse themselves in cruel pursuits, including horrific surgeries inflicted on unfortunate victims.

Just such a cruel underground race surfaced in the real world with the Shaver mysteries. As Michael Barkun documented, Doreal's writings were influential on early believers in the Shaver mysteries and the subsequent flying saucer community in the 1940s and 1950s. The Shaver mysteries are named for Richard Shaver, who claimed to hear in the noise of his arc welder the commands of evil, underground "detrimental robots" (deros) and the cries of their victims, whose sexually graphic tortures Shaver detailed in his letters and tales for *Amazing Stories* beginning in 1944. Shaver's claims to have visited these underground realms had to be modified to alleged astral projection when it became clear that he had been in a psychiatric hospital for eight years due to delusions regarding demons hunting him and his family. Shaver's stories and the letters to *Amazing Stories* by others claiming to have encountered the deros are considered by many to be the immediate predecessor to the flying saucer community. Editor Ray Palmer, who rewrote and promoted the Shaver stories, has been called "the man who invented the flying saucer."[138]

In August 1946, ten months before the coining of the term "flying saucer," the editors of *Amazing Stories* encouraged their audience to read Doreal's pamphlets. As a result, his Lovecraftian Reptilians became part of a mythology of ancient conflicts involving Atlanteans and Lemurians, underground tunnel systems and cities, the ancient extraterrestrial Rainbow City in Antarctica, and the prophecy that the dormant serpent men would rise from suspended animation in the earth to once again conquer the world. Extraterrestrial cities in the Antarctic, a hidden underworld, ancient conflicts bigger than humans, and sleeping aliens ready to strike when the stars are right are all Lovecraftian tropes from "The Call of Cthulhu," *At the Mountains of Madness*, and other pulp tales.[139]

The most infamous "nonfiction" version of the Reptilian myth today is that promoted by David Icke, who extensively cited Doreal's *Emerald Tablets* in his *Children of the Matrix* (2001), though Icke has his Egyptian priests place them in a trendier Mayan temple. However, after taking a more secular turn through UFO conspiracies, the Reptilian conspiracy theories are tied back into the folk Christian roots of serpents, Watchers, forbidden knowledge, and the destruction of paradise. The echoes of the Shaver mysteries, and arguably Lovecraft, Howard, and Bulwer-Lytton, can be found in various fragments of UFO lore, including the gold-loving reptilian Anunnaki in Mesopotamia (which enthusiasts equate with clay figurines from the Sumerian Ubaid culture) and hidden underground bases housing both aliens and human conspirators, possibly Satanic in nature, who practice horrifying experiments on abductees.[140]

The Cthulhu mythos influenced another major strand of alternative archaeology, the 2012 Mayan apocalypse. The Mayan apocalypse was first tentatively proposed by the mainstream archaeologist Michael Coe as a parallel of Mesoamerican beliefs about multiple world creations and destructions and Shiva's cyclical destruction of the world in Hindu cosmology. This comparison sprang in part from Coe's travels and studies in Southeast Asia after a stint in the CIA working against China during the Korean War.[141] Another possible source of inspiration was Coe's lifelong fandom of Lovecraft tales. Coe was attracted to the town of Heath, Massachusetts, where he retired in part due to it being reminiscent of a Lovecraft story. Coe is open to the suggestion that Lovecraft's writings of ancient eons-long apocalyptic cycles might have influenced his 2012 speculation.[142] An Ivy League archaeology professor in New England interprets ancient esoteric books and stone carvings found in the ruins of an exotic dead city to find that when the stars come right, a prophesized global apocalypse will lurch out of the past—this could describe either "The Call of Cthulhu" or Michael Coe's 2012 speculation.

The most influential 2012 prophet was Terence McKenna, a pioneer of DMT (dimethyltryptamine) research and a major figure in New Age circles. McKenna combined numerology, the divinatory Book of Changes (I Ching), and recent events and important dates in his own life in the computer program Timewave Zero, a profile of declining "novelty" in the world. He claimed inspiration from a voice he heard after consuming psilocybin-containing mushrooms in Colombia. After reading of Coe's 2012 idea, McKenna modified the end date of the Timewave Zero pattern to fit the thirteenth baktun of the Maya Long Count. The 2012 legend subsequently grew into almost uncountable varieties, including syncretic rejoinings with broader millenarian prophecies in indigenous Mayan communities.[143]

Not only does Timewave Zero strongly resemble the piecing together of disparate events and strange vision messages in "The Call of Cthulhu," but McKenna was specifically inspired to undertake his entheogenic research by Lovecraft's story "From Beyond" (1920), in which stimulation of the pineal gland and the alteration of perception allows one access to a parallel reality and its denizens.[144] McKenna's "machine elves" strongly resemble the shifting psychedelic, geometric forms that living creatures have in hyperspace in Lovecraft's story "The Dreams in the Witch House." In this tale, an advanced understanding of mathematics opens up new dimensions to brave travelers who unlock the ancient esoteric mysteries called "magic" by Western science. Could one better describe the holographic matrix of reality exposed by Timewave Zero?[145]

11

The Revenge of Alternative Archaeology

Closing the Barn Doors after That One Weird Horse Got the Hint and Left

Much of this book has been situated within antiquarianism, professional archaeology, and the impact of archaeology on the media and the public. I have examined members of the archaeological community who were spies, smugglers, occultists, and hunters of Atlantis and the yeti. Manuel Gamio conducted the first stratigraphic excavations in North America in the same time and place as the weird excavations of the museum supplier William Niven. As O. G. S. Crawford was pioneering the use of new aerial technology to see archaeological features under the landscape, Alfred Watkins was finding ley lines in the antiquarian landscape and Frederick Bligh Bond was peering under the soil with the help of the channeled memories of dead monks. Archaeologist-spies secretly played the great game for Britain in the Middle East. Thomas Gann was spying for the Americans one moment and smuggling a jade plaque sewn inside his coat in another, and he worked with the British Museum to support Mitchell-Hedges's excavations at Lubaantun, during which Anna Mitchell-Hedges later claimed she found a mystical crystal skull. Flinders Petrie went to Egypt to investigate mystical alignments. His student and colleague Margaret Murray went undercover looking for murderous occult conspiracies. At the time, one did not have to look far to find the mystical side-by-side with scientific archaeology, both preserved in a mountain of popular culture inspired by the reality of early archaeology.[1]

This is not the archaeology of today. With a handful of exceptions, the mystical is not a significant force in twenty-first-century archaeology.

Heritage management professionals are ensconced in a world of business and government. Academic archaeology and its theoretical disagreements occur on a spectrum ranging from hard physical science materialism, to a multivocal experiential approach to the past and the present, to a critical postcolonial political archaeology, all of which is acceptable within the limits of the orthodox academy. Topics such as ancient Egypt, which were integral to the field and which still fire the public imagination, have lost their academic value because of their popularity.[2] Within heritage or academic archaeology, one would be hard-pressed to find dowsing, ancient extraterrestrials, Atlantis, racial history, automatic writing, or curses other than in the occasional museum exhibit or partnership with a media company.

The agent of change was professionalization. The broad concept of professionalism—based on education rather than on patronage and position, and focused on a middle class with a purpose to serve others—emerged in the latter half of the nineteenth century.[3] The professionalization of archaeology was fought less over the control of financial resources or employment than over controlling the boundaries of method and theory. The emerging professional archaeological standards centered on excavation and the material rather than on the literary, folkloric, and religious aspects of antiquarianism.[4] Archaeological and antiquarian societies had existed since the seventeenth century, but the first academic and governmental positions in archaeology emerged in the middle of the nineteenth century and, in nonclassical archaeology, in the late nineteenth century. The classical-focused Disney Chair was endowed at Cambridge in 1851, and Flinders Petrie was appointed the Edwards Chair at University College London, the first professorship dedicated to teaching Egyptology, in 1893.[5] The beginning of a scientific archaeology might include John Lubbock's evolutionary *Pre-Historic Times* (1865), Flinders Petrie's abandonment of mystical numerology for an inductively scientific prehistory after 1877, Augustus Pitt Rivers's excavation techniques, and the collapse of the moundbuilder myth in the United States in 1890.[6]

Professionalization as a process of removing nonprofessionals, including but not limited to so-called cranks, from the research community accelerated after the Second World War and was largely concluded by 1960.[7] The increased state support for public universities and scientific research along with the radiocarbon-dating revolution expelled mythic theories and approaches in favor of first processual and then other theoretical forms of archaeology. The Gogmagog affair described in chapter 3 is a good example of the old guard clashing with the new professionals. At a time when archaeological data were analyzed in university laboratories to answer increasingly processual questions about prehistory, the museum-based T. C. Lethbridge was inspired by a local legend to use an almost dowsing-like technique to produce a mythic figure to illustrate prehistoric survivals and hyperdiffusion.

What happened after Gogmagog is even more important. Lethbridge found a new home in the world of dowsing, witch cults, and ancient astronauts, praised by the likes of paranormal outsider Colin Wilson. Lethbridge's trajectory embodied the creation of an alternative—a paranormal archaeology or a pseudoarchaeology—from the ruins of preprofessional archaeology and antiquarianism. The spooky spirits of archaeology did not vanish into the ether or dissolve into ectoplasmic residue. Ideas, practices, and styles that were once uncomfortably within archaeology have thrived on the outside and have come to dominate the public perception of the field and of the past.[8] In chapter 10, I examined how one new myth, the ancient extraterrestrial, began in the Victorian occult world of theosophy, in the Frazerian survival anthropology, in the folklore of Margaret Murray, and in the exploits of archaeological adventurers as reported by a post-Tutankhamun press. These are all forms of stigmatized knowledge.[9] The ancient extraterrestrial notion then moved through the pulp fiction of Lovecraft before resurfacing in the UFO subculture and the growing counterculture of the 1960s. Ley lines traced a similar path from the antiquarian world to midcentury defeat at the hands of professional archaeologists before revival by paranormal researchers and ufologists. Deeper examinations of sunken continents, hyperdiffusion, psychic archaeology, and other spooky topics generally show the same trajectory: the flourishing of supposedly vanished antiquarian practices in a new arena, a media-driven paranormal subculture without the scientific scruples of the academy, and then the artistic veil of the occult magical community.

The Invisible College of Alternative Archaeology

With the exception of some extreme cases of nationalist archaeology, a large portion of alternative archaeology has one unifying theme: opposition to professional mainstream archaeology and, more broadly, science.[10] As Atlantis author John Anthony West stated, "I don't have any [credentials], that's why I know something."[11] The ancient astronauts author Erich von Däniken said that his lack of formal education made him "completely free of all prejudices."[12] Alternative author John Michell resurrected a form of ley line geomancy that was animated by an opposition to evolutionary materialism and Marxism.[13] Alternative theorists paint professional archaeologists as willing stooges of a grand conspiracy that pays them to ignore alternative ideas or data, even if withholding such information might jeopardize human survival in future catastrophes.[14] Given the accusations of archaeologists' involvement in murderous conspiracies, we should not be surprised by calls from the alternative archaeology community for congressional hearings to investigate the Smithsonian and the profession of archaeology.[15] This call has made explicit the largely implicit agenda of alternative archaeology to return to the Victorian era before professional archaeology: "we need to wipe away the past 100 years and encourage the scientists [to] do the work with fresh, objective eyes."[16] The rejection of the moundbuilder myth, based on the work of Cyrus Thomas, is commonly identified as a key moment in the professionalization of American archaeology, yet critics have called it "the demise of American Archaeology" and "the scientific equivalent of the Dark Ages."[17] It is notable that similar rhetoric can be found among archaeological looters, who portray scientific investigation as pointless and archaeologists as elitists locking away information in basements.[18]

The paranormal community critiques authorities for accepting a less satisfying materialist and rational science over a more meaningful mythology and faith. This attack can be found in Victorian theosophical works, in Lethbridge's complaint that ancient mythology was being forgotten by science-obsessed archaeologists, and in present appeals to discard sterile Enlightenment science in favor of a universal memory and the indigenous secrets of extraterrestrial sky people.[19] So why does an alternative archaeology, with a claim to scientific investigation via archaeology, persist? Why are there alternative archaeologists or pseudoarchaeologists at all? There are plenty of religious and philosophical options for disagreeing with materialist and rationalist science. Why not take up a form of extrascience, such as magic or religion, that is unconcerned with scientific symbols and standards?

Alternative archaeology is a form of heteroscience, often labeled pseudoscience by critics. Heteroscience sits on the fringes of science, typically as a critique of the larger scientific community and following in the footsteps of catalogs of the wondrous, which were said to invalidate mainstream science and religion. This is also true of the larger label "paranormal," which can include conspiracy theories and their inherent opposition to official narratives. Belief in one of the domains labeled as conspiracy theory, paranormal, or pseudoscience correlates with belief in the others.[20]

Unlike other historical sciences, such as paleontology, archaeology studies the human past, the home of tradition. I have been alluding to this paradox, the science of mythic time, throughout this volume. Archaeologists abandoned the mystical in their study of the material past, but the powerful pull of the past for making meaning meant that the ground on which the mystical and the scientific past met would persevere. An invisible college of rejected antiquarian knowledge preserved the Romantic, traditional, and conservative and thus attracted paranormalists who embraced high-profile archaeological sites like Stonehenge.[21] Confrontations between archaeologists and the Universal Druid Brotherhood almost turned violent at Stonehenge in the 1910s and 1920s and flared again between the counterculture and the police in the 1970s and 1980s. Access to Stonehenge is now negotiated through stakeholder dialogue, but memories of past confrontations energize pagans and add to the meaning of the site.[22]

It has been suggested that pseudoarchaeologists routinely use outmoded scholarship and ideas because they have no alternatives.[23] I argue that the revival of Victorian theories is the entire point of alternative archaeology. Fairies, psychical research, sacred hieroglyphs, mythic identities, lost races and continents, and secret pagan survivals were all once part of archaeology before professionalization drove them out. Their persistence in the alternative archaeology community is a purposeful rejection of the professionals. The dismissal of expertise in order to go back to a previous imagined golden age is not unique to archaeology. It is manifest in the creationist, dentist, and former Texas Board of Education member Don McLeroy's exclamation that "Somebody's gotta stand up to experts!" and in politician Michael Gove's comment that "I think people in this country have had enough of experts" during his successful campaign to remove Britain from the European Union.[24]

Garrett Fagan noted that alternative theorists incorporate older sources for "art history; ancient epigraphy; comparative global mythology; comparative religion; philology; linguistics; mathematics; astronomy; and geophysics."[25] Marine biologist Barry Fell condemned North American archaeologists for not studying classical epigraphy.[26] Fell believed that America was covered in ancient Old World inscriptions, though many of his "inscriptions" have been otherwise interpreted as plow scars on field rocks. Fell's demands make no sense in the context of any actual archaeological remains found in North America. They make plenty of sense from a Victorian notion of protohistorical diffusion, the importance of text over material culture, and the chase for magical writing from the origins of civilization as the main job of archaeology. Compare Fagan's list with Posnansky. Or Lethbridge. Or Le Plongeon. Or Watkins. Or Kiss. Or Churchward. The puzzle-solving jack-of-all-trades explorer found in popular fiction and alternative archaeology circles is a cartoon version of preprofessional archaeology. The most prominent academic hyperdiffusionist, Grafton Elliot Smith, suggested that the Egyptians colonized the world in search of elixirs of immortality. Elliot Smith and his followers jumped from topic to topic pursuing broad but shallow examinations of cultural elements throughout time. When Elliot Smith was outside of his primary field of human anatomy, his ignorance of ethnological matters only made him more adamant in the rightness of his ideas.[27]

Victorian or "long nineteenth-century" imagery is prevalent in pseudoarchaeology and other forms of pseudoscience. In addition to raw nostalgia for European imperial dominance, such imagery invokes the rapid advances of Victorian science unfettered by professional community standards.[28] Rooted in theosophy and antiquarianism, alternative archaeology resembles the science fantasy genre of steampunk, which depicts a fantastical Victorian world of retrofuturistic technology. The community that enacts these ideals in part does so to protest the modern corporate consumer world. However, the steampunks have been criticized for also preserving and promoting the negative aspects of Victorian imperial culture, including racism, classism, and colonialism.[29] These same criticisms can be leveled at alternative archaeologists who promote the racially informed colonialist fantasies of hyperdiffusion, lost continents, lost races, angelic or demonic giants buried in indigenous monuments, ancient extraterrestrials, hybrid DNA, and others.

Opposition to the mainstream does not mean that loose "orthodoxies" do not emerge. Alternative Egyptologists Lynn Picknett and Clive Prince argued that such an "alternative orthodoxy" has arisen around Egypt and the Giza plateau, a notion confirmed by independent ethnography.[30] Not unlike some papers in established academia, their article contains unsubtle hints of ax grinding against rivals in the alternative archaeology community, such as Graham Hancock or the followers of Edgar Cayce. Picknett and Prince are better known for a conspiracy theory about ancient cults and modern secret societies dedicated to the worship of the Nine, ultradimensional entities that once appeared as the gods of classical Egypt.[31]

The core ideology of alternative Egyptology is dependent on much older dates for the monuments of Giza, especially the Sphinx. This difference with mainstream Egyptology is not just academic, but is tied directly into imminent apocalyptic events, which will emanate from the ancient monuments, which are foretold in the monuments, or about which the monuments encode vital information from an ancient civilization that is not the mundane Egypt of scientists and historians.[32]

Decades of alternative community support for field research and establishing a presence in Egypt paid off in the early 1990s. The explosion of cable television and Internet media, the declining government funding of educational media, and the resulting privatization and outsourcing of documentary production replaced academic and specialist media figures with telegenic presenters of mysterious themes. This new environment increased the influence of alternative archaeologists.[33]

Money and media influence moved Egyptologists and Egyptian government officials either to confront the claims of the alternative theorists or to cooperate with them. Followers of America's sleeping prophet, Edgar Cayce, a populist faith healer and Christian mystic, have worked with credentialed university scholars to gain access to Egyptian ruins for study and for documentary filmmaking. Their research efforts generally find little of archaeological interest, but they emphasize technological approaches, such as remote sensing surveys or fiber optic and robotic probes. The Association for Research and Enlightenment (ARE), a group based on Cayce's teachings, funded the education and work of archaeologist Mark Lehner who, like Flinders Petrie a century before, eventually discarded alternative ideas and became a powerful advocate for orthodox archaeology at Giza.[34]

In Cayce's hypnotized sessions, he channeled the past lives of people who had witnessed the destruction of Atlantis 50,000 years ago and reported that five races had left traces in the Pyrenees, Morocco, Belize, Yucatán, and North America. Cayce foretold the rising of Atlantis in 1968 or 1969, a prophecy metaphorically fulfilled by his followers with their allegations in 1968 that beach rocks off the coast of Bimini in the Bahamas were actually the ruins of Atlantis. Geological analysis determined "Bimini Road" to be natural beach rock formations, but the inclusion of scientific authorities in underwater expeditions gave short-term press attention to Cayce's supporters.[35]

Cayce spoke of a Hall of Records buried under the paws of the Sphinx at Giza, like those described in the Himalayas and elsewhere by Blavatsky.[36] This has spurred tremendous interest in redating the Sphinx and searching under it with remote sensing technology. The alternative Giza "academy" has interpreted weathering on the Sphinx as the result of rainfall from the late Pleistocene or early Holocene and therefore as evidence of Plato's Atlantis in 10,000 BCE. This date then appeared in Robert Bauval's claims for astronomical alignments at Giza and similar ideas in Graham Hancock's *Fingerprints of the Gods* in 1995.[37] The use of astronomical alignments to date megalithic structures backed Posnansky's attempts to make Tiwanaku the cradle of humanity in the Americas.

Prior to the Egyptian Revolution in 2011, archaeologist Zahi Hawass was the official in charge of the Giza plateau. Hawass is hated by many alternative archaeologists for allegedly denying them access to Egypt's lost knowledge. Yet Hawass several times gave these groups access to the pyramids, and he spoke at conferences hosted by Cayce's followers in the ARE and by the California-based Ancient and Mystical Order Rosae Crucis (the same group that endorsed the 1932 film *The Mummy*). A documentary that resulted from efforts of the ARE, *The Mystery of the Sphinx* (1993), aired on the NBC network, winning huge audiences and an Emmy. Hawass has been very critical of these individuals and their ideas, and they became an unavoidable and significant part of his job; such tensions have continued to the present. But starting in 2000 Hawass worked with various alternative theorists, including the lost civilization/Atlantis proponents John Anthony West, Robert Bauval, and Graham Hancock and paranormal media stars, such as radio host Art Bell. This new relationship was brokered by tourism concerns, including a New Age tour operator friendly with all parties, though it did not stop Hawass's criticism of their ideas.[38]

Can Archaeology Avoid/Afford Being Spooky?

The core thesis of this book is that much of the spooky image of archaeology derives from the history, practices, and nature of archaeology itself. Be it the common reconfiguration of the archaeological as supernatural, the importance of the mythic in the history of archaeology, or a roster of sketchy artifact smugglers and more reputable archaeologist-spies, our spooky history has persisted in the popular image of the field. Yet the predominant reaction by professional archaeologists has been to minimize or just ignore this image, with little success. Magic and the supernatural, demonstrably of great importance in all human societies, either have been the subject of incautious archaeological sensation or, more typically, have become taboo.[39]

This presents two questions. Can supernatural and mysterious themes be ignored away? Alternatively, can we invoke the spirits of magic and myth without damning our scientific achievements?

One school of thought would sympathetically group openly supernatural and nonscientific or antiscientific approaches to the past with postcolonial academic critiques of positivist materialist archaeology generally and modernity more broadly.[40] From this perspective, one would draw lines based not on scientific accuracy, but on whether a particular ideology (nationalism, creationism, postcolonialism) has the potential for creating political harm.[41] One might, for example, inclusively publish archaeological studies based in religious text and that are openly antagonistic to mainstream evolutionary biology as part of a heterogeneous discussion. More radically, one might proclaim the entire notion of scientific authority to be only situational and primarily appealing to those with an obedient attitude toward modern society. This approach elevates the mythic narrative of archaeology over methodology or results.[42]

Several of the works cited in the notes in the previous paragraph explicitly criticize those who debunk spooky ideas in defense of scientific method. More than fifty years ago, Glyn Daniel argued that if archaeologists cede their role as interpreters of the past due to self-doubting scruples, the unscrupulous will be more than happy to step in and take their place.[43] The debunker school decries the media power of alternative archaeology, pointing to television channels, bookshelves, and an Internet where the vast quantities of material about ancient extraterrestrials, Atlantis, earth energies, conspiracies, racially informed hyperdiffusion, and various flavors of creationism hugely outweigh the supposedly elite and socially valued scientific archaeology. These positivist critics respond to their postcolonial critics by suggesting that material reality trumps cultural relativity and that many fringe proponents engage in charlatanry rather than honest cultural resistance.[44]

Support and criticism of both camps can be found in the contradictions that emerged from Jasmine Day's analysis of mummies in fictional and museum representations and what these can tell us about public perspectives on these issues. Day argued that the human element of mummified remains and their prominence in the history of public perceptions of archaeology make mummies mirrors for archaeology and the public. Museum visitors have offered many criticisms of displaying mummies and other human remains, but mostly these were not about colonialism or the repatriation of indigenous remains. Many were simply uncomfortable with human remains, for either reasons of taste or fears over hygiene. Many others supported the displays, suggested that more mummies should be displayed, and would be disappointed in mummy-less exhibits.[45]

Museumgoers' hostility was driven more by envy of or disdain for professional archaeologists, who were seen as limiting access to the material past and its riches, than by any anticolonial concerns. Careless and callous archaeologists were blamed (rather than the ravages of time), especially by adult visitors, for any visible damage to mummies.[46] Feeling left out, many visitors felt most engaged when they imagined themselves as explorers and archaeologists inside the exhibits. These imaginings were primarily informed by supernatural tropes and popular stereotypes of tomb raiders and archaeologists, like Indiana Jones and Lara Croft, which was encouraged by museums' publicity materials about romantic adventurers "entering tombs."[47]

One of the primary appeals of the paranormal is that it provides room for intellectual play.[48] Visitors to University College London's Petrie Museum liked archaeology and its pop culture tropes but rejected academics as boring hoarders of information; they had little interest in archaeological ethics and rejected Greek, Roman, or Islamic era Egypt as lacking mystery.[49] Museum visitors rejected the authoritative voice of experts and embraced colonialist heroes who were dominant over "native" peoples. Television and other media producers keenly understand this and have followed in the style of Fell and von Däniken, questioning expert dogma by using a combination of preprofessional common sense and the esoteric, text-based wisdom of the ancients to find a hidden or forbidden history informed by colonialist tropes.

Both those who would include alternative archaeology and those who would debunk it make valid points and demonstrate critical flaws. Adam Stout and others connect the criticism of neo-druids and the debunking of ley line hunters with the triumphalist policing of boundaries: professionals within archaeology, amateurs without.[50] Concern for the veracity of claims over the social context of these claims can ignore the relationship between scientific authority and political power. However, the same could be said of those who argue for the inclusion of alternatives to a scientific archaeology. Trying to critique professional archaeology as classist, racist, sexist, and exclusionary by incorporating alternatives primarily informed by Victorian theory and culture seems like a stupendously bad idea. Alternative archaeology can be a major vector for spreading old racist ideologies into the present.[51]

Jasmine Day suggested that the appeal of colonialist treasure hunters rests in the acquisition of valuable items. There are two components of a treasure hunt: the hunt and the treasure. Museum visitors, fantasizing about being treasure hunters in the tomb-like low lighting of maze-like Egyptological museum exhibits, are playing at participating in the hunt. April Beisaw compares the role of participation in archaeology with ghost hunting. Unlike the occulted archaeologists Bond and Lethbridge, Beisaw isn't using spectral evidence to investigate the past. She takes her students on ghost hunts in old buildings on her college campus. Students who previously ignored these structures become fascinated by the idea of a haunting and the opportunity to investigate. Beisaw argues that when archaeologists address visitors to a site or a museum, they lecture too much about the fruits of their archaeological research. We archaeologists experience the adventure of archaeology, and then we tell others about it. Placed in the role of an investigator, Beisaw's students learn to ask questions, weigh evidence, check their results, and present their interpretations. By using the metaphors of the detective and the psychic investigator that we've already seen entangled with archaeology, Beisaw teaches her students about the scientific examination of the past.[52]

Much of the appeal of alternative archaeology and one reason that it goes hand in hand with conspiracy theory is that the conspiracy theorist or alternative thinker believes they are engaged in detective work or a quest themselves. They take pride in assembling theories for themselves out of evidence they have tracked through alternative sources. Michael Barkun discussed improvisational millennialism as the style of conspiracy culture, the creation of apocalyptic scenarios out of not one existing religious tradition, but a collage of many different sources, including existing religions and popular media. Conspiracy theorists create "real news" in opposition to mainstream knowledge.[53]

The hunt is important, but so is the treasure. Evan Parker echoed Jasmine Day in his analysis of archaeology on American cable television as part of a larger category of object-oriented shows in which acquisition is the primary motivation (house hunting, antique identification, archaeological digging).[54] However, I would argue that a greater issue is at play: purpose. Acquisition is a straightforward purpose. Popular and stereotypical archaeologists may be after gain, but the big adventures of fictional archaeologists, from Setne Khamwas to Lara Croft, are about recovering dangerously powerful supernatural artifacts that explain and control the nature of the world. These objects provide clear motivations either for the protagonist to safeguard such objects or for evil antagonists to try to use these artifacts to control the world. By contrast the academic stereotype, Professor Dryasdust, studies potsherds for reasons that aren't clear or interesting while ignoring valuable treasures of wealth, wisdom, and wonder.

The weird and pointless Professor Dryasdust reflects one of three attitudes toward science found in American culture and also more broadly.[55] The first is rooted in Protestant theology during the Enlightenment, a sacred exploration of creation through engaged but atheoretical doing (exploring, documenting, collecting, classifying). The wonder at creation and the demonstration of cosmological meaning through experience are found in the importance of artifacts and especially landscapes to myth and identity, the antiquarian impulse to find meaning in the land and in received history.

The second attitude celebrates practical science, the use of scientific discovery and technological advancement to better the individual and society. This is a common argument for funding and education in the hard sciences with the goal of economic, social, or military advancement. The hunt for supernaturally powerful artifacts makes practical sense (if they exist), and the trope of secret agents or societies racing to find such artifacts is common in fiction and conspiracy theories.

Professor Dryasdust embodies the third attitude, which values research science focused on the theoretical over the practical. The research scientist, stereotyped as the mad scientist, questions the universe and dares to write its rules. This hubris is compounded by unclear or unnatural motives. Research science for the sake of research gives us Professor Dryasdust and his pointless obsessions. When politicians attack archaeology, they are invoking Professor Dryasdust. In 2013 two US senators wrote an editorial attacking scientific projects they believed that the National Science Foundation should not be funding. Five of their nine examples of meritless science were archaeological.[56]

If archaeology's motives are not pointless, then they are hidden or unnatural. The archaeological equivalent of the mad scientist is the incompetent or conspiratorial archaeologist who is unable to see the mythic truth or is hiding it. Spending a lifetime to analyze broken pottery or fish ear bones doesn't make sense unless the archaeologist is a bit mad or has a hidden conspiratorial motivation.

Wrestling with a Spooky Past

The prevalence of people bringing mythic themes to museums or other archaeology experiences suggests that archaeologists must engage with those themes if they are to effectively communicate their work.[57] How has archaeology engaged with mythic and alternative claims?[58] Archaeologists initially engaged with such claims in a Romantic sense, attempting to materialize myth. I have examined numerous examples of this, including MacRitchie's fairy race, Bond's sacred Glastonbury, Evans's Palace of Minos, Schliemann's Agamemnon, numerous protohistoric national archaeologies, Woolley's deluge level at Ur, the attempts to discover Atlanteans or other colonists in the Mississippian or Mayan ruins of the Americas, and Margaret Murray's witch cult.

These mythic archaeologists, as well as numerous hoaxers, were confronted during the process of professionalization. I already mentioned the resistance to Lethbridge's Gogmagog and to the ley line hunters. Other efforts included the direct testing of extraordinary claims. Epigraphers and linguists were unimpressed with the allegedly ancient inscriptions in Old World languages on the Kensington Runestone and the Newark "holy stones." A late example of this kind of artifact debunking occurred in the 1950s, when Charles di Peso uncovered the hoaxing of clay dinosaurs and other strange figurines near Acambaro, Mexico.[59]

In a number of cases, archaeologists chose not just to examine artifacts, but to dig. I have already discussed the tremendous controversy over the Glozel case, whose claims fell apart after a team of archaeologists demonstrated the shortcomings of the Glozel diggers by burying their modern corkscrews at the site in a supposedly ancient context. A similar case had unraveled decades earlier when James Talmage undertook quiet excavations to investigate the "Michigan relics," which had started to appear in 1889. He found no evidence for their authenticity. Archaeologists also dug in response to hoaxed Latin-inscribed artifacts found near Tucson, Arizona.[60]

Perhaps the most formal example of digging to investigate the extraordinary is the tower of Newport, Rhode Island. According to historical records, colonial governor Benedict Arnold built a stone masonry windmill sometime around the 1670s. However, in 1837 the mill became a Viking "tower" in Carl Rafn's book *Antiquitates Americanae*, part of a popular and racially tinged nineteenth-century argument for Narragansett Bay being the Vinland of Norse sagas.[61] As already noted, the quite racist H. P. Lovecraft visited the site, loved the Viking concept, and wanted to make it part of a weird tale. The ultimate result of Lovecraft's interest included inhuman builders, foundation sacrifices, native legends, unexplainable construction techniques, hidden passages, and a history as part of an ancient underwater city subsequently thrust up from the depths.[62]

In 1942 Philip Ainsworth Means, an archaeologist who had worked with Hiram Bingham at Machu Picchu,[63] claimed that the Newport tower was built in 1120 CE. His offer to fund excavations was denied by Newport's Park Commission but inspired the Society for American Archaeology to organize a committee to address the issue. Despite objections that the investigation was a waste of time and money, excavations in 1948 and 1949 were directed by William S. Godfrey Jr., a graduate student attached to Harvard University's Peabody Museum. Artifacts and features associated with the excavation and construction of the tower foundations dated to the seventeenth century, supporting the historical record. Godfrey anticipated later theoretical arguments about power and the past by suggesting that the newly class-conscious elites of the nineteenth century had used the legend of very white and very Northern European Vikings to embellish their ancestry in a context of increased immigration.[64] An uncharitable reading might note that Godfrey, himself a descendant of Benedict Arnold, was a graduate student at America's most prestigious university and was ritually invoking a famous ancestor to claim professional authority over interlopers.

When I visited the Newport tower in 2011, the official tourist signs for historic Newport referred to the structure as the Old Stone Mill. I was unable to visit a nearby museum dedicated to the tower because of the Fourth of July holiday. In the storefront window, the museum noted that everyone from the Phoenicians to the Chinese to the Templars had been suggested as having built the tower, though they apparently preferred the tower to be an Elizabethan astronomical device. In 2003 another group, the Chronognostic Research Foundation (CRF), hired a cultural resource management firm to conduct remote sensing and archaeological excavations that once again found no evidence against a seventeenth-century construction.[65] Despite this, the CRF continued to use astronomical alignments, the method practiced by Arthur Posnansky, Graham Hancock, and other alternative archaeologists, to suggest a medieval construction date.[66] The excavations brought attention to CRF-involved media events, including the unveiling of a graphic to be used on U-Haul rental vehicles.[67] The graphic described the tower as "mysterious" and built by "unknown explorers." It was part of a series highlighting mysteries and wonders of the fifty American states, including Vermont's Lake Champlain monster,

New Mexico's Roswell UFO crash, and Nevada's allegedly extraterrestrial Area 51.

Another excavation of an alleged ancient European structure occurred at Pattee's Caves in southern New Hampshire in 1956. Beginning in 1935 the site, generally believed by archaeologists to be colonial, had been reconstructed into "Celtic" or other pre-Columbian European architecture. Excavation only produced nineteenth-century artifacts, yet the site is now known as "Mystery Hill" and "America's Stonehenge" and is the center of Celtic and Phoenician hyperdiffusion claims.[68] The site's management offers spirit walks with dowsing and electromagnetic field detectors to communicate with the spirits of the land and ancient people, as well as "paranormal investigation" close to Halloween.[69] The interest in numerous "megalithic" sites in the region inspired Vermont's state archaeologist to study the poorly documented rural colonial structures that mainstream archaeologists find at the heart of the New England megalith phenomenon.[70]

Beyond specific scientific inquiries, broader professional archaeological engagement with public mass media was once common. Top professional archaeologists, like Woolley, Sir Mortimer Wheeler, and Glyn Daniel, helped produce print material, radio shows, and television programming aimed at a general audience.[71] The establishment of archaeology in university departments favored other priorities, however. The last steps completing professionalization occurred in the 1950s and 1960s and can be seen in the Gogmagog affair and the formal rejection of hyperdiffusion.[72] This era boasted a "new archaeology" and subsequent theoretical reactions to this triumphant positivist science. Perhaps it is no accident that once archaeologists had to publish more in order to stay on the increasingly formal academic track, the old hyperdiffusionist and theosophical ideas reemerged outside of the profession. The popularization of ancient astronauts in the book *Chariots of the Gods?* made author Erich von Däniken the most famous archaeologist in the public mind for decades after its release.[73] This book inspired a television documentary featuring the *Twilight Zone* creator and host, Rod Serling, called *In Search of Ancient Astronauts*, which launched an entire genre of television: the paranormal documentary.[74] If the theosophists and antiquarians of archaeology's alchemical days were going to be driven from museums and universities, they would find a new home in the media that archaeology had abandoned.

The first professional critiques of what was coming to be called pseudo-archaeology followed about a decade later.[75] Following in the footsteps of Robert Wauchope, many of these and subsequent works aimed simultaneously to debunk what the authors saw as pseudoscientific claims and to teach the basics of science and critical thinking to a larger audience. These efforts were criticized from two ends. Like the critics of Godfrey's excavations of the Newport tower, many professionals refused to acknowledge what they saw as the lunatic fringe. Recognizing its existence, even to debunk it, dignified it. Alternatively, there were critiques of scientific and positivist archaeology that found the debunking efforts to be a gross form of gatekeeping for the establishment. As a result, the most common form of pseudoarchaeology critiqued in textbooks is that practiced for nationalist or ideological causes and organizations. Nazi or imperialist racial archaeology is inherently scientifically invalid and can simultaneously act as a critique of professionals acting badly on behalf of the powerful. There is something to offend everyone.[76]

The initial steps in examining spooky archaeology have led to a host of new studies of extreme archaeological claims, which call out bad scientific practices but do not forget the anthropological importance of context.[77] The Hebrew-inscribed Newark holy stones were a hoax (one of them replicated a nineteenth-century typeface), but they may have been a desperate attempt to scientifically debunk a racist ideology and head off the American Civil War.[78] Much of the information about archaeology and extrahumans in chapter 2 has its roots in folklore that emerged from archaeological interest in memory, identity, and the ancient reuse of the archaeological landscape. The Arthurian and spiritual claims for Glastonbury examined in chapter 3 inspired historical and archaeological research that produced important information on the nature of spirituality in modern Britain and the role of memory in the medieval construction of identity and political power. The discovery of the Mu stones didn't tell us a lot about the ancient mystical past but opened up a window into how and why Mesoamerican archaeology came to be. The shadowy histories of museums and spies in chapters 7 and 8 show the effects of empire on archaeological practices. And as I showed in chapters 9 and 10, the roots of modern alternative archaeology may lead back to theosophy or the Romantics, but they were planted in the archaeological community and watered by the practices discussed in this book.

Completely ignoring the sensational, supernatural, or suspect elements of archaeology's past and present is unrealistic. They are inherent to a science that studies the origins of human identities, that attempts to map territory that is both mythic and meaningful. The very notion of scientifically examining this past is part of modernity, and like other institutions archaeology shares in the contested and negative legacy of modernity. Archaeology's colonial history, when combined with the mythic aspect, transforms into not only orientalism, but supernatural exoticism. Ignoring this reality will not make it go away. Visitors to our museums, classrooms, and presentations bring this history with them and will often replace our messages with the supernatural and exotic. Accepting our checkered past and the inherently weird practice of digging into the mythic past should be an exercise in "constructively deconstructing."[79] The archaeologist's job is to look under rocks, find unexpected historical remnants, and explore their cultural meaning for the past and for the present. There is no reason that our own cultures should be exempt from such methods. The prominence of many of these issues, including their success outside the walled garden of academic and professional archaeology, makes them less like random potsherds and more like monumental pyramids begging for explanation. Like the real pyramids, we can't blame aliens or foreign colonists or "Hollywood" or "the media" or "the fringe" for their construction. We made them ourselves for reasons that made sense in their time and that help us make sense of our own.

CHRONOLOGY

ca. 2500 BCE	The apkallu of Sumerian and Babylonian lore starts a deep tradition in southwestern Asia of divine civilization bringers. This tradition inspires much of later alternative archaeology.
ca. 1279–1224 BCE	Lifetime of Khaemweset, *sem* priest, chief son of Ramesses II, restorer of the pyramid of Unas, and model for Setne Khamwas and *The Mummy*.
440 BCE	Herodotus inspires later concepts of time with *Histories*.
350 BCE	Plato creates the narrative of Atlantis.
ca. 300–200 BCE	Bronze Age monuments in Lebanon and elsewhere influence the Abrahamic traditions of the Watchers, including those found in the book of Enoch, key elements of later alternative archaeology. Earliest known date for story of Setne Khamwas.
ca. 100–500 CE	At least as early as the early Classic period, Mayan scribes reworked Olmec jades into heirlooms.
ca. 300–400	Horapollo's *Hieroglyphica* is produced. It will become a major influence on later views of Egyptian hieroglyphs.
ca. 500	Oldest evidence for occupation at Glastonbury Abbey. Anglo-Saxons in Britain reuse ancient burial mounds, including thinking of them as home to spirits and treasure.
ca. 944	Yemeni historian al-Hasan al-Hamdani inventories structures allegedly built by jinn.
ca. 1136	Geoffrey of Monmouth writes that the wizard Merlin magically constructed Stonehenge.
1191	Glastonbury monks dig and "find" the bones of Arthur and Guinevere.
ca. 1198	William of Newburgh records the legend of a man who raided the barrow of Willy Howe in East Riding, Yorkshire, for a fairy cup that ended up in the hands of Henry I and other kings.
1208	Saxo Grammaticus records that megalithic sites were the work of the giants and later occupied by fairies.

1278	The alleged bones of Arthur are reinterred at Glastonbury Abbey in the presence of King Edward I.
1419	Horapollo's *Hieroglyphica* is rediscovered on the Greek island of Andros.
1487	The *Malleus Maleficarum* provides a guidebook to hunting witches and likely inspires many of the "confessions" obtained under torture.
1493	Giovanni Nanni creates archaeological fakes to give the Borgias a fictional descent from the Egyptian god Osiris.
1520	Europeans first encounter Mesoamerican writing and compare it with Egyptian writing.
1535	Atlantis is suggested as an ancient record of the New World.
1544	Bishop Cristóbal de Pedraza records the first written account later interpreted as the legendary Ciudad Blanca in Honduras.
1549	A pseudo obelisk is raised in Paris.
1590	Accused Scottish witch Katherene Ross describes going into the hills to obtain "elf-arrow-heidis" for healing. Chinese writing is compared to Egyptian and Mexican hieroglyphs.
ca. 1600	Earliest versions of the Luck of Edenhall story.
1620	After Plymouth Puritans start grave robbing, the sachem of Passonagessit invokes his mother's ghost in protest, establishing a precedent for the "cursed native burial ground."
1628	Accused Scottish witch Stein Maltman describes the use of an elf arrowhead in healing an "elf-shot" woman.
1634	England's royal clockmaster, David Ramsay, leads a party of treasure hunters, including a dowser, at Westminster Abbey. Though demons plague the party, no treasure is found.
1652–1654	Athanasius Kircher writes the influential *Oedipus Aegyptiacus* and 15 years later creates his own symbolic hieroglyphic system.
1680	Mexican scholar Carlos de Sigüenza y Góngora suggests Atlantis as the source of Mexican civilization.
1689	King of Denmark obtains the fairy-made Oldenburg Horn.
1721	Publication and widespread popularity of the Luck of Edenhall story.
ca. 1775	Antiquarian John Aubrey collects firsthand account of a fairy assault in Wiltshire.
1781	Antoine Court de Gébelin claims the tarot encodes secrets of the Book of Thoth.

1783	First theosophical society founded in London.
1787	Captain Antonio del Río is first scholar to explore a Classic Maya ruin. His report on Palenque suggests it was the product of hyper-diffusion from the Old World. The Canaries and Azores are suggested to be Atlantean mountaintops.
1798	Napoleon invades Egypt. Scholars traveling with his army spark intense scientific work on Egypt, especially after the discovery of the Rosetta Stone. Public dedication of the cemetery at Marietta, Ohio, gives classical names to indigenous monuments allegedly built by Mexicans.
1801–1812	Lord Elgin begins removing the carved marbles of the Parthenon.
1803	Earliest suggestion that fairies may be a memory of ancient peoples in Europe.
1814	Removal of the Odin Stone at Stenness in the Orkneys, Scotland, generates local fury.
1818	John Cleves Symmes Jr. produces "Circular Number 1," urging expedition to the hollow earth.
1822	Charles Maclaren first suggests that Hisarlik is Troy.
1825	Bolivia's second president, Antonio José de Sucre, orders the excavation of the Gateway of the Sun at Tiwanaku, but later intellectuals ignore the site.
1827	Jane Webb Loudon's *The Mummy! A Tale of the Twenty-Second Century* is one of the first mummy stories.
1830	Walter Scott suggests the tie between ancient peoples and fairies.
1838	The US Exploring Expedition, inspired in part by John Symmes's promotion of the hollow earth expedition, helps lead to formation of Smithsonian Institution.
1841	John Lloyd Stephens and Frederick Catherwood bring the image of lost Mayan cities to a global audience, inspiring the development of Mayan archaeology.
1842	Joseph Smith translates Egyptian papyruses as *The Book of Abraham*.
1850	P. T. Barnum promotes the Iximaya hoax.
1851	First use of term "prehistory." The Great Exhibition in London features Egyptian monuments.

1859   Charles Darwin publishes *On the Origin of Species*.

1864   French newspaper *Le Pays* describes discovery of calcified "Martian mummy" and images of alien creatures in Colorado. Within a year, similar stories emerge and spread throughout Latin America in the 1870s.

　　　　　　Discovery of papyrus recording the tale *Setne Khamwas and Naneferkaptah*.

　　　　　　Lemuria is invented to account for the distribution of primates around the Indian Ocean.

1865   French emperor Napoleon III personally funds a statue of Vercingetorix, modeled on the emperor himself, at the site identified with the Battle of Alésia.

1867   George Hull commissions the Cardiff giant, the most famous archaeological hoax of its day.

　　　　　　Charles Warren secretly digs to the foundations of the Temple Mount, uncovering the first direct archaeological ties to the Bible in Jerusalem.

　　　　　　Brasseur de Bourbourg uses Mayan mythology and hieroglyphs to suggest an origin in Atlantis.

1871   Edward Bulwer-Lytton's novel *The Coming Race* is a major influence on science fiction and paranormal claims.

　　　　　　Heinrich Schliemann begins excavating at Hisarlik and two years later finds Priam's Treasure.

1873   Augustus and Alice Le Plongeon begin archaeological exploration of Yucatán.

1877   H. P. Blavatsky publishes her first major work in theosophy, *Isis Unveiled*.

1879   Edward Thompson publishes an article in *Popular Science Monthly* linking Atlantis to the Mayas.

1880   Flinders Petrie goes to Egypt to test the "pyramid inch."

1881   Antiquities dealer Eugène Boban unveils the crystal skull later acquired by the British Museum.

1882   Ignatius Donnelly's *Atlantis: The Antediluvian World* creates the modern hyperdiffusion myth of Atlantis.

1883   First of several articles in *Scientific American* by Augustus and Alice Le Plongeon about their archaeological work in Yucatán.

　　　　　　Flinders Petrie finds that the pyramid inch does not exist, but stays to study and protect Egyptian antiquities.

　　　　　　E. A. Wallis Budge begins efforts to triple the size of the British Museum's Egyptian holdings.

1885	The eruption of Krakatoa in 1883 inspires the notion that the Thera eruption in the Aegean may be related to the myth of Atlantis.
1886	H. Rider Haggard's *She* is published.
1887	Augustus Jessopp explores the haunted nature of antiquarian treasures, inspiring ghost story author M. R. James.
1888	H. P. Blavatsky publishes the magnum opus of theosophy, *The Secret Doctrine*. Founding of the first temple of the Hermetic Order of the Golden Dawn.
1890	David MacRitchie publishes the first of two works on his pygmy fairy race theory, *Testimony of Tradition*. A year later, formal debate of the theory by the Folklore Society does not resolve the question. Cyrus Thomas begins debunking the moundbuilder myth.
1892	Arthur Conan Doyle's "Lot No. 249" is early example of villainous mummy story. Amelia Edwards endows a professorship and museum to support Flinders Petrie at University College London.
1895	"The Shining Pyramid" is the first of several stories by Arthur Machen about a pygmy fairy race. Percival Lowell believes he has discovered canals on Mars.
1897	A supposed craft from Mars, containing "hieroglyphics," allegedly crashes into a windmill in Aurora, Texas. Later in the year, "Professor" Jeremiah MacDonald claims that an aerolite fell in Binghamton, New York, containing message from Mars. Marie Corelli's *Ziska, the Problem of a Wicked Soul* melds romance, reincarnation, and mysteries under the Great Pyramid. Corelli will later inspire the Tut curse.
1898	Kaiser Wilhelm II tours the Middle East and is fascinated by Baalbek. He funds German excavations that alarm Britain and France.
1899	Folklorist Charles Leland claims to have found a pagan survival of witch practices in Italy; he publishes *Aradia; or, The Gospel of the Witches*. Arthur Evans buys Knossos. First meeting of the Archaeological Institute of America.
1901	Arthur Conan Doyle visits the Devon home of Bertram Fletcher Robinson, a visit that inspires *The Hound of the Baskervilles*.
1903	Bram Stoker's story of reincarnation and a villainous mummy, *The*

Jewel of Seven Stars, is inspired by Howard Carter's discovery of tomb of Hatshepsut earlier in the year.

Despite later claims of discovery by Mitchell-Hedges, Thomas Gann and R. E. Merwin of the Peabody Museum work at Lubaantun, Belize.

1904   Aleister Crowley travels in Egypt for his honeymoon. After overnight rituals in the Great Pyramid, he channels *The Book of the Law*.

E. A. Wallis Budge first tells the story of the unlucky mummy to reporter Bertram Fletcher Robinson.

Arturo Posnansky begins digging at Tiwanaku in Bolivia, which he considers the "cradle of American man."

Sylvanus Morley writes a paper on deluge myths in Central America.

George Gustav Heye begins funding archaeological expeditions, sometimes participating in the field, as part of his collecting efforts.

1906   The United States passes the Antiquities Act to protect archaeological resources on federal land, partly in response to commercial digging in Chaco Canyon by Richard Wetherill.

1907   Sir Arthur Conan Doyle suggests "elemental" spirits caused the death of his friend Bertram Fletcher Robinson in connection with the unlucky mummy case. Panicked collectors send their Egyptian antiquities to the British Museum.

1908   Algernon Blackwood publishes "The Nemesis of Fire."

1911   Evans-Wentz suggests in *The Fairy-Faith in Celtic Countries* that fairies are likely real psychical phenomena.

M. R. James depicts the British Library as an occult battleground in "Casting the Runes."

Kaiser Wilhelm II begins excavations in Corfu, sparking an interest in the sun cult and gorgons.

Montague Brownlow Parker follows the psychic advice of Finnish medium Valter H. Juvelius to excavate the Temple Mount. The secret digging causes riots in Jerusalem as rumors spread that they have plundered the Temple Mount and found the Ark of the Covenant.

William Niven describes excavating a vast and ancient civilization around Mexico City.

1912   Sylvanus Morley successfully proposes the Carnegie Institution fund a 25-year archaeology program in the Mayan region.

Gustaf Kossinna publishes *German Prehistory, an Extraordinary National Science*, inspiring racial archaeology in Germany.

T. E. Lawrence and Leonard Woolley conduct espionage against German rail interests while digging at Carchemish.

"Paul Schliemann" tells how he "found" Atlantis.

1914   Sax Rohmer's *Brood of the Witch-Queen* includes the Book of Thoth and may have helped inspire *The Mummy*.

1915   The Ancient and Mystical Order Rosae Crucis is founded.

Archaeologists Gertrude Bell, Leonard Woolley, D. G. Hogarth, and T. E. Lawrence become the Oxford Four, directing British intelligence work in the Middle East during the First World War.

1916   Lawrence leads an Arab revolt against the Ottoman Empire.

Woolley is captured outside of Port Said.

Guatemalan troops ambush Sylvanus Morley's archaeological expedition to Waxaktun, killing two.

Mexican archaeologist Manuel Gamio criticizes William Niven as a charlatan.

1917   Lovecraft writes "Dagon," his first story about an ancient, ruined, underwater nonhuman city.

Sylvanus Morley volunteers to act as a spy for the US Office of Naval Intelligence, ultimately constructing a ring of several archaeologists working in Mexico and Central America.

Margaret Murray begins publishing articles about the witch cult.

Manuel Gamio founds the Dirección de Antropología in Mexico.

1919   Charles Fort publishes *The Book of the Damned*, launching Fortean studies.

Franz Boas criticizes the Mayan spy ring in the *Nation*, leading to his censure within professional anthropology.

1920   Ramón Mena uses William Niven's materials to propose a chronology of Mexico, prompting critics to discover that some of Niven's artifacts are fakes.

Lovecraft writes his one explicit Atlantis story, "The Temple."

1921   Lovecraft writes of an inhuman buried city inspired by Irem in "The Nameless City."

Frederick Bligh Bond reveals his psychic archaeology in *The Gate of Remembrance*. He is dismissed from his position the following year.

Margaret Murray lays out her theory in *The Witch-Cult in Western Europe*.

William Niven begins discovering "glyph tablets" at San Miguel Amantla.

1922	Gertrude Bell becomes director of the newly formed Baghdad Archaeological Museum (later the National Museum of Iraq).
	Howard Carter discovers Tutankhamun tomb, sends for Lord Carnarvon.
1923	Marie Corelli suggests that Lord Carnarvon has been poisoned, according to accounts she read in a translation of a medieval book on Hermetic Egyptian lore. When Carnarvon dies of an infection, this narrative is promoted by Arthur Conan Doyle, sparking the Tut curse legend.
	Artifacts from Chichén Itzá's Sacred Cenote are revealed to the public.
	Frans Blom, Sylvanus Morley, and Thomas Gann visit William Niven and, though initially thinking the glyph tablets to be hoaxes, see his workers excavate some. During this same trip, Morley is shown a jade plaque later purchased and smuggled out of Mexico by Thomas Gann.
	Archaeologists, ruins, and pagan survivals are featured in Lovecraft's "The Rats in the Walls." After reading Murray's *Witch-Cult*, Lovecraft incorporates the idea into "The Festival" and later into other stories.
1924	Manuel Gamio publishes the first stratigraphic sequence in Mexico.
	British Museum director Frederic Kenyon urges Mitchell-Hedges and Lady Richmond Brown to excavate at Lubaantun.
	Agatha Christie cites the unlucky mummy in the Tut-inspired "The Adventure of the Egyptian Tomb."
	Lovecraft ghostwrites "Under the Pyramids" for Houdini.
	Professor L. H. Dudley Buxton of the University of Oxford presents on William Niven's "partitioned skulls" from Mexico at the annual meeting of the British Association for the Advancement of Science.
	Count Byron Khun de Prorok begins promoting his Sahara expedition in New York.
1925	An anthropologist and a form of the hidden witch cult appear in Lovecraft's "The Horror at Red Hook." Lovecraft plots "The Call of Cthulhu."
	Alfred Watkins invents ley lines in *The Old Straight Track*.
1926	James Churchward publishes *The Lost Continent of Mu*.
	William Niven sends one of his tablets to Tulane University.
	Lovecraft finalizes "The Call of Cthulhu" in August. He mentions Tutankhamun in "Cool Air."
	Investigation of the Glozel affair.

1927	The robbery of F. A. Mitchell-Hedges gets tremendous press coverage, resulting in Mitchell-Hedges losing a libel suit the following year.
	Lovecraft's "The History of the Necronomicon" resembles Marie Corelli's claims of a mysterious book warning of Tut's curse.
1928	Glozel is increasingly considered a fake after an investigatory panel demonstrates incompetence of the diggers.
	Standing stones and Arthur Machen's pagan survivals inspire Lovecraft's "The Dunwich Horror."
1929	Charles Lindbergh partners with A. V. Kidder to conduct first aerial archaeological survey of Mayan ruins.
	Occultist Marie Emily "Netta" Fornario found dead on Sithean Mor.
	The Heye Museum of the American Indian and museums in Oxford and Cambridge accept Panamanian artifacts from Mitchell-Hedges and Lady Richmond Brown.
1930	Lovecraft ghostwrites the lost-race stories "The Mound" and "Medusa's Coil." He also transforms Arthur Machen's fairy race into alien abductors in "The Whisperer in Darkness."
	A German archaeologist is arrested in Iran on suspicion of being Lawrence of Arabia.
1931	Mitchell-Hedges plans expedition to Honduras. The Heye Museum will display its share of the artifacts in 1933 while the other half goes to the British Museum.
	Leonard Woolley links several discoveries at Ur to the Bible. He claims to have found evidence of the deluge.
	Lovecraft writes influential ancient extraterrestrials novella *At the Mountains of Madness*.
	Mortimer Wheeler is one of several scholars to hide on May Eve near the Cerne giant in the hope of seeing rituals by surviving pagans.
1932	A number of plot points in Lovecraft's "The Dreams in the Witch House" resemble details in Murray's *Witch-Cult*.
	The Mummy is released.
	Wendell Bennett excavates a massive monolith at Tiwanaku. Arturo Posnansky has it installed in La Paz despite substantial opposition.
1933	Margaret Murray details the witch cult in *The God of the Witches*.
	London art dealer Sydney Burney writes to George Vaillant at the American Museum of Natural History about the crystal skull he has obtained, later known as the Mitchell-Hedges skull.

Lovecraft ghostwrites "Out of the Aeons," featuring the continent of Mu.

Edgar Cayce has psychic readings of a Hall of Records in Egypt and later discusses a counterpart in Yucatán.

1934 Aleš Hrdlička of the Smithsonian explains claims of giants' bones as mistakes.

1935 The Nazi SS creates the Ahnenerbe to investigate historical, archaeological, and occult topics.

Katharine Maltwood proposes that landscape features around Glastonbury form an effigy of the zodiac.

1936 The British Museum and Burney (or Mitchell-Hedges) crystal skulls are profiled in *Man*.

Agatha Christie's novel *Murder in Mesopotamia* is published. The following year she writes the Egyptian historical play *Akhnaton*, though it is not published until 1973.

1937 Ahnenerbe agent Edmund Kiss publishes fiction and nonfiction work about the world ice theory and racial prehistory based on his work at Tiwanaku.

1940 Theodore Morde claims to have found the "city of the monkey god" in Honduras.

1942 The Office of Strategic Services employs many archaeologists as intelligence agents during World War II.

1943 The FBI severs ties to Dana and Ginger Lamb, who appear to be more interested in archaeological exploration and collecting artifacts for Nelson Rockefeller than in spying for the Allies.

1944 The Acambaro figurines begin appearing in Mexico.

F. A. Mitchell-Hedges buys the Burney crystal skull. He never provides its origins, though his daughter claims it was found decades earlier at Lubaantun, Belize.

Agatha Christie's *Death Comes as the End* is based on unpublished Egyptian papyruses.

1948 Walter W. Taylor's dissertation on the state of American archaeology inspires more explicit methodological and theoretical discussion within the profession.

1949 The invention of radiocarbon dating transforms archaeological theory.

A. V. Kidder describes the two stereotypes of archaeologist as "hairy-chested" adventurer and "hairy-chinned" professor.

1950 Crashed saucer legend first published in Frank Scully's *Behind the Flying Saucers*.

Press campaign by former Scotland Yard chief inspector Robert Fabian sparks witchcraft speculation about the murder of Charles Walton in 1945, inspiring Margaret Murray to investigate.

1951	William Godfrey concludes that the Newport tower was built in the seventeenth century.
1952	Yuri Knorozov provides the key phonetic breakthrough in the decipherment of Maya writing, though it will be mostly ignored in the West for 20 years.
1953	Margaret Murray becomes president of the Folklore Society.

Charles di Peso debunks the Acambaro figurines in *American Antiquity*.

Conclusion of CIA Operation TP-AJAX, the overthrow of the Iranian government, masterminded by Donald Wilber.

Decipherment of Linear B undercuts many of the Minoan fantasies inspired by Arthur Evans.

1954   F. A. Mitchell-Hedges discusses the "skull of doom" for the first time in *Danger My Ally*.

Margaret Murray is quietly rejected by other scholars for suggesting a historical pagan conspiracy behind the British throne in *The Divine King in England*. However, her ideas inspire Gerald Gardner's introduction of his version of Wicca in *Witchcraft Today*.

T. C. Lethbridge begins his survey of the alleged Gogmagog earthworks at Wandlebury.

J. Eric Thompson's *Rise and Fall of Maya Civilization* is the most influential version of the "peaceful Maya" model. It also suggests that Mayan civilization may have diffused relatively recently from Asia.

1956   Gary Vescelius's excavations find no prehistoric European presence at Pattee's Caves, New Hampshire, also known as "America's Stonehenge."

1957   T. C. Lethbridge publishes on the controversial Gogmagog affair.

1958   James Mellaart publishes images of the controversial Dorak treasure in *Illustrated London News*.

Erik Wahlgren declares the Kensington Runestone to be a "mystery solved."

1959   Archaeologist George Agogino organizes research efforts for Tom Slick's hunt for the yeti. Agogino is also engaged with the CIA, and Slick's expedition is widely believed to have been a cover for spying on Chinese activities in Tibet.

1960	Louis Pauwels and Jacques Bergier publish *Le Matin des Magiciens* (The Morning of the Magicians).
1962	Robert Wauchope attacks hyperdiffusionism in *Lost Tribes and Sunken Continents*.
	Ralegh Radford believes that his excavations at Glastonbury Abbey found the burial pit of Arthur, but later analysis refutes this.
1964	T. C. Lethbridge appears on the BBC as a ghost hunter.
	US Army Intelligence attempts to use anthropologists in Project Camelot, but the project is exposed and collapses within a year.
1966	The Ica Stones begin appearing in southern Peru.
	John Rowe authors a definitive attack on hyperdiffusionist explanations for pre-Columbian America.
	Carlo Ginzburg suggests that some witch trials may record folk religion survivals in *The Night Battles*.
1968	Erich von Däniken mainstreams the notion of ancient extraterrestrials with *Chariots of the Gods?*
	Two journalists investigate the Dorak affair, suspecting that archaeologist James Mellaart was the victim of a hoax.
1969	Ufologist Jacques Vallee explicitly links fairy lore with UFO accounts.
	Ivor Noël Hume lauds dowsing in his manual *Historical Archaeology*.
1971	The Hexham Heads are excavated. Archaeologist Anne Ross and others report spectral activity.
	Ian Graham helps track dealers trying to sell a Mayan monument.
1972	Desmond Craigie says he made the Hexham Heads, and a study soon confirms they are composed of rough concrete. Anne Ross is forced to admit error in dating the objects.
	Sibley Morrill suggests that F. A. Mitchell-Hedges was a secret intelligence agent seeking the crystal skull. The skull is displayed in the Heye Museum of the American Indian and in 1973 is popularized in a book.
	The BBC production *The Stone Tape* uses archaeological imagery to popularize the ideas of T. C. Lethbridge and other psychic archaeologists.
1973	Rod Serling adapts *Chariots of the Gods?* for television as *In Search of Ancient Astronauts*. This documentary spawns the

television series *In Search of . . .* (arguably the model for paranormal television shows into the 1990s).

Basilo Uschuya admits to making the Ica Stones.

1974	Edgar Cayce supporters dive at Bimini in search of Atlantis.
1977	*The Amityville Horror* breathes new life into "cursed native burial ground" trope.

The Dragon Project investigates alleged energies associated with ancient monuments and ley lines.

1978   Spies, detectives, and the occult are invoked numerous times during the scripting meetings in which Indiana Jones is created.

Battlestar Galactica, in places resembling Mormon theology, bases science fiction adventure on the ancient extraterrestrials model.

1979   The first of a series of public addresses and publications against "pseudoarchaeology" begin to appear.

1980   *The Roswell Incident* by Berlitz and Moore includes a description of writing like "Egyptian hieroglyphics" in the supposed UFO wreckage. Other similar claims would emerge after this time in other crash stories.

Crop circles begin to appear in England in earnest, especially in the archaeologically rich Wiltshire area.

Vermont state archaeologist Giovanna Neudorfer publishes a study of stone chambers claimed by others to be ancient European constructions.

Hangar 18 mixes ancient extraterrestrials and the Roswell crash legend.

1981   *Raiders of the Lost Ark* is released.

1982   Marshall McKusick critically examines psychic archaeology in the *Journal for Field Archaeology*.

1983   Tom Williamson and Liz Bellamy publish *Ley Lines in Question*.

1984   Ken Feder writes an article combating pseudoarchaeology in *American Antiquity*.

Bruce Trigger examines ideology and alternative archaeology in *Man*.

Public celebrations are banned at Stonehenge, leading to the Battle of the Beanfield.

1985   Robert Ballard's search for the *Titanic* acts as a cover for US Navy investigation of two of its sunken submarines.

1986   Donald Wilber reveals his role in planning Operation TP-AJAX.

1990	Michael Michlovic examines folk archaeology in *Current Anthropology*.
	Kenneth Feder publishes the first edition of *Frauds, Myths, and Mysteries*, a popular textbook critically examining pseudoarchaeology.
	The United States protects indigenous remains with the Native American Graves Protection and Repatriation Act.
	Archaeological investigation of the McMartin preschool finds no evidence of tunnels described as integral parts of alleged Satanic rites.
1991	Stephen Williams publishes *Fantastic Archaeology*.
1993	Archaeological digging is interpreted by a second investigation as confirming the presence of tunnels at the McMartin preschool.
1994	*Stargate* launches a franchise based on the ancient extraterrestrials meme.
1995	Graham Hancock's "world civilization" described in *Fingerprints of the Gods* resembles older conceptions of hyperdiffusionist Atlantis.
	The first suggestions of a prosaic explanation for the Roswell incident, a secret balloon program, include clarification that the mysterious hieroglyphics were tape used in creating the balloons.
1999	*The Mummy* is released.
2000	Donald Wilber's secret history of Operation TP-AJAX is leaked to the *New York Times*.
	Brad Lepper and Jeff Gill argue that the Newark holy stones were an attempt to bring national unity in the face of the approaching American Civil War.
	The American Association of Museums and the Archaeological Institute of America support opposite sides in repatriation of a golden vessel looted from Sicily.
2001	Archaeological reanalysis of the Michigan relics hoax.
2002	Reanalysis of the McMartin preschool excavation suggests the remains were not of a tunnel but a series of trash pits.
	The Bennett monolith is returned to Tiwanaku in a celebration of indigenous political power in Bolivia.
2005	Debate about alternative archaeology in *World Archaeology*.
	Analysis of Mellaart's papers suggest the Dorak affair was a hoax.
	The television show *Bones* becomes an influential media representation of anthropology and archaeology.

The American Anthropological Association retracts its 86-year-old censure of Franz Boas over the issue of academic spies.

2006   Bolivia's first indigenous president, Evo Morales, is inaugurated at Tiwanaku.

2007   Archaeological investigation of the Newport tower finds no evidence refuting seventeenth-century construction date.

Lithic scatters in Pacific Northwest suggested as human explanation for Sasquatch.

2008   Scientific comparison of the crystal skulls with excavated Mesoamerican lapidary work discovers evidence of modern manufacture.

Release of *Indiana Jones and the Kingdom of the Crystal Skull*.

2009   *Ancient Aliens* becomes a staple of the History channel.

The Smithsonian frames its Jamestown exhibit in terms of forensic science methods popularized by television.

2011   Egyptian troops and civilians protect the Cairo Museum from looters during the Egyptian Revolution.

The Penn Museum hosts psychic ghost hunters as part of a Halloween-themed event, "We See Dead People."

Reports suggest Sean Quinn lost his billions due to moving a fairy-enchanted megalithic structure in 1992.

2012   Archaeologists criticize the claim that LiDAR surveying may have discovered Ciudad Blanca in Honduras.

The discovery of English king Richard III through DNA evidence and bioarchaeology and the discovery of cannibalized remains at Jamestown draw broad comparisons to criminal forensic investigation.

Controversial legal allegations between Belizean officials and the Disney corporation over use of the Mitchell-Hedges crystal skull.

The Mayan apocalypse does not occur.

2013   Two US senators pen an open letter in *USA Today* attacking archaeology as unworthy of National Science Foundation funding.

2014   Four "Mu stones" from William Niven's excavations are rediscovered at Miami University.

2015   Ground exploration of sites previously identified by LiDAR are linked to Ciudad Blanca, setting off a controversy over sensational television versus science.

Reanalysis of the archaeology of Glastonbury Abbey revises earlier legends and archaeological reports.

NOTES

Chapter 1

1. Bader et al. 2010:46–51.
2. Wynn 2007:121.
3. Smith 2006:45–47.
4. Levi 1988.
5. Gosden and Lock 1998:4–6.
6. Finley 1965:288. Daniel (1963:18) paraphrases Sir Alfred Clapham as saying that archaeology begins where living history ends.
7. Errington 1993:210.
8. Chadwick and Gibson 2013:12.
9. Lucas 2005:85–86.
10. Eliade 1954:34–48.
11. Zerubavel 2003:25–36.
12. Lane (2013:51–53) notes some of the methodological problems with this term.
13. Daniel 1963:30.
14. Mayor 2000.
15. Levine 1986:95–96.
16. Rizvi 2013:149–51; Schmidt and Mrozowski 2013:9.
17. Moshenska 2006.
18. Moshenska 2012.
19. Gann 1929:57–58, 64.
20. Baines 1996:364; Finley 1965:284–85; Gosden and Lock 1998:4–5.
21. Smith 2006:174–77.
22. Lightfoot 2013:189–91.
23. Murray 2014 [2004].
24. Daniel 1963:189–90, 194–95.
25. Finley 1965.
26. Lane 2013:57; Lucas 2004.
27. Daniel 1963:185–86; Lane 2013:57.
28. Hiscock 2012.

29. Kostich-Lefebvre 1998:130.
30. Mayor 2000:223–27.
31. Moshenska 2006.
32. Wengrow 2014:20–23.
33. Mayor 2000:223–27.
34. McElwee 2007; Rieder 2008:76–77.
35. Gann 1929:253.
36. Blavatsky 2006a [1877] :xxxvii–xxxix, 264–65; Hornung 2001:141; Pels 2000.
37. Blavatsky 2006a [1877]:iv–viii, xviii–xix; Ellis 1998:70.
38. Blavatsky 2014a [1888]:xxi–xxii, xl, xliii.
39. Luckhurst 2012:214–15; Moreno García 2009; Williams 1991:142.
40. Blavatsky 2006a [1877]:107, 162–63; Goodrick-Clarke 2004:18–19.
41. Kripal 2011.
42. Scherzler 2012:77–78.

Chapter 2

1. Harkin 2011.
2. Devereux 2003:42.
3. Bennett 2011.
4. Fortune 1963:95–96; Topham 2010.
5. Ashliman 2006:145–46; Brown and Bowen 1999; Ellis 2004:114–24; Champion and Cooney 1999:198–99, 201–4; Holm 1999:225–26; Silver 1999:36; Thompson 2004.
6. Ashliman 2006:17; MacLeod 2012:12–13; Ross 1967:39–42, 59; Silver 1999:43; Thompson 2004.
7. Silver 1986:141–42; Williamson and Bellamy 1983:114–15.
8. Semple 1998:117–18, 120.
9. Hinson 2003:50–51; Hutton 2014:1138–44, 1155; Silver 1999:41–42; Thompson 2004.
10. Ashliman 2006:143; Semple 1998:113.
11. Hingley 1996; Holtorf 1998; Semple 1998; Williamson and Bellamy 1983:115–21.
12. Grinsell 1967:7, 10; Mackenzie 1937; MacRitchie 1890:107; Semple 1998:109–10.
13. Greenhalgh 1989:219; Grinsell 1967:11–15.
14. Jessopp 1887:51–55; Rankine 2009.
15. Rankine 2009:14.
16. Beard 1972 [1934]:36–38; Greenhalgh 1989:235–36; Grinsell 1967:16–18, 38.
17. Grinsell 1967:15–16; Semple 1998.
18. Evans 2013; Jessopp 1887:48–50.
19. Cusack 2012:143; Williamson and Bellamy 1983:191–92.
20. Ashliman 2006:145–46.
21. Hallen 1903:118–20.
22. Towrie 2016; Gibson et al. 2015.

23. Eckardt and Williams 2003:149–55.
24. Davidson 1956; Hall 2007:110–11.
25. Daniel 1963:47–48; Davidson 1956:149–50.
26. Cohn 1975:114; Davidson 1956:152; Hall 2005:26–29.
27. Donovan 2007.
28. Tolkien 2004:173–82, 1052.
29. Beard 1972 [1934]:36–37; Briggs 1971:233–34.
30. Ashliman 2006:157; Ashliman 2012.
31. Randle 2000:35–41.
32. See http://www.vam.ac.uk/content/articles/t/the-luck-of-edenhall-history-and-myths, accessed 1 August 2017.
33. Beckett 2016; Briggs 1971:305; http://collections.vam.ac.uk/item/O3311/the-luck-of-edenhall-beaker-and-case-unknown, accessed 1 August 2017.
34. Hutton 2014:1152; Silver 1986:148–49.
35. Hinson 2003:10.
36. Forsyth 1980:49.
37. Scott 1830:110; Silver 1986:143–44, 149–50; Silver 1999:10–15, 29–30.
38. MacRitchie 1893:xx–xxii; Silver 1999:7, 32–33, 45–50, 129–42.
39. Stout 2008:58.
40. MacRitchie 1890:8–13, 33–34, 37–38, 45–46, 133–34; Richards 1996:194–96.
41. MacRitchie 1890:67–72, 141–42.
42. MacRitchie 1893:xv–xvi.
43. MacRitchie 1893:xvii; Packer et al. 1980:32.
44. Joshi 2011:xi, xvii; Leslie-McCarthy 2007:77–78; Machen 1898:271–73.
45. Machen 2010 [1895].
46. Machen 2011b.
47. Machen 2011a:34–37.
48. Leslie-McCarthy 2007:24; Machen 2011a:60–64.
49. Machen 2011a:46–47.
50. Silver 1999:51–56.
51. Evans-Wentz 1911:457–58, 489–91; Hinson 2003:50.
52. Silver 1986:147; Silver 1999:38–40, 51–56.
53. Boone 2000:376–81; Carrasco 2000:76; Jones 1995:334; Umberger 1987:66–69, 97–98.
54. Stuart 2000:501–6.
55. Boone 2000:388–89; Hamann 2002:355; López Luján et al. 2000; Pasztory 1997:15.
56. Pasztory 1997:16.
57. Greenhalgh 1989:125–33.
58. Umberger 1987:67–68.
59. Boone 2000:372–73; Hamann 2002:354–57; Umberger 1987:64.
60. Jansen 1990:103–4; Smith 1973:68–71; Williams 2009:54, 105.
61. Davies 2014.
62. Miller and Taube 1993:60; Umberger 1987:73–74.

63. Hamann 2002:353–54; Umberger 1987:66.
64. Boone 2000:390–91n5; Hamann 2002:354; León-Portilla 2002:110.
65. Chuchiak 2009; Clendinnen 1987:47–48, 73–79, 85–86, 169–89; Cook and Offit 2013:144–49; León-Portilla 2002:5–7.
66. Gould 2013; Tilley 2005.
67. Cook and Offit 2013:24, 52–53; Samson 2007:93–100.
68. Gnecco 2011:57–64.
69. Evans 2004:47.
70. Blom and La Farge 1926:255; Gann 1926:50; Stewart 2013:225.
71. Clarke 2015:83–88, 148–52, 191, 195–96.
72. Montejo 2005:67–69.
73. Hutson 2010:166–67; Jones 1995:193, 272n58; Redfield 1962 [1950]:14.
74. Jones 1998.
75. Castañeda 1996:288–93.
76. Hamann 2002:355.
77. Redfield and Villa Rojas 1962 [1934]:11–12.
78. Breglia 2009:61–62.
79. Hamann 2002:355.
80. Bierhorst 1990:8–9; Gann 1925:100; Kintz 1990:53, fig. 3.4; Preuss 2012:450, 454, 461.
81. Benavides C. 2008:242–43; Re Cruz 1996:181–82n25; Redfield and Villa Rojas 1962 [1934]:12n1, 119–21, 175.
82. Castañeda 1996:294–95.
83. Redfield and Villa Rojas 1962 [1934]:113–14.
84. Preuss 2012:454.
85. Hutson 2010:167–68; Magnoni et al. 2008:215.
86. Astor-Aguilera 2010:205–6; Redfield 1962 [1950]:125.
87. Sherman Horn, personal communication, 20 January 2016.
88. Silver 1999:193–205; Stableford 2007a:327–28.
89. Clarke 2015:267–70.
90. Gann 1926:93–94.
91. Gann 1925:156.
92. Gann 1925:100–101.
93. Gann 1925:203–4.
94. Gann 1925:235–36; Gann 1929:165–68.
95. Mitchell-Hedges 1931:194–95.
96. Gann 1925:67–68; Mitchell-Hedges 1931:75; Sherman Horn, personal communication, 20 January 2016.
97. Gann 1918:40–41.
98. Annus 2010:301–7, 313; Fröhlich 2014:12.
99. Annus 2010:295–96; Chesnutt 2014:172–73; Davies 2009:8; Sullivan 2014:95–96.
100. Annus 2010:309–10; Ben-Dov 2013.

101. Coppens 2012:61–63; Partridge 2004:167.
102. Manassa 2013:12–13.
103. Grinsell 1947:349; Reeves 2000:26; Regier 2004:6.
104. Reeves 2000:58.
105. Jordan 1998:xv–xvi, 22.
106. Behlmer 1996; Haarmann 1996:607; Manassa 2013:35.
107. Mango 1963; Salih 2015:18–19.
108. Cook 1983; Dykstra 1994:59; Grinsell 1947:347–48; Haarmann 1996:612–14; Hornung 2001:82, 155–58; M. Smith 2007:9–13.
109. Hornung 2001:163–64; Picknett and Prince 2003.
110. Haarmann 1996:616.
111. Zivie-Coche 2002:16.
112. Drieskins and Lucarelli 2002:85–87; El-Zein 2009:32–33; Lebling 2010:28–29; Peterson 2007:94, 98–99; Stevens 2006 [1931]:105–11.
113. El-Zein 2009:27–28, 39–41.
114. Hornung 2001:75; Pinch 2006:170.
115. Blavatsky 2006b [1877]:26; Lebling 2010:236–38; Perry 1743:326–27.
116. Lebling 2010:44–45; Peterson 2007:97–98; Silberman 1982:102.
117. Lebling 2010:64–66, 70–72; Peterson 2007:95.
118. Peterson 2007:96–97.
119. Drieskins and Lucarelli 2002:84–85; Grinsell 1947:348–49; Hornung 2001:61.
120. Grinsell 1947; Zivie-Coche 2002:16.
121. Drieskins 2006:141; Drieskins and Lucarelli 2002:89–90; Trew 2014.
122. Bergland 2000:1–2, 29–32; Boyd and Thrush 2011:xv–xvi; Freeman 2011:215–16.
123. McGarry 2008:66–93.
124. Kavanagh 2011:151–55, 167–68.
125. Cutler 1798:34–36.
126. Evans 2004.
127. Woodward and McDonald 2001:252–55.
128. Loxton and Prothero 2013:249, 377n215.
129. Laycock 2008:79–80.
130. Anson 1977:115; Boyd and Thrush 2011:vii; Hanks 2015:160–61.
131. Caterine 2014:51–54.
132. Boyd and Thrush 2011:xxx–xxxiii; Freeman 2011:223.
133. Colwell-Chanthaphonh and Ferguson 2006; Kuwanwisiwma and Ferguson 2004; Reimer/Yumks 2007:24; Schaafsma and Tsosie 2009.
134. Boyd 2011:192–94, 200–203.
135. Buhs 2009:51–53; Loxton and Prothero 2013:34–35; Muckle 2012; Muckle and Tubelle de González 2015:44.
136. Bayanov and Bourtsev 1976; Porshnev et al. 1974; Strasenburgh 1975.
137. Colyer et al. 2015; Strain 2008, 2012.
138. Quinn 2011; Reimer/Yumks 2007; Woolheater 2013.

139. Boyd 2011:204–5.
140. Boyd and Thrush 2011:xxxiv; Gibson et al. 2013:6–8.

Chapter 3

1. Wheatley 2011.
2. Nickell 2001:70–75; Stacy 1999; Vallee 1969.
3. Bond and Camm 1909; Hopkinson-Ball 2007:8–10, 27–28, 33–37, 203.
4. Durant 2015; Gilchrist and Green 2015b:384–88; Green and Gilchrist 2015:110–11; Rahtz and Watts 2009:21–32.
5. Pennick 1996:83–84; Rahtz and Watts 2009:73–80.
6. Carley 1985:11–13, 81; Gilchrist 2015b:54; Scott 1981:53.
7. Gilchrist 2015b:60–61; Higham 2002:230–32; Rahtz and Watts 2009:55–56; Scott 1981:29, 83–85.
8. Greenhalgh 1989:190.
9. Carley 1985:xlix–l; Courtney et al. 2015:294–95, 309; Gilchrist 2015a:1; Gilchrist 2015b:56–59; Rahtz and Watts 2009:55, 59–62; Scott 1981:34–38.
10. Gilchrist 2015c:433–34; Sampson 2015:381.
11. Rahtz and Watts 2009:48–49.
12. Moreland 1999:207; Stout 2012:263–65.
13. Bond 1921:17–20, 44, 97–98, 183; Hopkinson-Ball 2007:40–43, 60–61, 148–51.
14. Lowe 2007; Wilson 1987:273–82.
15. Bond 1921:22–23.
16. *New York Times* 1911a, 1911b, 1911c; Silberman 1982:180–88.
17. Bond 1921:19, 124; Hopkinson-Ball 2007:40.
18. Bond 1921:32, 80.
19. Hopkinson-Ball 2007:118, 164, 175–78.
20. Hopkinson-Ball 2007:95–97.
21. Bond 1921:27–30, 35–36, 40.
22. van Leusen 1998:127–29.
23. Bond 1921:48; McKusick 1982:102–3.
24. Bond 1921:155–57.
25. Gilchrist 2015a.
26. Bond 1921:26, 79; Hopkinson-Ball 2007:105–6, 112–13, 140; Luckhurst 2012:46.
27. Willis 2000:64–65.
28. Hopkinson-Ball 2007:135–36, 144–56.
29. Bond 1921:20; Hopkinson-Ball 2007:191; McKusick 1982:104–5.
30. Gilchrist 2015a:17–19.
31. Gilchrist and Green 2015b:394.
32. Hopkinson-Ball 2007:181.
33. Gilchrist and Green 2015a:445.

34. Gilchrist and Green 2015b:406.
35. Gilchrist 2015b:56; Griffin 2013:50; Hopkinson-Ball 2007:121–23; Prince and Riches 2000:60, 93; Wheatley 2011.
36. Stout 2008:173–74; Wheatley 2011; Williamson and Bellamy 1983:162–70, 176.
37. Stout 2008:178.
38. Watkins 1925; Williamson and Bellamy 1983:13.
39. Crawford 1955:26–30; Deuel 1969:24–29.
40. Maxwell 1932:14, 20–24.
41. Maxwell 1933:vii–viii.
42. Stout 2008:190–202.
43. Williamson and Bellamy 1983:14–16.
44. Wheatley 2011.
45. Clarke and Roberts 2007:180–84.
46. Silver 1999:209–10; Stout 2008:201–7; Watkins 1925:184–88.
47. Maxwell 1932:133–34.
48. Devereux 2003:11–13; Phillips 2013:74–75; Wallis and Blain 2010.
49. Prince and Riches 2000:67–68.
50. My copy of *Glastonbury Abbey: Concise History of the Establishment, Growth and Confiscation*, published by the Central Somerset Gazette, has neither an author nor a publication date. The map and some of the images in the volume are reproduced courtesy of Bond and the Somerset Archaeological Society. Entries in WorldCat attribute the book to the Central Somerset Gazette in one case and to Bond in another. Most likely, this volume is based on Bond's work.
51. Blavatsky 2006a [1877]:162–64, 264; Cameron 1976:36–37; Holzer 1992:xxvii, 17–19, 57–86; McKusick 1982:105–6.
52. McKusick 1982:105.
53. Trwoga 2001:18.
54. See Lewis 2012:202–3.
55. Daniel 1963:28–29; Piccini 1996:S89.
56. Cusack 2012:144–45; Stout 2008.
57. Cusack 2012:148–49.
58. Day 2006:138–44.
59. Twenty-first-century remote sensing suggests that Stonehenge was part of a larger ritual landscape. See Ludwig Boltzmann Institute 2014.
60. Cusack 2012:145.
61. Stout 2008:164–65.
62. Stout 2008:117–18, quoting Doris Chapman's *Is This Your First Visit to Avebury?* (1939).
63. *New York Times* 1926b.
64. Feder 1984:532; van Leusen 1998:123–27.
65. Williamson and Bellamy 1983:172.
66. Noël Hume 1969:37–39.

67. Clarke and Roberts 1996:86–87.
68. Lilly 1822 [1715]:78–81; Rankine 2009:12–13.
69. Cameron 1976:47.
70. Goodman 1977:67–70, 87–89, 131–33.
71. Cameron 1976:106–7; Mumford et al. 1995:E4–5; van Leusen 1998:126.
72. Cameron 1976:35–39; Dispatch 1974.
73. van Leusen 1998.
74. Lethbridge 1957; Welbourn 2011:25–40.
75. Welbourn 2011:89–90.
76. Lethbridge 1957:1–4; Welbourn 2011:50, 147.
77. Lethbridge 1957:75, 84; Petrie 1926.
78. Mackley 2010.
79. Gibson 2013:42; Lethbridge 1957:99–101, 111–16, 159.
80. Clark and Bushnell 1957; Grimes 1957; Lethbridge 1957:54, 124–27; Lethbridge 1968; Murray 1957; Welbourn 2011:159; letter from C. J. Norris, Manea, to Margaret Murray, 8 November 1933, in Oates and Wood 1998:48–51, letter 10.
81. Stout 2008:119.
82. Clarke and Roberts 1996:53–60.
83. Lethbridge 1957:87–88, 154–55.
84. Jarus 2016.
85. Haarmann 1996:608; Hornung 2001:159–64.
86. Black 1872.
87. Drower 1985:27–31, 41, 51, 178.
88. Lethbridge 1957:vii, 34, 59, 81, 83.
89. Lethbridge 1957:vii, 41, 118–19.
90. Lethbridge 1957:154–55; Lethbridge 1972:97–98.
91. Welbourn 2011:151.
92. Lethbridge 1957:22, 57, 47–50.
93. Hutton 1999b:278–79; Welbourn 2011:152–61.
94. Lethbridge 1957:44; Welbourn 2011:163.
95. Hutton 1999b:274; Lethbridge 1972:11–18, 82–83.
96. Hutton 1999b:364; Wilson 1982.
97. Graves and Hoult 1982:214–64; Lethbridge 1972:90–98.
98. Lethbridge 1972:55–63; Welbourn 2011:248–58.
99. Graves and Hoult 1982:25–58; Lethbridge 1972:27–28, 110–12; Robins 1988:157–58; Screeton 2012:197; Welbourn 2011:40–45.
100. Murray 1963:180–82.
101. Lethbridge 1972:15, 37–41, 74–78; Welbourn 2011:234–37.

Chapter 4

1. Daniel 1963:13.

2. Rizvi 2013.
3. Pasztory 2005:77–79.
4. Bintliff 1984; Gordon 1982:124; Papadopoulos 2005:96–98; Robinson 2009:76.
5. Gordon 1982:135–36; Papadopoulos 2005:97–98, 125.
6. Gere 2009:12–13, 97–98.
7. Ellis 1998:110, 139–40.
8. Papadopoulos 2005:107–8.
9. Gere 2009:220–25.
10. Witzel 2006:218–20.
11. Gates 1978b [1932].
12. Carter 2015.
13. Tejeda F. 1950:249.
14. Thompson 1954:9, 168.
15. Schufeldt 1950:226–27.
16. Thompson 1954:137.
17. Taylor 1967 [1948]:48–65.
18. Thompson 1954:79–82, 165–70.
19. Thompson 1954:84, 87–88, 91–92, 267–68.
20. Coe 2012:124–25, 152–53, 162–65, 175–76.
21. Manassa 2013:74–75.
22. Burstein 1996; Dykstra 1994:58; Hornung 2001:9–25, 50, 80–81, 90; Iversen 1993:60, 76–77; Pinch 2006:28–29.
23. Hornung 2001:34–38; Jordan 1998:21; Manassa 2013:18, 49–50, 76–78.
24. Hornung 2001:1, 118–27, 141–42; Luckhurst 2012:215, 219–28; Pinch 2006:174.
25. Davies 2009:169; Hornung 2001:147–54.
26. Gange 2013:268–69; Vinson and Gunn 2015.
27. Hornung 2001:121–22, 153–54.
28. MacDonald (2003:88) is quoting unpublished research also used by MacDonald and Shaw 2004; see Fisher 2000.
29. Iversen 1993:41–46; Manassa 2013:34.
30. Hornung 2001:84, 90; Iversen 1993:47–49, 68–73.
31. Hornung 2001:12; Manassa 2013:71–72.
32. Iversen 1993:62–63.
33. Herva and Nordin 2015:123–25.
34. Hamann 2008; Iversen 1993:64–65; Jones 2015; Suhay 2014.
35. Hornung 2001:11–12.
36. Hamann 2008:14–15; Hornung 2001:136–37; Iversen 1993:81–82, 86, 132–33.
37. Hamann 2008:24–25; Hornung 2001:104; Iversen 1993:106–7; Keen 1971:63–64.
38. Hamann 2008:26–28.
39. Hamann 2008:29–31; Hornung 2001:100–101; Iversen 1993:92–97; Wheatcroft 2003:155.
40. Hamann 2008:35–39; Hornung 2001:98–99, 103; Iversen 1993:105–6.

41. Davies 2009:169–70.
42. Hornung 2001:177–78.
43. Fagan 1977:296; Luckhurst 2012:142.
44. Hamann 2008:45.
45. Aubeck 2002:8–10; Bartholomew 1998; Brooklyn Daily Eagle 1865.
46. *New York Times* 1897b.
47. *New York Times* 1897c.
48. *New York World* 1897.
49. Beauford 2011:2.
50. Binghamton Republican 1897.
51. Holbrook 1959:111; Seward 1924:3:147–48.
52. Cawley 1956; Cramp 1921:607.
53. All of these degrees and supporting documents are in the special collections of the Binghamton University library.
54. Seward 1924:3:40; notes from 1966 interview by Mrs. Susan Cardoza of Mrs. Marion J. Rury, one of the subsequent family owners of Atlas, part of research into the MacDonald patent business. Cardoza appears to have obtained the primary MacDonald and Atlas documents from Rury and then deposited them in the special collections of the Broome County Public Library and Binghamton University. I am not aware that she ever produced a publication from this research.
55. Binghamton Republican 1897; Williams 1897:46.
56. Jenkins 2011; Schmidt 2011.
57. Crossley 2011:72–74, 131–43; Rochester Democrat and Chronicle 1897.
58. Clark 1998a:54–55; Clark 1998b:261–63; Haydon 1897.
59. Scully 1950:117.
60. Berlitz and Moore 1980:79–80.
61. Moore 1997; Thomas 1995.
62. Randle 1995:99–100; Wickersham 2015.
63. The website http://www.dronehoax.com (accessed 26 June 2017) is an exhaustive resource on this case.
64. Hornung 2001:48–49.
65. Reeves 2000:57.
66. Clayton 2006:63; Oakes and Gahlin 2008:94; Pinch 2006:21–22, 50; Weeks 1998:255.
67. Clayton 2006:147.
68. Lichtheim 1980:125–27.
69. Lupton 2003:30–31.
70. Hornung 2001:48–49; Jasnow and Zauzich 2014:43–50, 124–25; Manassa 2013:81; Pinch 2006:22–23.
71. Griffith 1900:3; Lichtheim 1980:128; Maspero 1915:118–19.
72. Hornung 2001:57.
73. Vinson 2009:287n25.
74. Lichtheim 1980:128–29; Pinch 2006:61.

75. Jasnow and Zauzich 2014:22–29.

76. Lichtheim 1980:131–32.

77. S. Smith 2007:20–21.

78. Lichtheim 1980:132–35.

79. Lichtheim 1980:136–37.

80. S. Smith 2007:20.

81. Fagan 1977:358; James 2008:330; Murray 1999:297; *New York Times* 1924a, 1924b, 1924c; Reeves 2000:134–36.

82. Lupton 2003:33; S. Smith 2007:20.

83. Day 2006:67, 82, 190n4; Huckvale 2012:13, 18.

84. Fagan 2005:52; Woolley 1949 [1930]:21–22.

85. MacDonald 2003:89–90.

86. Liszka 2010:316; Lupton 2003:44.

87. Hornung 2001:177.

88. Lupton 2003:24–26.

89. Bleiler 1983:215; Stableford 2007b:321.

90. Blackman 1917; Luckhurst 2012:186, 191–94.

91. Bleiler 1983:126.

92. Luckhurst 2012:173; Lupton 2003:27.

93. Bleiler 1983:32; Guran 2007:387–90.

94. Day 1997:123; Hornung 2001:112–14; Huckvale 2012:13; Kripal 2011:47; Wynn 2007:235n10.

95. Drieskins and Lucarelli 2002:82–84, 88.

96. Luckhurst 2012:74–84, 98, 161.

97. Silberman 1982:152–53.

98. Cook 2014:59.

99. Luckhurst 2012:148–50.

100. Day 2006:46–47.

101. Bacon 1976:189–91; Day 2006:50–51.

102. *New York Times* 1923b.

103. Colavito 2016; *New York Times* 1923d.

104. Luckhurst 2012:31; *New York Times* 1923c.

105. Patzek et al. 2001 [1999]:298–400.

106. Hankey 2001:3–5; Luckhurst 2012:11–12; Weigall 2006 [1924].

107. Nelson 2002.

Chapter 5

1. Dyson 1989:131.

2. Woolley 1949 [1930]:99, 116.

3. Trigger 2003:409–10.

4. Pasztory 2005:61–68; Jordan 1998:7.

5. Sugiyama et al. 2013.
6. Hornung 2001:6, 26, 57.
7. Wengrow 2011:155; Wengrow 2014:40–43, 83.
8. Jones 2000:95–112; Pasztory 2005:70; Wengrow 2014:2, 62, 92–94.
9. Evans 1987:32; Wengrow 2014:83.
10. Carter 2015:1–2, 11.
11. Mackley 2010:123–25.
12. Hornung 2001:68–71.
13. Ellis 1998:108.
14. Daniel 1963:64–65.
15. Gere 2009:19–21; Klejn 1999b:109–14; Traill 1995:56–57.
16. Traill 1995:130–35, 304–5.
17. Klejn 1999b:115–18; Traill 1995:167–75.
18. Gere 2009:39–44.
19. Letter from Wilhelm II to Admiral Hollmann, 15 February 1903, quoted in Scheffler 1998:23.
20. *New York Times* 1931g, 1936b; Scheffler 1998:23–24, 35–41.
21. Jidejian 1975:11–12; Scheffler 1998:13–15; Silberman 1982:161–62.
22. Greenhalgh 1989:178.
23. Whitley 1988.
24. Williamson and Bellamy 1983:113–14.
25. Jansen 1990.
26. Daniel 19634:51–53; Stout 2008:166–67, 220–24.
27. Kelker and Bruhns 2010:37.
28. Bernal 1980:160–72.
29. Beisaw 2010.
30. Dietler 1994:585–87; Kennedy 2015; Piccini 1996:S88; Stout 2008:55–56, 120–21.
31. Daniel 1963:111.
32. Challis 2013:225–31.
33. Daniel 1963:75–76.
34. Thompson 1954:40–42.
35. Evans 2004:20.
36. Hutton 2011:1; Megaw and Megaw 1994:291.
37. Moreland 1999.
38. Watkins 1925:201; Williamson and Bellamy 1983:25, 49–55, 71–73, 77–81, 110, 204.
39. Ball 2014; Evans 2004:85–87.
40. Daniel 1963:114–17.
41. Cusack 2012:147; Dietler 1994:597–98; Murray 1993:176; Piccini 1996:S89.
42. Daniel 1963:44–45.
43. Daniel 1963:26–28; Gibson et al. 2013:4–5; Kennedy 2015; Pittock 1999:3–5.
44. Dietler 1994:585; Megaw and Megaw 1994:291–93; Piccini 1996; Pittock 1999.
45. Hutton 1999b:156–59; Luckhurst 2012:225.

46. Gibson 2014:349; Stout 2008:118–21.
47. Clarke and Roberts 1996.
48. Screeton 2012:12, 23, 236.
49. Clarke and Roberts 1996:124–35; Prag 2015.
50. Screeton 2012:14–15, 18, 21, 24–25, 28–30, 34–35.
51. Clarke and Roberts 1996:20; Ross 1967.
52. Clarke and Roberts 1996:131; Robins 1988:5–6; Screeton 2012:22, 37–39, 63–66, 204, 216, 221.
53. Clarke and Roberts 1996:130–31; Robins 1988:8; Screeton 2012:187–90; letter from Anne Ross to Peter Underwood, 1 March 1976, in Screeton 2012:42.
54. Robins 1988:15–21; Ross and Reynolds 1978; Screeton 2012:48–52, 56–57, 71–72, 74–75, 89–95, 115–17. See Clarke and Roberts (1996:22–60) for more on the survivals in northern England and their Victorian reworking.
55. Dietler 1998:77.
56. Herva and Nordin 2015:124; Lucas 2004:109–10.
57. Papadopoulos 2005.
58. Rice and MacDonald 2003:7–8.
59. Haikal 2003:127–30; Wynn 2007:79–81.
60. Kehoe 2013:31.
61. Effros 2003; Dietler 1994:589, 595–96; Dietler 1998:73–77, 84–85.
62. Errington 1993:223–28, 238–41; Florescano 1993:97–99.
63. Kelker and Bruhns 2010:173–75.
64. Evans 2004:101.
65. Anderson 2016.
66. Schmidt 2013:98–106.
67. Klejn 1999a:233–36; Link and Hare 2015:110–11; Trigger 1996:239–41.
68. Dietler 1994:588.
69. Klejn 1999a:239–42.
70. Klejn 1999a:244–45; Link and Hare 2015:111.
71. Goodrick-Clarke 2004:177–88; Pringle 2006:46–50, 78–81, 282–84.
72. Dietler 1998:82; Pittock 1999:25–26, 65–66.
73. Hutton 1999b:341–44, 360–61; Stout 2008:66–71.
74. Stout 2008:126–32.
75. Wynn 2007:105.
76. Scarborough 2008:1090–91.
77. Scarborough 2008:1093–94.
78. Posnansky 1945:1:9–10.
79. Posnansky 1945:2:42, 52n59, 115.
80. "Mestizo" is a widespread racial concept in Latin America and refers to someone of "mixed race" who is culturally Spanish instead of indigenous.
81. Fernández-Osco 2011:341; Posnansky 1945:2:185–88; Scarborough 2008.
82. Posnansky 1945:1:1–5, 11–12, 20–22, 32–33, 45–51, 56–57.

83. Posnansky 1945:2:1–2, 54, 89–91, 95–96.
84. Posnansky 1945:2:45–49.
85. Posnansky 1945:2:113n119, 131.
86. Goodrick-Clarke 2002:131–34; Kurlander 2015:144–49; Pringle 2006:179–82, 309–10.
87. Daniel 1963:101–2.
88. Wynn 2007:106.
89. Stout 2008:85–89, 108.
90. Forsyth 1980:77.
91. Forsyth 1980:20–25; Hornung 2001:191.
92. Ellis 1998:28–31.
93. Keen 1971:192; Orser 2004:64.
94. Herva and Nordin 2015:125–28.
95. Forsyth 1980:81–82.
96. Williams 1991:132–39.
97. Donnelly 1882:2–3.
98. Blavatsky 2014b [1888]:8.
99. Jordan 2001:281–83; Orser 2004:65–66.
100. Stout 2008:192–202.

Chapter 6

1. Hamann 2008:46–47n135.
2. Coe 2012:100–106.
3. Brasseur de Bourbourg 2001 [1869]; Mace 1973:298–308; Wauchope 1962:44–48.
4. Evans 2004:35.
5. Mace 1973:319–20.
6. Desmond 2009:236–37; Evans 2004:105–18, 129.
7. Desmond and Messenger 1988:25–29, 38–39; Wauchope 1962:8–10, 19–21.
8. Desmond and Messenger 1988:32–35, 102–3, 118–19; Evans 2004:141–48.
9. Augustus Le Plongeon 1883; Alice Le Plongeon 1884a, 1884b.
10. Desmond and Messenger 1988:112–15.
11. Desmond and Messenger 1988:106–7, 112–13, 121, 124.
12. Blavatsky 2014a [1888] :267; Blavatsky 2014b [1888]:34–35, 229, 506; Desmond 2009:267, 270.
13. Desmond 1989:146; Desmond 2009:334–39; Deuel 1969:196–211.
14. Schliemann 1912.
15. *New York Times* 1914; Traill 1995:299.
16. Gere 2009:153–57; Luckhurst 2012:188–90; Moshenska 2012:1198; Stout 2008:81.
17. Luckhurst 2012:188–95.
18. Gibson 2014:351–52.
19. Elson and Venzor 2016; Wicks and Harrison 1999:17–25.

20. Levine 1986:9, 31–32.
21. Niven 1897:217–18; *Los Angeles Times* 1913; *New York Times* 1897a; Wicks and Harrison 1999:xii, 38–39, 47–48.
22. Foshag and Leslie 1955.
23. Wicks and Harrison 1999:30–31.
24. Dunn 2009; Feilberg 1895:298; Gaddis 1994:58–59; Kearney 1986:49–50.
25. Wicks and Harrison 1999:31–32.
26. Spinden 1911.
27. Kelker and Bruhns 2010:177–78.
28. Elson and Venzor 2016; Wicks and Harrison 1999:61, 186, 246, 269.
29. Churchward 2011; Churchward 2014:7, 133–36.
30. Churchward 2005.
31. Churchward 2016.
32. An Archaeologist 1911; *Los Angeles Times* 1911.
33. Wicks and Harrison 1999:288.
34. Bernal 1980:160–64; Cobean and Mastache Flores 1999:327–29; Gamio 1924.
35. Wicks and Harrison 1999:173–75.
36. Wicks and Harrison 1999:222; Buxton 1924.
37. Bernal 1980:169.
38. Churchward 2014:9–14; Wicks and Harrison 1999:180.
39. Bernal 1980:164; Bonsal 1921; Wicks and Harrison 1999:165, 174, 176.
40. *New York Times* 1923a.
41. Niven 1926b.
42. *Los Angeles Times* 1919, 1922, 1925; Wicks and Harrison 1999:213–20, 237–53.
43. Gamio 1924.
44. Bruhns and Kelker 2010:183–86; Feder 2010:143; di Peso 1953; Pezzati 2005.
45. *New York Times* 1927f; Philip 1927; Rieth 1970:92–95.
46. *New York Times* 1927g; Rieth 1970:104.
47. *New York Times* 1926i, 1927d.
48. *New York Times* 1926e, 1926i, 1927d, 1927e, 1927f; Rieth 1970:96–100.
49. *New York Times* 1927g, 1927h, 1928b, 1928c, 1928d, 1929b; Rieth 1970:101–3.
50. Mena 1920.
51. Wicks and Harrison 1999:198–204, 227.
52. Analysis based on Montoya 2001 and Scott 2004.
53. Kelker and Bruhns 2010:129–34.
54. Mena 1920; Wicks and Harrison 1999:205–8.
55. Niven 1926b; Wicks and Harrison 1999:227.
56. Wicks and Harrison 1999:211.
57. Wicks and Harrison 1999:223–25.
58. Churchward 1926c.
59. Blom 1925.
60. Velarde 1926a, 1926b, 1926c.

61. Niven 1925.
62. Niven 1926a, 1926b.
63. Blom 1926a.
64. Blom 1926b.
65. Niven 1926b.
66. Wicks and Harrison 1999:153, 213–18.
67. Wicks and Harrison 1999:219.
68. Gann 1936:11–12.
69. Brunhouse 1971:192–93.
70. La Farge 1928.
71. Blom 1926a.
72. Wicks and Harrison 1999:152–53.
73. *Los Angeles Times* 1922.
74. Wicks and Harrison 1999:224–25.
75. Wicks and Harrison 1999:219, 249–53.
76. Wicks and Harrison 1999.
77. Wicks and Harrison 1999:235.
78. Elson and Venzor 2016.
79. Objects 28-1-20/C10585, 28-1-20/C10585.1, 28-1-20/C10585.2, among others donated by Niven, can be seen at http://pmem.unix.fas.harvard.edu:8080/peabody, accessed 7 August 2017.
80. Wicks and Harrison 1999:245.
81. Niven 1926b; Wicks and Harrison 1999:233–35.
82. Brown 1924:146–48.
83. Churchward 1926a:195; Desmond 2009:328.
84. Blavatsky 2014b [1888]:7–8; Ramaswamy 2004:21–23.
85. Churchward 1926a:170–83, 281, 286–88, 308–13.
86. Churchward 1926a:24–26, 33; Churchward 1931:15.
87. Churchward 1926a:64.
88. Churchward 1926a:2–4, 16; Wauchope 1962:36–42.
89. Churchward 1926a:300–307; Churchward 1931:16–17.
90. Blavatsky 2014b [1888]:317; Churchward 1926a:41, 56; Churchward 1931; Valentine 1931.
91. Churchward 1926a:206–18; Wicks and Harrison 1999:220–22.
92. Churchward 1926a:220–25, 235.
93. Churchward 1931:25–26, 28.
94. Churchward 1926a:241–44.
95. Churchward 1926a:246–47.
96. Churchward 1926a:239.
97. Churchward 1931:33.
98. Churchward 1926c.
99. Churchward 2014:2; Wicks and Harrison 1999:237–40, 247.
100. Churchward 1931:27.

Chapter 7

1. *Science News Letter* 1934.
2. Tribble 2009:37–38, 46–50.
3. Fitting 2004:5–6.
4. Fitting 2004:95–96; Klinger 2014:562n89; Vitelli 2014.
5. Ellis 2004:121; Grinsell 1947:357.
6. Salih 2015:17–29.
7. Gange 2013:263; James 1911; Luckhurst 2010; Luckhurst 2012:144–45, 177, 220.
8. Davies 2009:180, 183–84; Gange 2013:267; Luckhurst 2012:222.
9. Fortune 1963:95–96.
10. Falk and Dierking 2013:111–13.
11. Day 2006:136–44; Lane 2013:64.
12. Eckardt and Williams 2003:141–42.
13. Clarke and Roberts 1996:51–52; Prag 2015.
14. Falk and Dierking 2013:86, 189–90.
15. Effros 2003:264–65.
16. Kelker and Bruhns 2010:49–51.
17. Lothrop 1957:67.
18. Mallowan 1946:84–85, 192–95.
19. Wastiau 2006.
20. Levine 1986:17–18, 91.
21. Daniel 1963:21.
22. Boone 1993:329–30.
23. Lyons 2002.
24. Boone 1993:328; Luckhurst 2012:135.
25. Drower 1985:105.
26. Lothrop 1957:67.
27. Drower 1985:211.
28. Drower 1985:64, 125; Fagan 1977:295–302; Luckhurst 2012:137–39.
29. Moss and Baden 2015; Whitcomb 2017.
30. MacDonald and Shaw 2004:109–10.
31. Day 2006:130–31, 144–47; MacDonald 2003:89.
32. Luckhurst 2012:175.
33. Moshenska 2012:1194–96.
34. Landrum 2011:272–74.
35. Hernandez and Garcia 2016.
36. Clarke and Roberts 1996:138–39; Pye 2011.
37. Day 2006:54; Luckhurst 2012:27–33; Weigall 2006 [1924]:5–6.
38. Luckhurst 2012:39, 43–47, 53.
39. Davies 2009:184.
40. Luckhurst 2012:61–65, 72.

41. Luckhurst 2012:143.
42. Luckhurst 2012:38–40.
43. Xie 2011; Penn Museum 2011.
44. Day 2006:158.
45. Wieczorkiewicz 2006:53–54.
46. Hanks 2015:50–53.
47. Day 2006:154–55.
48. Harvey 2006:31.
49. Hill 2012.
50. American Museum of Natural History 2007.
51. MacManus 2012.
52. Hiscock 2012:158–59.
53. Lui 2011.
54. Campbell 2004.
55. Scherzler 2012:82.
56. Edmiston 2014.
57. Whittle 2004.
58. Lucas Museum of Narrative Art 2015.
59. National Geographic 2011.
60. Gardner 2012; Pappas 2012; News Belize 2012a, 2012b.
61. Mitchell-Hedges 1956 [1954]:238.
62. Garvin 1973:13, 48, photo 25.
63. Shirey 1972.
64. Kelker and Bruhns 2010:53; Kidwell 1999; Lothrop 1957:66; Stewart 2013:39–41.
65. Digby 1936; Morant 1936; Nickell 2007:69.
66. Nickell 2007:68–70.
67. Kelker and Bruhns 2010:193, 196–98; Sax et al. 2008:2752–57.
68. Morrill 1972; Nickell 2007:69.
69. Gann 1925:128.
70. Mitchell-Hedges 1931:42–43; *New York Times* 1926f, 1926h; letter from Frederic Kenyon to Lady M. Richmond Brown, 17 June 1924, in Brown 1924:xi–xii.
71. Gann 1918; Mitchell-Hedges 1931:92.
72. Hammond 1975:31–40.
73. Kelker and Bruhns 2010:196.
74. Gann 1925:137–39; Hammond 1975:36; Mitchell-Hedges 1931.
75. Gann 1929:22–23.
76. Wallace 2011.
77. *New York Times* 1927a, 1927b.
78. *New York Times* 1927a, 1927b, 1927c.
79. *New York Times* 1928a.
80. Brown 1924:148; *New York Times* 1930c.
81. See Mitchell-Hedges 1931 for numerous examples.

82. Brown 1924:41–42, 128–37; Mitchell-Hedges 1955 [1954]:136–45.

83. Mitchell-Hedges 1955 [1954]:122–23; *New York Times* 1926g.

84. Brown 1924:141–43; Mitchell-Hedges 1955 [1954]:144–45; Garvin 1973:41–42; British Museum 1972.

85. Keith 1950 [1928]:434; Montagu 1952:184–86; Stepan 1982:92, 108.

86. Brunhouse 1975:82–86; Mitchell-Hedges 1931:xviii.

87. *New York Times* 1931b.

88. Deuel 1969:194–211; *New York Times* 1929d.

89. Houlson 1934:275–84; Strong 1935.

90. *New York Times* 1931a, 1931e.

91. Chamberlain 1953:13–14.

92. *New York Times* 1931c. Notes in the British Museum ethnographic collection state that the Mitchell-Hedges artifacts came "c/o G G Heye Esq Mus of the American Indian."

93. The names of the specific islands were derived from notes in the British Museum ethnographic collection.

94. *New York Times* 1933c.

95. Houlson 1934:159.

96. Daily Star 1932; Mitchell-Hedges 1956 [1954]:207–13.

97. Brown 1924:261–62.

98. Cuddy 2007:67–68, 72, 84–86; Healy 1993:209, 212; Manahan 2004.

99. Healy 1993:203–4.

100. Dennett 2007:19; Healy 1993:195; Strong 1935:123–32, 136–39.

101. Houlson 1934:60, 152–53, 248–50, 255–57; Mitchell-Hedges 1955 [1954]:217–21.

102. Houlson 1934:76–77, 129–33, 161, 214–23.

103. Davidson 1974:143–44n1.

104. Mitchell-Hedges 1955 [1954]:277–78; *New York Times* 1931d.

105. *New York Times* 1915.

106. Spinden 1924.

107. Lancaster 1991; *New York Times* 1929a.

108. Mitchell-Hedges 1931:96; *New York Times* 1923e.

109. *New York Times* 1936a.

110. *New York Times* 1933a, 1934a; Raphael 1934; Stewart 2013:32–33.

111. *New York Times* 1934b; Raphael 1934.

112. Stewart 2013:10, 78.

113. Mitchell-Hedges 1931:192–93.

114. Stewart 2013:28–32, 203–5, 232.

115. *New York Times* 1940; Stewart 2013:49, 83–85, 190.

116. Morde 1940.

117. *New York Times* 1933b.

118. Regal 2011:24.

119. Morde 1940; Stewart 2013:177–79.

120. Morde 1940; *New York Times* 1940; Stewart 2013:165–66, 190–92.
121. Loxton and Prothero 2013:129–34, 243–44; Morde 1940.
122. *New York Times* 1931f.
123. *New York Times* 1930a, 1931b.
124. Raphael 1934.
125. See Stewart 2013 for a history of these attempts.
126. Preston 2015.
127. Preston 2015.
128. Joyce 2012, 2015; Yuhas 2015; Letter from International Scholars 2015.
129. Begley 2016; Preston 2013; Preston 2015:111; Stewart 2013.

Chapter 8

1. Graham 2010:429–30, 436–39.
2. Graham 2010:450–51.
3. Yates 2014a:32–33.
4. Graham 2010:387–89, 392–95.
5. Cholidis 2001 [1999]; Mallowan 1946; Morgan 2001 [1999]:19, 23; Winstone 1990:172–77.
6. Gut 2001 [1999]:87–88; Hawkes 1946; Trümpler 2001 [1999].
7. Suerbaum 2001 [1999]:418–19.
8. Gugliemi 2001 [1999]:351–53, 365–84.
9. Morgan 2001 [1999]:25.
10. Patzek et al. 2001 [1999]:394.
11. Daniel 1963:192–93; Neuhaus 2001 [1999]:429–32.
12. See Bahn 2001; Praetzellis 2000.
13. Fagan 1995:14–15, 19, 24–39; Holtorf 2007:75–81.
14. Bahn 2001:8–9.
15. Brittain and Clack 2007:15; Holtorf 2007:63–68, 96–97.
16. Lucas 2005:127–28.
17. Niiler 2015.
18. Wieczorkiewicz 2006:57–58; American Museum of Natural History 2015.
19. Boyle 2013; Smithsonian Institution 2009.
20. Pohlman 2004:268, 270, 273–74.
21. Pearson and Connor 1968:159–60; Watkins 2012.
22. Pearson and Connor 1968:30, 129–35, 165, 173–75.
23. Mazur 2005a, 2005b; Muscarella 2000:141–43; Pearson and Connor 1968:146–47.
24. Mazur 2005b.
25. Coe 2012:225–27; Kelker and Bruhns 2010:95–96; Yates 2014b.
26. Newitz 2016.
27. Ibanga 2008.
28. Numerous examples are found throughout Hanson and Oltean 2013.

29. Britton 2004:14.
30. Keefe 2013; Lucas et al. 1978.
31. Patzek et al. 2001 [1999]:393.
32. Price 2016:221; Wilford 2013:36–37.
33. Reeves 2000:19–20.
34. Coe 2006:64, 73–93.
35. Webster 2006:145.
36. Kidder 1950:94.
37. McEvoy 1950:130; Nusbaum 1950:177.
38. Browman and Williams 2013:321; Harrington 1950:72; Kidder 1950:94; Lister and Lister 1970:21–22; Ruz Lhuillier 1950:109–10.
39. Givens 1999:313–14; Lekson 2008:37, 50–51; Lister and Lister 1983:110–11, 134.
40. Thompson 1879, 1965 [1932]:21, 75–79.
41. Browman and Williams 2013:279–81; Evans 2004:129; Hinsley 1993:110; Thompson 1965 [1932]:16–18.
42. Givens 1999:313–16; Lister and Lister 1970:22–23.
43. Harris and Sadler 2003:40–41.
44. Andrews et al. 2003.
45. McEvoy 1950:138–39.
46. Schávelzon 1989:110–11.
47. Brunhouse 1971:78–79; McEvoy 1950:138–39.
48. Guthe 1950:68–69; Kidder 1950:98–99.
49. Journal of S. G. Morley, 27 May 1920, in Lister and Lister 1970:94.
50. Journal of S. G. Morley, 8 May 1921, in Lister and Lister 1970:126.
51. Lister and Lister 1970:29.
52. Journal of S. G. Morley, 22 May 1920, in Lister and Lister 1970:89.
53. Journal of S. G. Morley, 26 April 1916, in Lister and Lister 1970:33.
54. Gann 1929:103–4.
55. Brown 1924:80; Mitchell-Hedges 1931:121.
56. Blom and La Farge 1926:7–8.
57. Journal of S. G. Morley, including letters to Robert Woodward, president of the Carnegie Institution, 22 and 31 May 1916, in Carpenter 1950.
58. Browman and Williams 2013:347; Brunhouse 1971:113, 130; Givens 1999:319–20.
59. See Harris and Sadler 2003 for an extensive treatment of Morley's intelligence work.
60. Browman and Williams 2013:342; Meyrat 2014.
61. Graham 2010:464.
62. Harris and Sadler 2003:72–75; Long 1950:118–20.
63. Mitchell-Hedges 1931:234–50.
64. Harris and Sadler 2003:289–90.
65. Boas 2005 [1919]; Browman and Williams 2013:345–48; Brunhouse 1971:119.
66. Browman and Williams 2013:348; Coleman 2002:193; Harris and Sadler 2003:312.

67. Brunhouse 1971:119; Harris and Sadler 2003:284, 288–89; Lewis 2001:457.
68. American Anthropological Association 2005.
69. Long 1950:118; Scott 1950:230.
70. Brunhouse 1971:276–77; Givens 1999:321–22; Wauchope 1965:232–40.
71. Harris and Sadler 2003:161–62.
72. *New York Times* 1930b.
73. Brunhouse 1975:266–67; Gann 1925:102–7.
74. Wallace 2011:24–25.
75. Brunhouse 1971:195, 210–11; Gann 1936:38–39; Harris and Sadler 2003:297; McVicker and Palka 2001.
76. Silberman 1982:190–94.
77. Richter 2008:219; Winstone 1990:28–29, 34.
78. Woolley 1920:55–59.
79. Winstone 1990:35–36, 43.
80. Fagan 2005:52; Richter 2008:218–25; Winstone 1990:27–28, 53–57.
81. Harrison 1926; Richter 2008:217, 223–24; Winstone 1990:61.
82. Harrison 1926; Richter 2008:225.
83. Price 1930; Savage 1926.
84. Price 2016:222–25.
85. Wilber 1986:105; Wilford 2013:38–39.
86. Price 2016:39; Stewart 2013:206.
87. Price 2016:143–45.
88. Price 2016:258–62.
89. Wilber 1986:9.
90. Wilber 1986:192–93.
91. Wilber 1986:11, 17–22.
92. Wilber 1986:100–102.
93. Wilber 1986:135–39.
94. Wilber 1986:149–51, 209.
95. Wilber 1981, 1986:172, 195–205.
96. Wilford 2013:168.
97. Wilber 1981:149.
98. Risen 2000; Wilber 1969 [1954].
99. Wilber 1969 [1954]:vii, 1, 5, 20, 29, 36–37, 66–72, 86; Wilber 1986:9, 157, 187–89; Wilford 2013:162–64.
100. Preston 1995.
101. Hibben 1941.
102. Haynes and Agogino 1986.
103. Loxton and Prothero 2013:85–89; Regal 2011:32.
104. Coleman 2002:117–18, 204–5; Greenwell and King 1981; Regal 2011:43–44.
105. Coleman 2002:118, 126, 139, 148; Coleman 2003; McLeod 2009:156; Regal 2011:62.
106. Coleman 2002:81, 122; Coon 1962:27–28; Regal 2011:45–46, 94–95.

107. Coleman 2002:183–84, 192–94; Regal 2011:35–36, 44–45, 50–51; Wilford 2013:23–24.
108. Preston 1995; Price 2016:229.

Chapter 9

1. Cook 2014:2–3.
2. Machen 1902:20–21.
3. Kruse 2010; Willis 2007:157.
4. Cook 2014:7–8.
5. Delasara 2000:156.
6. Willis 2000:64–65.
7. Leslie-McCarthy 2007:157–58, 167, 209.
8. Lupton 2003:30–31.
9. Blackwood 1908; Cook 2014:20.
10. Cook 2014:29–30.
11. Leslie-McCarthy 2007:11.
12. Willis 2000:61–62.
13. Conan Doyle 2006a, 2006b.
14. Cook 2014:74, 78–79; Luckhurst 2012:30.
15. Stableford 1990:97–98.
16. Wace 1956.
17. Carroll 1981; Patzek et al. 2001 [1999]:396–97; Phillips and Witchard 2010; Spencer 1987.
18. Leslie-McCarthy 2007:54–55.
19. Leslie-McCarthy 2007:22.
20. Moreno García 2009:179–81.
21. Luckhurst 2012:125–26.
22. Caleb 2010:43–44.
23. Fishman 1988:217–26; Odell 2006.
24. Curtis 2006:187.
25. Frost and Kynvin 2015.
26. Curtis 2006:192–93; Fishman 1988:214–15; George 2006.
27. *Telegraph* 2011.
28. Sugden 1994:183–86, 342–43.
29. Richter 2008:216; Silberman 1982:90–99, 124–26.
30. Beisaw 2016.
31. Colavito 2008:54–58.
32. Duda 2006:1–2; Spencer 1987:92–93.
33. Gere 2009:8–9.
34. Leslie-McCarthy 2007:38.
35. Carroll 1987; Stewart 1982:44.

36. Carroll 1987:22, 56–57; Stewart 1982:33–34, 39; Weston et al. 2015:320.
37. Stewart 1982:44.
38. Carroll 1987; Leslie-McCarthy 2007:52–53, 122.
39. Spencer 1987:90–92.
40. Duda 2006:9–10.
41. Carroll 1987:57.
42. Cook 2014:37.
43. Zimmerman 2008:9–10, 28–29.
44. Stout 2008:214.
45. Weston et al. 2015:319.
46. Duda 2006:2–3, 54.
47. Laycock 2012b, 2015:249–66.
48. Mathews 2009:121–29.
49. Constantine 2013:160–64; Laycock 2012b:117–18.
50. Ellis 2000:117–18.
51. Stickel 1993.
52. Wyatt 2002.
53. Murray 1963:11–29, 62, 115–16, 207–8; Drower 1985:210, 395; Oates and Wood 1998:9–10.
54. Murray 1963:143–49.
55. Drower 1985:331; Drower 2004:115, 128–29.
56. Murray 1963:96–97.
57. Murray 1963:104; Oates and Wood 1998:18–19.
58. Hopkinson-Ball 2007:46–47, 103.
59. Drower 2004:123–24; Murray 1963:131–32, 207–8.
60. Grinsell 1973:76.
61. Murray 1963:175.
62. Mitchell-Hedges 1931:194.
63. Murray 1963:178.
64. Simpson 1994:89–90.
65. Murray 1963:179–83, 196–98.
66. Hutton 1999a:33–35.
67. Hornung 2001:152–53; Murray 1963:176–78; British Museum 1889.
68. Simpson 1994:90.
69. Murray 1917a:61–65; Murray 1921:238–39; Silver 1999:174–76.
70. Murray 1921:10, 14, 107–9, 194–95, 201, 245.
71. Hutton 1999a:31–33; Oates and Wood 1998:20–21, 25; Toland 2014:6–8; Van Luijik 2016:121–26; Watkins 1925:89–90.
72. Leland 1899:vii, 101–6, 111–14, 117.
73. Murray 1957.
74. Adler 1986:56–57; Hutton 1999b:120–31; Oates and Wood 1998:16.
75. Sidky 1997:54.

76. Ginzburg 1983, 1991; Hutton 2000:110–11.
77. Murray 1917a, 1917b, 1920, 1921, 1933.
78. Cohn 1975:107; Hutton 1999b:275–76; Murray 1929, 1963:104–5, 207–8; Oates and Wood 1998:10, 27–29; Simpson 1994:89.
79. Adler 1986:549; Gardner 2004 [1954]; Oates and Wood 1998:13.
80. Gardner 2004 [1954]:18; Hutton 2000:104.
81. Magliocco 2004:49–50.
82. Hutton 1999b:205, 223, 230.
83. Cusack 2012:147; Hutton 2000:105, 108, 112–13; Gardner 2004 [1954].
84. Gardner 1939; Hutton 1999b:223–25; Magliocco 2004:51.
85. Hutton 1999b:235–36.
86. Ellis 2000:145–51; Hutton 1999b:258, 262–68.
87. Medway 2001:141–62.
88. *Nottingham Evening Post* 1929.
89. Hutton 1999b:201.
90. Mahon 1950; Pullinger 1950; Stanley 1950.
91. Read 2014:161.
92. Argus 1950; Daily Mercury 1950.
93. McCormick 1968:74–75; *Worker* 1951; Metropolitan Police file MEPO 3/2290, United Kingdom National Archives, Kew, London.
94. Donald McCormick (1968:74–77) cited an article that allegedly appeared in the *Birmingham Post* on 2 September 1950. Ronald Hutton (1999b:201) was unable to find this article, and I did a manual search of the month of September 1950 of both the *Birmingham Post* and the *Birmingham Evening Post* in the archives of the British Library and found nothing about the murder investigation or Margaret Murray. The existence of equivalent stories from the dates in question in other newspapers suggests that McCormick may have made a mistake about the name of the paper in which he found Murray's interview.
95. Murray 1954:38–39; Sydney Morning Herald 1950.
96. Thomas 1950.
97. Young 1956b.
98. Young 1956b.
99. Fabian 1950, 1953:106–9.
100. Read 2014:50–51, 168–69.
101. Young 1956a, 1956c.
102. Thomas 1950.
103. Rollyson 2012:252.
104. Fabian 1954:92–94.
105. Read 2014:19–21, 160–61.
106. McCormick 1968:72.
107. McCormick 1968:83.
108. McCormick 1968:183.

109. McCormick 1968:81–82, 88–89; Read 2014:140–41; Vale 2013.
110. McCormick 1968:76–77.

Chapter 10

1. Lovecraft 1926a. For citations of Lovecraft's work, I have used the date when he wrote the story, rather than the date of publication. This is more useful to my analysis and avoids the complicated history of Lovecraft's publication in the pulps, in some cases posthumously. This also applies to Lovecraft's ghost-writing, including stories by Zealia Bishop, Adolphe de Castro, and Hazel Heald.

2. The contemporary analogue was the Archaeological Institute of America. The institute met in Toronto in 1908 (Archaeological Institute of America 1909), though it did meet in St. Louis in 1916 (Archaeological Institute of America 1917). The meetings were held numerous times in New England in the early part of the twentieth century, including in Providence in 1910 (Archaeological Institute of America 1911). This period is the least documented in Lovecraft's life (Joshi 1996:83–91), but it seems likely that if he attended, Lovecraft would have mentioned it in his later copious correspondence.

3. Black and Green 1992:56; Copeland 1982; Leick 1991:29; Lovecraft 1917.

4. Joshi (2008:16–18) gives a more in-depth definition.

5. Examples of sites: the frozen city in *At the Mountains of Madness*; the buried city in "The Shadow out of Time"; the partially excavated mound in "The Mound"; the megalithic sites in "The Dreams in the Witch House," "The Whisperer in Darkness," and "The Dunwich Horror"; the Pacific ruins in "The Shadow over Innsmouth"; and the fragment of Mu in "Out of the Aeons."

   Examples of artifacts: the soapstones of *At the Mountains of Madness*; the cylinder in "The Mound"; the black stone in "The Whisperer in Darkness" (which was strongly influenced by Arthur Machen's "The Novel of the Black Seal"); the tiara and other jewelry in "The Shadow over Innsmouth"; the mummies of "The Case of Charles Dexter Ward"; the mummy and scroll in "Out of the Aeons"; the hieroglyphic clock in "Through the Gates of the Silver Key"; the exhibits in "The Horror in the Museum" (ghostwritten for Heald); and the shining trapezohedron in "The Haunter of the Dark."

   Examples of stories with academic protagonists: "The Mound," "The Whisperer in Darkness," "The Shadow out of Time," and "Out of the Aeons" and a secondary character in "The Rats in the Walls." The Miskatonic geologists in *At the Mountains of Madness* take a crash course in archaeology. The specific disciplines of Professors Rice and Morgan are left unstated in "The Dunwich Horror." The cult leader in "The Haunter of the Dark" is an Egyptologist, and the cult leader in "The Horror at Red Hook" is an anthropologist.

6. Lovecraft 1965:114–15.
7. Lovecraft 2006a [1934]:220.
8. Lovecraft 2006a [1934]:225.
9. Waugh 1994:4.
10. Joshi 1996:22–26, 36–40, 50–54.
11. Pinch 2006:163.
12. Callaghan 2013:204–7.
13. Klinger 2014:103n1, 108–9n19; Lovecraft 1923b.
14. Lovecraft 2006a [1934]:225. Lovecraft's commonplace book entries are only dated by year, but are numbered in order.
15. Lovecraft 1971:178–83; Lovecraft 1976:297, 392–93.
16. Lovecraft (hereafter HPL) letter to Elizabeth Toldridge, 15 April 1929, in Lovecraft 1968:331, letter 352.
17. HPL letter to Elizabeth Toldridge, 1 July 1929, in Lovecraft 2014:81–85, letter 10; Lovecraft 1965:258; Lovecraft 1971:161–63; Stepan 1982:108; Waugh 1994.
18. HPL letter to Elizabeth Toldridge, 8 March 1929, in Lovecraft 2014:36–51, letter 4.
19. Lovecraft 1923a.
20. Lovecraft 1925b; Price 1990:44–45.
21. Bleiler 1983:111; see also Lovecraft 1971:225–26.
22. Gunter 2005:264.
23. Dziemianowicz 1991:176; Hite 2008:61–62.
24. Daniel 1963:69–73; Murray 1993:175–76, 179.
25. Murray 1921:15.
26. Lovecraft 1930.
27. Murray 1917a:59–60; Murray 1921:15, 21, 130–31.
28. Lovecraft 1932.
29. Callaghan 2013:181; Murray 1921:85–87.
30. Lovecraft 1968:202–3. Lovecraft never published this dream but gave it to protégé Frank Belknap Long, who incorporated it into his Cthulhu mythos novel *The Horror from the Hills*.
31. Lovecraft 2006a [1934]:227.
32. Lovecraft 1928, 1933.
33. Anson 1977; Caterine 2014:49–50.
34. Lovecraft 1925a.
35. Caterine 2014:40–44.
36. Joshi 2001:224.
37. Lovecraft 1924a, 2006a [1934]:221.
38. HPL letter to Frank Belknap Long, 11 December 1923, in Lovecraft 1965:275, letter 153.
39. Lovecraft 2006b.
40. HPL letter to Elizabeth Toldridge, 8 March 1929, in Lovecraft 1968:317–18, letter 346; HPL letter to Elizabeth Toldridge, 3 September 1929, in Lovecraft

2014:99–104, letter 17; HPL letter to Elizabeth Toldridge, 24 October 1930, in Lovecraft 2014:160–63, letter 33.

41. HPL letter to Elizabeth Toldridge, 1 October 1929, in Lovecraft 1971:28, letter 372; HPL letter to Frank Belknap Long, 14 March 1930, in Lovecraft 1971:131–32, letter 404.

42. HPL letter to Clark Ashton Smith, 13 December 1933, in Lovecraft 1976:335–36, letter 674.

43. Derleth 1966:311–12; Eddy 1966:244–45.

44. HPL letter to Elizabeth Toldridge, 24 August 1932, in Lovecraft 2014:219–20, letter 53.

45. Beherec 2008.

46. Bishop 1928, 1930a.

47. Warren 2007:147; HPL letter to Zealia Brown Reed [Bishop], 9 March 1928, in Lovecraft 1968:232–33, letter 322.

48. Cannon 1989:98.

49. Joshi 2007:102; Klinger 2014:133–34n31; Natural Resources Canada 2013.

50. Cannon and Joshi 1999:6; Hite 2008:59.

51. Lovecraft 1983:35; HPL letter to Elizabeth Toldridge, 31 July 1929, in Lovecraft 2014:89–93, letter 15; HPL letter to Elizabeth Toldridge, 1 October 1929, in Lovecraft 2014:107–10, letter 19.

52. Kripal 2010:98–99, 122–23.

53. Fort 1919:156; Kripal 2010:124–25.

54. Kripal 2010:130–31.

55. de Camp 1976:221; Lovecraft 1968:173–74.

56. Joshi 1996:336–37, 346, 387; Lovecraft 2006c [1924].

57. Joshi 2012a:410n20; *New York Times* 1929c.

58. Lovecraft 2006a [1934]:233.

59. Daniel 1963:85–86.

60. Lovecraft 1927b, 1968:201–2.

61. Leslie-McCarthy 2007:142–43; Luckhurst 2012:10, 178.

62. Davis 1971 [1948]; James 2008:354–78.

63. Lovecraft 1926b.

64. Joshi 2012a:377, 382n24; Lovecraft 1924b.

65. Lovecraft 1971:121.

66. *Telegraph* 2011.

67. *New York Times* 1924e, 1924g.

68. *New York Times* 1925a.

69. *New York Times* 1925b.

70. *New York Times* 1925c.

71. *New York Times* 1925e.

72. Hite 2008:51; *New York Times* 1925k, 1925L.

73. Lovecraft 1976:360.

74. *New York Times* 1925m, 1925n, 1925p.
75. Wilson 1926.
76. Harrison 1926; *New York Times* 1926d.
77. Lovecraft 1920, 1968:77.
78. Mariconda 1995b:61; *New York Times* 1925t.
79. HPL letter to Clark Ashton Smith, 17 June 1926, in Lovecraft 1968:57–58, letter 223; Price 1982; Trigger 1996:217–23.
80. Heald 1933; Mariconda 1995a:43.
81. Hite 2008:91–92; Joshi 2012b:454n8, 455n10; Lovecraft 1976:153; Lovecraft and Price 1933.
82. HPL letter to Elizabeth Toldridge, 20 November 1928, in Lovecraft 1968:253, letter 338; HPL letter to Zealia Bishop, 22 January 1929, in Branney and Leman 2015:138–43; HPL letter to Elizabeth Toldridge, 25 March 1933, in Lovecraft 1976:165–66, letter 610; HPL letter to E. Hoffmann Price, 13 January 1935, in Lovecraft 1976:86–87, letter 746; HPL letter to William Lumley, 6 December 1935, in Lovecraft 1976:213, letter 816.
83. HPL letter to Elizabeth Toldridge, 16 September 1929, in Lovecraft 1971:27, letter 371; HPL letter to William Lumley, 6 December 1935, in Lovecraft 1976:213, letter 816; HPL letter to Robert H. Barlow, 29 November 1933, in Lovecraft 2007:87–89, letter 58.
84. Casson 1934:96–97.
85. Khun de Prorok 1925a, 1925b, 1925c; May 1993:157–75; *New York Times* 1924f, 1925d, 1925h, 1925i; Pond 2003:17–18, 178; Reed 1924; Tarabulski 2003:6–8.
86. Khun de Prorok 2001:181.
87. Khun de Prorok 2001:3–4, 153; Pond 2003:17–18, 174, 184–85; Tarabulski 2003:5–11.
88. Ellis 1998:33–34; Forsyth 1980:98–101.
89. *New York Times* 1926a, 1926c.
90. de Castro 1927; Bishop 1930b.
91. Bishop 1930b; de Castro 1927; Khun de Prorok 1926:21; Lovecraft 1971:39; letter from H. P. Lovecraft to Zealia Brown Reed [Bishop], 22 September 1927, in Branney and Leman 2015:85–88; Murray 1983.
92. Khun de Prorok 2001:41, 166–69, 183–88.
93. Ellis 1998:34; Khun de Prorok 2001:95–96, 106–17, 120–23; Pond 2003:172–73.
94. Khun de Prorok 2001:46, 114; Tarabulski 2003:10.
95. Khun de Prorok 1925a, 1925b, 1925c; *New York Times* 1925d, 1925h, 1925i.
96. *New York Times* 1925j, 1925o, 1925q, 1925r.
97. Brunhouse 1971:197–200; Gates 1978a [1931]; *New York Times* 1924d; Thompson 1962:4.
98. Blom and La Farge 1926; McVicker 2008.
99. Kelker and Bruhns 2010:86; McVicker 2008:40.
100. Bleiler 1983:77, 297.
101. Blom and La Farge 1926:20–26; *New York Times* 1925f, 1925g.

102. Barr 1925a; *New York Times* 1925s.
103. Barr 1925b; *New York Times* 1925u.
104. Brunhouse 1975:129–33.
105. van Wormer and Gross 2006.
106. Gates 1969 [1910], 1978a [1931]:x.
107. Gates 1915; Lerner 2011:144.
108. *New York Times* 1922.
109. Gates 1978b [1932]:178.
110. Gates 1969 [1910]:44–45; Gates 1978b [1932]:178.
111. Gates 1969 [1910]:53, 57–58, 61–64.
112. The phrase "Cthulhu mythos" was invented by Lovecraft's posthumous publisher August Derleth.
113. Lovecraft 1976:70–71.
114. Colavito 2005; Garofalo and Price 1982.
115. Lovecraft 1971:193, emphasis in original.
116. Mariconda 1995a.
117. Joshi 1986:37–38.
118. Harms and Gonce 1998.
119. Lovecraft 1976:270–71.
120. Caterine 2014:47–48; Grant 1972:6, 115–18; Woodman 2004.
121. Lovecraft 1968:57–58; Lovecraft 1976:153, 155, 165, 213–14, 267–69; Lovecraft and Conover 1975:33; Price 1990:12–19.
122. Lovecraft 1931a.
123. Lovecraft and Conover 1975:33.
124. Colavito 2005:130–37; Colavito 2012, 2014a; Pauwels and Bergier 1963:160; von Däniken 1970.
125. Roberts and Gilbertson 1980.
126. Jones 2011.
127. Marrs 2013:xi.
128. Barkun 2003:29–36.
129. Loxton and Prothero 2013:129–34; Moseley and Pflock 2002:66; Peebles 1994:4–6; Radford 2011.
130. Picknett and Prince 2001.
131. Barkun 2003:114–15; Clark 1998c.
132. Barkun 2003:119–20; Colavito 2014c.
133. Lovecraft 1917, 1919, 1931b.
134. Lovecraft 1926c, 1930.
135. Howard 1929; Lovecraft 1921.
136. Bleiler 1983:105.
137. Bleiler 1983:459; Warren 2007:139.
138. Barkun 2003:115–19; Clark 1998d; Peebles 1994:3–6; Standish 2006:270–73.
139. Barkun 2003:90, 110–12, 117–21; Clark 1998c; Nadis 2013:76–82; Tierney 1985.

140. Barkun 2003:110–12, 120–24; Partridge 2004.
141. Coe 2006:63–99.
142. Coe 2006:182–84; Hoopes 2012:41.
143. Sitler 2012; Whitesides and Hoopes 2012:59, 62–63.
144. Solomon 2011.
145. Whitesides and Hoopes 2012:65.

Chapter 11

1. Vinson and Gunn 2015:108–9.
2. MacDonald and Shaw 2004:111–12.
3. Leslie-McCarthy 2007:153; Levine 1986:123–25.
4. Levine 1986:55–57, 70–71, 87–88; Stout 2008:17–19.
5. Drower 1999:225–28; Henson 2010:209; Levine 1986:143–44.
6. Chippindale 1989:28; Levine 1986:89; Williams 1991:61–76.
7. Stout 2008:46–47.
8. Levitt 2006:269–71.
9. Barkun 2003:26–29.
10. Holzer 1992:xxiv.
11. Wynn 2007:103.
12. Roggersdorf 1970 [1968].
13. Phillips 2013:79–80.
14. Hancock 1995:468–79; Kenyon 2005; Parsons 2005:67; Trento 1978:xx–xxi.
15. Colavito 2014b.
16. Wolter 2014.
17. McNeil 2005:14–15; Williams 1991:61–76.
18. Graham 2010:390–92.
19. Clarke 2015:13–14; Gange 2013:265; Robertson 2014:73–74.
20. Cook 2004:209–13; Laycock 2012a:6–9; Lobato et al. 2014; Wood et al. 2012.
21. Hetherington 1996:166–67; Levine 1986:64, 73–74; Lewis 2012.
22. Stout 2008:139–43; Wallis and Blain 2010:314–15.
23. Fagan 2006:30–31.
24. Branch 2010; Wright 2016.
25. Fagan 2006:36–37.
26. Fell 1989:12–13, 19–20.
27. Daniel 1963:109–13.
28. Clayton 2003:8.
29. Card 2016; Carrott and Johnson 2013:325; Donovan 2011:25; Stross 2010.
30. Wynn 2007:97–99.
31. Picknett and Prince 2001.
32. Picknett and Prince 2003:176–78.
33. Hale 2006; Kulik 2007:121–23; Schadla-Hall and Morris 2003:203–9.

34. Picknett and Prince 2003:181–87; Wynn 2007:97–99, 108–10.
35. Ellis 1998:72–75; Orser 2004:68–69; Shinn 2004.
36. Blavatsky 2014a [1888]:xxiv, xxxii–xxxiii.
37. Picknett and Prince 2003:184–86.
38. Hancock 2015; Picknett and Prince 2003:181–87; Wynn 2007:88, 99, 102, 111–12.
39. Houlbrook and Armitage 2015.
40. Andersson 2012:126–27; Cusack 2012:139; Derricourt 2012; Stout 2008:242–46.
41. Colwell-Chanthaphonh and Ferguson 2006:149–50; Lucas 2005:123–24; Ramaswamy 2004:10–15; Schadla-Hall 2004.
42. Cremo 2012; Holtorf 2005:546–48; Holtorf 2012; Simandiraki-Grimshaw and Stefanou 2012.
43. Daniel 1963:196. Laycock (2012a) made a related argument for studying the paranormal in religious studies.
44. Fagan and Feder 2005.
45. Day 2006:159–68.
46. Day 2006:131–33.
47. Wieczorkiewicz 2006:56, 58–59.
48. Laycock 2012a:10–11.
49. MacDonald and Shaw 2004:119–21, 124–26.
50. Stout 2008; Taylor 1995.
51. Orser 2004:72–73.
52. Beisaw 2016.
53. Barkun 2003:18–21.
54. Parker 2016.
55. Toumey 1996.
56. Cantor and Smith 2013.
57. MacDonald and Shaw 2004:129–30.
58. Card and Anderson 2016.
59. di Peso 1953; Kehoe 2005; Lepper and Gill 2000; Wahlgren 1958.
60. Ashurst-McGee 2001; Burgess 2009; Williams 1991:176–86.
61. Williams 1991:189–91.
62. Derleth 1966:311–12.
63. Browman and Williams 2013:336–37; Means 1934.
64. Godfrey 1951; Williams 1991:217–19.
65. Barstad 2007.
66. Chronognostic Research Foundation 2008a.
67. Chronognostic Research Foundation 2008b.
68. Vescelius 1956.
69. See http://www.stonehengeusa.com (accessed 26 June 2016).
70. Neudorfer 1980.
71. Kulik 2007:117; Woolley 1949 [1930].
72. Rowe 1966; Wauchope 1962.

73. Kulik 2007:118–21.
74. Colavito 2005.
75. Cole 1980; Daniel 1979; Feder 1980, 1984; McKusick 1982.
76. Trigger 1984.
77. Mainfort and Kwas 2004; Michlovic 1990; Stamps 2001.
78. Lepper and Gill 2000.
79. Piccini 1996:S98.

WORKS CITED

Adler, Margot
1986   *Drawing Down the Moon: Witches, Druids, Goddess-Worshippers, and Other Pagans in America Today.* Rev. ed. Beacon, Boston.

American Anthropological Association
2005   Uncensoring Franz Boas. 15 June. http://www.americananthro.org/ ConnectWithAAA/Content.aspx?ItemNumber=2134, accessed 23 June 2017.

American Museum of Natural History
2007   Mythic Creatures. Electronic document, http://www.amnh.org/exhibitions/ mythic-creatures, accessed 30 June 2016.
2015   Teen Programs: Crime Scene Neanderthal. Electronic document, http://www. amnh.org/learn-teach/grades-9-12/teen-programs/crime-scene-neanderthal, accessed 24 June 2016.

An Archaeologist
1911   Ancient America. *Theosophical Path* 1(5):323–28.

Anderson, David S.
2016   Black Olmec and White Egyptians: A Parable for Professional Archaeological Responses to Pseudoarchaeology. In *Lost City, Found Pyramid: Understanding Alternative Archaeologies and Pseudoscientific Practices*, edited by Jeb J. Card and David S. Anderson, 68–80. University of Alabama Press, Tuscaloosa.

Andersson, Pia
2012   Alternative Archaeology: Many Pasts in Our Present. *Numen* 59:125–37.

Andrews, Anthony P., E. Wyllys Andrews, and Fernando Robles Castellanos
2003   The Northern Maya Collapse and Its Aftermath. *Ancient Mesoamerica* 14(1):151–56.

Annus, Amar
2010   On the Origin of Watchers: A Comparative Study of the Antediluvian Wisdom in Mesopotamian and Jewish Traditions. *Journal for the Study of Pseudepigrapha* 19(4):277–320.

Anson, Jay

1977   *The Amityville Horror: A True Story.* Bantam, New York.

Archaeological Institute of America

1909   General Meeting of the Archaeological Institute of America, December 28–31, 1908. *American Journal of Archaeology* 13(1):49–68.

1911   General Meeting of the Archaeological Institute of America, December 27–30, 1910. *American Journal of Archaeology* 15(1):60–75.

1917   General Meeting of the Archaeological Institute of America, December 27–29, 1916. *American Journal of Archaeology* 21(1):83–90.

Argus

1950   Hunt for Witches Is on in England. 18 September:2. Melbourne, Australia. http://nla.gov.au/nla.news-article22905800, accessed 28 May 2015.

Ashliman, D. L.

2006   *Fairy Lore: A Handbook.* Greenwood Press, Westport, Connecticut.

2012   Fairy Cup Legends. http://www.pitt.edu/~dash/type6045.html, accessed 26 February 2016.

Ashurst-McGee, Mark

2001   Mormonism's Encounter with the Michigan Relics. *BYU Studies* 40(3):175–209.

Astor-Aguilera, Miguel Angel

2010   *The Maya World of Communicating Objects: Quadripartite Crosses, Trees, and Stones.* University of New Mexico Press, Albuquerque.

Aubeck, Chris

2002   Comets and UFO Crashes. *Mutual UFO Network UFO Journal* 411 (July):8–11.

Bacon, Edward (editor)

1976   *The Great Archaeologists.* Bobbs-Merrill, Indianapolis, Indiana.

Bader, Christopher D., F. Carson Mencken, and Joseph O. Baker

2010   *Paranormal America: Ghost Encounters, UFO Sightings, Bigfoot Hunts, and Other Curiosities in Religion and Culture.* New York University Press, New York.

Bahn, Paul (editor)

2001   *The Archaeology Detectives: How We Know What We Know about the Past.* Ivy Press, Lewes, England.

Baines, John

1996   Myth and Literature. In *Ancient Egyptian Literature: History and Forms,* edited by Antonio Loprieno, 361–77. Brill, Leiden.

Ball, Donald B.

2014 A Forgotten Tale of Archaeological Folklore: Aztec Children in Tennessee. *Newsletter of the SAA's History of Archaeology Interest Group* 4(1):3–7.

Barkun, Michael

2003 *A Culture of Conspiracy: Apocalyptic Visions in Contemporary America*. University of California Press, Berkeley.

Barr, Kenneth

1925a Find Amazing Relics of Mayas' Empire. *New York Times* 20 August:1, 6. New York.

1925b Tales of Maya Indians Recounted by Explorer. *New York Times* 30 August:XX6. New York.

Barstad, Jan

2007 The Newport Tower Project: An Archeological Investigation into the Tower's Past. Electronic document, http://www.chronognostic.org/pdf/tower_project_report_2007.pdf, accessed 25 August 2014.

Bartholomew, Robert E.

1998 Before Roswell: The Meaning behind the Crashed-UFO Myth. *Skeptical Inquirer* 22(3) (May–June):29–30, 59.

Bayanov, Dmitri, and Igor Bourtsev

1976 On Neanderthal vs. *Paranthropus. Current Anthropology* 17(2):312–18.

Beard, Charles R.

1972 [1934] *Lucks and Talismans: A Chapter of Popular Superstition*. Benjamin Blom, New York.

Beauford, R. E.

2011 Meteorwrongs Received by the Arkansas Center for Space and Planetary Sciences: Program Results and Potentials. 42nd Lunar and Planetary Science Conference. http://www.lpi.usra.edu/meetings/lpsc2011/pdf/1100.pdf, accessed 22 June 2017.

Beckett, Matthew

2016 Eden Hall. *Lost Heritage: England's Lost Country Houses*. http://www.lostheritage.org.uk/houses/lh_cumbria_edenhall.html, accessed 26 February 2016.

Begley, Christopher

2016 The Lost White City of the Honduras: Discovered Again (and Again). In *Lost City, Found Pyramid: Understanding Alternative Archaeologies and Pseudo-scientific Practices*, edited by Jeb J. Card and David S. Anderson, 35–45. University of Alabama Press, Tuscaloosa.

WORKS CITED

Beherec, Marc A.
2008   H. P. Lovecraft and the Archaeology of "Roman" Arizona. *Lovecraft Annual* 2:192–202.

Behlmer, Heike
1996   Ancient Egyptian Survivals in Coptic Literature: An Overview. In *Ancient Egyptian Literature: History and Forms*, edited by Antonio Loprieno, 567–90. Brill, Leiden.

Beisaw, April
2010   Memory, Identity, and NAGPRA in the Northeastern United States. *American Anthropologist* 112(2):244–56.
2016   Ghost Hunting as Archaeology: Archaeology as Ghost Hunting. In *Lost City, Found Pyramid: Understanding Alternative Archaeologies and Pseudoscientific Practices*, edited by Jeb J. Card and David S. Anderson, 185–98. University of Alabama Press, Tuscaloosa.

Benavides C., Antonio
2008   Edzná: A Lived Place through Time. In *Ruins of the Past: The Use and Perception of Abandoned Structures in the Maya Lowlands*, edited by Travis W. Stanton and Aline Magnoni, 223–55. University Press of Colorado, Boulder.

Ben-Dov, Jonathan
2013   Turning to Angels to Save Jewish Mythology. *Haaretz* 18 October. http://www.haaretz.com/weekend/.premium-1.553219, accessed 22 June 2017.

Bennett, Paul
2011   Sithean Mor, Shian, Iona. *Northern Antiquarian* 13 December. https://megalithix.wordpress.com/2011/12/13/sithean-mor, accessed 21 June 2016.

Bergland, Renée
2000   *The National Uncanny: Indian Ghosts and American Subjects*. University Press of New England, Hanover, New Hampshire.

Berlitz, Charles, and William L. Moore
1980   *The Roswell Incident*. Berkley Books, New York.

Bernal, Ignacio
1980   *A History of Mexican Archaeology: The Vanished Civilizations of Middle America*. Translated by Ruth Malet. Thames and Hudson, London.

Bierhorst, John
1990   *The Mythology of Mexico and Central America*. William Morrow, New York.

Binghamton Republican
1897   Sandstone Meteorite. 20 November. Binghamton, New York.

Bintliff, John L.

1984   Structuralism and Myth in Minoan Studies. *Antiquity* 58:33–38.

Bishop, Zealia

1928   The Curse of Yig. http://www.hplovecraft.com/writings/fiction/cy.aspx, accessed 22 June 2017.

1930a   The Mound. http://www.hplovecraft.com/writings/fiction/mo.aspx, accessed 22 June 2017.

1930b   Medusa's Coil. http://www.hplovecraft.com/writings/fiction/mc.aspx, accessed 22 June 2017.

Black, Jeremy, and Anthony Green

1992   *Gods, Demons, and Symbols of Ancient Mesopotamia: An Illustrated Dictionary.* British Museum Press for the Trustees of the British Museum, London.

Black, W. H.

1872   Notes on Wareham and on Early Customs and Monuments of Dorset. *Journal of the British Archaeological Association* 28:230–37.

Blackman, Aylward

1917   The Nugent and Haggard Collections of Egyptian Antiquities. *Journal of Egyptian Archaeology* 4(1):39–46.

Blackwood, Algernon

1908   The Nemesis of Fire. Electronic document, http://algernonblackwood.org/Z-files/Nemesis%20of%20Fire.pdf, accessed 7 August 2017.

Blavatsky, H. P.

2006a [1877]   *Isis Unveiled: A Master Key to the Mysteries of Ancient and Modern Science and Theology,* vol. 1: *Science.* Theosophy Trust, N.p.

2006b [1877]   *Isis Unveiled: A Master Key to the Mysteries of Ancient and Modern Science and Theology,* vol. 2: *Theology.* Theosophy Trust, N.p.

2014a [1888]   *The Secret Doctrine: The Synthesis of Science, Religion, and Philosophy,* vol. 1: *Cosmogenesis.* Theosophical University Press, N.p.

2014b [1888]   *The Secret Doctrine: The Synthesis of Science, Religion, and Philosophy,* vol. 2: *Anthropogenesis.* Theosophical University Press, N.p.

Bleiler, Everett F.

1983   *The Guide to Supernatural Fiction.* Kent State University Press, Kent, Ohio.

Blom, Frans

1925   Letter to William Niven, 28 October 1925. Middle American Research Institute, Tulane University, New Orleans.

1926a   Letter to A. B. Dinwiddie, 7 December 1926. Middle American Research Institute, Tulane University, New Orleans.

1926b   Letter to William Niven, 7 December 1926. Middle American Research Institute, Tulane University, New Orleans.

Blom, Frans, and Oliver La Farge
1926   *Tribes and Temples: A Record of the Expedition to Middle America Conducted by the Tulane University of Louisiana in 1925.* Tulane University, New Orleans.

Boas, Franz
2005 [1919]   Scientists as Spies. *Anthropology Today* 21(3) (June):27.

Bond, Frederick Bligh
1921   *The Gate of Remembrance: The Story of the Psychological Experiment Which Resulted in the Discovery of the Edgar Chapel at Glastonbury.* 4th ed. Dutton, New York.

Bond, Frederick Bligh, and Dom Bede Camm
1909   *Roodscreens and Roodlofts.* 2 vols. Pitman and Sons, London.

Bonsal, Stephen
1921   Mexico's Main Need. *New York Times* 17 July:80. New York.

Boone, Elizabeth Hill
1993   Collecting the Pre-Columbian Past: Historical Trends and the Process of Reception and Use. In *Collecting the Pre-Columbian Past: A Symposium at Dumbarton Oaks, 6th and 7th October 1990,* edited by Elizabeth Hill Boone, 315–50. Dumbarton Oaks Research Library and Collection, Washington, DC.
2000   Venerable Place of Beginnings: The Aztec Understanding of Teotihuacan. In *Mesoamerica's Classic Heritage: From Teotihuacan to the Aztecs,* edited by Davíd Carrasco, Lindsay Jones, and Scott Sessions, 371–95. University Press of Colorado, Boulder.

Boyd, Colleen E.
2011   "We Are Standing in My Ancestor's Longhouse": Learning the Language of Spirits and Ghosts. In *Phantom Past, Indigenous Presence: Native Ghosts in North American Culture and History,* edited by Colleen E. Boyd and Coll Thrush, 181–208. University of Nebraska Press, Lincoln.

Boyd, Colleen E., and Coll Thrush
2011   Introduction: Bringing Ghosts to Ground. In *Phantom Past, Indigenous Presence: Native Ghosts in North American Culture and History,* edited by Colleen E. Boyd and Coll Thrush, vii–xl. University of Nebraska Press, Lincoln.

Boyle, Alan
2013   CSI Jamestown: Anthropologists Lay Out Evidence of Colonial Cannibalism. *Cosmic Log NBC News,* 1 May. http://cosmiclog.nbcnews.com/_news/2013/05/01/18002011-csi-jamestown-anthropologists-lay-out-evidence-of-colonial-cannibalism, accessed 26 May 2016.

Branch, Glenn

2010   McLeroy Booted in Texas. *National Center for Science Education*, 3 March. http://ncse.com/news/2010/03/mcleroy-booted-texas-005354, accessed 24 June 2016.

Branney, Sean, and Andrew Leman (editors)

2015   *H. P. Lovecraft: The Spirit of Revision: Lovecraft's Letters to Zealia Brown Reed Bishop*. H. P. Lovecraft Historical Society, Glendale, California.

Brasseur de Bourbourg, Charles Étienne

2001 [1869]   Letter to Léon de Rosny. In *The Decipherment of Ancient Maya Writing*, edited by Stephen Houston, Oswaldo Chinchilla Mazariegos, and David Stuart, 60–67. University of Oklahoma Press, Norman.

Breglia, Lisa

2009   When Patrimonies Collide: The Case of Chunchucmil, Yucatán. In *Ethnographies and Archaeologies: Iterations of the Past*, edited by Lena Mortensen and Julie Hollowell, 55–70. University Press of Florida, Gainesville.

Briggs, Katharine M.

1971   *A Dictionary of British Folk-Tales in the English Language*. Part B, *Folk Legends*, Vol. 1. Indiana University Press, Bloomington.

British Museum

1889   The Unlucky Mummy. No. EA22542. http://www.britishmuseum.org/research/collection_online/collection_object_details.aspx?objectId=117233&partId=1, accessed 10 September 2015.

1972   Human Remains: Charm. No. As1972,Q.2279.a. http://www.britishmuseum.org/research/collection_online/collection_object_details.aspx?objectId=552652&partId=1, accessed 30 June 2016.

Brittain, Marcus, and Timothy Clack

2007   Introduction: Archaeology and the Media. In *Archaeology and the Media*, edited by Timothy Clack and Marcus Brittain, 11–65. Left Coast Press, Walnut Creek, California.

Britton, Wesley

2004   *Spy Television*. Praeger, Westport, Connecticut.

Brooklyn Daily Eagle

1865   Remarkable Phenomenon: A Piece of the Moon Found in the Rocky Mountains. 14 November:4. Brooklyn, New York.

Browman, David L., and Stephen Williams

2013   *Anthropology at Harvard: A Biographical History, 1790–1940*. Peabody Museum Press, Harvard University, Cambridge, Massachusetts.

Brown, Martin, and Pat Bowen

1999   The Last Refuge of the Faeries: Archaeology and Folklore in East Sussex. In
        Archaeology and Folklore, edited by Amy Gazin-Schwartz and Cornelius
        Holtorf, 255–73. Routledge, London.

Brown, M. Richmond

1924   *Unknown Tribes, Uncharted Seas*. Hazell, Watson, and Viney, London.

Bruhns, Karen O., and Nancy L. Kelker

2010   *Faking the Ancient Andes*. Left Coast Press, Walnut Creek, California.

Brunhouse, Robert L.

1971   *Sylvanus G. Morley and the World of the Ancient Mayas*. University of Okla-
        homa Press, Norman.

1975   *Pursuit of the Ancient Maya: Some Archaeologists of Yesterday*. University of
        New Mexico Press, Albuquerque.

Buhs, Joshua Blu

2009   *Bigfoot: The Life and Times of a Legend*. University of Chicago Press, Chicago.

Burgess, Don

2009   Romans in Tucson? The Story of an Archaeological Hoax. *Journal of the South-
        west* 51(1):3–135.

Burstein, Stanley M.

1996   Images of Egypt in Greek Historiography. In *Ancient Egyptian Literature: His-
        tory and Forms*, edited by Antonio Loprieno, 591–604. Brill, Leiden.

Buxton, L. H. Dudley

1924   Abstract: Skulls of the Valley of Mexico. In *Report of the Ninety-Second
        Meeting (Ninety-Fourth Year) of the British Association for the Advancement
        of Science, Toronto, 6–13 August 1924*, 421. Office of the British Association,
        London.

Caleb, Amanda Mordavsky

2010   "A City of Nightmares": Suburban Anxiety in Arthur Machen's London
        Gothic. In *London Gothic: Place, Space and the Gothic Imagination*, edited by
        Lawrence Phillips and Anne Witchard, 41–49. Continuum, London.

Callaghan, Gavin

2013   *H. P. Lovecraft's Dark Arcadia: The Satire, Symbology and Contradiction*.
        McFarland, Jefferson, North Carolina.

Cameron, Constance

1976   Archaeology and Parapsychology. MA thesis, Department of Anthropology,
        California State University, Fullerton. University Microfilms, Ann Arbor,
        Michigan.

Campbell, Don (writer and director)
2004   *Quest for King Arthur*. Partisan Pictures.

Cannon, Peter
1989   *H. P. Lovecraft*. Twayne, Boston.

Cannon, Peter, and S. T. Joshi (editors)
1999   *More Annotated H. P. Lovecraft*. Swordsmith Productions and the Wildside Press, Dell, New York.

Cantor, Eric, and Lamar Smith
2013   Rethinking Science Funding. *USA Today* 30 September. http://www.usatoday.com/story/opinion/2013/09/30/cantor-gop-budget-science spending-column/2896333, accessed 15 June 2016.

Card, Jeb J.
2016   Steampunk Inquiry: A Comparative Vivisection of Discovery Pseudosciences. In *Lost City, Found Pyramid: Understanding Alternative Archaeologies and Pseudoscientific Practices*, edited by Jeb J. Card and David S. Anderson, 68–80. University of Alabama Press, Tuscaloosa.

Card, Jeb J., and David S. Anderson
2016   Alternatives and Pseudosciences: A History of Archaeological Engagement with Extraordinary Claims. In *Lost City, Found Pyramid: Understanding Alternative Archaeologies and Pseudoscientific Practices*, edited by Jeb J. Card and David S. Anderson, 1–18. University of Alabama Press, Tuscaloosa.

Carley, James P.
1985   *The Chronicle of Glastonbury Abbey: An Edition, Translation and Study of John of Glastonbury's "Cronica sice Antiquitates Glastoniensis Ecclesie."* Translated by David Townsend. Boydell Press, Woodbridge, Suffolk, United Kingdom.

Carpenter, Arthur
1950   The Death of Lafleur: Two Letters from Morley. In *Morleyana: A Collection of Writings in Memoriam Sylvanus Griswold Morley (1883–1948)*, 21–48. School of American Research and the Museum of New Mexico, Santa Fe.

Carrasco, David
2000   *Quetzalcoatl and the Irony of Empire: Myths and Prophecies in the Aztec Tradition*. Rev. ed. University Press of Colorado, Boulder.

Carroll, Noël
1981   Nightmare and the Horror Film: The Symbolic Biology of Fantastic Beings. *Film Quarterly* 34(3):16–25.
1987   The Nature of Horror. *Journal of Aesthetics and Art Criticism* 46(1):51–59.

Carrott, James H., and Brian David Johnson
2013   *Vintage Tomorrows*. O'Reilly Media, Sebastopol, California.

Carter, Nicholas P.
2015   Once and Future Kings: Classic Maya Geopolitics and Mythic History on the Vase of the Initial Series from Uaxactun. *PARI Journal* 15(4):1–15.

Casson, Stanley
1934   *Progress of Archaeology*. Whittlesey House, McGraw-Hill, New York.

Castañeda, Quetzil E.
1996   *In the Museum of Maya Culture: Touring Chichén Itzá*. University of Minnesota Press, Minneapolis.

Caterine, Darryl V.
2014   Heirs through Fear: Indian Curses, Accursed Indian Lands, and White Christian Sovereignty in America. *Nova Religio: The Journal of Alternative and Emergent Religions* 18(1):37–57.

Cawley, Tom
1956   Old MacDonald Had a Charm. *Binghamton Press*, 5 October:17. Binghamton, New York.

Chadwick, Adrian M., and Catriona D. Gibson
2013   "Do You Remember the First Time?": A Preamble through Memory, Myth and Place. In *Memory, Myth and Long-Term Landscape Inhabitation*, edited by Adrian M. Chadwick and Catriona D. Gibson, 1–31. Oxbow, Oxford.

Challis, Debbie
2013   *The Archaeology of Race: The Eugenic Ideas of Francis Galton and Flinders Petrie*. Bloomsbury, London.

Chamberlain, Robert S.
1953   *The Conquest and Colonization of Honduras: 1502–1550*. Carnegie Institution of Washington, Washington, DC.

Champion, Sara, and Gabriel Cooney
1999   Naming the Places, Naming the Stones. In *Archaeology and Folklore*, edited by Amy Gazin-Schwartz and Cornelius Holtorf, 196–213. Routledge, London.

Chesnutt, Randall D.
2014   The Descent of the Watchers and Its Aftermath According to Justin Martyr. In *The Watchers in Jewish and Christian Traditions*, edited by Angela Kim Harkins, Kelley Coblentz Bautch, and John C. Endres, 167–80. Fortress Press, Minneapolis, Minnesota.

Chippindale, Christopher
1989   "Social Archaeology" in the Nineteenth Century: Is It Right to Look for

Modern Ideas in Old Places? In *Tracing Archaeology's Past: The Historiography of Archaeology*, edited by Andrew L. Christenson, 21–33. Southern Illinois University Press, Carbondale.

Cholidis, Nadja
2001 [1999]   "The Glamour of the East": Some Reflections on Agatha Christie's *Murder in Mesopotamia*. In *Agatha Christie and Archaeology*, edited by Charlotte Trümpler, 334–49. Translated by Anthea Bell. British Museum Press, London.

Chronognostic Research Foundation
2008a   Discovery over Touro Park. Electronic document, http://www.chronognostic. org/over_touro_park.html, accessed 11 October 2014.
2008b   Rhode Island U-Haul Truck Unveiling at Touro Park. Electronic document, http://www.chronognostic.org/daily_logs.php?id=7, accessed 11 October 2014.

Chuchiak, John F., IV
2009   *De Descriptio Idolorum*: An Ethnohistorical Examination of the Production, Imagery, and Functions of Colonial Yucatec Maya Idols and Effigy Censers, 1540–1700. In *Maya Worldview at Conquest*, edited by Leslie G. Cecil and Timothy W. Pugh, 135–58. University Press of Colorado, Boulder.

Churchward, Jack
2005   About My-Mu. http://www.my-mu.com/aboutmymu.html, accessed 30 June 2016.
2011   *Lifting the Veil on the Lost Continent of Mu, Motherland of Men*. Ozark Mountain Publishing, Huntsville, Arkansas.
2014   *The Stone Tablets of Mu*. Ozark Mountain Publishing, Huntsville, Arkansas.
2016   Dr. Jeb Card and the Mu Stones. Electronic document, http://blog.my-mu. com/?p=2367, accessed 30 June 2016.

Churchward, James
1926a   *The Lost Continent of Mu: The Motherland of Man*. William Edwin Rudge, New York.
1926b   Undated manuscript interpreting Tablet No. 339. Included in 1926 packet of material sent to Tulane University. Middle American Research Institute, Tulane University, New Orleans.
1926c   Undated manuscript interpreting Tablet No. 1154. Included in 1926 packet of material sent to Tulane University. Middle American Research Institute, Tulane University, New Orleans.
1931   *The Children of Mu*. Ives Washburn, New York.

Clark, Jerome
1998a   Airship Sightings in the Nineteenth Century. In *The UFO Encyclopedia: The Phenomenon from the Beginning*, edited by Jerome Clark, 44–63. Omnigraphics, Detroit, Michigan.

1998b   Crashes and Retrievals of UFOs in the Nineteenth Century. In *The UFO Encyclopedia: The Phenomenon from the Beginning*, edited by Jerome Clark, 257–64. Omnigraphics, Detroit, Michigan.

1998c   Hollow Earth and UFOs. In *The UFO Encyclopedia: The Phenomenon from the Beginning*, edited by Jerome Clark, 520–24. Omnigraphics, Detroit, Michigan.

1998d   Shaver Mystery. In *The UFO Encyclopedia: The Phenomenon from the Beginning*, edited by Jerome Clark, 845–48. Omnigraphics, Detroit, Michigan.

Clark, J. G. D., and G. H. S. Bushnell
1957   British Archaeology. *The Times* 15 May:11. London.

Clarke, Ardy Sixkiller
2015   *Sky People: Untold Stories of Alien Encounters in Mesoamerica*. New Page, Pompton Plains, New Jersey.

Clarke, David, and Andy Roberts
1996   *Twilight of the Celtic Gods: An Exploration of Britain's Hidden Pagan Traditions*. Blandford, London.
2007   *Flying Saucerers: A Social History of UFOlogy*. Alternative Albion, Wymeswold, Loughborough, United Kingdom.

Clayton, Jay
2003   *Charles Dickens in Cyberspace: The Afterlife of the Nineteenth Century in Postmodern Culture*. Oxford University Press, New York.

Clayton, Peter A.
2006   *Chronicle of the Pharaohs: The Reign-by-Reign Record of the Rulers and Dynasties of Ancient Egypt*. Thames and Hudson, New York.

Clendinnen, Inga
1987   *Ambivalent Conquests: Maya and Spaniard in Yucatan, 1517–1570*. Cambridge University Press, Cambridge.

Cobean, Roberto, and Alba Guadalupe Mastache Flores
1999   Manuel Gamio (1883–1960). Translated by Judith Braid. In *Encyclopedia of Archaeology: The Great Archaeologists*, edited by Tim Murray, 1:325–33. ABC-CLIO, Santa Barbara, California.

Coe, Michael D.
2006   *Final Report: An Archaeologist Excavates His Past*. Thames and Hudson, New York.
2012   *Breaking the Maya Code*. 3rd ed. Thames and Hudson, New York.

Cohn, Norman
1975   *Europe's Inner Demons: An Enquiry Inspired by the Great Witch-Hunt*. Basic, New York.

Colavito, Jason

2005   *The Cult of Alien Gods: H. P. Lovecraft and Extraterrestrial Pop Culture.* Prometheus, Amherst, New York.

2008   *Knowing Fear: Science, Knowledge, and the Development of the Horror Genre.* McFarland, Jefferson, North Carolina

2012   Lovecraftian Themes in Bergier's Later Work. Electronic document, http://www.jasoncolavito.com/lovecraft-in-bergier.html, accessed 16 June 2016.

2014a   Pauwels, Bergier, and Lovecraft: Establishing a Cthulhu-Ancient Astronaut Connection. Electronic document, http://www.jasoncolavito.com/pauwels-bergier-and-lovecraft.html, accessed 16 June 2016.

2014b   Scott Wolter Calls for Congressional Investigation of the Smithsonian; Brien Foerster Discusses Alien DNA. Electronic document, http://www.jasoncolavito.com/blog/scott-wolter-calls-for-congressional-investigation-of-the-smithsonian-brien-foerster-discusses-alien-dna, accessed 16 June 2016.

2014c   "The Emerald Tablets of Thoth": A Lovecraftian Plagiarism. Electronic document, http://www.jasoncolavito.com/blog/the-emerald-tablets-of-thoth-a-lovecraftian-plagiarism, accessed 5 October 2016.

2016   The Secret Source behind the Curse of King Tut. Electronic document, http://www.jasoncolavito.com/blog/the-secret-source-behind-the-curse-of-king-tut, accessed 28 June 2016.

Cole, John R.

1980   Cult Archaeology and Unscientific Method and Theory. *Advances in Archaeological Method and Theory* 3:1–33.

Coleman, Loren

2002   *Tom Slick: True Life Encounters in Cryptozoology.* Craven Street, Fresno, California.

2003   George Allen Agogino: 1921–2000. Electronic document, http://lorencoleman.com/archives/george-allen-agogino, accessed 25 June 2016.

Colwell-Chanthaphonh, Chip, and T. J. Ferguson

2006   Memory Pieces and Footprints: Multivocality and the Meanings of Ancient Times and Ancestral Places among the Zuni and Hopi. *American Anthropologist* 108(1):148–62.

Colyer, Daryl G., Alton Higgins, Brian Brown, Kathy Strain, Michael C. Mayes, and Brad McAndrews

2015   The Ouachita Project, Version 1.1. Electronic document, http://media.texasbigfoot.com/OP_paper_media/OuachitaProjectMonograph_Version1.1_03112015.pdf, accessed 17 January 2016.

Conan Doyle, Arthur

2006a [1890]   The Ring of Thoth. In *Into the Mummy's Tomb: Mysterious Tales of*

Mummies and Ancient Egypt, edited by John Richard Stephens, 45–60. Barnes and Noble, New York.

2006b [1892]   Lot No. 249. In *Into the Mummy's Tomb: Mysterious Tales of Mummies and Ancient Egypt*, edited by John Richard Stephens, 208–38. Barnes and Noble, New York.

Constantine, Alex
2013   *Virtual Government: CIA Mind Control Operations in America*. Feral House, Port Townsend, Washington.

Cook, Garrett W., and Thomas A. Offit, with a contribution from Rhonda Taube
2013   *Indigenous Religion and Cultural Performance in the New Maya World*. University of New Mexico Press, Albuquerque.

Cook, Michael
1983   Pharaonic History in Medieval Egypt. *Studia Islamica* 57:67–103.
2014   *Detective Fiction and the Ghost Story: The Haunted Text*. Palgrave Macmillan, Houndmills, Basingstoke, Hampshire, United Kingdom.

Cook, Ryan Jonathan
2004   Weather-Workers, Saucer Seekers, and Orthoscientists: Epistemic Authority in Central Mexico. PhD dissertation, Department of Anthropology, University of Chicago. University Microfilms, Ann Arbor, Michigan.

Coon, Carleton S.
1962   *The Story of Man: From the First Human to Primitive Culture and Beyond*. 2nd ed. Knopf, New York.

Copeland, Harold Hadley
1982   The Real Father Dagon. *Crypt of Cthulhu* 9. http://crypt-of-cthulhu.com/realfatherdagon.htm, accessed 22 June 2017.

Coppens, Philip
2012   *The Ancient Alien Question: A New Inquiry into the Existence, Evidence, and Influence of Ancient Visitors*. New Page, Pompton Plains, New Jersey.

Courtney, Paul, Geoff Eagan, and Roberta Gilchrist, with a contribution from John Cherry
2015   Small Finds. In *Glastonbury Abbey: Archaeological Excavations, 1904–79*, edited by Roberta Gilchrist and Cheryl Green, 293–311. Society of Antiquaries of London, London.

Cramp, Arthur J. (editor)
1921   *Nostrums and Quackery*. Vol. 2. Press of American Medical Association, Chicago.

Crawford, Osbert Guy Stanhope

1955 *Said and Done: The Autobiography of an Archaeologist.* Weidenfeld and Nicolson, London.

Cremo, Michael A.

2012 An Insider's View of an Alternative Archaeology. In *From Archaeology to Archaeologies: The "Other" Past,* edited by Anna Simandiraki-Grimshaw and Eleni Stefanou, 14–19. Archaeopress, Oxford.

Crossley, Robert

2011 *Imagining Mars: A Literary History.* Wesleyan University Press, Middletown, Connecticut.

Cuddy, Thomas W.

2007 *Political Identity and Archaeology in Northeast Honduras.* University Press of Colorado, Boulder.

Curtis, L. Perry, Jr.

2006 Responses to the Ripper Murders: Letters to Old Jewry. In *Ripperology,* edited by Paul Begg, 184–96. Barnes and Noble, New York.

Cusack, Carole M.

2012 Charmed Circle: Stonehenge, Contemporary Paganism, and Alternative Archaeology. *Numen* 59:138–55.

Cutler, Reverend Doctor, of Hamilton

1798 The Charge. In *A Sermon Preached August the 15th, 1798, at Hamilton, at the Ordination of the Rev. Daniel Story: To the Pastoral Care of the Church in Marietta, and Its Vicinity, in the Territory of the United States, North-West of the River Ohio* by Isaac Story, 30–36. Thomas C. Cushing, Salem, Massachusetts. http://trove.nla.gov.au/work/29997381, accessed 7 August 2017.

Daily Mercury

1950 Sacrificial Slaying? 28 September:5. Mackay, Queensland, Australia. http://nla. gov.au/nla.news-article171309799, accessed 28 May 2015.

Daily Star

1932 Will Give Air Talk on "Lost Atlantis." 30 January, evening edition:7. Long Island City, New York.

Daniel, Glyn

1963 *The Idea of Prehistory.* World Publishing, Cleveland, Ohio.

1979 The Forgotten Mile Stones and Blind Alleys of the Past. *Royal Anthroplogical Institute News* 33:3–6.

Davidson, Thomas

1956 Elf-Shot Cattle. *Antiquity* 30:149–55.

Davidson, William V.

1974   *Historical Geography of the Bay Islands, Honduras: Anglo-Hispanic Conflict in the Western Caribbean*. Southern University Press, Birmingham, Alabama.

Davies, Diane

2014   Reuse of the Past: A Case Study from the Ancient Maya. *Historian* 123 (Autumn):32–36.

Davies, Owen

2009   *Grimoires: A History of Magic Books*. Oxford University Press, Oxford.

Davis, Sonia H.

1971 [1948]   Lovecraft as I Knew Him. In *Something about Cats and Other Pieces* by H. P. Lovecraft, 234–46. Collected by A. Derleth. Books for Libraries Press, Plainview, New York.

Day, Howard David

1997   *A Treasure Hard to Attain: Images of Archaeology in Popular Film, with a Filmography*. Scarecrow Press, Lanham, Maryland.

Day, Jasmine

2006   *The Mummy's Curse: Mummymania in the English-Speaking World*. Routledge, London.

de Camp, L. Sprague (editor)

1976   *To Quebec and the Stars: H. P. Lovecraft*. Donald M. Grant, West Kingston, Rhode Island.

de Castro, Adolphe

1927   The Last Test. http://www.hplovecraft.com/writings/fiction/lt.aspx, accessed 22 June 2017.

Delasara, Jan

2000   PopLit, PopCult, and *The X-Files*: A Critical Exploration. McFarland, Jefferson, North Carolina.

Dennett, Carrie Lynd

2007   The Río Claro Site (AD 1000–1530), Northeast Honduras: A Ceramic Classification and Examination of External Connections. Master's thesis, Department of Anthropology, Trent University, Peterborough, Ontario, Canada.

Derleth, August

1966   Final Notes. In *The Dark Brotherhood and Other Pieces* by H. P. Lovecraft and Divers Hands, 302–21. Arkham House, Sauk City, Wisconsin.

Derricourt, Robin

2012   Pseudoarchaeology: The Concept and Its Limitations. *Antiquity* 86:524–31.

Desmond, Lawrence G.

1989   Of Facts and Hearsay: Bringing Augustus Le Plongeon into Focus. In *Tracing Archaeology's Past: The Historiography of Archaeology*, edited by Andrew L. Christenson, 139–50. Southern Illinois University Press, Carbondale.

2009   *Yucatán through Her Eyes: Alice Dixon Le Plongeon, Writer and Expeditionary Photographer.* University of New Mexico Press, Albuquerque.

Desmond, Lawrence Gustave, and Phyllis Mauch Messenger

1988   *A Dream of Maya: Augustus and Alice Le Plongeon in Nineteenth-Century Yucatan.* University of New Mexico Press, Albuquerque.

Deuel, Leo

1969   *Flights into Yesterday: The Story of Aerial Archaeology.* St. Martin's, New York.

Devereux, Paul

2003   *Spirit Roads: An Exploration of Otherworldly Routes.* Collins and Brown, London.

Dietler, Michael

1994   "Our Ancestors the Gauls": Archaeology, Ethnic Nationalism, and the Manipulation of Celtic Identity in Modern Europe. *American Anthropologist* 96(3):584–605.

1998   A Tale of Three Sites: The Monumentalization of Celtic Oppida and the Politics of Collective Memory and Identity. *World Archaeology* 30(1):72–89.

Digby, Adrian

1936   Comments on the Morphological Comparison of Two Crystal Skulls. *Man* 36:107–9.

di Peso, Charles C.

1953   The Clay Figurines of Acambaro, Guanajuato, Mexico. *American Antiquity* 18(4):388–89.

Dispatch

1974   Sunken Treasure Finds Justify Man's Predictions. 18 July:12. Lexington, North Carolina. https://news.google.com/newspapers?nid=1734&dat=19740717&id=5XkcAAAAIBAJ&sjid=51EEAAAAIBAJ&pg=4066,1828774&hl=en, accessed 22 June 2015.

Donnelly, Ignatius

1882   *Atlantis: The Antediluvian World.* Harper and Brothers, New York.

Donovan, Art

2011   Introduction. In his *The Art of Steampunk: Extraordinary Devices and Ingenious Contraptions from the Leading Artists of the Steampunk Movement*, 24–29. Fox Chapel Publishing, East Petersburg, Pennsylvania.

Donovan, Leslie A.

2007   Elf-Shot. In *J. R. R. Tolkien Encyclopedia: Scholarship and Critical Assessment*, edited by Michael D. C. Drout, 148–49. Routledge, New York.

Drieskins, Barbara

2006   *Living with Djinns: Understanding and Dealing with the Invisible in Cairo.* SAQI, London.

Drieskins, Barbara, and Rita Lucarelli

2002   Untying the Magic of the Pharaoh. In *Egyptological Essays on State and Society*, edited by Rosanna Pirelli, 79–93. Dipartimento di Studi e Ricerche su Africa e Paesi Arabi, Naples.

Drower, Margaret S.

1985   *Flinders Petrie: A Life in Archaeology.* Victor Gollancz, London.

1999   Sir William Matthew Flinders Petrie (1853–1942). In *Encyclopedia of Archaeology: The Great Archaeologists*, edited by Tim Murray, 1:221–32. ABC-CLIO, Santa Barbara, California.

2004   Margaret Alice Murray, 1863–1963. In *Breaking Ground: Pioneering Women Archaeologists*, edited by Getzel M. Cohen and Martha Sharp Joukowsky, 109–41. University of Michigan Press, Ann Arbor.

Duda, Heather Lynn

2006   An Examination of the Contemporary Monster Hunter in Popular Culture: Murderers and Men of God. PhD dissertation, Department of English, Indiana University of Pennsylvania. University Microfilms, Ann Arbor, Michigan.

Dunn, David

2009   *The Successful Treasure Hunter's Secret Manual: Discovering Treasure Auras in the Digital Age.* True Treasure, Whitstable, United Kingdom.

Durant, Jennifer, with a contribution by Roger T. Taylor

2015   Roman Tile. In *Glastonbury Abbey: Archaeological Excavations, 1904–79*, edited by Roberta Gilchrist and Cheryl Green, 246–48. Society of Antiquaries of London, London.

Dykstra, Darrell

1994   Pyramids, Prophets, and Progress: Ancient Egypt in the Writings of 'Alī Mubārak. *Journal of the American Oriental Society* 114(1):54–65.

Dyson, Stephen L.

1989   The Role of Ideology and Institutions in Shaping Classical Archaeology in the Nineteenth and Twentieth Centuries. In *Tracing Archaeology's Past: The Historiography of Archaeology*, edited by Andrew L. Christenson, 127–35. Southern Illinois University Press, Carbondale.

Dziemianowicz, Stefan

1991   Outsiders and Aliens: The Uses of Isolation in Lovecraft's Fiction. In *An Epi-cure in the Terrible: A Centennial Anthology of Essays in Honor of H. P. Love-craft*, 159–87. Fairleigh Dickinson University Press, Rutherford, New Jersey.

Eckardt, Hella, and Howard Williams

2003   Objects without a Past? The Use of Roman Objects in Early Anglo-Saxon Graves. In *Archaeologies of Remembrance: Death and Memory in Past Societies*, edited by Howard Williams, 141–70. Kluwer Academic/Plenum, New York.

Eddy, C. M., Jr.

1966   Walks with H. P. Lovecraft. In *The Dark Brotherhood and Other Pieces* by H. P. Lovecraft and Divers Hands, 242–45. Arkham House, Sauk City, Wisconsin.

Edmiston, Jake

2014   Kathleen Wynne Warns against Marketing Stunts That Scare People after Bell's Lake Ontario "Shark" Hoax. *National Post* 15 July. http://news.nationalpost.com/news/canada/possible-shark-sighting-in-lake-ontario-greeted-with-fear-and-scepticism, accessed 27 February 2016.

Effros, Bonnie

2003   Memories of the Early Medieval Past: Grave Artifacts in Nineteenth-Century France and Early Twentieth-Century America. In *Archaeologies of Remem-brance: Death and Memory in Past Societies*, edited by Howard Williams, 255–80. Kluwer Academic/Plenum, New York.

Eliade, Mircea

1954   *The Myth of the Eternal Return; or, Cosmos and History.* Translated by Wil-lard R. Trask. Princeton University Press, Princeton, New Jersey.

Ellis, Bill

2000   *Raising the Devil: Satanism, New Religions, and the Media.* University Press of Kentucky, Lexington.

2004   *Lucifer Ascending: The Occult in Folklore and Popular Culture.* University Press of Kentucky, Lexington.

Ellis, Richard

1998   *Imagining Atlantis.* Knopf, New York.

Elson, Christina M., and Kathryn Venzor

2016   Meso-American Archaeological Collection. *American Museum of Natural History.* http://www.amnh.org/our-research/anthropology/collections/collections-history/meso-american-archaeology, accessed 21 March 2016.

El-Zein, Amira

2009   *Islam, Arabs, and the Intelligent World of the Jinn.* Syracuse University Press, Syracuse, New York.

Errington, Shelly

1993 Progressivist Stories and the Pre-Columbian Past: Notes on Mexico and the United States. In *Collecting the Pre-Columbian Past: A Symposium at Dumbarton Oaks, 6th and 7th October 1990*, edited by Elizabeth Hill Boone, 209–49. Dumbarton Oaks Research Library and Collection, Washington, DC.

Evans, Dewi

2013 Frivola (1896). *Mystery and Imagination*, 4 August. https://gothictexts. wordpress.com/category/augustus-jessopp-1823-1914, accessed 22 June 2017.

Evans, Jonathan D.

1987 The Dragon. In *Mythical and Fabulous Creatures: A Source Book and Research Guide*, edited by Malcolm South, 27–58. Greenwood Press, New York.

Evans, R. Tripp

2004 *Romancing the Maya: Mexican Antiquity in the American Imagination, 1820–1915*. University of Texas Press, Austin.

Evans-Wentz, W. Y.

1911 *The Fairy-Faith in Celtic Countries*. Oxford University Press, London.

Fabian, Robert

1950 The "Witchcraft" Murder Mystery. *Truth* 8 January:18. Sydney, Australia. http://trove.nla.gov.au/newspaper/article/167907737, accessed 21 March 2017.

1953 *Fabian of the Yard*. British Book Centre, New York.

1954 *London after Dark*. British Book Centre, New York.

Fagan, Brian

1977 *The Rape of the Nile: Tomb Robbers, Tourists, and Archaeologists in Egypt*. MacDonald and Jane's, London.

1995 *Time Detectives: How Scientists Use Modern Technology to Unravel the Secrets of the Past*. Simon and Schuster, New York.

2005 Short History of Archaeological Methods, 1870 to 1960. In *Handbook of Archaeological Methods*, edited by Herbert D. G. Maschner and Christopher Chippindale, 1:40–72. AltaMira, Lanham, Maryland.

Fagan, Garrett G.

2006 Diagnosing Pseudoarchaeology. In *Archaeological Fantasies: How Pseudoarchaeology Misrepresents the Past and Misleads the Public*, edited by Garrett G. Fagan, 23–46. Routledge, London.

Fagan, Garrett G., and Kenneth L. Feder

2005 Crusading against Straw Men: An Alternative View of Alternative Archaeologies. *World Archaeology* 38(4):718–29.

Falk, John, and Lynn Dierking

2013 *The Museum Experience Revisited*. Left Coast Press, Walnut Creek, California.

Feder, Kenneth L.

1980   Foolsgold of the Gods. *Humanist* 40(1):20–23.

1984   Irrationality and Popular Archaeology. *American Antiquity* 49(3):525–41.

2010   *Encyclopedia of Dubious Archaeology: From Atlantis to Walam Olum*. Greenwood, Santa Barbara, California.

2017 [1990]   *Frauds, Myths, and Mysteries: Science and Pseudoscience in Archaeology*. 9th ed. Oxford University Press, New York.

Feilberg, H. F.

1895   Ghostly Lights. *Folk-lore* 6:288–300.

Fell, Barry

1989   *America B.C.: Ancient Settlers in the New World*. Rev. ed. Pocket, New York.

Fernández-Osco, Marcelo

2011   Bolivian Archaeology: Another Link in the Chain of Coloniality? In *Indigenous Peoples and Archaeology in Latin America*, edited by Cristóbal Gnecco and Patricia Ayala, 333–44. Left Coast Press, Walnut Creek, California.

Finley, M. I.

1965   Myth, Memory, and History. *History and Theory* 4(3):281–302.

Fisher, S.

2000   Exploring People's Relationships with Egypt: Qualitative Research for the Petrie Museum. Petrie Museum, University College London.

Fishman, W. J.

1988   *East End 1888: A Year in a London Borough among the Labouring Poor*. Duckworth, London.

Fitting, Peter (editor)

2004   *Subterranean Worlds: A Critical Anthology*. Wesleyan University Press, Middletown, Connecticut.

Florescano, Enrique

1993   The Creation of the Museo Nacional de Antropología of Mexico and Its Scientific, Educational, and Political Purposes. In *Collecting the Pre-Columbian Past: A Symposium at Dumbarton Oaks, 6th and 7th October 1990*, edited by Elizabeth Hill Boone, 81–103. Dumbarton Oaks Research Library and Collection, Washington, DC.

Forsyth, Phyllis Young

1980   *Atlantis: The Making of Myth*. McGill-Queen's University Press, Montreal.

Fort, Charles

1919   *The Book of the Damned*. Boni and Liveright, New York.

Fortune, Dion
1963   *Psychic Self-Defense.* Weiser, Boston.

Foshag, William F., and Robert Leslie
1955   Jadeite from Manzanal, Guatemala. *American Antiquity* 21(1):81–83.

Freeman, Victoria
2011   Indigenous Hauntings in Settler-Colonial Spaces: The Activism of Indigenous Ancestors in the City of Toronto. In *Phantom Past, Indigenous Presence: Native Ghosts in North American Culture and History,* edited by Colleen E. Boyd and Coll Thrush, 209–54. University of Nebraska Press, Lincoln.

Fröhlich, Ida
2014   Mesopotamian Elements and the Watchers Traditions. In *The Watchers in Jewish and Christian Traditions,* edited by Angela Kim Harkins, Kelley Coblentz Bautch, and John C. Endres, 11–24. Fortress Press, Minneapolis, Minnesota.

Frost, Adam, and Jim Kynvin
2015   Sherlock Holmes: Examining the Evidence—in Charts. *Guardian* 29 June. http://www.theguardian.com/books/gallery/2015/jun/29/sherlock-holmes-examining-the-evidence-in-charts?CMP=twt_gu&CMP=twt_gu, accessed 29 June 2015.

Gaddis, Vincent H.
1994   *Mysterious Fires and Lights.* Borderland Sciences, Garberville, California.

Gamio, Manuel
1924   The Sequence of Cultures in Mexico. *American Anthropologist* 26(3):307–22.

Gange, David
2013   *Dialogues with the Dead: Egyptology in British Culture and Religion, 1822–1922.* Oxford University Press, Oxford.

Gann, Thomas W. F.
1918   *The Maya Indians of Southern Yucatan and Northern British Honduras.* US Government Printing Office, Washington, DC.
1925   *Mystery Cities of the Maya: Exploration and Adventure in Lubantuun.* Duckworth, London.
1926   *Ancient Cities and Modern Tribes: Exploration and Adventure in Maya Lands.* Duckworth, London.
1929   *Discoveries and Adventures in Central America.* Scribner's, New York.
1936   *Mexico: From the Earliest Times to the Conquest.* Lovat Dickson, London.

Gardner, Eriq
2012   "Indiana Jones" Lawsuit Seeks Hollywood Profits from Alleged Crystal Skull Theft. *Hollywood Reporter* 7 December. http://www.hollywoodreporter.com/thr-esq/indiana-jones-lawsuit-seeks-hollywood-399236, accessed 22 June 2017.

Gardner, Gerald Brosseau

1939   Witchcraft. *Folklore* 50(2):188–90.

2004 [1954]   *Witchcraft Today.* Additional material by Judy Harrow, Ronald Hutton, Wren Walker, and Tara Nelsen. Citadel Press, New York.

Garofalo, Charles, and Robert M. Price

1982   Chariots of the Old Ones? *Crypt of Cthulhu* 1(5). http://crypt-of-cthulhu.com/chariotsofoldones.htm, accessed 22 June 2017.

Garvin, Richard M.

1973   *The Crystal Skull.* Doubleday, Garden City, New York.

Gates, William E.

1915   *The Spirit of the Hour in Archaeology.* Aryan Theosophical Press, Point Loma, California.

1969 [1910]   *Commentary upon the Maya-Tzental Perez Codex, with a Concluding Note upon the Linguistic Problem of the Maya Glyphs.* Peabody Museum, Cambridge, Massachusetts. Kraus Reprint, New York.

1978a [1931]   *An Outline Dictionary of Maya Glyphs, with a Concordance and Analysis of Their Relationships.* Dover, New York.

1978b [1932]   Glyph Studies. In his *An Outline Dictionary of Maya Glyphs, with a Concordance and Analysis of Their Relationships*, 175–204. Dover, New York.

George, Christopher T.

2006   Díosy and D'Onston: Black Magic and Jack the Ripper. In *Ripperology*, edited by Paul Begg, 59–65. Barnes and Noble, New York.

Gere, Cathy

2009   *Knossos and the Prophets of Modernism.* University of Chicago Press, Chicago.

Gibson, Gayle, Meg Morden, and Willie Rowbotham

2015   "The Standing Stones of Stenness." *Odyssey: Adventures in Archaeology.* Electronic document, http://www.odysseyadventures.ca/articles/stone-circles/orcadian/article_stenness.htm#, accessed 26 June 2017.

Gibson, Marion

2013   Old Deities, New Worlds: The Return of the Gods in Fiction. In *Mysticism, Myth, and Celtic Identity*, edited by Marion Gibson, Shelley Trower, and Garry Tregidga, 38–48. Routledge, London.

2014   Melting the Ice Gods: The Creation and Destruction of Old and New Gods in British Fiction, 1880–1955. *Preternature* 3(2):339–66.

Gibson, Marion, Shelley Trower, and Garry Tregidga

2013   Mysticism, Myth, and Celtic Identity. In *Mysticism, Myth, and Celtic Identity*, edited by Marion Gibson, Shelley Trower, and Garry Tregidga, 1–20. Routledge, London.

Gilchrist, Roberta

2015a   Excavations at Glastonbury Abbey. In *Glastonbury Abbey: Archaeological Excavations, 1904–79*, edited by Roberta Gilchrist and Cheryl Green, 1–19. Society of Antiquaries of London, London.

2015b   A Sense of Place: History, Buildings and Landscape. In *Glastonbury Abbey: Archaeological Excavations, 1904–79*, edited by Roberta Gilchrist and Cheryl Green, 51–79. Society of Antiquaries of London, London.

2015c   Conclusions. In *Glastonbury Abbey: Archaeological Excavations, 1904–79*, edited by Roberta Gilchrist and Cheryl Green, 415–35. Society of Antiquaries of London, London.

Gilchrist, Roberta, and Cheryl Green (editors)

2015a   *Glastonbury Abbey: Archaeological Excavations, 1904–79*. Society of Antiquaries of London, London.

Gilchrist, Roberta, and Cheryl Green

2015b   Chronological Summary. In *Glastonbury Abbey: Archaeological Excavations, 1904–79*, edited by Roberta Gilchrist and Cheryl Green, 383–414. Society of Antiquaries of London, London.

Ginzburg, Carlo

1983 [1966]   *The Night Battles: Witchcraft and Agrarian Cults in the Sixteenth and Seventeenth Centuries*. Translated by John Tedeschi and Anne Tedeschi. Penguin, New York.

1991   *Ecstasies: Deciphering the Witches' Sabbath*. Translated by Raymond Rosenthal. Pantheon, New York.

Givens, Douglas R.

1999   Sylvanus Griswold Morley (1883–1948). In *Encyclopedia of Archaeology: The Great Archaeologists*, edited by Tim Murray, 1:313–24. ABC-CLIO, Santa Barbara, California.

Gnecco, Cristóbal

2011   Native Histories and Archaeologists. In *Indigenous Peoples and Archaeology in Latin America*, edited by Cristóbal Gnecco and Patricia Ayala, 53–66. Left Coast Press, Walnut Creek, California.

Godfrey, William S., Jr.

1951   The Archaeology of the Old Stone Mill in Newport, Rhode Island. *American Antiquity* 17(2):120–29.

Goodman, Jeffrey

1977   *Psychic Archaeology: Time Machine to the Past*. Berkley Books, New York.

Goodrick-Clarke, Nicholas

2002   *Black Sun: Aryan Cults, Esoteric Nazism and the Politics of Identity*. New York University Press, New York.

2004   *The Occult Roots of Nazism: Secret Aryan Cults and Their Influence on Nazi Ideology.* Tauris Parke, London.

Gordon, Cyrus H.
1982   *Forgotten Scripts: Their Ongoing Discovery and Decipherment.* Rev. ed. Basic, New York.

Gosden, Chris, and Gary Lock
1998   Prehistoric Histories. *World Archaeology* 30(1):2–12.

Gould, D. Rae
2013   Cultural Practice and Authenticity: The Search for Real Indians in New England in the "Historical" Period. In *The Death of Prehistory,* edited by Peter R. Schmidt and Stephen A. Mrozowski, 241–66. Oxford University Press, Oxford.

Graham, Ian
2010   *The Road to Ruins.* University of New Mexico Press, Albuquerque.

Grant, Kenneth
1972   *The Magical Revival.* Frederick Muller, London.

Graves, Tom, and Janet Hoult (editors)
1982   *The Essential T. C. Lethbridge.* Granada, London.

Green, Cheryl, and Roberta Gilchrist
2015   The Cemetery and Church. In *Glastonbury Abbey: Archaeological Excavations, 1904–79,* edited by Roberta Gilchrist and Cheryl Green, 80–123. Society of Antiquaries of London, London.

Greenhalgh, Michael
1989   *The Survival of Roman Antiquities in the Middle Ages.* Duckworth, London.

Greenwell, J. Richard, and James E. King
1981   Attitudes of Physical Anthropologists toward Reports of Bigfoot and Nessie. *Current Anthropology* 22(1):79–80.

Griffin, Justin E.
2013   *Glastonbury and the Grail: Did Joseph of Arimathea Bring the Sacred Relic to Britain?* McFarland, Jefferson, North Carolina.

Griffith, Francis Llewellyn
1900   *Stories of the High Priests of Memphis: The Sethon of Herodotus and the Demotic Tales of Khamuas.* Clarendon, Oxford.

Grimes, W. F.
1957   British Archaeology. *The Times* 15 May:11. London.

Grinsell, L. V.
1947   The Folklore of Ancient Egyptian Monuments. *Folklore* 58(4):345–60.

1967   Barrow Treasure in Fact, Tradition, and Legislation. *Folklore* 78(1):1–38.

1973   Witchcraft at Some Prehistoric Sites. In *The Witch Figure: Folklore Essays by a Group of Scholars in England Honouring the 75th Birthday of Katharine M. Briggs*, edited by Venetia Newall, 72–79. Routledge and Kegan Paul, London.

Gugliemi, Waltraud

2001 [1999]   Agatha Christie and Her Use of Ancient Egyptian Sources. In *Agatha Christie and Archaeology*, edited by Charlotte Trümpler, 350–89. Translated by Anthea Bell. British Museum Press, London.

Gunter, Michael M.

2005   The Kurdish Minority Identity in Iraq. In *Nationalism and Minority Identities in Islamic Societies*, edited by Maya Shatzmiller, 263–82. McGill-Queen's University Press, Kingston, Ontario.

Guran, Paula

2007   The Mummy. In *Icons of Horror and the Supernatural: An Encyclopedia of Our Worst Nightmares*, edited by S. T. Joshi, 1:375–407. Greenwood Press, Westport, Connecticut.

Gut, Renate

2001 [1999]   Nineveh. In *Agatha Christie and Archaeology*, edited by Charlotte Trümpler, 72–88. Translated by Anthea Bell. British Museum Press, London.

Guthe, Carl E.

1950   Journey to Petén. In *Morleyana: A Collection of Writings in Memoriam Sylvanus Griswold Morley (1883–1948)*, 65–69. School of American Research and the Museum of New Mexico, Santa Fe.

Haarmann, Ulrich

1996   Medieval Muslim Perceptions of Pharaonic Egypt. In *Ancient Egyptian Literature: History and Forms*, edited by Antonio Loprieno, 605–27. Brill, Leiden.

Haikal, Fayza

2003   Egypt's Past Regenerated by Its Own People. In *Consuming Ancient Egypt*, edited by Sally MacDonald and Michael Rice, 123–38. Institute of Archaeology, UCL Press, London.

Hale, Christopher

2006   The Atlantean Box. In *Archaeological Fantasies: How Pseudoarchaeology Misrepresents the Past and Misleads the Public*, edited by Garrett G. Fagan, 235–58. Routledge, London.

Hall, Alaric

2005   Getting Shot of Elves: Healing, Witchcraft, and Fairies in the Scottish Witchcraft Trials. *Folklore* 116(1):19–36.

2007   *Elves in Anglo-Saxon England: Matters of Belief, Health, Gender and Identity.* Boydell Press, Woodbridge, Suffolk, United Kingdom.

Hallen, A. W. Cornelius (editor)
1903   *The Scottish Antiquary; or, Northern Notes and Queries.* Vol. 7. University Press, Edinburgh.

Hamann, Byron Ellsworth
2002   The Social Life of Pre-Sunrise Things: Indigenous Mesoamerican Archaeology. *Current Anthropology* 43(3):351–82.
2008   How Maya Hieroglyphs Got Their Name: Egypt, Mexico, and China in Western Grammatology since the Fifteenth Century. *Proceedings of the American Philosophical Society* 152(1):1–68.

Hammond, Norman
1975   *Lubaantun: A Classic Maya Realm.* Peabody Museum of Archaeology and Ethnology, Harvard University, Cambridge, Massachusetts.

Hancock, Graham
1995   *Fingerprints of the Gods.* Three Rivers Press, New York.
2015   Zahi Hawass vs. Graham Hancock: The April 2015 "Debate" Debacle. Electronic document, https://grahamhancock.com/hancockg15, accessed 1 July 2016.

Hankey, Julie
2001   *A Passion for Egypt: Arthur Weigall, Tutankhamun and the "Curse of the Pharaohs."* Tauris, London.

Hanks, Michele
2015   *Haunted Heritage: The Cultural Politics of Ghost Tourism, Populism, and the Past.* Left Coast Press, Walnut Creek, California.

Hanson, William S., and Ioana A. Oltean (editors)
2013   *Archaeology from Historical Aerial and Satellite Archives.* Springer, New York.

Harkin, Greg
2011   Former Billionaire Sean Quinn's Downfall "Caused by Fairies." *Belfast Telegraph* 23 November. http://www.belfasttelegraph.co.uk/news/local-national/republic-of-ireland/former-billionaire-sean-quinns-downfall-caused-by-fairies-28683988.html#ixzz1fEs16rHB, accessed 22 June 2017.

Harms, Daniel, and John Wisdom Gonce III
1998   *The Necronomicon Files: The Truth behind the Legend.* Nightshade, Mountain View, California.

Harrington, John P.
1950   Little Hummingbird. In *Morleyana: A Collection of Writings in Memoriam*

Sylvanus Griswold Morley (1883–1948), 71–72. School of American Research and the Museum of New Mexico, Santa Fe.

Harris, Charles H., III, and Louis R. Sadler
2003   *The Archaeologist Was a Spy: Sylvanus G. Morley and the Office of Naval Intelligence*. University of New Mexico Press, Albuquerque.

Harrison, Marguerite
1926   Gertrude Bell a Desert Power. *New York Times* 18 July:XX12. New York.

Harvey, Penelope
2006   Memorialising the Future: The Museum of Science and Industry in Manchester. In *Science, Magic, and Religion: The Ritual Processes of Museum Magic*, edited by Mary Bouquet and Nuno Porto, 29–50. Berghahn, Oxford.

Hawkes, Jacquetta
1946   Introduction. In *Come Tell Me How You Live* by Agatha Christie Mallowan. William Morrow, New York.

Haydon, S. E.
1897   A Windmill Demolishes It. *Dallas Morning News* 19 April:5. Dallas, Texas. https://en.wikipedia.org/wiki/File:Haydon_article,_Aurora,_Texas,_UFO_incident,_1897.jpg, accessed 26 July 2015.

Haynes, C. Vance, Jr., and George A. Agogino
1986   *Geochronology of Sandia Cave*. Smithsonian Institution Press, Washington, DC.

Heald, Hazel
1932   The Horror in the Museum. http://www.hplovecraft.com/writings/texts/fiction/hm.aspx, accessed 7 August 2017.
1933   Out of the Aeons. http://www.hplovecraft.com/writings/fiction/oa.aspx, accessed 22 June 2017.

Healy, Paul
1993   Northeastern Honduras. In *Pottery of Prehistoric Honduras: Regional Classification and Analysis*, edited by John S. Henderson and Marilyn Beaudry-Corbett, 194–213. UCLA Institute of Archaeology, Regents of the University of California, Los Angeles.

Henson, Don
2010   The Academy and the Public. In *Unquiet Pasts: Risk Society, Lived Cultural Heritage, Re-Designing Reflexivity*, edited by Stephanie Koerner and Ian Russell, 209–22. Ashgate, Farnham, United Kingdom.

Hernandez, Erica, and Adrian Garcia
2016   Haunted South Texas Museum Comes to Life at Night. Electronic document,

http://www.ksat.com/holidays/halloween/haunted-south-texas-museum-comes-to-life-at-night, accessed 24 February 2016.

Herva, Vesa-Pekka, and Jonas M. Nordin
2015   Unearthing Atlantis and Performing the Past: Ancient Things, Alternative Histories, and the Present Past in the Baroque World. *Journal of Social Archaeology* 15(1):116–35.

Hetherington, Kevin
1996   The Utopics of Social Ordering: Stonehenge as a Museum without Walls. In *Theorizing Museums: Representing Identity and Diversity in a Changing World*, edited by Sharon Macdonald and Gordon Fyfe, 153–76. Blackwell Publishers and the Sociological Review, Oxford.

Hibben, Frank C.
1941   *Evidences of Early Occupation in Sandia Cave, New Mexico, and Other Sites in the Sandia-Manzano Region.* Smithsonian Institution, Washington, DC.

Higham, N. J.
2002   *King Arthur: Myth-Making and History.* Routledge, London.

Hill, Sharon
2012   Military UFOs Secrets Revealed Sept 22 at National Atomic Testing Museum. *Doubtful News* 4 September. http://doubtfulnews.com/2012/09/military-ufos-secrets-revealed-sept-22-at-national-atomic-testing-museum, accessed 30 June 2016.

Hingley, Richard
1996   Ancestors and Identity in the Later Prehistory of Atlantic Scotland: The Reuse and Reinvention of Neolithic Monuments and Material Culture. *World Archaeology* 28(2):231–43.

Hinsley, Curtis M.
1993   In Search of the New World Classical. In *Collecting the Pre-Columbian Past: A Symposium at Dumbarton Oaks, 6th and 7th October 1990*, edited by Elizabeth Hill Boone, 105–21. Dumbarton Oaks Research Library and Collection, Washington, DC.

Hinson, David H.
2003   Comparing Stories of Extraterrestrials with Stories of Fairies. MA thesis, University of North Carolina, Asheville. University Microfilms, Ann Arbor, Michigan.

Hiscock, Peter
2012   Cinema, Supernatural Archaeology, and the Hidden Human Past. *Numen* 59:156–77.

Hite, Kenneth
2008   *Tour de Lovecraft: The Tales*. Atomic Overmind Press, Alexandria, Virginia.

Holbrook, Stewart H.
1959   *The Golden Age of Quackery*. Macmillan, New York.

Holm, Ingunn
1999   Clearance Cairns: The Farmers' and the Archaeologists' Views. In *Archaeology and Folklore*, edited by Amy Gazin-Schwartz and Cornelius Holtorf, 214–29. Routledge, London.

Holtorf, Cornelius
1998   The Life-Histories of Megaliths in Mecklenburg-Vorpommern (Germany). *World Archaeology* 30(1):23–38.
2005   Beyond Crusades: How (Not) to Engage with Alternative Archaeologies. *World Archaeology* 37(4):544–51.
2007   *Archaeology Is a Brand! The Meaning of Archaeology in Contemporary Pop Culture*. Left Coast Press, Walnut Creek, California.
2012   The Colours of the Past. In *From Archaeology to Archaeologies: The "Other" Past*, edited by Anna Simandiraki-Grimshaw and Eleni Stefanou, 102–5. Archaeopress, Oxford.

Holzer, Hans
1992   *Long before Columbus: How the Ancients Discovered America*. Bear, Santa Fe, New Mexico.

Hoopes, John W.
2012   The Hidden History of 2012. *Fortean Times* 285 (April):40–43.

Hopkinson-Ball, Tim
2007   *The Rediscovery of Glastonbury: Frederick Bligh Bond, Architect of the New Age*. Sutton Publishing, Stroud, Gloucestershire, United Kingdom.

Hornung, Erik
2001   *The Secret Lore of Egypt: Its Impact on the West*. Translated by David Lorton. Cornell University Press, Ithaca, New York.

Houlbrook, Ceri, and Natalie Armitage
2015   Introduction: The Materiality of the Materiality of Magic. In *The Materiality of Magic*, edited by Ceri Houlbrook and Natalie Armitage, 1–13. Oxbow, Oxford.

Houlson, Jane Harvey
1934   *Blue Blaze: Danger and Delight in Strange Islands of Honduras*. Bobbs-Merrill, Indianapolis, Indiana.

Howard, Robert E.
1929   The Shadow Kingdom. https://en.wikisource.org/wiki/The_Shadow_Kingdom, accessed 12 August 2016.

Huckvale, David

2012   *Ancient Egypt in the Popular Imagination: Building a Fantasy in Film, Literature, Music, and Art.* McFarland, Jefferson, North Carolina.

Hutson, Scott R.

2010   *Dwelling, Identity, and the Maya: Relational Archaeology at Chunchucmil.* AltaMira, Lanham, Maryland.

Hutton, Ronald

1999a   Modern Pagan Witchcraft. In *Witchcraft and Magic in Europe: The Twentieth Century*, edited by Bengt Ankarloo and Stuart Clark, 1–79. University of Pennsylvania Press, Philadelphia.

1999b   *The Triumph of the Moon: A History of Modern Pagan Witchcraft.* Oxford University Press, Oxford.

2000   Paganism and Polemic: The Debate over the Origins of Modern Pagan Witchcraft. *Folklore* 111(1):103–17.

2011   Romano-British Reuse of Prehistoric Ritual Sites. *Britannia* 42:1–22.

2014   The Making of the Early Modern British Fairy Tradition. *Historical Journal* 57(4):1135–56.

Ibanga, Imaeyen

2008   Search for Titanic Really Was Cover-Up Mission. *ABC News* 2 June. http://abcnews.go.com/GMA/AroundTheWorld/story?id=4978391, accessed 21 June 2016.

Iversen, Erik

1993   *The Myth of Egypt and Its Hieroglyphs in European Tradition.* Princeton University Press, Princeton, New Jersey.

James, Montague Rhodes

1911   Casting the Runes. Electronic document, https://en.wikisource.org/wiki/Casting_the_Runes, accessed 7 August 2017.

James, T. G. H.

2008   *Howard Carter: The Path to Tutankhamun.* Tauris Parke Paperbacks, New York.

Jansen, Maarten

1990   The Search for History in Mixtec Codices. *Ancient Mesoamerica* 1:99–112.

Jarus, Owen

2016   Great Pyramid of Giza Is Slightly Lopsided. *Live Science* 20 June. http://www.livescience.com/55118-great-pyramid-giza-is-slightly-lopsided.html, accessed 1 July 2016.

Jasnow, Richard, and Karl-Theodor Zauzich

2014   *Conversations in the House of Life: A New Translation of the Ancient Egyptian Book of Thoth.* Harrassowitz, Wiesbaden, Germany.

Jenkins, Phil
2011   A True Ottawa Eccentric. *Ottawa Citizen* 6 June. https://www.pressreader.
        com/canada/ottawa-citizen/20110606/281749855960374, accessed 7 August 2017.

Jessopp, Augustus
1887   Hill-Digging and Magic. *Nineteenth Century* 21:40–58.

Jidejian, Nina
1975   *Baalbek: Heliopolis "City of the Sun."* Dar el-Machreq Publishers, Beirut,
        Lebanon.

Jones, Alex
2011   Alex Jones, DMT, and the Clockwork Elves. *YouTube.* https://www.youtube.
        com/watch?v=0BKzuzjjCro, accessed 1 July 2016.

Jones, David E.
2000   *An Instinct for Dragons.* Routledge, London.

Jones, Grant D.
1998   *The Conquest of the Last Maya Kingdom.* Stanford University Press, Stanford,
        California.

Jones, Jonathan
2015   Emoji Is Dragging Us Back to the Dark Ages—And All We Can Do Is
        Smile. *Guardian* 27 May. http://www.theguardian.com/artanddesign/
        jonathanjonesblog/2015/may/27/emoji-language-dragging-us-back-to-the-
        dark-ages-yellow-smiley-face, accessed 2 July 2015.

Jones, Lindsay
1995   *Twin City Tales: A Hermeneutical Reassessment of Tula and Chichén Itzá.* Uni-
        versity Press of Colorado, Boulder.

Jordan, Paul
1998   *Riddles of the Sphinx.* New York University Press, New York.
2001   *The Atlantis Syndrome.* Sutton Publishing, Thrupp, Stroud, Gloucestershire,
        United Kingdom.

Joshi, S. T.
1996   *H. P. Lovecraft: A Life.* Necronomicon Press, West Warwick, Rhode Island.
2001   *A Dreamer and a Visionary: H. P. Lovecraft in His Time.* Liverpool University
        Press, Liverpool, England.
2007   The Cthulhu Mythos. In *Icons of Horror and the Supernatural: An Encyclope-
        dia of Our Worst Nightmares,* edited by S. T. Joshi, 1:97–128. Greenwood Press,
        Westport, Connecticut.
2008   *The Rise and Fall of the Cthulhu Mythos.* Mythos, Poplar Bluff, Missouri.
2011   Introduction. In *The White People and Other Weird Stories* by Arthur Machen,
        xi–xxviii. Edited by S. T. Joshi. Penguin, New York.

2015 Introduction. In *H. P. Lovecraft: The Spirit of Revision: Lovecraft's Letters to Zealia Brown Reed Bishop*, edited by Sean Branney and Andrew Leman, 7–14. H. P. Lovecraft Historical Society, Glendale, California.

Joshi, S. T. (editor)

1986 *H. P. Lovecraft: Uncollected Letters*. Necronomicon Press, West Warwick, Rhode Island.

2012a *The Annotated Revisions and Collaborations of H. P. Lovecraft*, vol. 1: *The Crawling Chaos and Others*. Arcane Wisdom, Welches, Oregon.

2012b *The Annotated Revisions and Collaborations of H. P. Lovecraft*, vol. 2: *Medusa's Coil and Others*. Arcane Wisdom, Welches, Oregon.

Joyce, Rosemary

2012 Good Science, Big Hype, Bad Archaeology. *Berkeley Blog*, 7 June. http://blogs.berkeley.edu/2012/06/07/good-science-big-hype-bad-archaeology, accessed 30 June 2016.

2015 There's a Real Archaeological Surprise in Honduras . . . *Berkeley Blog*, 3 March. http://blogs.berkeley.edu/2015/03/03/theres-a-real-archaeological-surprise-in-honduras, accessed 30 June 2016.

Kavanagh, Sarah Schneider

2011 Haunting Remains: Educating a New American Citizenry at Indian Hill Cemetery. In *Phantom Past, Indigenous Presence: Native Ghosts in North American Culture and History*, edited by Colleen E. Boyd and Coll Thrush, 151–78. University of Nebraska Press, Lincoln.

Kearney, Michael

1986 *The Winds of Ixtepeji: World View and Society in a Zapotec Town*. Waveland Press, Long Grove, Illinois.

Keefe, Patrick Radden

2013 Spitballing Indy. *New Yorker* 25 March. http://www.newyorker.com/culture/culture-desk/spitballing-indy, accessed 1 June 2016.

Keen, Benjamin

1971 *The Aztec Image in Western Thought*. Rutgers University Press, New Brunswick, New Jersey.

Kehoe, Alice Beck

2005 *The Kensington Runestone: Approaching a Research Question Holistically*. Waveland Press, Long Grove, Illinois.

2013 "Prehistory's" History. In *The Death of Prehistory*, edited by Peter R. Schmidt and Stephen A. Mrozowski, 31–46. Oxford University Press, Oxford.

Keith, Arthur

1950 [1928] The Evolution of the Human Races. In *This Is Race: An Anthology Selected from the International Literature on the Races of Man*, edited by Earl W. Count, 426–35. Henry Schuman, New York.

Kelker, Nancy L., and Karen O. Bruhns

2010   *Faking Ancient Mesoamerica*. Left Coast Press, Walnut Creek, California.

Kennedy, Maeve

2015   From Monsters to Manga: Golden Age of Art by the Celtic Race That Never Was. *Guardian* 9 July. http://www.theguardian.com/artanddesign/2015/jul/10/from-monsters-to-manga-golden-age-of-art-by-the-celtic-race-that-never-was, accessed 24 July 2015.

Kenyon, J. Douglas

2005   Exposing a Scientific Cover-Up: *Forbidden Archaeology* Coauthor Michael Cremo Talks about the "Knowledge Filter" and Other Means for Cooking the Academic Books. In *Forbidden History: Prehistoric Technologies, Extraterrestrial Intervention, and the Suppressed Origins of Civilization*, edited by J. Douglas Kenyon, 22–28. Bear, Rochester, Vermont.

Khun de Prorok, Byron

1925a   Seeking Africa's Lost Glories. *New York Times* 8 March:SM1–2. New York.
1925b   Key to Carthage Sought in Old Utica. *New York Times* 29 March:SM3–18. New York.
1925c   Hunts Lost Towns in Sands of Sahara. *New York Times* 9 April:25. New York.
1926   *Digging for Lost African Gods: The Record of Five Years Archaeological Excavation in North Africa*. Translation by Edgar Fletcher Allen. Putnam's, New York.
2001   *Mysterious Sahara: The Land of Gold, of Sand, and of Ruin*. Narrative Press, Santa Barbara, California.

Kidder, Alfred Vincent

1950   Sylvanus Griswold Morley, 1883–1948. In *Morleyana: A Collection of Writings in Memoriam Sylvanus Griswold Morley (1883–1948)*, 93–102. School of American Research and the Museum of New Mexico, Santa Fe.

Kidwell, Clara Sue

1999   Every Last Dishcloth: The Prodigious Collecting of George Gustav Heye. In *Collecting Native America, 1870–1960*, edited by Shepard Krech III and Barbara A. Hail, 232–58. Smithsonian Institution Press, Washington, DC.

Kintz, Ellen R.

1990   *Life under the Tropical Canopy: Tradition and Change among the Yucatec Maya*. Holt, Rinehart and Winston, Fort Worth, Texas.

Klejn, Leo

1999a   Gustaf Kossinna (1858–1931). In *Encyclopedia of Archaeology: The Great Archaeologists*, edited by Tim Murray, 1:233–46. ABC-CLIO, Santa Barbara, California.

1999b   Heinrich Schliemann (1822–1890). In *Encyclopedia of Archaeology: The Great Archaeologists*, edited by Tim Murray, 1:109–25. ABC-CLIO, Santa Barbara, California.

Klinger, Leslie S. (editor)
2014   *The New Annotated H. P. Lovecraft*. Liveright, New York.

Kostich-Lefebvre, Gordana Ana
1998   Political Vases: The Architectural Uses of Etruscan Urns/Vases in the Formation of Medicean Political Symbolism under Cosmo I, Magnus Dux Aetruriae. In *Building as a Political Act: 1997 ACSA International Conference*, edited by Randall Ott, 129–32. ACSA Press, New York.

Kripal, Jeffrey J.
2010   *Authors of the Impossible: The Paranormal and the Sacred*. University of Chicago Press, Chicago.
2011   *Mutants and Mystics: Science Fiction, Superhero Comics, and the Paranormal*. University of Chicago Press, Chicago.

Kruse, Corinna
2010   Producing Absolute Truth: CSI Science as Wishful Thinking. *American Anthropologist* 112(1):79–91.

Kulik, Karol
2007   A Short History of Archaeological Communication. In *Archaeology and the Media*, edited by Timothy Clack and Marcus Brittain, 111–24. Left Coast Press, Walnut Creek, California.

Kurlander, Eric
2015   Hitler's Supernatural Sciences: Astrology, Anthroposophy, and World Ice Theory in the Third Reich. In *Revisiting the "Nazi Occult": Histories, Realities, Legacies*, edited by Monica Blak and Eric Kurlander, 132–56. Camden House, Rochester, New York.

Kuwanwisiwma, Leigh J., and T. J. Ferguson
2004   Ang Kuktota: Hopi Ancestral Sites and Cultural Landscapes. *Expedition* 46(2):24–29.

La Farge, Oliver
1928   Letter to A. B. Dinwiddie, 16 January. Middle American Research Institute, Tulane University, New Orleans.

Lancaster, Roger N.
1991   Skin Color, Race, and Racism in Nicaragua. *Ethnology* 30(4):339–53.

Landrum, Cynthia
2011   Shape-Shifters, Ghosts, and Residual Power: An Examination of Northern Plains Spiritual Beliefs, Location, Objects, and Spiritual Colonialism. In

Phantom Past, Indigenous Presence: Native Ghosts in North American Culture and History, edited by Colleen E. Boyd and Coll Thrush, 255–79. University of Nebraska Press, Lincoln.

Lane, Paul

2013   Presencing the Past: Implications for Bridging the History/Prehistory Divide. In *The Death of Prehistory*, edited by Peter R. Schmidt and Stephen A. Mrozowski, 47–66. Oxford University Press, Oxford.

Laycock, Joseph P.

2008   Mothman: Monster, Disaster and Community. *Fieldwork in Religion* 3(1):70–86.

2012a   Approaching the Paranormal. *Nova Religio: The Journal of Alternative and Emergent Religions* 18(1):5–15.

2012b   Carnal Knowledge: The Epistemology of Sexual Trauma in Witches' Sabbaths, Satanic Ritual Abuse, and Alien Abduction Narratives. *Preternature: Critical and Historical Studies on the Preternatural* 1(1):100–129.

2015   *Dangerous Games: What the Moral Panic over Role-Playing Games Says about Play, Religion, and Imagined Worlds.* University of California Press, Berkeley.

Lebling, Robert

2010   *Legends of the Fire Spirits: Jinn and Genies from Arabia to Zanzibar.* Counterpoint, Berkeley, California.

Leick, Gwendolyn

1991   *A Dictionary of Ancient Near Eastern Mythology.* Routledge, London.

Lekson, Stephen H.

2008   *A History of the Ancient Southwest.* School for Advanced Research Press, Santa Fe, New Mexico.

Leland, Charles G.

1899   *Aradia; or, The Gospel of the Witches.* David Nutt, London.

León-Portilla, Miguel

2002   *Bernardino de Sahagún: First Anthropologist.* Translated by Mauricio J. Mixco. University of Oklahoma Press, Norman.

Le Plongeon, Alice

1884a   Dr. Le Plongeon's Latest and Most Important Discoveries among the Ruined Cities of Yucatan. *Scientific American Supplement* 18(405) (2 August):7143–47.

1884b   Astonishing Discovery: Deified Mayas That Lived in America Thousands of Years Ago Found among the Gods and Goddesses of Japan. *Scientific American Supplement* 18(459) (18 October):7333–34.

Le Plongeon, Augustus

1883   Are the Ruined Monuments of Yucatan Ancient or Modern? *Scientific American Supplement* 16(405) (6 October):6468.

Lepper, Bradley T., and Jeff Gill

2000   The Newark Holy Stones. *Timeline* 17(3):16–25.

Lerner, Jesse

2011   *The Maya of Modernism: Art, Architecture, and Film.* University of New Mexico Press, Albuquerque.

Leslie-McCarthy, Sage

2007   The Case of the Psychic Detective: Progress, Professionalisation and the Occult in Psychic Detective Fiction from the 1880s to the 1920s. PhD dissertation, School of Arts, Griffith University. University Microfilms, Ann Arbor, Michigan.

Lethbridge, T. C.

1957   *Gogmagog: The Buried Gods.* Routledge and Kegan Paul, London.

1968   *Witches.* Citadel Press, New York.

1972   *The Legend of the Sons of God: A Fantasy?* Arkana, London.

Letter from International Scholars

2015   Archaeological Finds in Honduras. 6 March. Electronic document, https://realhonduranarchaeology.wordpress.com/letter-from-international-scholars-archaeological-finds-in-honduras-2, accessed 30 June 2016.

Levi, J. M.

1988   Myth and History Reconsidered: Archaeological Implications of Tzotzil-Maya Mythology. *American Antiquity* 53(3):605–19.

Levine, Philippa

1986   *The Amateur and the Professional: Antiquarians, Historians and Archaeologists in Victorian England, 1838–1886.* Cambridge University Press, Cambridge.

Levitt, Norman

2006   The Colonization of the Past and the Pedagogy of the Future. In *Archaeological Fantasies: How Pseudoarchaeology Misrepresents the Past and Misleads the Public*, edited by Garrett G. Fagan, 259–85. Routledge, London.

Lewis, Herbert S.

2001   The Passion of Franz Boas. *American Anthropologist* 103(2):447–67.

Lewis, James R.

2012   Excavating Tradition: Alternative Archaeologies as Legitimation Strategies. *Numen* 59:202–21.

Lichtheim, Miriam

1980   *Ancient Egyptian Literature: A Book of Readings*, vol. 3: *The Late Period*. Gustave E. von Grunebaum Center for Near Eastern Studies, University of California Press, Berkeley.

Lightfoot, Kent G.

2013   Rethinking the Archaeology of Human/Environmental Interactions in Deep Time History. In *The Death of Prehistory*, edited by Peter R. Schmidt and Stephen A. Mrozowski, 183–200. Oxford University Press, Oxford.

Lilly, William

1822 [1715] *William Lilly's History of His Life and Times, from the Year 1602 to 1681*. Charles Baldwin, London.

Link, Fabian, and J. Laurence Hare

2015   Pseudoscience Reconsidered: SS Research and the Archaeology of Haithabu. In *Revisiting the "Nazi Occult": Histories, Realities, Legacies*, edited by Monica Blak and Eric Kurlander, 105–31. Camden House, Rochester, New York.

Lister, Robert H., and Florence C. Lister

1983   *Those Who Came Before: Southwestern Archeology in the National Park System*. 3rd printing. Southwest Parks and Monuments Association, Globe, Arizona.

Lister, Robert H., and Florence C. Lister (editors)

1970   *In Search of Maya Glyphs: From the Archaeological Journals of Sylvanus G. Morley*. Museum of New Mexico Press, Santa Fe.

Liszka, Kate

2010   "Medjay" (No. 188) in the Onomasticon of Amenemope. In *Millions of Jubilees: Studies in Honor of David P. Silverman*, vol. 1, edited by Zahi Hawass and Jennifer Houser Wegner, 315–31. Publications du Conseil Suprême des Antiquités de l'Égypte, Cairo.

Lobato, Emilio, Jorge Mendoza, Valerie Sims, and Matthew Chin

2014   Examining the Relationship between Conspiracy Theories, Paranormal Beliefs, and Pseudoscience Acceptance among a University Population. *Applied Cognitive Psychology* 28(5):617–25.

Long, Boaz

1950   Legation and Embassy Reminiscences. In *Morleyana: A Collection of Writings in Memoriam Sylvanus Griswold Morley (1883–1948)*, 117–25. School of American Research and the Museum of New Mexico, Santa Fe.

López Luján, Leonardo, Hector Neff, and Saburo Sugiyama

2000   The 9-Xi Vase: A Classic Thin Orange Vessel Found at Tenochtitlan. Translated by Scott Sessions. In *Mesoamerica's Classic Heritage: From Teotihuacan to the Aztecs*, edited by Davíd Carrasco, Lindsay Jones, and Scott Sessions, 219–49. University Press of Colorado, Boulder.

Los Angeles Times
1911   An Old King's Seal. 14 May:V20. Los Angeles, California.
1913   Centuries Old City in Mexico. 16 February:V120. Los Angeles, California.
1919   Links Mexico with Orient. 12 January:III14. Atzcapotzalco, Mexico.
1922   Mexicans of Chinese Origin. 2 January:I2. Monterey, Mexico.
1925   Aid Americans to See Mexico. 17 May:F5. Tampico, Mexico.

Lothrop, Samuel K.
1957   George Gustav Heye (1874–1956). *American Antiquity* 23(1):66–67.

Lovecraft, Howard Phillips
1917   Dagon. http://www.hplovecraft.com/writings/texts/fiction/d.aspx, accessed 22 June 2017.
1919   The Doom That Came to Sarnath. http://www.hplovecraft.com/writings/texts/fiction/ds.aspx, accessed 22 June 2017.
1920   The Temple. http://www.hplovecraft.com/writings/texts/fiction/te.aspx, accessed 22 June 2017.
1921   The Nameless City. http://www.hplovecraft.com/writings/texts/fiction/nc.aspx, accessed 22 June 2017.
1923a The Rats in the Walls. http://www.hplovecraft.com/writings/texts/fiction/rw.aspx, accessed 22 June 2017.
1923b The Festival. http://www.hplovecraft.com/writings/texts/fiction/f.aspx, accessed 22 June 2017.
1924a The Shunned House. http://www.hplovecraft.com/writings/texts/fiction/sh.aspx, accessed 22 June 2017.
1924b Under the Pyramids. http://www.hplovecraft.com/writings/texts/fiction/up.aspx, accessed 22 June 2017.
1925a He. http://www.hplovecraft.com/writings/texts/fiction/he.aspx, accessed 22 June 2017.
1925b The Horror at Red Hook. http://www.hplovecraft.com/writings/texts/fiction/hrh.aspx, accessed 22 June 2017.
1926a The Call of Cthulhu. http://www.hplovecraft.com/writings/texts/fiction/cc.aspx, accessed 22 June 2017.
1926b Cool Air. http://www.hplovecraft.com/writings/texts/fiction/ca.aspx, accessed 22 June 2017.
1926c Pickman's Model. http://www.hplovecraft.com/writings/texts/fiction/pm.aspx, accessed 22 June 2017.
1927a The Case of Charles Dexter Ward. http://www.hplovecraft.com/writings/texts/fiction/cdw.aspx, accessed 7 August 2017.
1927b The History of the Necronomicon. http://www.hplovecraft.com/writings/texts/fiction/hn.aspx, accessed 22 June 2017.

1928   The Dunwich Horror. http://www.hplovecraft.com/writings/texts/fiction/ dh.aspx, accessed 22 June 2017.

1930   The Whisperer in Darkness. http://www.hplovecraft.com/writings/texts/ fiction/wid.aspx, accessed 22 June 2017.

1931a   *At the Mountains of Madness.* http://www.hplovecraft.com/writings/fiction/ mm.aspx, accessed 6 August 2017.

1931b   The Shadow over Innsmouth. http://www.hplovecraft.com/writings/fiction/ soi.aspx, accessed 22 June 2017.

1932   The Dreams in the Witch House. http://www.hplovecraft.com/writings/texts/ fiction/dwh.aspx, accessed 22 June 2017.

1933   The Thing on the Doorstep. http://www.hplovecraft.com/writings/texts/ fiction/td.aspx, accessed 22 June 2017.

1935a   The Shadow out of Time. http://www.hplovecraft.com/writings/texts/fiction/ sot.aspx, accessed 7 August 2017.

1935b   The Haunter of the Dark. http://www.hplovecraft.com/writings/texts/fiction/ hd.aspx, accessed 7 August 2017.

1965   *Selected Letters*, vol. 1: *1911–1924.* Edited by August Derleth and Donald Wandrei. Arkham House, Sauk City, Wisconsin.

1968   *Selected Letters*, vol. 2: *1925–1929.* Edited by August Derleth and Donald Wandrei. Arkham House, Sauk City, Wisconsin.

1971   *Selected Letters*, vol. 3: *1929–1931.* Edited by August Derleth and Donald Wandrei. Arkham House, Sauk City, Wisconsin.

1976   *Selected Letters*, vol. 4: *1932–1934.* Edited by August Derleth and James Turner. Arkham House, Sauk City, Wisconsin.

2006a [1934] Commonplace Book. Originally transcribed by R. H. Barlow. In *Collected Essays*, vol. 5: *Philosophy, Autobiography and Miscellany*, edited by S. T. Joshi, 219–37. Hippocampus Press, New York.

2006b [mid-1930s] Of Evil Sorceries Done in New-England, of Daemons in No Humane Shape. In *Collected Essays*, vol. 5: *Philosophy, Autobiography and Miscellany*, edited by S. T. Joshi, 254–56. Hippocampus Press, New York.

2006c [1924] Advertisement in the *New York Times*. In *Collected Essays*, vol. 5: *Philosophy, Autobiography and Miscellany*, edited by S. T. Joshi, 283–84. Hippocampus Press, New York.

2007   *O Fortunate Floridian: H. P. Lovecraft's Letters to R. H. Barlow.* Edited by S. T. Joshi and David E. Schultz. University of Tampa Press, Tampa, Florida.

2014   *Letters to Elizabeth Toldridge and Anne Tillery Renshaw.* Edited by David E. Schultz and S. T. Joshi. Hippocampus Press, New York.

Lovecraft, H. P., and Willis Conover
1975   *Lovecraft at Last.* Carrollton-Clark, Arlington, Virginia.

Lovecraft, H. P., with E. Hoffmann Price
1933   Through the Gates of the Silver Key. http://www.hplovecraft.com/writings/ texts/fiction/tgsk.aspx, accessed 22 June 2017.

Lowe, N. J.

2007   Gilbert Murray and Psychic Research. In *Gilbert Murray Reassessed: Helle-nism, Theatre and International Politics*, edited by Christopher Stray, 349–70. Oxford University Press, Oxford.

Loxton, Daniel, and Donald R. Prothero

2013   *Abominable Science: Origins of the Yeti, Nessie, and Other Famous Cryptids.* Columbia University Press, New York.

Lucas, Gavin

2004   Modern Disturbances: On the Ambiguities of Archaeology. *Modernism/modernity* 11(1):109–20.

2005   *The Archaeology of Time.* Routledge, London.

Lucas, George, Steven Spielberg, and Larry Kasdan

1978   "Raiders of the Lost Ark" Story Conference Transcript, 23–28 January. Electronic document, http://maddogmovies.com/almost/scripts/raidersstoryconference1978.pdf, accessed 1 June 2016.

Lucas Museum of Narrative Art

2015   The Exhibition: Indiana Jones and the Adventure of Archaeology. http://www.indianajonestheexhibition.com, accessed 13 October 2012.

Luckhurst, Roger

2010   An Occult Gazetteer of Bloomsbury: An Experiment in Method. In *London Gothic: Place, Space and the Gothic Imagination*, edited by Lawrence Phillips and Anne Witchard, 50–62. Continuum, London.

2012   *The Mummy's Curse: The True History of a Dark Fantasy.* Oxford University Press, Oxford.

Ludwig Boltzmann Institute

2014   Remains of Major New Prehistoric Stone Monument at Durrington Walls Discovered. Electronic document, http://lbi-archpro.org/cs/stonehenge, accessed 27 June 2016.

Lui, Debora

2011   Evaluating Pop Culture Museum Engagements: Pedagogies of, about, and with Harry Potter. *Working Papers in Educational Linguistics* 26(2):111–31.

Lupton, Carter

2003   "Mummymania" for the Masses: Is Egyptology Cursed by the Mummy's Curse? In *Consuming Ancient Egypt*, edited by Sally MacDonald and Michael Rice, 23–46. Institute of Archaeology, UCL Press, London.

Lyons, Claire L.

2002   Objects and Identities: Claiming and Reclaiming the Past. In *Claiming the Stones, Naming the Bones: Cultural Property and the Negotiation of National and Ethnic Identity*, edited by Elazar Barkan and Ronald Bush, 116–37. Getty Research Institute, Los Angeles, California.

MacDonald, Sally

2003   Lost in Time and Space: Ancient Egypt in Museums. In *Consuming Ancient Egypt*, edited by Sally MacDonald and Michael Rice, 87–99. Institute of Archaeology, UCL Press, London.

MacDonald, Sally, and Catherine Shaw

2004   Uncovering Ancient Egypt: The Petrie Museum and Its Public. In *Public Archaeology*, edited by Nick Merriman, 109–31. Routledge, London.

Mace, Carroll Edward

1973   Charles Etienne Brasseur de Bourbourg, 1814–1874. In *Guide to Ethnohistorical Sources*, part 2, edited by Howard F. Cline, 298–325. Handbook of Middle American Indians, Vol. 13. Robert Wauchope, general editor. University of Texas Press, Austin.

Machen, Arthur

1898   Folklore and Legend of the North. Review of *Les Vieux Chants Populaires Scandinaves* by M. Leon Pineau. *Literature* 49 (24 September):271–73.

1902   *Hieroglyphics*. Grant Richards, London.

2010 [1895] The Shining Pyramid. In *The Great God Pan, The Shining Pyramid, The White People*, 77–110. Library of Wales, Parthian, Cardigan, United Kingdom.

2011a   The Novel of the Black Seal. In *The White People and Other Weird Stories*, edited by S. T. Joshi, 29–66. Penguin, New York.

2011b   The Red Hand. In *The White People and Other Weird Stories*, edited by S. T. Joshi, 83–110. Penguin, New York.

Mackenzie, W. Mackay

1937   The Dragonesque Figure in Maeshowe, Orkney. *Proceedings of the Society of Antiquaries of Scotland* 71:157–73.

Mackley, J. S.

2010   Gog and Magog: Guardians of the City. In *London Gothic: Place, Space and the Gothic Imagination*, edited by Lawrence Phillips and Anne Witchard, 121–39. Continuum, London.

MacLeod, Sharon Paice

2012   *Celtic Myth and Religion: A Study of Traditional Belief, with Newly Translated Prayers, Poems and Songs*. McFarland, Jefferson, North Carolina.

MacManus, Chistopher

2012   Massive "Indiana Jones" Exhibit Headed to U.S. *CNet* 1 October. http://news. cnet.com/8301-17938_105-57523029-1/massive-indiana-jones-exhibit-headed-to-u.s., accessed 13 October 2012.

MacRitchie, David

1890   *The Testimony of Tradition.* Kegan Paul, Trench, Trübner, London.

1893   *Fians, Fairies, and Picts.* Kegan Paul, Trench, Trübner, London.

Magliocco, Sabina

2004   *Witching Culture: Folklore and Neo-Paganism in America.* University of Pennsylvania Press, Philadelphia.

Magnoni, Aline, Scott R. Hutson, and Travis W. Stanton

2008   Landscape Transformations and Changing Perceptions at Chunchucmil, Yucatán. In *Ruins of the Past: The Use and Perception of Abandoned Structures in the Maya Lowlands*, edited by Travis W. Stanton and Aline Magnoni, 193–222. University Press of Colorado, Boulder.

Mahon, G.

1950   Memorandum from G. Mahon, Superintendent, Criminal Investigation Department, Metropolitan Police, to Chief Superintendent, Metropolitan Police, 5 April. Metropolitan Police file MEPO 3/2290, 17A. National Archives, United Kingdom, Kew, London.

Mainfort, Robert C., and Mary L. Kwas

2004   The Bat Creek Stone Revisited: A Fraud Exposed. *American Antiquity* 69(4):761–69.

Mallowan, Agatha Christie

1946   *Come, Tell Me How You Live.* William Morrow, New York.

Manahan, T. Kam

2004   The Way Things Fall Apart: Social Organization and the Classic Maya Collapse of Copan. *Ancient Mesoamerica* 15:107–25.

Manassa, Colleen (editor)

2013   *Echoes of Egypt: Conjuring the Land of the Pharaohs: An Exhibition at the Peabody Museum of Natural History, 13 April 2013 through 4 January 2014.* Yale University Press, New Haven, Connecticut.

Mango, Cyril

1963   Antique Statuary and the Byzantine Beholder. *Dumbarton Oaks Papers* 17:53, 55–75.

Mariconda, Steven J.

1995a   Toward a Reader-Response Approach to the Lovecraft Mythos. In *On the Emergence of "Cthulhu" and Other Observations*, edited by Steven J. Mariconda, 29–44. Necronomicon Press, West Warwick, Rhode Island.

1995b   On the Emergence of "Cthulhu." In *On the Emergence of "Cthulhu" and Other Observations*, edited by Steven J. Mariconda, 59–62. Necronomicon Press, West Warwick, Rhode Island.

Marrs, Jim

2013   *Our Occulted History: Do the Global Elite Conceal Ancient Aliens?* William Morrow, New York.

Maspero, G. (editor)

1915   *Popular Stories of Ancient Egypt.* Translated by C. H. W. Johns from the fourth French edition. Putnam's, New York.

Mathews, Chris

2009   *Modern Satanism: Anatomy of a Radical Subculture.* Praeger, Westport, Connecticut.

Maxwell, Donald

1932   *A Detective in Surrey: Landscape Clues to Invisible Roads.* John Lane the Boadley Head, London.

1933   *A Detective in Essex: Landscape Clues to an Essex of the Past.* John Lane the Boadley Head, London.

May, Antoinette

1993   *Passionate Pilgrim: The Extraordinary Life of Alma Reed.* Paragon House, New York.

Mayor, Adrienne

2000   *The First Fossil Hunters: Paleontology in Greek and Roman Times.* Princeton University Press, Princeton, New Jersey.

Mazur, Susan

2005a   Dig of the Century: Getting to the Bottom of the Dorak Affair. *Scoop* 27 August. http://www.scoop.co.nz/stories/HL0508/S00224.htm, accessed 26 May 2016.

2005b   Is This the Dorak Affair's Final Chapter? *Scoop* 10 October. http://www.scoop.co.nz/stories/HL200510/S00120.htm, accessed 26 May 2016.

McCormick, Donald

1968   *Murder by Witchcraft: A Study of the Lower Quinton and Hagley Wood Murders.* Arrow, Tiptree, Essex, United Kingdom.

McElwee, Pamela

2007   Of Rice, Mammals, and Men: The Politics of "Wild" and "Domesticated" Species in Vietnam. In *Where the Wild Things Are Now: Domestication Reconsidered*, edited by Rebecca Cassidy and Molly Mullin, 249–76. Berg, Oxford.

McEvoy, J. P.

1950   The Great Maya Whodunit. In *Morleyana: A Collection of Writings in Memoriam Sylvanus Griswold Morley (1883–1948)*, 130–47. School of American Research and the Museum of New Mexico, Santa Fe.

McGarry, Molly

2003   *Ghosts of Futures Past: Spiritualism and the Cultural Politics of Nineteenth-Century America*. University of California Press, Berkeley.

McKusick, Marshall

1982   Psychic Archaeology: Theory, Method, and Mythology. *Journal for Field Archaeology* 9(1):99–118.

McLeod, Michael

2009   *Anatomy of a Beast: Obsession and Myth on the Trail of Bigfoot*. University of California Press, Berkeley.

McNeil, William F.

2005   *Visitors to Ancient America: The Evidence for European and Asian Presence in America Prior to Columbus*. McFarland, Jefferson, North Carolina.

McVicker, Donald

2008   Institutional Autonomy and Its Consequences: The Middle American Research Institute at Tulane University. *Histories of Anthropology Annual* 4:34–57.

McVicker, Donald, and Joel W. Palka

2001   A Maya Carved Shell Plaque from Tula, Hidalgo, Mexico. *Ancient Mesoamerica* 12:175–97.

Means, Philip Ainsworth

1934   New Clues to Early American Culture. *New York Times* 20 May:SM12, 19. New York.

Medway, Gareth J.

2001   *Lure of the Sinister: The Unnatural History of Satanism*. New York University Press, New York.

Megaw, Ruth, and Vincent Megaw

1994   Through a Window on the European Iron Age Darkly: Fifty Years of Reading Early Celtic Art. *World Archaeology* 25(3):287–303.

Mena, Ramón

1920   *Un Gran Descubrimiento Arqueológico: Los Tecpaneca en el Valle de Mexico (Exploraciones de Wm. Niven)/A Great Archaeological Discovery: The Ancient Tecpanecs in the Valley of Mexico (Explorations of Wm. Niven)*. Imprenta Nacional, Mexico.

Meyrat, Pierre

2014   Hieroglyphs for Your Eyes Only: Samuel K. Lothrop and His Use of Ancient Egyptian as Cipher. *Mesoweb*. http://www.mesoweb.com/articles/meyrat/Meyrat2014.pdf, accessed 8 August 2015.

Michlovic, Michael G.

1990   Folk Archaeology in Anthropological Perspective. *Current Anthropology* 31(1):103–7.

Miller, Mary, and Karl Taube

1993   *An Illustrated Dictionary of the Gods and Symbols of Ancient Mexico and the Maya.* Thames and Hudson, New York.

Mitchell-Hedges, Frederick Albert

1931   *Land of Wonder and Fear.* Century, New York.

1955 [1954]   *Danger My Ally.* Little, Brown, Boston.

1956 [1954]   *Danger My Ally.* Pan, London.

Montagu, M. F. Ashley

1952   *Man's Most Dangerous Myth.* 3rd ed. Harper, New York.

Montejo, Victor D.

2005   *Maya Intellectual Renaissance: Identity, Representation, and Leadership.* University of Texas Press, Austin.

Montoya, Janet

2001   Terracotta Figurines from the Pyramid of the Moon at Teotihuacán, México. Electronic document, http://www.famsi.org/reports/98060/98060Montoya01.pdf, accessed 29 June 2016.

Moore, Charles B.

1997   The Early New York University Balloon Flights. In *UFO Crash at Roswell: The Genesis of a Modern Myth*, edited by Benson Saler, Charles A. Ziegler, and Charles B. Moore, 74–114. Konecky and Konecky, Old Saybrook, Connecticut.

Morant, G. M.

1936   A Morphological Comparison of Two Crystal Skulls. *Man* 36:105–7.

Morde, Theodore

1940   In the Lost City of Ancient America's Monkey God. *Milwaukee Sunday News Sentinel* 22 September.

Moreland, John

1999   The World(s) of the Cross. *World Archaeology* 31(2):194–213.

Moreno García, Juan Carlos

2009   From Dracula to Rostovtzeff; or, The Misadventures of Economic History in Early Egyptology. *IBAES* 10:175–98.

Morgan, Janet

2001 [1999]   Agatha Christie (1890–1976). In *Agatha Christie and Archaeology*, edited by Charlotte Trümpler, 18–37. Translated by Anthea Bell. British Museum Press, London.

Morrill, Sibley S.

1972   *Ambrose Bierce, F. A. Mitchell-Hedges, and the Crystal Skull.* Caledon Press, San Francisco, California.

Moseley, James W., and Karl T. Pflock

2002   *Shockingly Close to the Truth! Confessions of a Grave-Robbing Ufologist.* Prometheus Books, Amherst, New York.

Moshenska, Gabriel

2006   The Archaeological Uncanny. *Public Archaeology* 5:91–99.

2012   M. R. James and the Archaeological Uncanny. *Antiquity* 86:1192–1201.

Moss, Candida, and Joel Baden

2015   Exclusive: Feds Investigate Hobby Lobby Boss for Illicit Artifacts. *Daily Beast* 26 October. http://www.thedailybeast.com/articles/2015/10/26/exclusive-feds-investigate-hobby-lobby-boss-for-illicit-artifacts.html, accessed 25 June 2016.

Muckle, Robert

2012   Archaeology and Bigfoot. *Anthropology News* 53(10):S12.

Muckle, Robert, and Laura Tubelle de González

2015   *Through the Lens of Anthropology: An Introduction to Human Evolution and Culture.* University of Toronto Press, Ontario.

Mumford, Michael D., Andrew M. Rose, and David A. Goslin

1995   An Evaluation of Remote Viewing: Research and Applications. American Institutes of Research, 29 September. Electronic document, https://www.cia.gov/library/readingroom/docs/CIA-RDP96-00791R000200180006-4.pdf, accessed 8 August 2017.

Murray, Margaret Alice

1917a   The God of the Witches. *Journal of the Manchester Egyptian and Oriental Society* 6:49–65.

1917b   Organisations of Witches in Great Britain. *Folk-lore* 28:228–58.

1920   Witches and the Number Thirteen. *Folk-lore* 28:204–9.

1921   *The Witch-Cult in Western Europe: A Study in Anthropology.* Oxford University Press, London.

1929   Witchcraft. In *Encyclopedia Britannica.* 14th ed., 23:686–88. Encyclopedia Britannica, London.

1933   *The God of the Witches.* Sampson Low, Marston, London.

1954   *The Divine King in England.* Faber and Faber, London.

1957   English Archaeology. *The Times* 10 May:13. London.

1963   *My First Hundred Years.* William Kimber, London.

Murray, Tim

1993   Archaeology and the Threat of the Past: Sir Henry Rider Haggard and the Acquisition of Time. *World Archaeology* 25(2):175–86.

1999   Howard Carter (1874–1939). In *Encyclopedia of Archaeology: The Great Archaeologists*, edited by Tim Murray, 1:289–99. ABC-CLIO, Santa Barbara, California.

2014 [2004]   Archbishop Ussher and Archaeological Time. In his *From Antiquarian to Archaeologist: The History and Philosophy of Archaeology*, 157–73. Pen and Sword Archaeology, Barnsley, South Yorkshire, England.

Murray, Will
1983   Mysteries of the Hoggar Religion. *Crypt of Cthulhu* 3(1):32, 39.

Muscarella, Oscar White
2000   *The Lie Became Great: Forgery of Ancient Near Eastern Cultures.* Styx Publications, Groningen, Netherlands.

Nadis, Fred
2013   *The Man from Mars: Ray Palmer's Amazing Pulp Journey.* Tarcher/Penguin, New York.

National Geographic
2011   Indiana Jones and the Adventure of Archaeology. Electronic document, http://events.nationalgeographic.com/events/exhibits/indiana-jones, accessed 13 October 2012.

Natural Resources Canada
2013   The 1925 Magnitude 6.2 Charlevoix-Kamouraska Earthquake. http://www.earthquakescanada.nrcan.gc.ca//historic-historique/events/19250301-eng.php, accessed 11 October 2013.

Nelson, Mark R.
2002   The Mummy's Curse: Historical Cohort Study. *BMJ: British Medical Journal* 325(7378):1482–84.

Neudorfer, Giovanna
1980   Vermont's Stone Chambers: An Inquiry into Their Past. Vermont Historical Society, Montpelier.

Neuhaus, Volker
2001 [1999]   The Archaeology of Murder. In *Agatha Christie and Archaeology*, edited by Charlotte Trümpler, 425–35. Translated by Anthea Bell. British Museum Press, London.

Newitz, Annalee
2016   Confirmed: Mysterious Ancient Maya Book, Grolier Codex, Is Genuine. *Ars Technica* 11 September. http://arstechnica.com/science/2016/09/confirmed-mysterious-ancient-maya-book-grolier-codex-is-genuine, accessed 22 October 2016.

News Belize

2012a   Director of Archaeology Says He Wants No Part of Crystal Skull Lawsuit. 11 December. http://www.7newsbelize.com/sstory.php?nid=24166, accessed 25 June 2017.

2012b   Archeology Attorney Says Jaime Awe Signed Off on Lawsuit. 12 December. http://www.7newsbelize.com/sstory.php?nid=24180&frmsrch=1, accessed 25 June 2017.

New York Times

1897a   Prehistoric Mexican City. 24 July. New York.

1897b   Message Perhaps from Mars: Strange Characters Found in an Aerolite Which Struck the Earth Near Binghamton. 14 November:1. New York.

1897c   Wiggins on the Aerolite: Thinks It Was a Message from Mars: Sacred Books Received from Heaven of Old Make It Possible. 18 November:5. New York.

1911a   Fear Diggers Took Ark of Covenant. 4 May:5. New York.

1911b   [Untitled]. 5 May. New York.

1911c   Have Englishmen Found the Ark of the Covenant? 7 May:Part 5, 1. New York.

1914   To Be New Greek Minister. 8 January:3. New York.

1915   Relics of Lost City Found in Honduras. 30 September:13. New York.

1922   Deciphering Key to Maya Writings. 18 December:3. New York.

1923a   Mexican Interest in Ruins. 2 March:3. New York.

1923b   Topics of the Times: Eliminates Spirit Guardians. 26 March:12. New York.

1923c   Carnarvon Is Dead of an Insect's Bite at Pharaoh's Tomb. 5 April:1. New York.

1923d   Carnarvon's Death Spreads Theories about Vengeance. 6 April:1. New York.

1923e   Finds "Missing Link" of Ancient Culture. 2 May:5. New York.

1924a   Carter Denounces Affronts by Cairo and Shuts Up Tomb. 14 February:1. New York.

1924b   Egyptologists Join in Carter's Protest. 15 February:5. New York.

1924c   Carter Assailed by Egyptian Press. 18 February:17. New York.

1924d   To Unravel History of Maya Race. 3 April:25. New York.

1924e   H. G. Evelyn White a Suicide in Leeds. 10 September:11. New York.

1924f   Ruins of Carthage Seen Here in Films. 24 November:15. New York.

1924g   To Delve in Ruins of Incas. 31 December:25. New York.

1925a   Dr. Joseph C. Hoppin Dies. 1 February:E7. New York.

1925b   Dr. David B. Spooner Dies in Agra, India. 2 February:17. New York.

1925c   Rev. Wm. C. Winslow Dies. 3 February:13. New York.

1925d   Americans Ready to Dig at Carthage. 6 March:13. New York.

1925e   H. V. Hilprecht Dies, Noted Paleologist. 20 March:19. New York.

1925f   Tulane Explorers Find Sacred Island. 29 March:E4. New York.

1925g   Mayan Ruins Found Near Puerto. 2 April:14. New York.

1925h   First Skyscrapers Built in Carthage. 2 April:23. New York.

1925i   Prehistoric Homes Explored at Djerba. 15 April:6. New York.

1925j   Ebbing Lake Bares Ancient City in Arizona, with Apartments Bigger than Park Avenue's. 25 April:3. New York.

1925k   Seager, American Explorer, Is Dead. 14 May:19. New York.

1925L   Impressive Funeral for Seager in Crete. 18 May:15. New York.

1925m   Prof. Chas D. Curtis, Archaeologist, Dead. 9 June:21. New York.

1925n   Senator Boni Near Death. 9 July:19. New York.

1925o   Ancient Granite Appears. 24 July:13. New York.

1925p   Dr. Alexander Scott. 29 July:21. New York.

1925q   The Arcturus' Cargo. 1 August:10. New York.

1925r   Finds London Is Sinking. 15 August:24. New York.

1925s   Marvels in Tomb of Maya Monarch. 21 August:1, 6. New York.

1925t   City Discovered under Sea: Soviet Captain Sees Buildings and Streets at Bottom of Caspian. 29 October:5. New York.

1925u   Back with Relics of Ancient Mayas. 24 November:13. New York.

1926a   Scientists Here Await Full Data. 26 June:5. New York.

1926b   Divining Rod's Part in Fossil Find Told. 27 June:E3. New York.

1926c   Locating the Lost Atlantis. 9 July:18. New York.

1926d   Iraq's Uncrowned Queen. 14 July:20. New York.

1926e   Tablets 6,000 Years Old. 29 August:2. New York.

1926f   Bring Back Relics of Chibohas Indians. 4 October:9. New York.

1926g   Fight Huge Escaped Boa. 5 October:11. New York.

1926h   Ancient Mayan City Reveals High Culture. 28 October:14. New York.

1926i   French Ruling Near on Alphabet Relics. 14 November:16. New York.

1927a   Mitchell-Hedges Robbed in England. 16 January:15. New York.

1927b   Knows Reason for Robbery. 16 January:15. New York.

1927c   Six Youths Remind Him of Lecture on Pluck. 17 January:2. New York.

1927d   Peasant's Plow Begins a War of Scientists. 6 November:XX6. New York.

1927e   Says Glozel Shows Writing in 3000 B.C. 13 November:N1. New York.

1927f   The Spirit of Glozel. 4 December:E4. New York.

1927g   The School of Savants. 26 December:22. New York.

1927h   Inquiry Is Started on Glozel Relics. 6 November:28. New York.

1928a   Explorer Loses Libel Suit. 15 February:5. New York.

1928b   France Abandons Glozelian Field. 23 February:22. New York.

1928c   Finds Corkscrews in Glozel Diggings. 26 February:29. New York.

1928d   Glozel Takes a Place among Historic Fakes. 28 October:132. New York.

1929a   Negroes Alarm Honduras. 19 January:6. New York.

1929b   Glozel Relics Fake, French Expert Says. 11 May:3. New York.

1929c   Coronado's Route Traced into Kansas. 29 September:N3. New York.

1929d   Archaeologist Lauds Lindbergh Flights. 19 November:24. New York.

1930a   Finley Presents Globe. 22 January:5. New York.

1930b   Dr. Gann to Marry Miss Mary Wheeler. 2 October:17. New York.

1930c   Museum Here Gets Rare Indian Finds. 29 December:59. New York.

1931a   Excavations in Ur Verify Book of Daniel. 10 January:3. New York.

1931b   Seeks Cradle of Race in American Jungle. 24 January:1. New York.

1931c   Museum Endorses F. A. Mitchell-Hedges. 25 January:29. New York.

1931d   Says Idle Vessels Clog Foreign Ports. 11 February:25. New York.

1931e   Science Confirms Noah's Great Deluge. 15 February:128. New York.

1931f   Says Explorers Aid Trade. 9 June:55. New York.

1931g   Ex-Kaiser Gets Model of Ancient Olympia; American Pays for Study of Historic Games. 21 August. New York.

1932   Will Give Talk on "Lost Atlantis." 30 January:7. New York.

1933a   Educated Indian Boy to Aid Study of His Native Wilds in Honduras. 7 June:23. New York.

1933b   To Hunt Strange Apes. 25 July:5. New York.

1933c   Relics from Islands in Caribbean Shown. 16 November:25. New York.

1934a   Scientist Departs for Honduran Wilds. 18 February:N3. New York.

1934b   Explorer Returns with Indian Relics. 14 July:9. New York.

1936a   Scientist to Study Nicaraguan Tribe. 8 March:N2. New York.

1936b   Ex-Kaiser Writes a Book about Gorgons. 8 November:N3. New York.

1940   Honduran Jungles Yield Indian Data. 2 August:17. New York.

1959   Frederick Mitchell-Hedges Dies; British Explorer and Author, 76. 13 June:21. New York.

New York World

1897   Is This Meteor a Message from Far Away Mars? 21 November:45. New York. http://www.fultonhistory.com/Newspaper%2011/New%20York%20NY%20World/New%20York%20NY%20World%201897/New%20York%20NY%20World%201897%20-%208611.pdf#xml=, accessed 22 June 2011.

Nickell, Joe

2001   *Investigating the Paranormal.* Barnes and Noble, New York.

2007   *Adventures in Paranormal Investigation.* University Press of Kentucky, Lexington.

Niiler, Eric

2015   "CSI" Meets History: Piecing Together the Long-Lost Bones of Richard III. *Washington Post* 30 March. https://www.washingtonpost.com/national/health-science/what-the-skeleton-under-the-parking-lot-revealed-about-richard-iii/2015/03/30/c8df01c2-d172-11e4-ab77-9646eea6a4c7_story.html, accessed 26 May 2016.

Niven, William

1897   Omitlán, a Prehistoric City in Mexico. *Journal of the American Geographical Society of New York* 29(2):217–22.

1925   Letter to Frans Blom, 3 November. Middle American Research Institute, Tulane University, New Orleans.

1926a   Letter to William Harold Davis, 18 October. Middle American Research Institute, Tulane University, New Orleans.

1926b   Letter to Frans Blom, 15 December. Middle American Research Institute, Tulane University, New Orleans.

Noël Hume, Ivor

1969   *Historical Archaeology*. Knopf, New York.

Nottingham Evening Post

1929   "Witches" Secrets Revealed. 12 June. https://www.academia.edu/15240856/Margaret_Murray_Interview_1929, uploaded by Simon Young, accessed 10 November 2016.

Nusbaum, Rosemary

1950   Morley and His People. In *Morleyana: A Collection of Writings in Memoriam Sylvanus Griswold Morley (1883–1948)*, 174–78. School of American Research and the Museum of New Mexico, Santa Fe.

Oakes, Lorna, and Lucia Gahlin

2008   *Ancient Egypt: An Illustrated Reference to the Myths, Religions, Pyramids and Temples of the Land of the Pharaohs*. Hermes House, London.

Oates, Caroline, and Juliette Wood

1998   *A Coven of Scholars: Margaret Murray and Her Working Methods*. Folklore Society, London.

Odell, Robin

2006   Jack the Redeemer. In *Ripperology*, edited by Paul Begg, 170–81. Barnes and Noble, New York.

Orser, Charles E., Jr.

2004   *Race and Practice in Archaeological Interpretation*. University of Pennsylvania Press, Philadelphia.

Packer, Alison, Stella Beddoe, and Lianne Jarrett

1980   *Fairies in Legend and the Arts*. Cameron and Tayleur in association with David and Charles, London.

Papadopoulos, John K.

2005   Inventing the Minoans: Archaeology, Modernity and the Quest for European Identity. *Journal of Mediterranean Archaeology* 18(1):87–149.

Pappas, Stephanie

2012   Indiana Jones Crystal Skull Lawsuit Raises Questions of Hoax. *LiveScience* 10 December. http://www.livescience.com/25410-indiana-jones-crystal-skull-lawsuit-hoax.html, accessed 23 June 2017.

Parker, Evan A.
2016   The Proliferation of Pseudoarchaeology through "Reality" Television Programming. In *Lost City, Found Pyramid: Understanding Alternative Archaeologies and Pseudoscientific Practices*, edited by Jeb J. Card and David S. Anderson, 149–66. University of Alabama Press, Tuscaloosa.

Parsons, Steve
2005   The Perils of Planetary Amnesia: As Evidence of Ancient Cataclysm Mounts, the Legacy of a Rejected Genius Is Reconsidered. In *Forbidden History: Prehistoric Technologies, Extraterrestrial Intervention, and the Suppressed Origins of Civilization*, edited by J. Douglas Kenyon, 61–68. Bear, Rochester, Vermont.

Partridge, Christopher
2004   Alien Demonology: The Christian Roots of the Malevolent Extraterrestrial in UFO Religions and Abduction Spiritualties. *Religion* 34:163–89.

Pasztory, Esther
1997   *Teotihuacan: An Experiment in Living*. University of Oklahoma Press, Norman.
2005   *Thinking with Things: Toward a New Vision of Art*. University of Texas Press, Austin.

Patzek, Barbara, Regina Hauses, and Andreas Dudde
2001 [1999]   The Detective and the Archaeologist. In *Agatha Christie and Archaeology*, edited by Charlotte Trümpler, 390–409. Translated by Anthea Bell. British Museum Press, London.

Pauwels, Louis, and Jacques Bergier
1963   *The Morning of the Magicians*. Translated by Rollo Myers. Avon, New York.

Pearson, Kenneth, and Patricia Connor
1968   *The Dorak Affair*. Atheneum, New York.

Peebles, Curtis
1994   *Watch the Skies! A Chronicle of the Flying Saucer Myth*. Smithsonian Institution Press, Washington, DC.

Pels, Peter
2000   Occult Truths: Race, Conjecture, and Theosophy in Victorian Anthropology. In *Excluded Ancestors, Inventible Traditions: Essays toward a More Inclusive History of Anthropology*, edited by Richard Handler, 11–41. University of Wisconsin Press, Madison.

Pennick, Nigel
1996   *Celtic Sacred Landscapes*. Thames and Hudson, New York.

Penn Museum
2011   We See Dead People. https://www.penn.museum/collections/videos/
        video/909, accessed 13 October 2012.

Perry, Charles
1743   *A View of the Levant: Particularly of Constantinople, Syria, and Greece in
        Which Their Antiquities, Government, Politics, Maxims, Manners, and Cus-
        toms (with Many Other Circumstances and Contingencies) Are Attempted to Be
        Described and Treated Upon.* T. Woodward and C. Davis, and J. Shuckburgh,
        London.

Peterson, Mark Allen
2007   From Jinn to Genies: Intertextuality, Media, and the Making of Global Folk-
        lore. In *Folklore/Cinema: Popular Film as Vernacular Culture*, edited by Sha-
        ron R. Sherman and Mikel J. Koven, 93–112. Utah State University Press,
        Logan.

Petrie, Flinders
1926   *The Hill Figures of England.* Royal Anthropological Institute of Great Britain
        and Ireland, London.

Pezzati, Alex
2005   Mystery at Acámbaro, Mexico. *Expedition* 47(3):6–7.

Philip, P. J.
1927   Paris Recalls Stay of Legion Happily. *New York Times* 2 October:E7. New
        York.

Phillips, Carl
2013   "The Truth against the World": Spectrality and the Mystic Past in Late Twen-
        tieth-Century Cornwall. In *Mysticism, Myth, and Celtic Identity*, edited by
        Marion Gibson, Shelley Trower, and Garry Tregidga, 70–83. Routledge,
        London.

Phillips, Lawrence, and Anne Witchard (editors)
2010   *London Gothic: Place, Space and the Gothic Imagination.* Continuum,
        London.

Piccini, Angela
1996   Filming through the Mists of Time: Celtic Constructions and the Documen-
        tary. In *Anthropology in Public*, special issue, *Current Anthropology*
        37(1):S87–111.

Picknett, Lynn, and Clive Prince
2001   *The Stargate Conspiracy: Revealing the Truth behind Extraterrestrial Contact,
        Military Intelligence and the Mysteries of Ancient Egypt.* Berkley Books, New
        York.

2003   Alternative Egypts. In *Consuming Ancient Egypt*, edited by Sally MacDonald and Michael Rice, 175–93. Institute of Archaeology, UCL Press, London.

Pinch, Geraldine
2006   *Magic in Ancient Egypt*. British Museum Press, London.

Pittock, Murray G. H.
1999   *Celtic Identity and the British Image*. Manchester University Press, Manchester, England.

Pohlman, Don
2004   Catching Science in the Act: Mysteries of Çatalhöyük. In *Creating Connections: Museums and the Public Understanding of Research*, edited by David Chittenden, Graham Farmelo, and Bruce V. Lewenstein, 267–75. AltaMira, Walnut Creek, California.

Pond, Alonzo W.
2003   *Veiled Men, Red Tens, and Black Mountain: Adventures of an Expedition of the First Pneumatic-Tired Automobiles to Cross the Algerian Sahara (1925)*. Narrative Press, Santa Barbara, California.

Porshnev, B. F., Dmitri Bayanov, and Igor Bourtsev
1974   The Troglodytidae and the Hominidae in the Taxonomy and Evolution of Higher Primates. *Current Anthropology* 15(4):449–56.

Posnansky, Arthur
1945   *Tihuanacu: The Cradle of American Man*. 2 vols. Translated by James F. Shearer. Augustin, New York.

Praetzellis, Adrian
2000   *Death by Theory: A Tale of Mystery and Archaeological Theory*. AltaMira, Lanham, Maryland.

Prag, A. J. N. W.
2015   The Little Mannie with His Daddy's Horns. In *The Materiality of Magic*, edited by Ceri Houlbrook and Natalie Armitage, 171–81. Oxbow, Oxford.

Preston, Douglas
1995   The Mystery of Sandia Cave. *New Yorker* 12 June:66–83.
2013   The El Dorado Machine. *New Yorker* 6 May:34–40.
2015   Lure of the Lost City. *National Geographic* 228(4):102–21.

Preuss, Mary H.
2012   The Lights Dim but Don't Go Out on the Stars of Yucatec Maya Oral Literature. In *Parallel Worlds: Genre, Discourse, and Poetics in Contemporary, Colonial, and Classic Period Maya Literature*, edited by Kerry M. Hull and Michael D. Carrasco, 449–70. University Press of Colorado, Boulder.

Price, Clair

1930   The Most Famous Private in Any Army. *New York Times* 21 December:71. New York.

Price, David

2016   *Cold War Anthropology: The CIA, the Pentagon, and the Growth of Dual Use Anthropology*. Duke University Press, Durham, North Carolina.

Price, Robert M.

1982   The Monsters of Mu: The Lost Continent in the Cthulhu Mythos. *Crypt of Cthulhu* 1(5). http://crypt-of-cthulhu.com/monstersmu.htm, accessed 23 June 2017.

1990   *H. P. Lovecraft and the Cthulhu Mythos*. Starmont House, Mercer Island, Washington.

Prince, Ruth, and David Riches

2000   *The New Age in Glastonbury: The Construction of Religious Movements*. Berghahn, New York.

Pringle, Heather

2006   *The Master Plan: Himmler's Scholars and the Holocaust*. Hyperion, New York.

Pullinger, Agnes

1950   Statement to Scotland Yard, 4 April. Metropolitan Police file MEPO 3/2290. National Archives, United Kingdom, Kew, London.

Pye, Catherine

2011   Turton Tower Plans First Ever Midnight Ghost Hunts after Years of Sightings. *Lancashire Telegraph* 24 October. http://www.lancashiretelegraph.co.uk/news/9322246.Turton_Tower_plans_first_ever_midnight_ghost_hunts_after_years_of_sightings, accessed 23 March 2016.

Quinn, Virginia (director)

2011   *Bigfoot: The Definitive Guide*. Handel Productions.

Radford, Benjamin

2011   *Tracking the Chupacabra: The Vampire Beast in Fact, Fiction, and Folklore*. University of New Mexico Press, Albuquerque.

Rahtz, Philip, and Lorna Watts

2009   *Glastonbury: Myth and Archaeology*. History Press, Stroud, Gloucestershire, United Kingdom.

Ramaswamy, Sumathi

2004   *The Lost Land of Lemuria: Fabulous Geographies, Catastrophic Histories*. University of California Press, Berkeley.

Randle, Kevin D.
1995   *A History of UFO Crashes*. Avon, New York.
2000   *The Roswell Encyclopedia*. HarperCollins, New York.

Rankine, David
2009   *The Book of Treasure Spirits*. Avalonia, London.

Raphael, Leona
1934   Explorer Seeks Fabled Lost City; Spurns Weaker Sex Companionship. *Calgary Daily Herald* 16 June:34. Calgary, Alberta, Canada.

Read, Simon
2014   *The Case That Foiled Fabian: Murder and Witchcraft in Rural England*. History Press, Stroud, Gloucestershire, United Kingdom.

Re Cruz, Alicia
1996   *The Two Milpas of Chan Kom: Scenarios of a Maya Village Life*. State University of New York Press, Albany.

Redfield, Robert
1962 [1950]   *A Village That Chose Progress: Chan Kom Revisited*. University of Chicago Press, Chicago.

Redfield, Robert, and Alfonso Villa Rojas
1962 [1934]   *Chan Kom: A Maya Village*. Abridged ed. University of Chicago Press, Chicago.

Reed, Alma
1924   Science Hunts for the Lost Atlantis. *New York Times* 16 November:SM4, 15. New York.

Reeves, Nicholas
2000   *Ancient Egypt: The Great Discoveries: A Year-by-Year Chronicle*. Thames and Hudson, London.

Regal, Brian
2011   *Searching for Sasquatch: Crackpots, Eggheads, and Cryptozoology*. Palgrave Macmillan, New York.

Regier, Willis Goth
2004   *Book of the Sphinx*. University of Nebraska Press, Lincoln.

Reimer/Yumks, Rudy
2007   Smaylilh or Wild People Archaeology. *Nexus* 20:8–30.

Rice, Michael, and Sally MacDonald
2003   Introduction: Tea with a Mummy: The Consumer's View of Egypt's Immemorial Appeal. In *Consuming Ancient Egypt*, edited by Sally MacDonald and Michael Rice, 1–22. Institute of Archaeology, UCL Press, London.

Richards, Colin

1996   Monuments as Landscape: Creating the Centre of the World in Late Neolithic Orkney. *World Archaeology* 28(2):190–208.

Richter, Tobias

2008   Espionage and Near Eastern Archaeology: A Historiographical Survey. *Public Archaeology* 7(4):212–40.

Rieder, John

2008   *Colonialism and the Emergence of Science Fiction.* Wesleyan University Press, Middletown, Connecticut.

Rieth, Adolf

1970   *Archaeological Fakes.* Translated by Diana Imber. Barrie and Jenkins, London.

Risen, James

2000   Secrets of History: The C.I.A. in Iran: A Special Report. *New York Times* 16 April. http://www.nytimes.com/2000/04/16/world/secrets-history-cia-iran-special-report-plot-convulsed-iran-53-79.html?pagewanted=all, accessed 7 June 2016.

Rizvi, Uzma Z.

2013   Creating Prehistory and Protohistory: Constructing Otherness and Politics of Contemporary Indigenous Populations in India. In *The Death of Prehistory,* edited by Peter R. Schmidt and Stephen A. Mrozowski, 141–57. Oxford University Press, Oxford.

Roberts, Anthony, and Geoff Gilbertson

1980   *The Dark Gods.* Rider/Hutchinson, London.

Robertson, David G.

2014   Transformation: Whitley Strieber's Paranormal Gnosis. *Nova Religio: The Journal of Alternative and Emergent Religions* 18(1):58–78.

Robins, Don

1988   *The Secret Language of Stone.* Rider, London.

Robinson, Andrew

2009   *Lost Languages: The Enigma of the World's Undeciphered Scripts.* Thames and Hudson, New York.

Rochester Democrat and Chronicle

1897   Binghamton's Message from Mars. 16 November:6. Rochester, New York.

Roggersdorf, Wilhelm

1970 [1968]   About Erich von Däniken. In *Gods from Outer Space: Return to the Stars or Evidence for the Impossible* by Erich von Däniken, 7–8. Translated by Michael Heron. Putnam's, New York.

Rollyson, Carl
2012   *Hollywood Enigma: Dana Andrews*. University Press of Mississippi, Jackson.

Ross, Anne
1967   *Pagan Celtic Britain: Studies in Iconography and Tradition*. Routledge and Kegan Paul, London, and Columbia University Press, New York.

Ross, Anne, and Peter Reynolds
1978   Ancient Vermont. *Antiquity* 52:100–107.

Rowe, John Howland
1966   Diffusionism and Archaeology. *American Antiquity* 31(3):334–37.

Ruz Lhuillier, Alberto
1950   The Likeness of Sylvanus Griswold Morley. In *Morleyana: A Collection of Writings in Memoriam Sylvanus Griswold Morley (1883–1948)*, 106–16. School of American Research and the Museum of New Mexico, Santa Fe.

Salih, Sarah
2015   Idol Theory. *Preternature* 4(1):13–36.

Sampson, Jerry
2015   Gothic Sculpture and Worked Stone. In *Glastonbury Abbey: Archaeological Excavations, 1904–79*, edited by Roberta Gilchrist and Cheryl Green, 358–82. Society of Antiquaries of London, London.

Samson, C. Mathews
2007   *Re-Enchanting the World: Maya Protestantism in the Guatemalan Highlands*. University of Alabama Press, Tuscaloosa.

Savage, Raymond
1926   Lawrence of Arabia in a New Disguise. *New York Times* 7 March:SM3, 22. New York.

Sax, Margaret, Jane M. Walsh, Ian C. Freestone, Andrew H. Rankin, and Nigel D. Meeks
2008   The Origins of Two Purportedly Pre-Columbian Mexican Crystal Skulls. *Journal of Archaeological Science* 35:2751–60.

Scarborough, Isabel
2008   The Bennett Monolith: Archaeological Patrimony and Cultural Restitution in Bolivia. In *The Handbook of South American Archaeology*, edited by Helaine Silverman and William H. Isbell, 1089–1101. Springer, New York.

Schaafsma, Polly, and Will Tsosie
2009   Xeroxed on Stone: Times of Origin and the Navajo Holy People in Canyon

Landscapes. In *Landscapes of Origin in the Americas: Creation Narratives Linking Ancient Places and Present Communities*, edited by Jessica Joyce Christie, 15–31. University of Alabama Press, Tuscaloosa.

Schadla-Hall, Tim

2004   The Comforts of Unreason: The Importance and Relevance of Alternative Archaeology. In *Public Archaeology*, edited by Nick Merriman, 255–71. Routledge, London.

Schadla-Hall, Tim, and Genny Morris

2003   Ancient Egypt on the Small Screen: From Fact to Faction in the UK. In *Consuming Ancient Egypt*, edited by Sally MacDonald and Michael Rice, 195–214. Institute of Archaeology, UCL Press, London.

Schávelzon, Daniel

1989   The History of Mesoamerican Archaeology at the Crossroads: Changing Views of the Past. In *Tracing Archaeology's Past: The Historiography of Archaeology*, edited by Andrew L. Christenson, 107–12. Southern Illinois University Press, Carbondale.

Scheffler, Thomas

1998   The Kaiser in Baalbek: Tourism, Archaeology, and the Politics of the Imagination. In *Baalbek: Image and Monument, 1898–1998*, edited by Hélène Sader, Thomas Scheffler, and Angelika Neuwirth, 13–49. Orient-Institut der DMG and Deutsches Archäologisches Institut, Stuttgart, Germany.

Scherzler, Diane

2012   A Look in the Mirror and the Perspective of Others: On the Portrayal of Archaeology in the Mass Media. In *From Archaeology to Archaeologies: The "Other" Past*, edited by Anna Simandiraki-Grimshaw and Eleni Stefanou, 77–85. Archaeopress, Oxford.

Schliemann, Paul

1912   How I Found the Lost Atlantis, the Source of All Civilization. *New York American* 20 October. http://www.sacred-texts.com/atl/hif/hifoo.htm, accessed 23 June 2017.

Schmidt, Barbara

2011   Prophecy. Electronic document, http://www.twainquotes.com/Prophecy.html, accessed 24 June 2011.

Schmidt, Peter R.

2013   Historical Archaeology, Colonial Entanglements, and Recuperating "Timeless" Histories through Structuralism. In *The Death of Prehistory*, edited by Peter R. Schmidt and Stephen A. Mrozowski, 92–116. Oxford University Press, Oxford.

Schmidt, Peter R., and Stephen A. Mrozowski

2013   The Death of Prehistory: Reforming the Past, Looking to the Future. In *The Death of Prehistory*, edited by Peter R. Schmidt and Stephen A. Mrozowski, 1–28. Oxford University Press, Oxford.

Schufeldt, P. W.

1950   Reminiscences of a Chiclero. In *Morleyana: A Collection of Writings in Memoriam Sylvanus Griswold Morley (1883–1948)*, 224–29. School of American Research and the Museum of New Mexico, Santa Fe.

Science News Letter

1934   Measure Your Giant Carefully and His Size Will Shrink. 25(672) (24 February):118.

Scott, H. D.

1950   A Letter from Morley. In *Morleyana: A Collection of Writings in Memoriam Sylvanus Griswold Morley (1883–1948)*, 230–33. School of American Research and the Museum of New Mexico, Santa Fe.

Scott, John

1981   *The Early History of Glastonbury: An Edition, Translation and Study of William of Malmesbury's "De Antiquitate Glastonie Ecclesie."* Boydell Press, Woodbridge, Suffolk, United Kingdom.

Scott, Sue

2004   The Terracotta Figurines from Sigvald Linné's Excavations at Teotihuacán, México. Electronic document, http://www.famsi.org/reports/99100/99100Scott01.pdf, accessed 29 June 2016.

Scott, Walter

1830   *Letters on Demonology and Witchcraft*. Harper, New York.

Screeton, Paul

2012   *Quest for the Hexham Heads*. Fortean Words, Bideford, North Devon, United Kingdom.

Scully, Frank

1950   *Behind the Flying Saucers*. Popular Library, New York.

Semple, Sarah

1998   A Fear of the Past: The Place of the Prehistoric Burial Mound in the Ideology of Middle and Later Anglo-Saxon England. *World Archaeology* 30(1):109–26.

Seward, William Foote (editor in chief)

1924   *Binghamton and Broome County, New York: A History*. 3 vols. Lewis Historical Publishing, New York.

Shinn, Eugene A.

2004   A Geologist's Adventures with Bimini Beachrock and Atlantis True Believers. *Skeptical Inquirer* 28(1). http://www.csicop.org/si/show/geologists_adventures_with_bimini_beachrock, accessed 10 June 2015.

Shirey, David L.

1972   Museum of American Indian Displays Skull Masks. *New York Times* 4 November:30. New York.

Sidky, Homayun

1997   *Witchcraft, Lycanthropy, Drugs, and Disease: An Anthropological Study of the European Witch-Hunts.* Peter Lang, New York.

Silberman, Neil Asher

1982   *Digging for God and Country: Exploration, Archeology, and the Secret Struggle for the Holy Land, 1799–1917.* Knopf, New York.

Silver, Carole

1986   On the Origin of Fairies: Victorians, Romantics, and Folk Belief. *Browning Institute Studies* 14:141–56.

1999   *Strange and Secret Peoples: Fairies and Victorian Consciousness.* Oxford University Press, Oxford.

Simandiraki-Grimshaw, Anna, and Eleni Stefanou

2012   From Archaeology to Archaeologies: Themes, Challenges and Borders of the "Other" Past. In *From Archaeology to Archaeologies: The "Other" Past*, edited by Anna Simandiraki-Grimshaw and Eleni Stefanou, 9–13. Archaeopress, Oxford.

Simpson, Jacqueline

1994   Margaret Murray: Who Believed Her, and Why? *Folklore* 105:89–96.

Sitler, Robert K.

2012   The 2012 Phenomenon Comes of Age. *Nova Religio: The Journal of Alternative and Emergent Religions* 16(1):61–87.

Smith, Laurajane

2006   *Uses of Heritage.* Routledge, London.

Smith, Martyn

2007   Pyramids in the Medieval Islamic Landscape: Perceptions and Narrative. *Journal of the American Research Center in Egypt* 43:1–14.

Smith, Mary Elizabeth

1973   The Relationship between Mixtec Manuscript Painting and the Mixtec Language: A Study of Some Personal Names in the Codices Muro and Sánchez Solís. In *Mesoamerican Writing Systems*, edited by Elizabeth P. Benson, 47–98. Dumbarton Oaks, Washington, DC.

Smith, Stuart Tyson

2007   Unwrapping the Mummy: Hollywood Fantasies, Egyptian Realities. In *Box Office Archaeology: Refining Hollywood's Portrayals of the Past*, edited by Julie M. Schablitsky, 16–33. Left Coast Press, Walnut Creek, California.

Smithsonian Institution

2009   Written in Bone: Forensic Files of the Seventeenth-Century Chesapeake. http://anthropology.si.edu/writteninbone, accessed 26 May 2016.

Solomon, Avi

2011   Interview: Dennis McKenna. *BoingBoing*, 9 June. http://boingboing.net/2011/06/09/mck.html, accessed 23 March 2017.

Spencer, Kathleen

1987   Victorian Urban Gothic: The First Modern Fantastic Literature. In *Intersections: Fantasy and Science Fiction*, edited by George E. Slusser and Eric S. Rabkin, 87–96. Southern Illinois University Press, Carbondale.

Spinden, Herbert J.

1911   An Ancient Sepulcher at Placeres del Oro, State of Guerrero, Mexico. *American Anthropologist* 13:29–55.

1924   Adventuring in Archaeology. *New York Times* 25 May:SM9. New York.

Stableford, Brian

1990   Early Modern Horror Fiction, 1897–1949. In *Horror Literature: A Reader's Guide*, edited by Neil Barron, 93–159. Garland, New York.

2007a   The Cosmic Horror. In *Icons of Horror and the Supernatural: An Encyclopedia of Our Worst Nightmares*, edited by S. T. Joshi, 1:65–96. Greenwood Press, Westport, Connecticut.

2007b   The Immortal. In *Icons of Horror and the Supernatural: An Encyclopedia of Our Worst Nightmares*, edited by S. T. Joshi, 1:307–40. Greenwood Press, Westport, Connecticut.

Stacy, Dennis

1999   Crop Circles. In *Unexplained! Strange Sightings, Incredible Occurrences and Puzzling Physical Phenomena*, edited by Jerome Clark, 146–59. Visible Ink, Detroit, Michigan.

Stamps, Richard B.

2001   Tools Leave Marks: Material Analysis of the Scotford-Soper-Savage Michigan Relics. *BYU Studies* 40(3):211–38.

Standish, David

2006   *Hollow Earth: The Long and Curious History of Imagining Strange Lands, Fantastical Creatures, Advanced Civilizations, and Marvelous Machines below the Earth's Surface*. Da Capo, Cambridge, Massachusetts.

Stanley, J.

1950   Memorandum to the Commissioner, Criminal Investigation Division, Scotland Yard, 30 March. Metropolitan Police file MEPO 3/2290. National Archives, United Kingdom, Kew, London.

Stepan, Nancy

1982   *The Idea of Race in Science: Great Britain, 1800–1960.* Macmillan, London, in association with St. Anthony's College, Oxford.

Stevens, E. S. (editor and translator)

2006 [1931]   *Folktales of Iraq.* Dover, Mineola, New York.

Stewart, Christopher

2013   *Jungleland: A Mysterious Lost City, a WWII Spy, and a True Story of Deadly Adventure.* HarperCollins, New York.

Stewart, Susan

1982   The Epistemology of the Horror Story. *Journal of American Folklore* 95(375):33–50.

Stickel, E. Gary

1993   Archaeological Investigations of the McMartin Preschool Site, Manhattan Beach, California. McMartin Tunnel Project. http://members.shaw.ca/sharshenin/files/Archaeological_Investigations_of_the_McMartin_Preschool_Site_by_E._Gary_Stickel__Ph.D.%5B1%5D.pdf, accessed 24 February 2016.

Stout, Adam

2008   *Creating Prehistory: Druids, Ley Hunters and Archaeologists in Pre-War Britain.* Blackwell, Oxford.

2012   Grounding Faith at Glastonbury: Episodes in the Early History of Alternative Archaeology. *Numen* 59:249–69.

Strain, Kathy Moskowitz

2008   *Giants, Cannibals, and Monsters: Bigfoot in Native Culture.* Hancock House, Surrey, British Columbia, and Blaine, Washington.

2012   Mayak Datat: The Hairy Man Pictographs. *Relict Hominid Inquiry* 1:1–12.

Strasenburgh, Gordon

1975   On *Paranthropus* and "Relic Hominoids." *Current Anthropology* 16(3):486–87.

Strong, William Duncan

1935   *Archeological Investigations in the Bay Islands, Spanish Honduras.* Smithsonian Institution, Washington, DC.

Stross, Charlies

2010   The Hard Edge of Empire. 27 October. http://www.antipope.org/charlie/blog-static/2010/10/the-hard-edge-of-empire.html, accessed 16 June 2016.

Stuart, David
2000 "The Arrival of Strangers": Teotihuacan and Tollan in Classic Maya History. In *Mesoamerica's Classic Heritage: From Teotihuacan to the Aztecs*, edited by David Carrasco, Lindsay Jones, and Scott Sessions, 465–513. University Press of Colorado, Boulder.

Suerbaum, Ulrich
2001 [1999] Rules of the Game: Agatha Christie's Construction of the Detective Story. In *Agatha Christie and Archaeology*, edited by Charlotte Trümpler, 410–24. Translated by Anthea Bell. British Museum Press, London.

Sugden, Philip
1994 *The Complete History of Jack the Ripper.* Carrol and Graf, New York.

Sugiyama, Nawa, Saburo Sugiyama, and Alejandro Sarabia G.
2013 Inside the Sun Pyramid at Teotihuacan, Mexico: 2008–2011 Excavations and Preliminary Results. *Latin American Antiquity* 24(4):403–32.

Suhay, Lisa
2014 30-Day Emoji Challenge: Are We the New Egyptians? *Christian Science Monitor* 19 August. http://www.csmonitor.com/Technology/Tech-Culture/2014/0819/30-day-emoji-challenge-Are-we-the-new-Egyptians, accessed 2 July 2015.

Sullivan, Kevin
2014 The Watchers Traditions in 1 Enoch 6–16: The Fall of Angels and the Rise of Demons. In *The Watchers in Jewish and Christian Traditions*, edited by Angela Kim Harkins, Kelley Coblentz Bautch, and John C. Endres, 91–103. Fortress Press, Minneapolis, Minnesota.

Sydney Morning Herald
1950 Woman Scientist Suspects Ritual Murder in U.K. 5 September:3. Sydney, Australia. http://nla.gov.au/nla.news-article18176618, accessed 28 May 2015.

Tarabulski, Michael
2003 Editor's Introduction of Author. In *Veiled Men, Red Tents, and Black Mountains: Adventures of an Expedition of the First Pneumatic-Tired Automobiles to Cross the Algerian Sahara (1925)* by Alonzo W. Pond, 1–13. Edited by Michael Tarabulski. Narrative Press, Santa Barbara, California.

Taylor, Brian
1995 Amateurs, Professionals, and the Knowledge of Archaeology. *British Journal of Sociology* 46(3):499–508.

Taylor, Walter W.
1967 [1948] *A Study of Archeology.* Southern Illinois University Press, Carbondale.

Tejeda F., Antonio

1950   Morleyana Anecdotes. In *Morleyana: A Collection of Writings in Memoriam Sylvanus Griswold Morley (1883–1948)*, 248–51. School of American Research and the Museum of New Mexico, Santa Fe.

Telegraph

2011   Curse of Tutankhamun May Have Been Work of Satanist Killer. 8 November. http://www.telegraph.co.uk/news/worldnews/africaandindianocean/ egypt/8878314/Curse-of-Tutankhamun-may-have-been-work-of-Satanist-killer.html, accessed 24 November 2011.

Thomas, Aubrey

1950   Murdered Man Was a Witch, Doctor Heard. *Adelaide News* 16 September:4. Adelaide, Australia. http://nla.gov.au/nla.news-article131229659, accessed 28 May 2015.

Thomas, David E.

1995   The Roswell Incident and Project Mogul: Scientist Participant Supports Direct Links. *Skeptical Inquirer* 19(4) (July–August):15–18.

Thompson, Edward Herbert

1879   Atlantis Not a Myth. *Popular Science Monthly* 15(6):759–64.

1965 [1932]   *People of the Serpent: Life and Adventure among the Mayas*. Capricorn, New York.

Thompson, J. Eric

1950   Some Anecdotes about Vay. In *Morleyana: A Collection of Writings in Memoriam Sylvanus Griswold Morley (1883–1948)*, 252–56. School of American Research and the Museum of New Mexico, Santa Fe.

1954   *The Rise and Fall of Maya Civilization*. University of Oklahoma Press, Norman.

1962   *A Catalog of Maya Hieroglyphs*. University of Oklahoma Press, Norman, in cooperation with the Carnegie Institution of Washington.

Thompson, Tok

2004   The Irish *Sí* Tradition: Connections between the Disciplines, and What's in a Word? *Journal of Archaeological Method and Theory* 11(4):335–68.

Tierney, Richard L.

1985   The Brotherhood of Cthulhu. *Crypt of Cthulhu* 4(5):6–7.

Tilley, Virginia Q.

2005   *Seeing Indians: A Study of Race, Nation, and Power in El Salvador*. University of New Mexico Press, Albuquerque.

Toland, Eleanor

2014   And Did Those Hooves: Pan and the Edwardians. Master's thesis, Department of English, Victoria University, Wellington.

Tolkien, J. R. R.

2004 *The Lord of the Rings*. Houghton Mifflin, Boston.

Topham, Ian

2010 Netta Fornario: Iona's Occult Mystery. *Mysterious Britain and Ireland*. https://web.archive.org/web/20101212112851/http://www.mysteriousbritain.co.uk/scotland/occult/netta-fornario-ionas-occult-mystery.html, accessed 9 August 2017.

Toumey, Christopher

1996 *Conjuring Science: Scientific Symbols and Cultural Meanings in American Life*. Rutgers University Press, New Brunswick, New Jersey.

Towrie, Sigurd

2016 "The Odin Stone and the Orcadian Wedding." *Orkneyjar: The Heritage of the Orkney Islands*. Electronic document, http://www.orkneyjar.com/history/odinstone/odwedd.htm, accessed 26 June 2017.

Traill, David A.

1995 *Schliemann of Troy: Treasure and Deceit*. John Murray, London.

Trento, Salvatore Michael

1978 *The Search for Lost America: The Mysteries of the Stone Ruins*. Contemporary, Chicago.

Trew, Bel

2014 Egyptian Tomb-Robbing Market Explodes on eBay. *Daily Beast* 31 May. http://www.thedailybeast.com/articles/2014/05/31/egyptian-tomb-robbing-market-explodes-on-ebay.html, accessed 23 June 2017.

Tribble, Scott

2009 *A Colossal Hoax: The Giant from Cardiff That Fooled America*. Rowman and Littlefield, Lanham, Maryland.

Trigger, Bruce G.

1984 Alternative Archaeologies: Nationalist, Colonialist, Imperialist. *Man* 19:355–70.

1996 *A History of Archaeological Thought*. 2nd ed. Cambridge University Press, Cambridge.

2003 *Understanding Early Civilizations: A Comparative Study*. Cambridge University Press, Cambridge.

Trümpler, Charlotte

2001 [1999] "A Dark-Room Has Been Allotted to Me . . .": Photography and Filming by Agatha Christie on the Excavation Sites. In *Agatha Christie and Archaeology*, edited by Charlotte Trümpler, 229–57. Translated by Anthea Bell. British Museum Press, London.

Trwoga, Chris
2001   *Grail Quest in the Vales of Avalon.* Speaking Tree, Glastonbury, Somerset, United Kingdom.

Umberger, Emily
1987   Antiques, Revivals, and References to the Past in Aztec Art. *RES: Anthropology and Aesthetics* 13:62–105.

Vale, Allison
2013   Is This the Bella in the Wych Elm? Unravelling the Mystery of the Skull Found in a Tree Trunk. *Independent* 22 March. http://www.independent.co.uk/news/uk/home-news/is-this-the-bella-in-the-wych-elm-unravelling-the-mystery-of-the-skull-found-in-a-tree-trunk-8546497.html, accessed 23 June 2017.

Valentine, Uffington
1931   Mu, the Lost Atlantis of the Pacific Ocean. Review of James Churchward's *The Children of Mu. New York Times* 7 June:BR5. New York.

Vallee, Jacques
1969   *Passport to Magonia: From Folklore to Flying Saucers.* Henry Regnery, Chicago.

van Leusen, Martijn
1998   Dowsing and Archaeology. *Archaeological Prospection* 5:123–38.

Van Luijik, Ruben
2016   *Children of Lucifer: The Origins of Modern Religious Satanism.* Oxford University Press, New York.

van Wormer, Stephen R., and G. Timothy Gross
2006   Archaeological Identification of an Idiosyncratic Lifestyle: Excavation and Analysis of the Theosophical Society Dump, San Diego, California. *Historical Archaeology* 40(1):100–118.

Velarde, C. J.
1926a   Were Mongoloids the First Californians. *Los Angeles Times* 13 June:K11. Los Angeles, California.
1926b   A New Reckoning in Mexican Archaeology. *Los Angeles Times* 1 August:K13. Los Angeles, California.
1926c   New Names in Mexican Archaeology. *Los Angeles Times* 15 August:K21. Los Angeles, California.

Vescelius, Gary S.
1956   Excavations at Pattee's Caves. *Bulletin of the Eastern States Archaeological Federation* 15:13–14.

Vinson, Steve
2009   The Names "Naneferkaptah," "Ihweret," and "Tabubue" in the "First Tale of Setne Khaemwas." *Journal of Near Eastern Studies* 68(4):283–303.

Vinson, Steve, and Janet Gunn
2015   Studies in Esoteric Syntax: The Enigmatic Friendship of Aleister Crowley and
        Battiscombe Gunn. In *Histories of Egyptology: Interdisciplinary Measures*,
        edited by William Carruthers, 97–112. Routledge, London.

Vitelli, Romeo
2014   Exploring the Hollow Earth. *Providentia* 16 March. http://drvitelli.typepad.com/
        providentia/2014/03/exploring-the-hollow-earth.html, accessed 9 August 2017.

von Däniken, Erich
1970   *Chariots of the Gods? Unsolved Mysteries of the Past.* Translated by Michael
        Heron. Bantam, Toronto.

Wace, A. J. B.
1956   St. George the Vampire. *Antiquity* 30:156–62.

Wahlgren, Erik
1958   *The Kensington Stone: A Mystery Solved.* University of Wisconsin Press,
        Madison.

Wallace, Colin
2011   Reconnecting Thomas Gann with British Interest in the Archaeology of Meso-
        america: An Aspect of the Development of Archaeology as a University Sub-
        ject. *Bulletin of the History of Archaeology* 21(1):23–36. doi:10.5334/bha.2113,
        accessed 23 June 2017.

Wallis, Robert J., and Jenny Blain
2010   Sites, Sacredness, and Stories: Interactions of Archaeology and Contemporary
        Paganism. *Folklore* 114(3):307–21.

Warren, Alan
2007   The Curse. In *Icons of Horror and the Supernatural: An Encyclopedia of Our
        Worst Nightmares*, edited by S. T. Joshi, 1:129–59. Greenwood Press, Westport,
        Connecticut.

Wastiau, Boris
2006   The Scourge of Chief Kansabala: The Ritual Life of Two Congolese Master-
        pieces at the Royal Museum for Central Africa (1884–2001). In *Science, Magic,
        and Religion: The Ritual Processes of Museum Magic*, edited by Mary Bouquet
        and Nuno Porto, 95–115. Berghahn, Oxford.

Watkins, Alfred
1925   *The Old Straight Track: Its Mounds, Beacons, Moats, Sites and Mark Stones.*
        Methuen, London.

Watkins, Trevor
2012   James Mellaart: 14 November 1925–29 July 2012. *Antiquity.* http://antiquity.
        ac.uk/tributes/mellaart.html, accessed 26 May 2016.

Wauchope, Robert
1962   *Lost Tribes and Sunken Continents: Myth and Method in the Study of American Indians.* University of Chicago Press, Chicago.

Wauchope, Robert (editor)
1965   *They Found the Buried Cities: Exploration and Excavation in the American Tropics.* University of Chicago Press, Chicago.

Waugh, Robert H.
1994   Dr. Margaret Murray and H. P. Lovecraft: The Witch-Cult in New England. *Lovecraft Studies* 31:2–10.

Webster, David
2006   The Mystique of the Ancient Maya. In *Archaeological Fantasies: How Pseudoarchaeology Misrepresents the Past and Misleads the Public,* edited by Garrett G. Fagan, 129–53. Routledge, London.

Weeks, Kent R.
1998   *The Lost Tomb.* William Morrow, New York.

Weigall, Arthur
2006 [1924]   The Malevolence of Ancient Egyptian Spirits. In *Into the Mummy's Tomb: Mysterious Tales of Mummies and Ancient Egypt,* edited by John Richard Stephens, 1–15. Barnes and Noble, New York.

Welbourn, Terry
2011   *T. C. Lethbridge: The Man Who Saw the Future.* O-Books, Winchester, United Kingdom.

Wengrow, David
2011   Gods and Monsters: Image and Cognition in Neolithic Societies. *Paléorient* 37(1):153–63.
2014   *The Origins of Monsters: Image and Cognition in the First Age of Mechanical Reproduction.* Princeton University Press, Princeton, New Jersey.

Weston, Gavin, Jamie F. Lawson, Mwenza Blell, and John Hayton
2015   Anthropologists in Films: "The Horror! The Horror!" *American Anthropologist* 117(2):316–28.

Wheatcroft, Andrew
2003   "Wonderful Things": Publishing Egypt in Word and Image. In *Consuming Ancient Egypt,* edited by Sally MacDonald and Michael Rice, 151–63. Institute of Archaeology, UCL Press, London.

Wheatley, Maria
2011   Ley Lines and Earth Energies of Avalon. Celestial Songs Press, Marlborough, Wiltshire, United Kingdom.

Whitcomb, Dan

2017   Hobby Lobby to Forfeit Ancient Iraqi Artifacts in Settlement with U.S. DOJ. *Reuters*, 5 July, http://www.reuters.com/article/us-usa-iraqiartifacts-idUSKBN19Q33Q.

Whitesides, Kevin A., and John W. Hoopes

2012   Seventies Dreams and 21st Century Realities: The Emergence of 2012 Mythology. *Zeitschrift für Anomalistik* 12:50–74.

Whitley, James

1988   Early States and Hero Cults: A Re-Appraisal. *Journal of Hellenic Studies* 108:173–82.

Whittle, Christopher H.

2004   Development of Beliefs in Paranormal and Supernatural Phenomena. *Skeptical Inquirer* 28(2). http://www.csicop.org/si/show/development_of_beliefs_in_paranormal_and_supernatural_phenomena, accessed 27 February 2016.

Wickersham, Bill

2015   The 1941 Cape Girardeau UFO Crash. *Columbia Daily Tribune* 3 February. Columbia, Missouri. http://www.columbiatribune.com/opinion/oped/the-cape-girardeau-ufo-crash/article_687f4bcb-edff-5ce7-9111-ab3d9a0a5463.html, accessed 4 August 2015.

Wicks, Robert S., and Roland H. Harrison

1999   *Buried Cities, Forgotten Gods: William Niven's Life of Discovery and Revolution in Mexico and the American Southwest.* Texas Tech University Press, Lubbock.

Wieczorkiewicz, Anna

2006   Unwrapping Mummies and Telling Their Stories: Egyptian Mummies in Museum Rhetoric. In *Science, Magic, and Religion: The Ritual Processes of Museum Magic*, edited by Mary Bouquet and Nuno Porto, 51–71. Berghahn, Oxford.

Wilber, Donald N.

1969 [1954]   Overthrow of Premier Mossadeq: November 1952–August 1953. *National Security Archive*, George Washington University. http://nsarchive.gwu.edu/NSAEBB/NSAEBB28, accessed 7 June 2016.

1981   *Iran Past and Present: From Monarchy to Islamic Republic.* 9th ed. Princeton University Press, Princeton, New Jersey.

1986   *Adventures in the Middle East: Excursions and Incursions.* Darwin, Princeton, New Jersey.

Wilford, Hugh

2013   *America's Great Game: The CIA's Secret Arabists and the Shaping of the Modern Middle East.* Basic, New York.

Williams, J. E. (compiler)

1897 *Williams' Binghamton City Directory for 1897.* Binghamton Publishing, Binghamton, New York.

Williams, Robert Lloyd

2009 *Lord Eight Wind of Suchixtlan and the Heroes of Ancient Oaxaca: Reading History in the Codex Zouche-Nuttall.* University of Texas Press, Austin.

Williams, Stephen

1991 *Fantastic Archaeology: The Wild Side of North American Prehistory.* University of Pennsylvania Press, Philadelphia.

Williamson, Tom, and Liz Bellamy

1983 *Ley Lines in Question.* World's Work, Kingswood, Surrey, United Kingdom.

Willis, Chris

2000 Making the Dead Speak: Spiritualism and Detective Fiction. In *The Art of Detective Fiction*, edited by Warren Chernaik, Martin Swales, and Robert Vilain, 60–74. Macmillan, London, and St. Martin's, New York, in association with Institute of English Studies, School of Advanced Study, University of London.

Willis, Martin

2007 Jack the Ripper, Sherlock Holmes and the Narrative of Detection. In *Jack the Ripper: Media, Culture, History*, edited by Alexandra Warwick and Martin Willis, 144–58. Manchester University Press, Manchester, England.

Wilson, Colin

1982 Foreword. In *The Essential T. C. Lethbridge*, edited by Tom Graves and Janet Hoult, 7–16. Granada, London.

Wilson, Duncan

1987 *Gilbert Murray OM: 1866–1957.* Clarendon, Oxford.

Wilson, P. W.

1926 Pharaoh's Curse Clings to His Tomb. *New York Times* 11 April:SM3, 16. New York.

Winstone, H. V. F.

1990 *Woolley of Ur: The Life of Sir Leonard Woolley.* Secker and Warburg, London.

Witzel, Michael

2006 Rama's Realm: Indocentric Rewritings of Early South Asian Archaeology and History. In *Archaeological Fantasies: How Pseudoarchaeology Misrepresents the Past and Misleads the Public*, edited by Garrett G. Fagan, 203–32. Routledge, London.

Wolter, Scott

2014   The Smithsonian Responds to *America Unearthed*: "Lost Relics of the Bible"
        Episode. 6 February. http://scottwolteranswers.blogspot.com/2014
        /02/the-smithsonian-responds-to-america.html, accessed 16 June 2016.

Wood, Michael J., Karen M. Douglas, and Robbie M. Sutton

2012   Dead and Alive: Belief in Contradictory Conspiracy Theories. *Social Psychology and Personality Science* 3(6):767–73.

Woodman, Justin

2004   Alien Selves: Modernity and the Social Diagnostics of the Demonic in "Lovecraftian Magick." *Journal for the Academic Study of Magic* 2:13–47.

Woodward, Susan L., and Jerry N. McDonald

2001   *Indian Mounds of the Middle Ohio Valley: A Guide to Mounds and Earthworks of the Adena, Hopewell, Cole, and Fort Ancient People.* McDonald and Woodward, Granville, Ohio.

Woolheater, Craig

2013   Archaeology and Bigfoot. *Cryptomundo* 29 March. http://cryptomundo.com/bigfoot-report/archaeology-and-bigfoot, accessed 17 January 2016.

Woolley, C. Leonard

1920   *Dead Towns and Living Men: Being Pages from an Antiquary's Notebook.* Humphrey Milford, Oxford University Press, London.

1949 [1930]   *Digging Up the Past.* Penguin, Harmondsworth, Middlesex, United Kingdom.

The Worker

1951   Old Murder Probed by Woman of Eighty. 1 January:5, 7. Brisbane, Queensland, Australia. http://nla.gov.au/nla.news-article71395755, accessed 28 May 2015.

Wright, Ben

2016   There's a Sinister Strain of Anti-Intellectualism to Gove's Dismissal of "Experts." *Telegraph* 21 June. http://www.telegraph.co.uk/business/2016/06/21/in-defence-of-experts-whether-they-support-leave-or-remain, accessed 23 June 2016.

Wyatt, W. Joseph

2002   What Was under the McMartin Preschool? A Review and Behavioral Analysis of the "Tunnels" Find. *Behavior and Social Issues* 12:29–39.

Wynn, L. L.

2007   *Pyramids and Nightclubs: A Travel Ethnography of Arab and Western*

Imaginations of Egypt from King Tut and a Colony of Atlantis to Rumors of Sex Orgies, Urban Legends about a Marauding Prince, and Blonde Belly Dancers. University of Texas Press, Austin.

Xie, Julie

2011   "DP" Reporter Explores the Secrets of Penn Museum. *Daily Pennsylvanian* 30 October. http://www.thedp.com/index.php/article/2011/10/dp_reporter_explores_the_secrets_of_penn_museum, accessed 30 June 2016.

Yates, Donna

2014a   Displacement, Deforestation, and Drugs: Antiquities Trafficking and the Narcotics Support Economies of Guatemala. In *Cultural Property Crimes: An Overview and Analysis of Contemporary Perspectives and Trends*, edited by Joris Kila and Mark Balcells, 23–36. Brill, Leiden.

2014b   Maya Artefacts and Mexican Bandits: Trafficking Tall Tales. *Anonymous Swiss Collector* 1 July. http://www.anonymousswisscollector.com/2014/07/maya-artefacts-and-mexican-bandits-trafficking-tall-tales.html, accessed 30 June 2016.

Young, G. W.

1956a   "Grey Magic": Peril in Britain. *Reveille* 784 (25 May):5.

1956b   Waits 11 Years for Witchcraft Killer. *Reveille* 786 (1 June):9.

1956c   Underworld of Black Mass Maniacs. *Reveille* 788 (8 June):9.

Yuhas, Alan

2015   Archaeologists Condemn National Geographic over Claims of Honduran "Lost Cities." *Guardian* 11 March. https://www.theguardian.com/world/2015/mar/11/honduras-lost-cities-open-letter-national-geographic-report, accessed 30 June 2016.

Zerubavel, Eviatar

2003   *Time Maps: Collective Memory and the Social Shape of the Past.* University of Chicago Press, Chicago.

Zimmerman, Virginia

2008   *Excavating Victorians.* State University of New York Press, Albany.

Zivie-Coche, Christiane

2002   *Sphinx: History of a Monument.* Translated by David Lorton. Cornell University Press, Ithaca, New York.

INDEX

Page numbers in italics indicate illustrations.